DO YOU KNOW:

- Why chopsticks are used to eat Chinese food?
- What the final Supreme Court decision about the internment of Japanese Americans during World War II was?
- How Korean-American self-help credit organizations operate?
- What the special relationship between the United States and the Philippines was?
- How to tell Sikhs from other immigrants from India?
- Why cultural attitudes toward different ethnic groups are very different in Hawaii from the rest of the United States?
- How many Americans of Asian descent there are in our country today?

EVERYTHING YOU NEED TO KNOW ABOUT ASIAN-AMERICAN HISTORY

Himilce Novas is the author of seven books, including several highly acclaimed works of fiction, and *Everything You Need to Know About Latino History* (available from Plume). She has contributed to *The New York Times, The Christian Science Monitor, Connoisseur, Cuisine,* and other publications. She taught American Literature at the University of Southern California-Santa Barbara, and is currently teaching at Tulane University. She lives in New Orleans.

Lan Cao is a professor of international business law at the College of William & Mary Marshall-Wythe School of Law. Born in Vietnam, she now lives in Virginia.

Rosemary Silva is a teacher and the author of several books on culture. She holds a Ph.D. from Yale University and has taught at Mount Holyoke College and Amherst College.

EVERYTHING YOU NEED TO KNOW ABOUT ASIAN-AMERICAN HISTORY

2004 Edition

Himilce Novas and Lan Cao

with Rosemary Silva

A PLUME BOOK

PLUME
Published by the Penguin Group
Penguin Group (USA) Inc., 375 Hudson Street, New York, New York 10014, U.S.A.
Penguin Books Ltd, 80 Strand, London WC2R 0RL, England
Penguin Books Australia Ltd, 250 Camberwell Road, Camberwell, Victoria 3124, Australia
Penguin Books Canada Ltd, 10 Alcorn Avenue, Toronto, Ontario, Canada M4V 3B2
Penguin Books India (P) Ltd, 11 Community Centre,
Panchsheel Park, New Delhi –110 017, India
Penguin Books (N.Z.) Ltd, Cnr Rosedale and Airborne Roads,
Albany, Auckland 1310, New Zealand
Penguin Books (South Africa) (Pty) Ltd, 24 Sturdee Avenue,
Rosebank, Johannesburg 2196, South Africa

Penguin Books Ltd, Registered Offices: 80 Strand, London WC2R 0RL, England

First published by Plume, a member of Penguin Group (USA) Inc.

First Printing, August 2004
10 9 8 7 6 5 4 3 2 1

LIBRARY OF CONGRESS CATALOGING-IN-PUBLICATION DATA
Novas, Himilce.
Everything you need to know about Asian American history / Novas Himilce
and Lan Cao with Rosemary Silva.— 2004 ed.
p. cm.
Includes bibliographical references and index.
ISBN 0-452-28475-9
1. Asian Americans—History—Miscellanea. I. Cao, Lan, 1961–
II. Silva, Rosemary, 1962– III. Title.

E184.A75N68 2004
973'.0495'02—dc22
2003065622

Printed in the United States of America
Set in New Baskerville

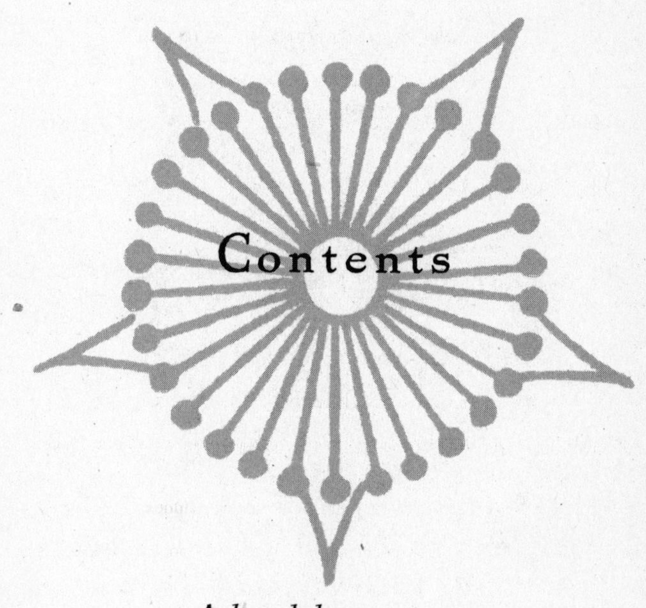

Contents

Acknowledgments

We owe thanks to the staff and librarians of the Library of Congress, the New York Public Library, the Clapp Library at Wellesley College, and the Davidson Library at the University of California, Santa Barbara, for their assistance in our research. Our thanks also go to the Smithsonian Institution, the Duke University Law School, and the cultural institutions devoted to Asian Pacific Islander Americans across the nation. Finally, we wish to express our gratitude to Professor Lorraine Elena Roses and Professor Winifred J. Wood at Wellesley College, to the poet Jonathan Roses, Susan Herner, Carlos Espinosa, Richard Silva, Genevieve Silva, Thomas Grohmann, Brigitta Grohmann, Dr. Daniel Spurlock, Carla Spurlock, Professor George Sparling, Bobbi Sparling, Harlan Margaret Van Cao, Professor William Van Alstyne at Duke University and our wonderful editor Ryan Harbage.

How to Read This Book

We have organized *Everything You Need to Know About Asian-American History* in a modular, question-and-answer format, allowing the reader to zoom in on aspects of Asian-American and Pacific Islander American history and culture that are of most interest to her or him. Of course, the book can be read linearly, from cover to cover, so that all the pieces of Asian-American and Pacific Islander American life form a complete picture.

We have divided the book according to the various Asian-American subgroups. Chinese Americans, Japanese Americans, Korean Americans, and Filipino Americans are afforded their own chapters, while South Asian Americans (Americans with roots in India, Pakistan, Bangladesh, Sri Lanka, Nepal,

Bhutan, and Maldives) appear together in one chapter, most of which is given over to Asian-Indian Americans due to their large numbers. All Southeast Asian Americans (Americans with roots in Vietnam, Laos, Cambodia, Thailand, Indonesia, Malaysia, Burma, Singapore, and Brunei), except for Filipino Americans, are organized together in another chapter, and all Pacific Islander Americans (Native Hawaiians, Samoans, Guamanians/Chamorros, Tongan Americans, and other Pacific Islander Americans) are grouped together in a final chapter.

The chapters are organized not in descending order of population, but according to the length of time that the various Asian-American subgroups have existed as recognizable communities in the United States. Since Chinese-American history goes back all the way to 1848 and the California gold rush, Chinese Americans are featured first, followed by Japanese Americans, whose immigration to the United States reached significant proportions after 1876; Korean Americans, who arrived in sizable numbers beginning in 1903; Filipino Americans, who came to America in abundant numbers beginning in 1907; South Asian Americans, who also first ventured to American shores in sizable numbers in 1907; and Southeast Asian Americans, who took refuge in the United States in large numbers beginning in the 1970s. We have placed the chapter on Pacific Islander Americans last because of the special nature of Pacific Islander American history: The overwhelming majority of Pacific Islander Americans (Native Hawaiians, American Samoans, and Guamanians) have been American citizens since birth, thanks to U.S. imperialism in the South Pacific at the end of the nineteenth century, and their movement to the fifty states is considered the internal migration of Americans and not immigration.

We have sought not to merely compile important dates and events in Asian-American and Pacific Islander American history, but to shed light on a diverse peoples who have dramatically altered the fabric of American life with their rich cultures, values, accomplishments, and sacrifices at the same time that American life has altered them. In the process, we have illuminated Asian and Pacific Islander subgroups in the United States that have hitherto been rather neglected by the American mainstream, have taken aim at some insidious stereotypes of Asian Americans and Pacific Islander Americans, have confronted the civil rights record as it relates to persons of Asian and Pacific Islander heritage, and have given credit and recognition where it was long overdue or underemphasized.

Introduction
Asian Americans

Who are the Asian Americans, who are the Pacific Islander Americans, and who are the Asian Pacific Islander Americans?

In the last two centuries, many peoples from Asia have ventured to the United States to forge new lives. The matter of classifying them in terms of race and ethnicity has become very complicated in recent decades, igniting heated debate. From the standpoint of the U.S. Bureau of the Census, Asia—a continent of the Eastern Hemisphere that forms a single landmass with Europe and includes numerous offshore islands and island archipelagos—is comprised of the East Asian nations (and one territory) of China, Taiwan, Hong Kong (which, along with its adjacent territories, was under British control from 1840 until July 1, 1997, when it reverted to Chinese control), Japan, and Korea; the South Asian nations of India, Pakistan, Bangladesh, Sri Lanka, Nepal, Bhutan, and Maldives; and the Southeast Asian nations of the Philippines, Vietnam, Laos, Cambodia, Thailand, Indonesia, Malaysia, Burma, Singapore, and Brunei. (A more liberal definition of Asia would include Afghanistan in South Asia, as well as the Central Asian nations of Kazakhstan, Kyrgyzstan, Tajikistan, Turkmenistan and Uzbekistan [which were all republics of the Soviet Union until it collapsed in 1991], and the numerous countries of the Middle East.)

All residents of the United States who are descended from the original peoples of the nations and one territory (Hong Kong) of Asia (as the U.S. Bureau of the Census defines it) are known as Asian Americans (if they possess U.S. citizenship) and as Asian nationals (if they do not possess U.S. citizenship). Asian Americans are also categorized by their particular country of origin, that is, as Chinese Americans, Filipino Americans, Asian-Indian Americans (they are called Asian Indians to distinguish them from Native Americans), Japanese Americans, Korean Americans, and so on. It should be noted that the U.S. Bureau of the Census has also created a few special Asian subgroups for those U.S. residents for whom regional or ethnic identity overrides national consciousness. The Hmong, a distinct ethnic group from the northern mountains of Laos who have no nation of their own, are one such subgroup. The Census Bureau assigned the Hmong their own category separate from Laotians because they produced a sizable immigration to the United States beginning in the mid-1970s.

Another special subgroup is the Iwo Jimans, those who identify first and foremost with the island of Iwo Jima and not with Japan, to which it belongs. (Iwo Jima was occupied by the United States until 1968, when it was returned to Japan.) Just 78 Iwo Jimans were counted in Census 2000. A third special

Asian subgroup is the Okinawans, those who identify with the Japanese island group of Okinawa before the nation of Japan, to which it belongs. (The United States occupied Okinawa until 1972, when the island group was returned to Japan.) Census 2000 tallied 10,599 Okinawans. A fourth special subgroup is the Indochinese, those who identify with French Indochina, which until 1945 was a federation of states in Southeast Asia comprised of the French colony of Cochin China and the French protectorates of Tonkin, Annam, Laos, and Cambodia, and which no longer exists. (Cochin China, Tonkin, and Annam were united in 1945 to form Vietnam.) Just 199 persons classified themselves as Indochinese on Census 2000. In the minds of some, the addition of these special subgroups to the U.S. census constitutes splitting hairs and has only complicated the matter of defining Asian Americans.

It is important to note that for Census 2000, the U.S. Bureau of the Census revised the census form to allow respondents to report one or more races to describe their racial identities. For example, a respondent could check both Asian and White on the census form. The Census Bureau tallied the results in what are known as "alone or in combination" totals. For instance, those who described themselves as Asian and White on the 2000 census form were counted both in the "White alone or in combination" category and in the "Asian alone or in combination" category. (Only a small number of people who filled out Census 2000 actually chose more than one race. In fact, nearly 98 percent of respondents to Census 2000 reported only one race.) The U.S. Bureau of the Census counted 11,898,828 Asian Americans and nationals, alone or in combination with another race, in the United States in 2000; of those, 10,242,998 identified themselves as Asian alone.

As for the various Asian-American subgroups, the U.S. Bureau of the Census in 2000, in what also amounts to hair splitting to some, broke down the total population of each Asian ethnic subgroup by single ethnicity (for instance, Japanese), two or more Asian ethnicities (for instance, Japanese and Filipino), and by Asian and at least one other race (for instance, Japanese and White). Of the Asian Americans (and Asian nationals) counted in Census 2000, Chinese Americans constituted the largest subgroup, with 2,734,841 (alone or in combination with at least one other race or Asian ethnicity), followed by Filipino Americans, with 2,364,815; Asian-Indian Americans, with 1,899,599; Korean Americans, with 1,228,427; Vietnamese Americans, with 1,223,736; Japanese Americans, with 1,148,932; Cambodian Americans, with 206,052; Pakistani Americans, with 204,309; Laotian Americans, with 198,203; Hmong Americans, with 186,310; Thai Americans, with 150,293; Taiwanese Americans, with 144,795; Indonesian Americans, with 63,073; Bangladeshi Americans, with 57,412; Sri Lankan Americans, with 24,587; Malaysian Americans, with 18,566; Burmese Americans, with 16,720; Nepalese Americans, with 9,399; Singaporean Americans, with 2,394; and each of the remaining subgroups with under 1,000.

According to the U.S. Bureau of the Census, Pacific Islander Americans and nationals (also called Pacific Americans) are those residents of the fifty states and the District of Columbia (inhabitants of U.S. dependencies and possessions are not included in the count) who on the census form classify themselves as predominantly ethnic Pacific Islander; that is, as descendants of the original peoples who inhabited the Pacific Islands—even if they may be of mixed blood (most probably are given the multiethnic nature of numerous Pacific Islands). The Pacific Islands include the 287 islands of Polynesia, most notably Hawaii, the Cook Islands, French Polynesia, American Samoa (an unincorporated and unorganized U.S. territory), Western Samoa, Tonga, Niue, Pitcairn Island, Easter Island, Tokelau, Tuvalu, Wallis Island, and Furtuna Island; the many islands of Micronesia, most notably the Marshall Islands, Guam (an organized, unincorporated U.S. territory), the Northern Mariana Islands (a U.S. commonwealth), the Federated States of Micronesia, Kiribati, Nauru, and Palau; and the islands of Melanesia, most notably New Caledonia, Papua New Guinea, Fiji, Irian Jaya, the Solomon Islands, and Vanuatu.

Census 2000 was the first census to designate Native Hawaiians and Other Pacific Islanders as a racial group distinct from Asians. On Census 2000, 874,414 persons in the United States identified themselves as Native Hawaiian and Other Pacific Islanders (alone or in combination with at least one other race). Of the 874,414 counted, 398,835 classified themselves as Native Hawaiian and Other Pacific Islander alone. Of the various Pacific Islander American subgroups, Native Hawaiians were the largest, with 401,162 (alone or in combination with at least one other race); followed by Samoans, with 133,281; Guamanians/Chamorros, with 92,611; Tongan Americans, with 36,840; and Fijian Americans, with 13,581. (The remaining Pacific Islands have contributed negligible numbers to the American mosaic.) Since most Pacific Islander Americans hail from the fiftieth state of Hawaii and from the U.S. territories of Guam and American Samoa, most were U.S. citizens at birth. Furthermore, Pacific Islander Americans, for the most part, unlike Asian Americans, are not minorities who crossed America's borders, or whose ancestors did, and then slowly acculturated to American society. They have roots in islands that during a brief window in time, from 1893 to 1899, were taken over by the United States. Thus, they or their forebears never crossed the U.S. border. The border crossed them.

As for Asian Pacific Islander Americans, they are a combination of all the highly diverse peoples mentioned above. By claiming a panethnic identity, by forging a common identity from disparate pasts and places, Americans of Asian and Pacific Islander descent have gained in numbers and, therefore, in political clout. Of course, in the best of all possible worlds, Asian Pacific Islander Americans also known by the abbreviation APIA, would do without the umbrella terms "Asian Americans," "Pacific Islander Americans," and "Asian Pacific

Islander Americans" and would simply refer to themselves as most Americans do, that is, by their country of origin—as Japanese Americans, Filipino Americans, Asian-Indian Americans, Chinese Americans, Korean Americans, Bangladeshi Americans, and so on.

Why don't Asian Americans want to be called Orientals?

Derived from the Latin *oriens,* the word "Orient" in the strictest sense refers to the countries of the East and to the part of the horizon where the sun first appears in the morning. (Thus "to orient" something, such as a church or a body for burial, is to situate it facing east.) Due to European colonial ventures in the Orient, or the East, this vast region incorporating most corners of Asia and the Middle East came to be viewed as a cohesive whole that existed in opposition to the West, the Occident. Scholar **Edward Said,** who currently teaches at Columbia University, elaborates on this notion in his key work entitled *Orientalism* (1978): "The Orient is not only adjacent to Europe; it is also the place of Europe's greatest and richest and oldest colonies, the source of its civilizations and languages, its cultural content, and one of its deepest and most recurring images of the Other. In addition the Orient has helped to define Europe (or the West) as its contrasting image, idea, personality, experience." Orientalism, that is, the image of the Orient as the other, has pervaded American depictions of Asians in both Asia and in the United States. To rid themselves of this Orientalism, of otherness, which has served only to disorient, to distort perceptions, Americans of Asian ancestry have embraced the umbrella term "Asian American." And so, in this age of multicultural enlightenment, Oriental is a rug, a perennial poppy (*Papaver orientale*), a spruce tree (*Picea orientalis*), and a little fishing village on the Neuse River in North Carolina. Asian is a race.

What myths and stereotypes have arisen around Asian Americans?

The myth of Asians as "the yellow peril" developed soon after the first Chinese laborers came ashore to pursue their dreams of riches during the California gold rush. By the 1870s, "Chinamen" bore the full brunt of racist hatred at the hands of nativist Americans, who threw sticks and stones and called them names that hurt, such as "heathen Chinee" and "stolid Asiatics." In the minds of Anglo-Saxon Americans, the "heathen Chinee" inhabited exotic, secret, and perilous places, including dark alleys, hidden bordellos, and opium dens, and exhibited negative traits, such as "Oriental inscrutability," "Oriental passivity," and "Oriental despotism." With the release in 1912 of Irish writer **Sax Rohmer**'s first Fu Manchu novel, which introduced to readers of the day the villainous Dr. Fu Manchu, a Chinese master criminal who plots to conquer the world, Americans could put a name to the Chinese menace, the yellow peril, in their midst. In 1931 the yellow peril acquired a female face. That year Fu Manchu's female counterpart, the deceptive dragon lady and sexual temptress, made her entrance in the Fu Manchu thriller *Daughter of the Dragon.*

As if to render Fu Manchu (and, thus, the yellow peril) harmless, in the mid-1920s Americans adopted the good-natured Chinese detective Charlie Chan, the main character of six novels written between 1925 and 1932 by American novelist and playwright **Earl Derr Biggers** and of forty-four Hollywood motion pictures by 1949. The truth is that Charlie Chan was just another Asian stereotype, that of the effeminate, nerdy, inscrutable Asian male, the prototype of the Asian-American "model minority." In the 1960s the antidote to the dragon lady appeared: Suzie, the Hong Kong prostitute, a naive Chinese girl, in the 1961 film version of **Richard Mason**'s hit novel *The World of Suzie Wong* (1957).

Only when **Pearl S. Buck** and Pearl Harbor made heroes out of the Chinese and villains out of the Japanese in America did another Asian subgroup bear the brunt of American racist hatred. With the Empire of Japan's unprovoked attack on the U.S. Pacific fleet moored at Pearl Harbor on December 7, 1941, overnight the Japanese on America's shores became known across the land as "the dirty Japs," "the goddamn Japs," and the "yellow Japs." ("Jap" became so rooted in the American vernacular that it lost its venom, and friendly whites began greeting Japanese men with "Hello, Mr. Jap.") During World War II (and until 1946), Japanese Americans and Japanese nationals suffered forced internment at camps set up in remote areas of the country. Since World War II, as before, all Asians in America have endured their share of racially motivated harassment, hate violence, and more subtle forms of discrimination. In the wake of the September 11, 2001, terrorist attacks, the South Asian community in America has endured more than its share. South Asian Americans and nationals, and especially Sikhs, with their beards and turbans, have frequently been mistaken for Arabs in the post–September 11 backlash. Hate crimes and bias incidents—from name-calling to denial of services, to fatal attacks—have occurred with such frequency in Sikh communities in America that the Sikh Coalition, which formed in the immediate aftermath of the September 11 attacks to provide an "accurate voice" for Sikh Americans, keeps a running list of bias-related incidents on its Web site.

Since the 1990s, white America has portrayed Asian Americans in terms of another stereotype, that of "model minority." According to this stereotype, Asian-American students are Albert Einsteins who consistently outperform their peers academically, especially in math and the sciences. And once in the workforce, Asian Americans work longer, harder, and better than everyone else. Hollywood has contributed to the stereotyping of Asian Americans by presenting image after image of nerdy Asian adolescent math geniuses and brainy Asian scientists who speak Charlie Chan English. While Asian Americans have contributed much and deserve recognition for their accomplishments, the myth of the model minority is terribly misleading. At best, it ignores the "lost generations" of Asian-American youths who have done poorly in America's classrooms and undermines serious discussion of the racial discrimination and inequities that Asian Americans continue to face, and at its worst, it fans the flames of racism in mainstream American society by raising fears of unfair competition.

FACTS AND FIGURES

1. According to the U.S. Bureau of the Census, Asian Americans and nationals numbered 11,898,828 (alone or in combination) in 2000, constituting 4.2 percent of the total U.S. population. Of those, 10,242,998 identified themselves as Asian alone. Another 874,414 persons in the United States identified themselves on Census 2000 as Pacific Islander (alone or in combination).

2. Between 1990 and 2000 all of the Asian subgroups in the United States grew in number except for the Japanese, who declined in number by nearly 10 percent.

3. Just over half of the Asian population (alone or in combination) in the United States resided in just three states in 2000: California, New York, and Hawaii. The greatest number, 4,155,685, called California home, followed by New York with 1,169,200, and then Hawaii with 703,232.

4. The three American metropolises with the largest Asian population (alone or in combination) in 2000 were New York City with 872,777 (and 787,047 alone), Los Angeles with 407,444 (and 369,254 alone), and Chicago with 140,517 (and 125,974 alone).

5. In 2000 Los Angeles County was the only county in the nation with more than one million persons of Asian ancestry.

6. In 2000 Asians comprised less than 1 percent of the population in nine states: Alabama, Kentucky, Mississippi, West Virginia, North Dakota, South Dakota, Montana, Wyoming, and Maine.

7. Of the 28.4 million foreign-born persons living in the United States in the year 2000, 7.2 million, or 26 percent, were born in Asia. Of the 7.2 million foreign-born Asians counted in 2000, 41.4 percent entered the United States in the 1990s; 35 percent in the 1980s; 17 percent in the 1970s; and 6 percent in the 1960s.

8. In the year 2000, 86 percent of persons of Asian and Pacific Islander ancestry in the United States had at least a high school education.

9. Between 1903 and 2000, 31 persons of Asian Pacific Islander descent served in the U.S. Congress. Thirteen of those were Resident Commissioners from the Philippines who served in Congress from 1907 to 1946.

ONE

Chinese Americans

THE FIRST CHINESE IN AMERICA

When does the history of Chinese America begin?

Could the Chinese have discovered the New World before the Europeans did?

GAM SAAN ("GOLD MOUNTAIN"); OR, ROLLING OUT THE WELCOME MAT IN CALIFORNIA

What's Gam Saan, and how did it generate the first significant wave of Chinese immigration to America?

Why were the Chinese invited to participate in President Taylor's funeral service in 1850?

"California for Americans"?

Were the Chinese who labored in America in the latter half of the nineteenth century eligible for U.S. citizenship?

What was California's Foreign Miners' License Tax Law?

Why did the Chinese go on "California dreaming" in the face of all this nativist hatred?

WORKIN' ON THE RAILROAD . . . AND IN THE FACTORY . . . AND IN THE FIELDS

How did America's rapid expansion westward create jobs for the Chinese in the post–gold rush decades?

Were the Chinese given credit for their part in building the transcontinental railroad?

Why did the Chinese settle in Chinatowns?

What were the Chinese Six Companies?

How did the Chinese build California's agricultural industry?

How did the Bing cherry get its name, and why does the Florida orange owe a debt of gratitude to a Chinese American?

MORE ANTI-CHINESE HOSTILITY IN THE WEST

Why did Californians call the Chinese evil in the 1870s?

Did San Franciscans actually harass the Chinese over their hairstyles, laundry services, and gong playing in the 1870s?

How did the Chinese in Butte, Montana, get started in the laundry business?

EASTWARD HO!

What brought the Chinese to the South after the American Civil War?

Why did a large number of Chinese settle in northeastern cities in the final decades of the nineteenth century?

Is it true that P. T. Barnum put Chinese people on display in his museum in New York City?

What are tongs, *and why have they been labeled the Chinese Mafia?*

CHINESE WOMEN IN AMERICA

Who was called "a hundred men's wife"?

What was the Page Law of 1875, and why was it an insult to Chinese women?

ANTI-CHINESE LEGISLATION

What was the Chinese Exclusion Act?

Since the Page Law and the Chinese Exclusion Act made it nearly impossible for Chinese women to come to America, did Chinese bachelors marry "out"?

What was the Scott Act of 1888, and how was it yet another setback for Chinese in America?

What was the Geary Act of 1892, and how did it manage to further demean Chinese immigrants?

FIGHTING BACK: THE PAPER SONS

Who were the "paper sons," and how did the San Francisco earthquake of 1906 actually facilitate Chinese immigration?

To what lengths did the U.S. government go in attempting to counter the paper son phenomenon?

What happened to those Chinese who got caught at immigration in San Francisco between 1910 and 1940?

Where did some of the first civil rights protests by Chinese in America take place?

PEARL HARBOR AND PEARL BUCK; OR, HOW AMERICAN SINOPHOBIA BECAME SINOPHILIA

Why were Pearl Harbor and Pearl S. Buck considered blessings for the Chinese in America?

How did Time *magazine teach Americans to distinguish the Chinese ally from the Japanese foe in the aftermath of the attack on Pearl Harbor?*

How did America's affection for the Chinese translate into the repeal of the Chinese Exclusion Act?

Why were so many Chinese in America drafted during World War II?

How were the seeds for a Chinese-American middle class sown on the East Coast during World War II?

THE RED SCARE: A TIME OF TROUBLES IN CHINESE AMERICA

Why did the Communist takeover of China put the Chinese in America on red alert?

How did McCarthyism intensify Chinese fears of a new era of persecution?

How did World War II and the Cold War lead to a change in U.S. immigration policies?

What was the Confession Program?

STEPS TOWARD EQUALITY

What was the Immigration Act of 1965?

How did the Chinese-American community change radically after 1965?

What are the "new" Chinatowns of the 1980s, 1990s, and the new millennium?

How many people of Chinese ancestry were counted by Census 2000, and where do they live?

FIGHTING CULTURAL STEREOTYPES AND FORGING CULTURAL HERITAGE

Who killed Vincent Chin, and why were his murderers given probation?

Who are the Chinese Americans in the political arena?

Who is Fu Manchu?

Who is Charlie Chan, and why is he so unpopular among most Asian Americans?

What is the dragon lady/lotus blossom dichotomy?

Who are the leading Chinese-American fiction writers?

Who are the great Chinese-American actors and filmmakers?

Who is Yo-Yo Ma?

Who are some of the leading Chinese-American scientists and medical researchers?

Who are some other prominent Chinese Americans?

Who are the world-class Chinese-American athletes?

How has Confucius contributed to both Chinese and Chinese-American society's devotion to order, respect, and patriarchy?

What is Taoism?

Which variety of Buddhism did the Chinese bring to America, and which religions do they practice nowadays?

How does traditional Chinese medicine differ from Western medicine?

What is t'ai chi ch'uan, *and what is kung fu?*

Which Chinese holidays do Chinese Americans typically celebrate?

What are some of the Chinese delicacies that Chinese Americans enjoy?

How did chow mein, chop suey, and the fortune cookie come to America?

Chinese Americans and Chinese nationals comprised the largest Asian subgroup in the United States at the dawn of the new millennium. For the sake of clarity, Chinese Americans are citizens of the United States who originated, or whose ancestors originated, from China, Hong Kong (which became part of mainland China on July 1, 1997, when British sovereignty over the territory ended), and Taiwan. (It should be noted that the descendants in America of Chinese who migrated to Taiwan many generations ago view themselves not as Chinese Americans but as Taiwanese Americans, while those descended from the Chinese who settled in Taiwan in the late 1940s, as the Communists overtook mainland China, consider themselves Chinese Americans and Taiwan a province of China.)

The Chinese first ventured to American shores in significant numbers in 1849, soon after the news reached Kwangtung Province in southeast China that **James W. Marshall,** an American contractor who was constructing a sawmill for **John Sutter** at Coloma in the Sacramento Valley of California, had struck gold. Once gold fever subsided in California, the Chinese made their way to various corners of the United States. From the mid-nineteenth century until after World War II, they made invaluable contributions to the development of the mining, railroad, agricultural, and manufacturing industries, despite encountering all along the way severe hostility from nativist Americans, who went to extreme ends to rid the country of the "heathen Chinee." In more recent decades, Americans whose roots are in China have been joined by their rich cousins from Taiwan and Hong Kong, who were either driven to the United States by fears that an economic and political crisis would erupt after Hong Kong's transfer from Great Britain to the People's Republic of China in 1997 or have found the United States a suitable place for settling.

THE FIRST CHINESE IN AMERICA

When does the history of Chinese America begin?

You might say that it begins in the late eighteenth century, when, according to various records, a few adventuresome Chinese crossed the oceans and settled in lands that presently constitute the United States. Evidence suggests, for instance, that in the final decades of the eighteenth century, Chinese men accompanied Spanish on their expeditions north along the coast of California. And a document preserved in the National Archives in Washington, D.C., tells of three Chinese sailors, known only as **Ah Cun, Ah Sing,** and **Ah Chuan,** from the Chinese trading vessel the *Pallas,* who sailed into Baltimore Harbor in 1785 and were left stranded there when the ship's captain, an American named **James O'Donnell,** went off to get married and did not schedule a return voyage to China. Apparently the three Chinese requested that Congress cover their living expenses and were looked after for nearly a year by a merchant in the China trade by the name of **Levi Hollingsworth.** Other sources indicate that in 1796 five Chinese servants accompanied the Canton agent for the Dutch East India Company, a Dutchman named **Andrea van Braam Houckgeest,** to the United States, settling not far from Philadelphia.

Could the Chinese have discovered the New World before the Europeans did?

Even before the eighth century A.D., Chinese vessels had navigated the waters of the Red Sea and the Persian Gulf. In 1405, at the height of the Ming dynasty, the Chinese Imperial Palace dispatched Chinese mariner **Cheng Ho,** known as Three Jewel Eunuch, on a mission westward, the first of seven major voyages he would undertake between 1405 and 1433. A common assumption is that the Chinese emperor commissioned Cheng Ho and the Imperial Fleet of sixty-two vessels to search for one of his relatives, who had allegedly fled west in 1403. Whatever the original motive for Cheng Ho's voyages, it is clear that they served a diplomatic purpose—that is, to exact "tributes" from other countries for presentment to the Chinese emperor. In fact, Cheng Ho and the Imperial Fleet diligently dropped anchor in Champa, Java, Sumatra, Ceylon, Siam, Bengal, Brunei, South Arabia, Mecca, Malindi, and at other ports of call to collect tributes.

Cheng Ho was unaware that the Chinese emperor had died while the voyages were under way and that his successor, in an abrupt switch in foreign policy, had done away with the tributes and had suspended China's maritime exploration in the 1420s. The new emperor was so isolationist that he issued an order to halt the building of oceangoing vessels. By 1500 the Chinese Imperial Palace had criminalized the construction of oceangoing ships with more than two masts, and in 1551 going to sea in a multimasted ship was declared an act of treason. Although it is pure conjecture, many historians assert that if Chinese emperors had remained committed to maritime exploration during the Ming dynasty (A.D. 1368–1644), China would not only have discovered Europe before Europe discovered China but would have had a strong foothold in the New World by the time the Europeans ventured along.

GAM SAAN ("GOLD MOUNTAIN"); OR, ROLLING OUT THE WELCOME MAT IN CALIFORNIA

What's Gam Saan, and how did it generate the first significant wave of Chinese immigration to America?

Gam Saan, which is Cantonese for "Gold Mountain," is the name that the Chinese gave to California after gold was discovered in the Sacramento Valley on January 24, 1848, changing forever the course of American history. The news that the Americans had struck gold electrified the Chinese. In 1848 and 1849 only a few hundred Chinese prospectors, who hailed mainly from the poor rural areas of south China made their way to California. However, by 1851 some 2,716 Chinese with gold on their minds had braved the rough ocean crossing to America, and by 1852 that figure had increased nearly tenfold, to 20,026. Historians are divided in their opinions as to how the Chinese financed their voyages to the New World. Some argue that the majority of Chinese entered into credit contracts that essentially turned them into slaves. Other historians maintain that some Chinese paid their own way and that even those with credit contracts could exercise free will.

Why were the Chinese invited to participate in President Taylor's funeral service in 1850?

The Californians didn't seem to mind when, in 1849, more than eighty thousand fortune seekers from the American East and Midwest and from such distant places as Europe, Asia, and Latin America descended on the gold mines that sprung up around Sutter's Mill. Euphoric over gold, the state of California rolled out the welcome mat to miners from far and near. In a gesture of good will, Californians invited Chinese gold miners to join them at ceremonies marking California's admission into the Union in 1850. At the celebration, **Nathaniel Bennett,** a justice of the California state supreme court, addressed the Chinese: ". . . You stand among us in all respects equals. . . . Henceforth we have one country, one hope, one destiny."

Californians' hospitality did not end there. That same year, San Francisco mayor **John White Geary** and some of his fellow citizens presented the Chinese in the city with gifts of Chinese books and paper, along with an invitation to attend commemorative funeral services for President **Zachary Taylor.** Californians were so at ease with the Chinese in their midst that in 1852 California governor **John McDougal** recommended that a system of land grants be established to encourage the Chinese to immigrate and settle in California. He did not foresee that Californians' benevolence toward the Chinese would soon turn to rancor.

"California for Americans"?

By 1852, as foreigners continued to pour into California's gold mines, white miners grew increasingly concerned that their piece of the pie was shrinking fast. Exclusionist cries of "California for Americans!" began to ring out across the state. Despite such squawking in California in the early 1850s over the "invaders" from distant lands, who had caused white gold miners' profits to plummet, the U.S. Congress refused to pass laws forbidding foreigners from mining for gold in the state of California, and the California state legislature seconded the motion by insisting that decisions about regulations be left up to local authorities. With little sympathy from the federal and state governments, Californians vented their outrage directly on foreign miners, dispensing "justice" as they saw fit. Numerous mining camps in the state passed hateful resolutions outlawing mining by foreigners. Californians also violently attacked the Chinese—even murdering some—and dispossessed them of their property.

One Chinese miner who was murdered in California around this time was **Ling Sing**. In 1853 **George W. Hall** and two others were tried for the crime, and one white and three Chinese witnesses testified on behalf of the prosecution in the case. The judge found only George Hall guilty of Ling Sing's murder. However, Hall's attorney appealed the case, arguing that a California statute enacted in 1849 that provided that "no Black or Mulatto person, or Indian, shall be allowed to give evidence for or against a white man" should also apply to the Chinese. In 1854 the California Supreme Court, in *People v. Hall*, reversed Hall's conviction on the grounds that the words "Indian, Negro, Black, and White" were "generic terms," and therefore non-whites, such as the Chinese, could not testify against whites. In his opinion, Chief Justice **Hugh G. Murray** reasoned that "Indian as commonly used refers only to the North American Indian, yet in the days of Columbus all shores washed by Chinese waters were called the Indies. In the second place the word 'white' necessarily excludes all races other than Caucasian; and in the third place, even if this were not so, I would decide against the testimony of Chinese on grounds of public policy."

With the California Supreme Court's decision in *People v. Hall*, the Chinese in the state were stripped of legal protection, and they became easy prey for white attackers. When the Civil War ended in 1865, the California state legislature removed the restrictions on the testimony of African Americans called for in the 1849 California statute, but those on the testimony of Mongolians, Chinese, and Indians were left intact.

Were the Chinese who labored in America in the latter half of the nineteenth century eligible for U.S. citizenship?

The Naturalization Act of 1790 specified that only "free white aliens" were eligible for naturalized U.S. citizenship once they completed two years of residence in the United States. With the ratification on July 28, 1868, of the Fourteenth Amendment to the U.S. Constitution, which is also known as the Reconstruction Amendment because former slaves were granted citizenship, "persons of African descent" were added to the short list of those eligible for naturalization. At the same time, the U.S. Congress took up the issue of whether naturalization rights should be extended to Asians in the United States. Efforts by Senator **Charles Sumner** of Massachusetts and then by Senator **Lyman Trumbull** of Illinois to extend the privilege of naturalization to persons "born in the Chinese Empire" both failed. The question of Asian naturalization would not be solved for many decades to come.

Without the right of naturalization, most Chinese in the United States considered themselves strangers in a strange land and "sojourners" abroad. Consequently, they sought to make an honest living toiling in America and then to one day set sail for home, where they would pay off their debts, join or start their families, and forge a better life on Chinese soil.

What was California's Foreign Miners' License Tax Law?

In an effort to appease California's nativists, whose concerns over sharing the state's gold with foreigners had escalated into violence, and egged on by California governor **John Bigler,** the California state legislature passed the Foreign Miners' License Tax Law in mid-1852. In keeping with the law, persons who were neither native-born nor naturalized U.S. citizens were required to purchase pricey mining licenses in order to mine for gold in California. California lawmakers knew very well that the Chinese were ineligible for U.S. citizenship (the Naturalization Act of 1790 extended that privilege only to "free white aliens") and that the Chinese gold miners in the state could not afford to buy mining licenses. Thus, the Foreign Miners' License Tax Law essentially amounted to a nativist measure aimed at halting the influx of Chinese workers to California and discouraging those already in the state from staying.

Unwilling to throw in the towel, the Chinese miners in California struggled to pay the license tax and to stay on in the gold mines. Between 1855 and 1870, when the federal Civil Rights Act of 1870 voided the Foreign Miners' License Tax Law, virtually all of the license tax collected in California—a sum of almost $5 million—came out of Chinese pockets. Since the Chinese had bowed but had not broken from the weight of the Foreign Miners' License Tax, California nativists grew even more enraged and searched frantically for a way to stem the tide of Chinese immigration. Clutching at straws, the U.S. House Committee on Mines and Mining, which was created on December 19, 1865, to address issues related to mining interests, charged that since the Chinese had arrived in the United States under credit contracts, such contracts should be declared null and void, and the Chinese should be forbidden to work as miners. Although both the committee and Governor Bigler favored such legislation, it did not pass. Angry Californians reacted by intensifying their efforts to oust the Chinese from their state.

Not every Californian was against the Chinese. In fact, in response to an increase in the Foreign Miners' License Tax, fair-minded citizens of the state of California, with the support of newspapers in the mining districts, presented petitions to the California state legislature in 1856 requesting that the tax be reduced. Nativist Californians fought back: In 1858 they managed to stem the flow of Chinese immigrants into California with the passage of legislation that forbade the Chinese from disembarking from ships on the Pacific coast except in cases of extreme emergency. In keeping with the law, the captain of any ship carrying Chinese citizens that docked along the coast could be fined up to $600 or imprisoned for up to a year.

Why did the Chinese go on "California dreaming" in the face of all this nativist hatred?

The Opium Wars, which China waged against the British between 1839 and 1842 and between 1859 and 1860, and the country's struggles to quell domestic revolts during the Taiping Rebellion from 1850 to 1864—during which an estimated twenty million Chinese perished—reduced China's ruling Qing dynasty (1644–1912) to a state of abject poverty. Those Chinese peasants who did not lose their lives during these decades of military defeat endured intense suffering: A large number lost their homes, their land, and their meager savings. Many pinned their hopes on California, "Gold Mountain," as the only way out of the economic morass.

WORKIN' ON THE RAILROAD . . . AND IN THE FACTORY . . . AND IN THE FIELDS

How did America's rapid expansion westward create jobs for the Chinese in the post-gold rush decades?

In the decades leading up to the California gold rush, the young American republic had embraced Manifest Destiny as its guiding principle, that is, extending the nation's borders to the edges of the continent to allow for "the free development of our multiplying millions." The rapid expansion westward in the first half of the nineteenth century ultimately necessitated the construction of a transportation system that would facilitate the movement of workers and goods. In 1862 the U.S. Congress enacted legislation providing for the construction of a transcontinental railroad to link the nation from east to west. The U.S. government gave federal land grants to the Union Pacific Railroad to break ground at Omaha, Nebraska, and build westward to Promontory Point, Utah, and to the Central Pacific Railroad to begin construction at Sacramento, California, and build eastward to Utah.

When the Chinese proved to be the most dependable workers on the transcontinental railroad, employers with the Central Pacific sought them out as their main source of labor. The Chinese were eager to take jobs on the railroad because by the early 1860s gold was growing scarce in the mines of California and virulent nativism in that state had made life rather unbearable. As pressure mounted to complete construction on the railroad within the time frame that Congress had specified, the Central Pacific dispatched an agent to China to recruit Chinese laborers. With little opportunity in an impoverished China and convinced that America was the land of golden opportunity, a good number of Chinese took the Central Pacific up on its job offers. However, most could not afford the high fare of forty dollars for passage, so their future employers prepaid the sum. In return, the Chinese signed contracts that committed them to working for no pay for a specified time period.

Unfortunately, many of the Chinese workers on the railroad could not read the contracts they signed, and their employers took advantage of the situation by cheating them out of pay, forcing them to work for nothing well beyond their contracts. When they were compensated, the Chinese made far less than fellow white laborers performing equivalent work. And they generally worked longer hours than whites, were subjected to greater occupational hazards, and were often beaten by their employers. In June 1867 about two thousand Chinese railroad workers with the Central Pacific went on strike, calling for an end to maltreatment and unfair wages. The railroad responded by withholding food from the strikers, who, as isolated as they were in the wilds, had no other choice but to return to work.

Were the Chinese given credit for their part in building the transcontinental railroad?

The construction of the Central Pacific Railroad line was a feat accomplished in large measure by Chinese workers. Approximately one-half of the ten thousand laborers in the Central Pacific's construction gangs were Chinese. They cleared trees and brush, blasted rock with explosives, shoveled debris and carted it away, and laid the tracks. And more than one thousand Chinese lost their lives in the effort, falling victim to such perils as avalanches in the Sierra Nevada.

Yet, on May 10, 1869, when the two railways linking east and west were finally joined at Promontory Point, Utah, before a large crowd, and a golden spike was driven in to commemorate the momentous occasion, the Chinese were absent. Despite their invaluable contributions to the construction of the transcontinental railroad—and their monumental sacrifices—Chinese laborers had been purposely excluded from the ceremonies and from the famous photograph of the Americans who drove the golden spike. Then, to add insult to injury, the Central Pacific laid off almost all of the Chinese in its employ. Thousands of these laid-off Chinese railroad workers poured into San Francisco, where they joined Chinese ex-miners in manufacturing. The Chinese found low-paying jobs in knitting mills, woolen mills, paper mills, tanneries, garment factories, and cigar factories. Thanks to this influx of workers, between 1860 and 1870 San Francisco's Chinese community swelled from 2,719 to 12,022. Had it not been for the thousands of Chinese willing to work hard for rock-bottom pay, San Francisco might never have become a leading manufacturing city in America in the latter half of the nineteenth century.

Why did the Chinese settle in Chinatowns?

Around the time of the California gold rush, most Chinese in America congregated in small enclaves in rural areas, a number of which eventually grew into self-sufficient Chinatowns. In the 1850s a Chinatown took shape in the heart of San Francisco, around what was then Portsmouth Square. The thousands of Chinese who ventured to the city after the transcontinental railroad was completed settled in this Chinatown, and by 1870 it was home to 24 percent of all the Chinese in California and had come to be known as *Dai Fou*, or "Big City." Settling in Chinatowns was not always a voluntary act for the Chinese. Even though the Chinese were specifically denied the right to become naturalized American citizens, Americans took further steps to alienate them by passing laws aimed at segregating them from the community at large. For instance, in 1879 the California legislature passed a law, subsequently struck down as unconstitutional, that required towns and cities to remove the Chinese from their streets. And, in 1885 the citizens of Tucson organized a petition drive to require Chinese to settle in a Chinatown, where they could be better monitored. Such legislation, as well as the general atmosphere of xenophobia, caused many

Chinese who had previously lived in rural areas among America's citizenry to flee to Chinatowns.

What were the Chinese Six Companies?

By the late 1850s the Chinese in America were forming associations geared at shielding them from xenophobia and assisting newcomers. Clan associations protected all those with a common ancestral lineage, while district associations looked out for Chinese from the same districts of Kwangtung Province, whence most of the immigrants had come. As their numbers grew, district associations came under the jurisdiction of an umbrella organization called the Chinese Consolidated Benevolent Association, later known as the Chinese Six Companies, or Six Companies.

Formed in the 1860s and headquartered in San Francisco, the Chinese Six Companies and its branches operated like mini–welfare states in every Chinese quarter, fulfilling benevolent functions on behalf of members of the community and new arrivals. For instance, they sent agents to greet incoming ships with Chinese passengers on board; helped with housing arrangements for newcomers; aided the elderly, the infirm, and the unemployed; and arranged for the shipment back to China of the bones of the deceased for burial in ancestral grounds. The Chinese Six Companies also served as representatives of their community before the California state legislature. During periods of intense anti-Chinese sentiment and agitation, they hired white attorneys to represent Chinese interests.

How did the Chinese build California's agricultural industry?

While a sizable percentage of Chinese railroad workers entered San Francisco's manufacturing industries after the transcontinental railroad was completed in 1869, many who had once farmed in the Pearl River Delta in Kwangtung Province found work in California's agricultural belts, imparting their expertise to American farmers who were turning their wheat fields into fruit orchards and vegetable croplands and to those who were transforming the state's countless undeveloped acres into fertile farmland. For instance, near the confluence of the San Joaquin and Sacramento Rivers at Suisin Bay, the Chinese provided the know-how and the muscle to turn marshes into arable land, which they accomplished by constructing an intricate system of drainage channels. Chinese laborers also dug miles of ditches to drain California's Salinas Valley and, in the process, raised the value of the land from twenty-eight dollars an acre in 1875 to one hundred dollars an acre in 1877.

In 1870 only 18 percent of farm workers in California were Chinese. However, once California farmers saw how effective the Chinese were in their agricultural methods—and how willing they were to work for low wages—virtually all of the state's farmland was "turned over" to their care. By 1880 the Chinese represented 86 percent of farm workers in Sacramento County, 85 percent in Yuba County, and 67 percent in Solano. Still, in the 1870s a good number of Chinese farmers quickly tired of digging ditches and taking orders; they hungered for a piece of land to cultivate on their own terms. Through a system of tenancy, some of these Chinese signed contracts with white landowners that allowed them to cultivate the land with borrowed farm equipment and then split the profits.

How did the Bing cherry get its name, and why does the Florida orange owe a debt of gratitude to a Chinese American?

Beginning in the 1850s, Chinese farm laborers also made invaluable contributions to the development of agriculture in the Pacific Northwest and elsewhere. In 1855 a Chinese immigrant named **Ah Bing** went to work in the Lewelling family's orchards in Milwaukie, Oregon. There he played a significant role in the creation, by grafting, of a new variety of cherry, the popular Bing cherry, which bears his name. When anti-Chinese sentiment grew fierce in Oregon in 1885, Bing and his fellow Chinese workers at the orchards found refuge in the Lewelling home. In 1889, after working in the Lewelling orchards for thirty years, Bing sailed back to China for a visit. Due to anti-Chinese immigration laws on the books (namely, the Exclusion Act of 1882), he never again stepped foot in America.

In the same year that Ah Bing was taking refuge in the Lewelling house, another Chinese immigrant, **Lue Gim Gong,** who was born in 1860 in Canton, China, went to work in the orange groves of Deland, Florida. Known as the Citrus Wizard, Lue devoted a great deal of time in the groves to experimenting with the fruit. By cross-pollinating a Hart's Late with a Mediterranean Sweet, he succeeded in developing in 1911 a revolutionary orange that ripened in early autumn and was more resistant to frost than common varieties. The Lue Gim Gong orange represented an extremely important step forward for American agriculture: Its development enabled Florida's nascent citrus industry to get off the ground.

MORE ANTI-CHINESE HOSTILITY IN THE WEST

Why did Californians call the Chinese evil in the 1870s?

In 1873 the exorbitant cost of waging the American Civil War and of constructing the railroads, inflated credit, and losses from high-risk commercial ventures threw the United States into an economic depression that would persist until 1889. California's boom turned to doom, and the state's unemployment rate soared. Before long anti-Chinese nativist cries of "California for Americans!" reached a feverish pitch in the state once again as unemployed Californians, searching for a convenient scapegoat to blame their troubles on, again targeted the Chinese. Even though foreign-born Irish, German, and Scandinavian workers far outnumbered Chinese workers in California, the unfortunate Chinese, with their queues, basket hats, loose-fitting clothes, and "yellow skin and almond eyes," bore the brunt of nativist Californians' hostility because they could not fade into the background as easily as their European counterparts.

For exclusionist Californians, **Bret Harte**'s poem "Plain Language from Truthful James," also known as "The Heathen Chinee," which was first published in the *Overland Monthly* in 1870, put into words their very sentiments about the Chinese, the seeming source of their woe: "That for ways that are dark/And for tricks that are vain/The heathen Chinee is peculiar." Newspapers throughout the land reprinted Harte's poem over and over, and before long the phrase "heathen Chinee" was on the lips of many Americans. Unfortunately Californians expressed their hostility toward the Chinese in more vicious forms than reciting poems and singing songs. All over California, from the Redwood Forest to San Diego, signs reading "No Chinese Need Apply" cropped up, and restaurants, hotels, and barbershops commonly turned would-be Chinese patrons away at the door. In the late 1870s the hostility escalated into violence as anti-Chinese riots erupted all over the state. In 1877 irate mobs set twenty-five Chinese laundries ablaze in San Francisco, and in 1878 the citizens of Truckee chased out all the Chinese. Physical attacks against the Chinese became so commonplace in California that a San Francisco newspaper warned: "It is scarcely safe for a Chinaman to walk the streets in certain parts of this city. When seen, whether by day or night, they are mercilessly pelted with stones by the young scapegraces. . . ."

In 1877 an alarmed California Senate appointed a committee to ascertain the extent to which Chinese immigrants threatened the state's welfare. The committee published and distributed a formal report entitled *Address to the People of the*

United States upon the Evils of Chinese Immigration, which was designed to alert Congress about the dangers that the Chinese posed to the welfare of California. The report claimed that the Chinese were chiefly engaged in prostitution, criminal rings, and *coolie* traffic, and that they were not equipped to assimilate into the American mainstream: "During their entire settlement in California, they have never adapted themselves to our habits . . . never discovered the difference between right and wrong, never ceased the worship of their idol gods, or advanced a step beyond the traditions of their native hive."

Did San Franciscans actually harass the Chinese over their hairstyles, laundry services, and gong playing in the 1870s?

As California's nativists, seething from the economic depression that had taken hold, lashed out with ferocity at the Chinese in the 1870s, anti-Chinese ordinances were passed with startling regularity in the state. For example, in 1873 San Francisco put into effect the Queue Ordinance, which granted prison officials the right to cut off a Chinese prisoner's queue, or single braid hanging from the back of the head (a style that dates back to the seventeenth century). And in 1873 and 1876, San Franciscans, targeting the numerous Chinese laundries in their city, passed the Laundry License Ordinances, which put in place a licensing fee system for laundries that was grossly unfair to the Chinese in the business. Laundries that depended on one horse for deliveries incurred a two-dollar fee, those that used two horses were charged a four-dollar licensing fee, and those without horses had to pay a fifteen-dollar fee. Since Chinese laundries did not rely on horses to make deliveries, they were saddled with the heaviest taxes.

Other inane and malicious ordinances were written into the books in the 1870s that made it illegal for San Francisco

Chinese to carry vegetable and clothes baskets on poles on the sidewalks, stage theatrical performances, and play the gong. An ordinance was even passed that forbade the Chinese from sending the bones of the deceased back to China for burial, a sacred gesture symbolizing the return of the spirit to its home.

How did the Chinese in Butte, Montana, get started in the laundry business?

While 77 percent of all Chinese in America dwelled in California in 1870, a small percentage found their way to Idaho, Montana, and Nevada, where jobs in mining were growing more abundant. The mining industry had been established in Butte, Montana, in 1862, and first the mining of gold and then the mining of silver dominated the local economy. When copper was discovered in Butte in 1880, and the Anaconda Copper Mining Company talked of exploiting the "richest hill on earth," young adventurers swarmed to the pioneer town with high hopes of getting rich quick. Among them were young Chinese men, who arrived in such numbers that in 1880 the Chinese comprised 21.1 percent of the town's population.

Just as in the gold mines of California in previous decades, the Chinese miners in Butte soon encountered intense hostility from Anglo-Saxon miners, who wanted to hoard the copper. Mining in Butte lost its charm for the Chinese in 1883, when the Montana Territorial Supreme Court declared that all mining claims held by aliens ineligible for citizenship, such as the Chinese, would be void. In the face of such discrimination, a number of Chinese miners in Butte and other frontier towns turned to other occupations. Since towns like Butte had very few women to do the cooking and cleaning, the Chinese found a niche for themselves doing "women's work." In the 1880s they hired themselves out as domestic servants or set up restaurants, tailor shops, and laundries.

The laundry business was an especially suitable venture for the Butte Chinese, as it was for Chinese elsewhere in America, since it required only a minimal knowledge of English and a relatively small capital investment, it could be mastered in a short time through an apprenticeship with a clansman, and it was easy to exit should a Chinese "sojourner" desire to return home to China. By 1905 the citizens of Butte had their choice of thirty-two Chinese laundries. The Chinese would come to dominate the laundry business beyond the frontier towns. By the first decade of the twentieth century, nearly every American city had its share of Chinese laundries, and 25 percent of all employed Chinese men in the United States worked in a laundry.

EASTWARD HO!

What brought the Chinese to the South after the American Civil War?

Even though the Chinese settled west of the Rockies for the most part until the 1880s, some headed to the southern states in the months after President **Abraham Lincoln** issued the Emancipation Proclamation, freeing the slaves on January 1, 1863. The reason was simple. During the era of Reconstruction, former slaves who remained on the plantations were no longer willing to break their backs in the fields. Plantation owners determined that one way to force their former slaves to work harder was to hire Chinese laborers to compete for their jobs. In the 1870s Louisiana and Mississippi planters brought hundreds of Chinese laborers, some from abroad, to work on their land, pitting them against freed slaves.

The Chinese, however, did not stick around on the southern plantations for very long. They preferred manufacturing jobs in the cities over toiling in the hot fields. By 1880 an appreciable number of Chinese laborers in the South had gravitated to New Orleans to work as laundry operators, cooks, cigar makers, domestic servants, and gardeners. Planters contributed to this trend by laying off Chinese laborers once they regained an upper hand over the former slaves.

Why did a large number of Chinese settle in northeastern cities in the final decades of the nineteenth century?

As the nineteenth century wound down, an appreciable proportion of the Chinese population in the West could no longer take the stress of living among an exclusionist American citizenry with all its anti-Chinese laws and regulations. In the 1880s and 1890s significant numbers of Chinese in the West headed to large cities in the Northeast, especially New York City and Boston, where they joined the Chinese already living in nascent Chinatowns. This movement of Chinese from west to east was so significant that when the nineteenth century came to a close, only half of all the Chinese in the United States dwelled in the state of California.

The Chinatown in Lower Manhattan, nowadays the largest in the United States, began as a small Chinese neighborhood that sprang up on Doyer's Farm near the Bowery around the 1860s. The first Chinese person to move into the neighborhood was a Kwangtung merchant named **Wo Kee,** who took up residence at 8 Mott Street in 1858. At first the neighborhood attracted few Chinese: In 1870 it was home to only about fifty Chinese, who inhabited uncomfortable attics and dank, dimly lit cellars, and sold cigars and newspapers on the streets to eke out a meager living. The sizable migration of Chinese across the Rockies beginning in the 1880s transformed the little Chinese neighborhood into a self-sufficient Chinatown, the heart of which was Mott Street. The early inhabitants of Manhattan's Chinatown opened restaurants, noodle shops, tea parlors, laundries, and garment sweatshops. They kept mostly to themselves: Only a small number ventured out of the neighborhood by day to hawk tickets to the popular Chinatown lottery.

Is it true that P. T. Barnum put Chinese people on display in his museum in New York City?

By 1850 Americans in the West had caught a glimpse of the Chinese, but for New Yorkers they were the epitome of exoticism. American showman **Phineas T. Barnum,** whose circuses and museum filled with assorted freaks of nature and "curiosities"—often fake—attracted huge throngs, saw a need (dollar signs) in New York City and filled it. In April 1850 he put an aristocratic Chinese women named **Pwan-Yekoo** and her Chinese servants on display at his American Museum, which was housed in a building at the corner of Broadway and Ann Street in Lower Manhattan from 1841 to 1865, when it burned down. An article in the *New York Courier and Enquirer* about Pwan-Yekoo and her entourage—mistakenly called "The Living Chinese Family" in an 1850 Currier lithograph—on opening day, April 22, 1850, reveals the degree of excitement that the exhibit generated among New Yorkers: "It is next to impossible to catch even a glimpse of a lady of distinction in China itself. Miss Pwan-Yekoo is naturally, therefore, the great sought-after by all the curious in New York. Her tiny feet, her polished manners, her *distingué* air, her pretty face and charming vivacity, interest all who behold her."

P. T. Barnum's fascination with the Chinese did not begin in 1850. In the 1840s he had other Chinese exhibits on display, including his "Chinese Museum," a life-size replica of the entrance to a Chinese temple, and a wax figure of conjoined twins **Chang** and **Eng Bunker,** who were born in 1811 to Chinese parents in Siam (present-day Thailand). In 1860 the real Bunker twins did a six-week stint at the American Museum in order to raise funds to support their twenty-two children from their marriages to the Caucasian sisters **Sarah Yates** and **Adelaide Yates.** At some point, Barnum also had on display **Chang-Yu Sing,** an eight-foot Chinese giant.

What are tongs, *and why have they been labeled the Chinese Mafia?*

The Chinese Six Companies—the benevolent associations that the Chinese first formed in San Francisco in the 1860s as a way to promote the welfare of members of the community and new arrivals—functioned aboveboard. However, the community-oriented organizations known as *tongs*, which started out as benevolent associations and trade unions, were modeled on the Triad Society, a fiercely political, antiforeign, anti-Qing secret organization that originated in Kwangtung Province, and functioned in total antiestablishment secrecy in Chinatowns. Most Chinese belonged to a district association in their community, but only a select group belonged to *tongs*.

Early on, the *tongs* tried to gain access to the political arena and to wrest control of Chinatowns from the Chinese Six Companies. When they were unsuccessful, they devolved into criminal rings akin to the Italian Mafia, running brothels, gambling joints, and opium dens in Chinatowns. They ruled by terrorizing fellow Chinese and demanding protection money from Chinese businesses. In an effort to spread their influence, the *tongs* fought each other with knives and guns for control of the streets in almost every Chinatown in America. In Manhattan's Chinatown, the *tongs* known as the Hip Sings managed by spilling blood to take over Pell and Doyer Streets, while the On Leongs seized control of Mott Street. Their gruesome turf wars stole the headlines of New York papers from the 1910s until the 1930s, when rival *tongs* finally drew a turf boundary down the middle of Mott Street.

To this day, *tongs* in New York City are still involved in both legitimate and illicit enterprises. Nowadays they extort money from the majority of restaurants and other businesses in the city's Chinatowns. They also control a large percentage of the heroin traffic in New York City, which they supply through links with drug rings in Southeast Asia.

CHINESE WOMEN IN AMERICA

Who was called "a hundred men's wife"?

A Chinese prostitute, known colloquially as a singsong girl, was also called a hundred men's wife. According to U.S. Census records, 61 percent of the 3,536 Chinese women in California in 1870 made a living on the streets as prostitutes, mainly in mining and railroad towns across the state and in the Chinatowns of Sacramento, San Francisco, and Marysville. A large percentage of them had been sold, abducted or tricked into the trade, and most were slaves to madams or pimps, who paid extortion money to the *tongs.* Chinese prostitution was rampant in 1870 (and in later decades) because the Chinese community in the United States then was overwhelmingly male, as it had been since the first Chinese gold miners labored in California. In 1880, for example, there were 70,000 Chinese men documented in California but fewer than 4,000 Chinese women. Chinese women came to America in such scant numbers in the nineteenth century due to financial constraints, cultural considerations (women were not supposed to travel alone), the severe limitations on Chinese immigration, and the difficult working conditions and anti-Chinese hostility in the United States.

What was the Page Law of 1875, and why was it an insult to Chinese women?

In 1875 the U.S. Congress passed a statute, commonly referred to as the Page Law, that prohibited the immigration of Chinese contract laborers and the importation of Chinese women for immoral purposes—purportedly in response to U.S. law enforcement claims that an organized network was trafficking Chinese prostitutes into the United States. The Page Law had a profound effect on Chinese prostitution in America. The number of Chinese women working as prostitutes in

California dropped from 61 percent in 1870 to just 24 percent in 1880, while the number of Chinese women employed as housekeepers jumped from 21 percent in 1870 to 46 percent in 1880. It should be noted that some of these housekeepers were former prostitutes who had paid off their debts or escaped the vicious *tongs* and had moved on to less volatile employment.

Unfortunately, another effect of the Page Law was that it cast doubt on the virtues of all Chinese women seeking to immigrate to the United States. Many resorted to securing certificates of good character to present to U.S. immigration officials, but even such certificates did not ensure entrance into the United States. Their virtue in question and interrogations at immigration checkpoints tougher, many Chinese women who might have ventured to America decided to stay home: Between 1875 and 1882, one-third fewer Chinese women immigrated to the United States than in the years just prior to the enactment of the Page Law.

ANTI-CHINESE LEGISLATION

What was the Chinese Exclusion Act?

In 1882 the U.S. Congress caved in to demands by powerful American labor unions to halt Chinese immigration by enacting the Chinese Exclusion Act, the first and only exclusionary federal immigration law in American history to target a specific nationality. It was also the first major victory that nativist Americans enjoyed in their campaign to rid the United States of Chinese immigrants. Among other things, the Chinese Exclusion Act of 1882 prohibited the immigration of Chinese to the United States for a period of ten years. Only merchants, diplomats, travelers, and students were exempt from exclusion. Those Chinese already on American soil were free to come and go, provided they obtain special certificates, what became popularly known as Section 6 certificates, confirming their legal status, as stipulated in Section 6 of the Chinese Exclusion Act. In addition, the act expressly prohibited the Chinese in the United States from becoming naturalized American citizens.

The 1882 Chinese Exclusion Act came as a shock to the Chinese community in America and dampened the spirits of its scores of Chinese men. The almost complete ban on Chinese immigration meant that Chinese bachelors had few prospects of finding mates in America and that those men whose wives or fiancées were still in China had little chance of being reunited with them on American soil. This lopsided male-female ratio among Chinese in the United States, perpetuated by the Chinese Exclusion Act, accounts for the very small numbers of Chinese Americans born in the late nineteenth and early twentieth centuries.

In 1892 the Chinese Exclusion Act was extended another ten years, and in 1902 it was extended indefinitely. The act was not repealed until 1943, when by a curious twist of fate China allied itself with the United States in World War II and the U.S. government determined that a more fair Chinese immigration policy was necessary to ensure the success of the wartime alliance. With the repeal of the Chinese Exclusion Act, the Chinese in America were permitted to become naturalized U.S. citizens—for the first time in the nearly one hundred years that they had been coming in significant waves to the United States—and the door to Chinese immigration opened. But not very widely. The Chinese seeking to come to America's shores were confronted by an immigration quota of 105.

Since the Page Law and the Chinese Exclusion Act made it nearly impossible for Chinese women to come to America, did Chinese bachelors marry "out"?

Chinese men in nineteenth-century America rarely courted women of other ethnicities. In the first place, most non-Chinese women shunned their company, and second, the Chinese considered their race superior to all others and did not want to jeopardize the ethnic purity of their lineage. Over the course of time, as Chinese men assimilated to American life as best they could and tired of bachelor life, a good number adopted more liberal attitudes about fraternizing with and marrying women of other ethnic backgrounds. Some were enticed by the benefits that came with marrying American citizens: As the spouses of citizens, Chinese men could skirt anti-Asian laws that made it impossible for them to own land, and thus they could finally drive roots into the American soil and build families. Opportunities also opened up for Chinese women who married Americans: Most importantly, they could circumvent naturalization and become American citizens.

By the 1920s, as more and more children were born to Chinese alien parents in the United States and thus were automatically American citizens, and as Chinese aliens married American citizens and achieved citizenship, the U.S. government determined that the nation's Anglo-Saxon way of life was under threat and passed the draconian, antimiscegenation Cable Act in 1922. The Cable Act essentially punished American women who married aliens ineligible for citizenship by revoking the women's citizenship and prohibited female aliens ineligible for citizenship from circumventing naturalization laws by marrying American citizens. Until the Cable Act was repealed in 1936, American women, for the most part, steered clear of eligible Chinese bachelors.

The Cable Act was preceded by a host of state laws aimed at stopping interracial marriage. For instance, in 1866 Oregon's antimiscegenation law, originally aimed at African Americans, was extended to include Hawaiians, Native Americans, and persons more than half Chinese. And, California's antimiscegenation law of 1880 prohibited marriage between a white and a "negro, mulatto, or Mongolian."

What was the Scott Act of 1888, and how was it yet another setback for the Chinese in America?

The Scott Act of 1888 was designed to further reduce the small number of Chinese entering the United States. It accomplished this by limiting the use of Section 6 certificates—which, in keeping with the 1882 Chinese Exclusion Act, guaranteed Chinese laborers the right to reenter the United States after a trip back to China—to those Chinese laborers who had a lawful wife, child, or parent in the United States or had U.S. real estate holdings valued at one thousand dollars or more. Since most Chinese in America were bachelors and did not own land, the negative effect of the Scott Act was widespread. At the time the act went into effect, approximately twenty thousand Chinese laborers possessing Section 6 certificates were overseas. They were forced to abandon their plans of returning to America. The approximately six hundred Chinese in transit to the United States when the Scott Act took effect were denied entry when they reached U.S. ports.

Upon signing the Scott Act, President **Grover Cleveland** declared it necessary because the "experiment of blending the social habits and mutual race idiosyncrasies of the Chinese laboring classes with those of the great body of the people of the United States . . . proved . . . in every sense unwise, impolitic, and injurious to both nations." Several U.S. senators and the Chinese government did not see the Scott Act quite the same way, declaring it a violation of the 1880 treaty between the United States and China, which allowed for the free entry and exit of those Chinese laborers already on American soil. The Chinese in America were equally up in arms over the Scott Act and promptly raised one hundred thousand dollars to challenge it in the courts. They got nowhere; lower federal courts, as well as the U.S. Supreme Court, upheld the Scott Act. It would not be repealed until 1894.

What was the Geary Act of 1892, and how did it manage to further demean Chinese immigrants?

In 1892 the U.S. Congress, succumbing to complaints that all Chinese looked and sounded alike, passed the Geary Act, which instituted a national registration system solely for the Chinese so that Americans could distinguish legal Chinese aliens from illegal aliens. All persons of Chinese ancestry in the United States were required to register with U.S. internal revenue authorities by providing a photograph and a description of their unique characteristics. They were then issued a certificate of residence, essentially an internal passport, stating that they were permitted to be in the United States. They were required to keep the certificate of residence on their person at all times and to present it whenever asked. Those Chinese who failed to register were to be deported by a federal judge—even if they were lawful residents—unless they could show with the aid of "at least one credible white witness" that they were U.S. residents at the time when the Geary Act was passed but had been unable to secure their certificate of residence.

The Geary Act was considered a more draconian measure than the Scott Act because it placed the burden of proving the legality of a Chinese person's presence in the United States on the Chinese person himself, denied bail to those arrested for Geary Act violations, required that white witnesses testify in cases involving Chinese, and allowed for arrests without warrants. Many Chinese refused to register. Others simply could not be bothered. A Chinese man named **Fong Yue Ting,** who had resided in New York City since 1879, did not take the time to register and was arrested when he was caught without a certificate of residence. He fought back, challenging the Geary Act on the grounds that it was unconstitutionally selective and discriminatory. In *Fong Yue Ting v. United States* (1893), the U.S. Supreme Court held that it was within Congress's power to exclude and expel aliens from the

United States. Justice **Horace Gray** summarized for the court: "Congress, having the right, as it may see fit, to expel aliens of a particular class, or to permit them to remain, has undoubtedly the right to provide a system of registration and identification of the members of that class within the country, and to take all proper means to carry out the system which it provides."

FIGHTING BACK: THE PAPER SONS

Who were the "paper sons," and how did the San Francisco earthquake of 1906 actually facilitate Chinese immigration?

After the Chinese Exclusion Act of 1882 was passed, reducing Chinese immigration to the United States to a mere trickle, the Chinese resorted to devising illegal methods, often entailing misrepresentation, to enter the country. A common strategy around exclusion legislation that they employed was to prove that they were, in fact, the sons or grandsons of U.S. citizens and, thus, were eligible for citizenship themselves. This was achieved through the purchase of fraudulent documents, "papers," establishing fictional relationships between Chinese Americans and their "sons," who became known as "paper sons" (there were few "paper daughters"). After memorizing all the facts about their new families, many a paper son managed to prove a relationship that did not exist in interrogations by U.S. immigration officials and thereby entered the United States.

The San Francisco earthquake and fire of April 8, 1906, which destroyed most of the city's vital records, presented an unprecedented opportunity for the Chinese to claim U.S. citizenship and bring actual family members and paper sons to America. When it became known that most of San Francisco's birth and citizenship records had been lost in the devastation that befell the city in 1906, a good number of Chinese men created fictitious American identities, declaring falsely that they had been born in the United States and, thus, were American citizens. As American citizens, they were entitled to bring family members to the United States. The new U.S. citizens routinely sold their papers to people from their villages or to complete strangers, causing the number of paper sons to surge.

To what lengths did the U.S. government go in attempting to counter the paper son phenomenon?

San Francisco immigration officials caught on to the fraudulent claims of U.S. citizenship by the Chinese. As one U.S. State Department report from that period noted, if every claim submitted were true, then "every known Chinese woman in San Francisco before the earthquake would have to have had 800 children." With few records to rely on, U.S. immigration officials responded to the paper son phenomenon by intensifying their interrogations, even of the Chinese who were exempt from exclusion under the Chinese Exclusion Act, such as students, teachers, and merchants.

The paper sons, and all prospective Chinese immigrants, resorted to memorizing facts and figures about "their forebears" in order to dodge traps laid by immigration officials. Transcripts of some of these paper son interrogations reveal that a good many questions covered details so minute that not even a real son could have known the answers: "Who occupied the house on the fifth lot of your row in your native village?" "How many water buffaloes does your village have?" "How many of those water buffaloes were male, and how many were female?"

Long after they had assimilated to American life, paper sons safeguarded their true identities, in some cases actually keeping them from family members, out of fear that they would be deported or worse if their real identities were discovered. Some paper sons even clung to their fake names for their entire lives and revealed their true identities only posthumously, when their real names were inscribed on their tombstones. For added protection, some requested that their real names be inscribed on their tombstones only in Chinese, next to inscriptions of their fake names in English.

What happened to those Chinese who got caught at immigration in San Francisco between 1910 and 1940?

In 1910 a special immigration station—complete with an administration building, hospital, detention barracks, and employee cottages—opened on Angel Island, the largest island in San Francisco Bay. Called the "Guardian of the Western Gate" by the Immigration Service, the facility was designed expressly as a holding area for Pacific Rim immigrants, mostly Chinese, whose right to enter the United States was under scrutiny. Between 1910 and 1940, approximately 175,000 Chinese aliens were held in the detention barracks on Angel Island until they could somehow convince immigration authorities that they were entitled to entry into the United States. For the majority, this process took two to three weeks, but for some it consumed months and even up to two years. Most detainees endured numerous humiliating interrogations by inspectors on even the most minuscule details of their family histories. (Although Angel Island has been called the "Ellis Island of the West," the comparison is terribly misleading. The average immigrant who came ashore at Ellis Island spent a mere three to five hours being processed by U.S. immigration authorities before they were on their way.)

As the enisled Chinese immigrants waited—packed in unsanitary, crowded quarters—for their fate, entry or deportation, to be decided, some vented their frustration and anger over emigration, exile, and incarceration by carving poems in the barrack walls. Many of these poems are still visible today. One unknown poet wrote:

For what reason must I sit in jail?
It is only because my country is weak and my family poor.
. . . . .
How many people ever return from battles?
. . . . .
Leaving behind my writing brush and removing my sword, I came to America.
Who was to know two streams of tears would flow upon arriving here?

In 1940, after three decades of operation, the U.S. government decided to close the Angel Island Immigration Station. On November 5, 1940, the last group of detainees—200 hopefuls, 150 of whom were Chinese—were transferred from the island to facilities in San Francisco. In 1941 the property was handed back to the army, which transformed it into the North Garrison of Fort McDowell. During World War II, the U.S. military processed German and Japanese prisoners in the Immigration Station's old detention barracks before shipping them to permanent detention camps on the U.S. mainland. When the war was over, the Immigration Station was abandoned, and in 1970 several of its now-dilapidated buildings were scheduled for demolition. Through the efforts of concerned citizens and the Angel Island Immigration Station Historical Advisory Committee, the buildings were saved and special legislation was passed that provided $250,000 for the restoration of the barracks. In 2000, Californians passed Proposition 12, earmarking $15 million for the restoration and preservation of the entire Angel Island Immigration Station.

Where did some of the first civil rights protests by Chinese in America take place?

Between 1895 and 1906, labor unions in Butte, Montana, in conjunction with the local chamber of commerce, organized a boycott of Chinese businesses with the intent of driving the

Chinese out of town. The Chinese fought back by hiring Colonel **Wilbur Fisk Sanders,** a prominent white attorney and a former U.S. senator from Montana, to initiate a lawsuit against the unions. As it turned out, Sanders won the case, and the Chinese held their ground in Butte. When news of their legal victory reached the Chinese Six Companies in San Francisco, its leaders supposedly declared: "The Butte Chinese are the smartest anywhere in the United States."

Chinese laundry owners also held their own in New York City in the early 1930s. White laundry operators in the city had introduced washing machines and steam presses, and the Chinese, who could not afford cutting-edge machinery, responded by lowering prices and offering free mending or free pickup and delivery. The white laundry operators retaliated by successfully lobbying the New York Board of Aldermen to pass a laundry ordinance requiring one-person laundries to post a thousand-dollar bond when they applied for a license. Chinese laundry operators fought back. In 1933 they formed the Chinese Hand Laundry Alliance, hired two lawyers, and challenged the bond ordinance. The Chinese Hand Laundry Alliance was able to convince the New York Board of Aldermen that the bond requirement discriminated against small laundries, and the bond was consequently reduced from one thousand dollars to one hundred dollars.

PEARL HARBOR AND PEARL BUCK; OR, HOW AMERICAN SINOPHOBIA BECAME SINOPHILIA

Why were Pearl Harbor and Pearl S. Buck considered blessings for the Chinese in America?

While the Empire of Japan's unprovoked surprise attack on the U.S. Pacific Fleet moored at Pearl Harbor on December 7, 1941, was "a date which will live in infamy" for all Americans, it was also a kind of blessing for the Chinese in America. On the day after the attack, President **Franklin Delano Roosevelt** declared war on the Japanese empire. Since the outbreak of the Second Sino-Japanese War in 1937, China, under the leadership of **Chiang Kai-shek,** had been battling Japanese forces for control of the Chinese mainland, and so on December 8, 1941, the United States and China found themselves confronting the same enemy. In his "A Call for Sacrifice" speech delivered before Congress on April 28, 1942, President Roosevelt not only asked Americans on the home front to work and sacrifice, following the example of the nation's "fighting men," but also acknowledged, as a way to signal his administration's willingness to forge a U.S.-China alliance, China's long-standing efforts in opposing Japanese aggression: "We remember that the Chinese people were the first to stand up and fight against the aggressors in this war; and in the future a still unconquerable China will play its proper role of maintaining peace and prosperity, not only in eastern Asia but in the whole world."

American goodwill toward China and Chiang Kai-shek spilled over to the Chinese on American soil, much to their relief. Nearly a century of insults and violence aimed at the "Chinamen," "heathen Chinee," and the "Chinks" in America gave way to gratitude that the Chinese and the Americans had joined together in the fight against the "dirty Japs." American novelist **Pearl Sydenstricker Buck** utilized the warming of U.S.-China relations during World War II to call for an end to anti-Chinese discrimination in the United States. Born on June 26, 1892, to Southern Presbyterian missionaries who were home on leave from their work in China, Pearl Buck was just three months old when the family returned to China so that her parents could resume their missionary efforts. Pearl spent most of her years in China up until 1934, when she returned permanently to the United States. Her experiences in China had a profound impact on her writing, as she acknowledged in her Nobel Lecture in 1938: "My earliest knowledge of story, of how to tell and write stories, came to me in China." The Chinese figure heavily in the more than seventy fiction and nonfiction works she published over the course of her life, including her novels *China Sky* (1941), *Dragon Seed* (1942), *Peony* (1948), *Kinfolk* (1949), and *Imperial Woman* (1956).

One of Pearl Buck's most celebrated works is the novel *The Good Earth* (1931), a compassionate portrayal of the struggle for survival of peasants in China's Anwei Province in the early twentieth century, which garnered Buck the Pulitzer Prize in Letters & Drama (Novel) in 1932. She was the first woman ever to receive the honor. In 1937 *The Good Earth* was made into a motion picture by the same name, starring **Paul Muni** and **Luise Rainer.** (Chinese-American actress **Anna May Wong**—the first internationally acclaimed Asian-American actress—was passed over for the female lead because the studio had selected a white leading man, and in those days Hollywood did not permit actors of different ethnic backgrounds to kiss on-screen.) In 1938 Pearl Buck became the first American woman to be honored with the Nobel Prize in Literature. Her literary accomplishments, as well as her direct appeals for the better treatment of America's Chinese, served over the decades to improve America's opinion of the Chinese people both in the United States and in China.

After she returned to America for good in 1934, Buck committed herself to promoting human rights, tolerance, and cultural understanding around the world, and to improving the quality of children's lives in many corners of the globe. In 1942 the distinguished writer established the East and West Association, which promoted cultural exchange and understanding between Asian and Western nations. Seven years later, in 1949, she founded Welcome House, the world's first international interracial adoption agency, and in 1964 she set up the Pearl S. Buck Foundation to provide monetary aid to impoverished children in several Asian countries. In 1991 Welcome House and the Pearl S. Buck Foundation merged into one organization, Pearl S. Buck International, whose mission is to improve the lives of children in need.

Pearl S. Buck's legacy endures not only in her humanitarian organizations but at her large estate, a National Historical Landmark, in Bucks County, Pennsylvania. Visitors can tour the farmhouse on the estate, which was home to the writer for thirty-eight years and which houses Chinese and nineteenth-century Pennsylvania art and an array of Pearl Buck's literary and humanitarian awards, among them her Nobel and Pulitzer prizes.

How did Time *magazine teach Americans to distinguish the Chinese ally from the Japanese foe in the aftermath of the attack on Pearl Harbor?*

Lest Americans confuse their Asian friends with their Asian foes, the December 22, 1941, issue of *Time* magazine published an article, "How to Tell Your Friends from the Japs," filled with helpful tips for distinguishing the Chinese and the Japanese, complete with photographs of a young Chinese man, a middle-aged Chinese man, a young Japanese man, and a middle-aged Japanese man for purposes of illustration. The article urges readers to bear in mind a few rules of thumb, including that "Japanese are likely to be stockier and broader-hipped than short Chinese," "Chinese, not as hairy as Japanese, seldom grow impressive mustache," "Most Chinese avoid horn-rimmed spectacles," "The Chinese expression is likely to be more placid, kindly, open; the Japanese more positive, dogmatic, arrogant," "Japanese are hesitant, nervous in conversation, laugh loudly at the wrong time," and "Japanese walk stiffly erect, hard heeled. Chinese, more relaxed, have an easy gait, sometimes shuffle."

Some Chinese were naturally unconvinced that Americans would be able to tell their friends from the Japs. When U.S. federal agents began rounding up Japanese after the attack on Pearl Harbor, some Chinese residents resorted to wearing signs declaring their Chinese ethnicity. A photograph in the University of Southern California's archival collections shows a Chinese worker with a sign attached to the back of his jacket that reads: ME CHINESE PLEASE NO JAP.

How did America's affection for the Chinese translate into the repeal of the Chinese Exclusion Act?

In response to both America's newfound compassion for the Chinese (thanks to Pearl Harbor and **Pearl S. Buck**) and the pressing need to strengthen the Sino-American alliance at a time when the world was engulfed in war, President **Roosevelt** and the U.S. Congress began to seriously consider repealing the nation's Chinese exclusion laws. On May 25, 1943, a group of American intellectuals formed in New York City the Citizens Committee to Repeal Chinese Exclusion and Place Immigration on a Quota Basis to push for an end to exclusion. Among the committee's spokespersons, who addressed Congress on the issue, were such prominent Americans as Pearl Buck; **Richard J. Walsh,** publisher of the John Day Company and editor of *Collier's Weekly, Judge, Asia Magazine,* and *United Nations World* (and Pearl Buck's husband); **Henry R. Luce,** the legendary founder of *Time, Fortune, Life,* and *Sports Illustrated* magazines; **Roger Baldwin** of the American Civil Liberties Union; the socialist academician **Broadus Mitchell;** and retired admiral **Harry E. Yarnell.**

In an effort to appeal to the average American, whose affection for the Chinese only went so far, the Citizens Committee argued that the elimination of exclusion in favor of a quota system would grant the Chinese equality as far as immigration was concerned, while at the same time actually reducing the number of Chinese laborers in the United States, since such an egalitarian policy would induce Chinese emigration authorities to cooperate with the United States and crack down on illegals leaving China.

The efforts of the Citizens Committee paid off. A law repealing Chinese exclusion was enacted in late 1943. It was based on a bill introduced by Congressman **Warren Magnuson,** a Democrat representing Washington, who served in the House from 1937 to 1942 and in the Senate from 1943 until 1980. In keeping with the law, all or part of the fifteen exclusionary statutes passed between 1882 and 1913 were repealed, the Naturalization Act was amended to allow "Chinese persons or persons of Chinese descent" to become eligible for naturalization, and an annual quota of 105 for "persons of the Chinese race" was instituted. Although the law was a step forward for the Chinese, the quota of 105 severely restricted access to immigration and was inherently discriminatory in its implementation from the standpoint that persons of Chinese ancestry, regardless of their country of origin, were categorized under the quota as "persons of Chinese race." Thus, Chinese born in Canada fell into this special category, while persons of European ancestry born in Canada could enter the United States as non-quota Canadian immigrants. The Chinese did not achieve immigration parity with other ethnic groups until the mid-1960s, when U.S. immigration laws were completely revamped.

The Republic of China gave the repeal of the Chinese Exclusion Act its stamp of approval, as evidenced by a press statement that the Chinese consul in Seattle issued: "The repeal of the Chinese Exclusions Acts places the Chinese people on a footing of actual equality with races of Caucasian or colored descent and it will constitute a milestone in the furtherance of friendship and mutual understanding between our two peoples." Still some voiced concern that issues affecting the quality of life of the Chinese in America were irrelevant to the deliberation and passage of the repeal of the Chinese Exclusion Act. For instance, a bill introduced in 1943 by Congressman **John Lesinski** of Michigan that would have granted the noncitizen wives of Chinese Americans the right to enter the United States without regard to the yearly ceiling of 105 was completely ignored by President Roosevelt. Three more years would pass before this bill, so critical to the issue of family unification, would become law and Chinese men could petition to have their spouses join them in America.

Why were so many Chinese in America drafted during World War II?

Until the mid-1940s, generations of Chinese men lived in a state of perpetual bachelorhood, thanks to anti-Chinese laws on the books, including the Page Law and the Chinese Exclusion Act. Since the majority of Chinese men in 1940s America had neither families nor dependents on U.S. soil, they were among the first to be drafted to fight in World War II. Altogether, about twenty thousand Chinese, over 30 percent foreign-born, were drafted into, or enlisted in, the U.S. armed forces between 1940 and 1946. In the decades after the war, the sacrifices, bravery, and loyal service of Chinese-American soldiers, sailors, marines, and airmen were largely unacknowledged and forgotten.

Fifty-four years after World War II ended, Chinese-American filmmaker **Montgomery Hom**'s 1999 docu-feature film *We Served With Pride: The Chinese American Experience in World War II* did much to bring Chinese Americans' contributions to the war effort to light. Narrated by actress **Ming-Na** and television journalist **David Louie,** the film weaves together the stories of twenty-seven Chinese Americans, men and women, who either answered the nation's call to duty during World War II or lent their support to fellow Chinese Americans in uniform. The premiere of *We Served With Pride* took place in Washington, D.C., on October 26, 1999, which the **Clinton** White House officially declared a National Day of Recognition for Chinese American Veterans of World War II.

How were the seeds for a Chinese-American middle class sown on the East Coast during World War II?

When Japanese troops invaded the northern provinces of China in 1937 and Chinese resistance unleashed the Second Sino-Japanese War, numerous Chinese professionals, scientists, and engineers visiting the United States were stranded abroad. Many settled in Manhattan's Chinatown, where they laid the foundation for the emergence of a middle class. This process was helped along by Chinese high school students in New York City, who in the 1940s outperformed their non-Asian peers and went on to college in greater numbers than any other ethnic group in the city.

World War II, which generated jobs in numerous industries, provided a unique opportunity for the Chinese in America to consider career options beyond running small businesses, such as restaurants and laundries. A significant number found higher-paying defense industry jobs in shipyards, manufacturing plants, and airplane factories. The job market also opened up for college-educated Chinese, who were able to find excellent employment in certain fields of specialization, such as engineering.

THE RED SCARE: A TIME OF TROUBLES IN CHINESE AMERICA

Why did the Communist takeover of China put the Chinese in America on red alert?

In the aftermath of World War II, hostilities between Chinese Nationalists and Communists in China escalated into a full-fledged war as both factions tried desperately to seize territory evacuated by the Japanese. In 1947 the Communists gained the upper hand, and by April 1950 they had overrun all of mainland China. A few months later, Communist Chinese forces intervened in the Korean War by intercepting United Nations forces headed toward the Manchurian border. As "Red China" loomed as a global threat, the pro-Chinese sentiment of 1930s and 1940s America rapidly gave way to suspicion and fear.

In 1950 the U.S. Congress passed the McCarran Internal Security Act, authorizing the internment of Communists during a state of national emergency. The U.S. attorney general was vested with the authority to detain any person if there were reasonable grounds to assume that he or she was engaged in espionage or sabotage. Again the Chinese in America had cause for alarm, for they knew by now that their welfare rested on U.S. foreign policy toward China. Furthermore, they had witnessed how Imperial Japan's hostility toward the United States in World War II had devastated the Japanese community in America, landing honest, hardworking Japanese in American internment camps.

The Chinese Consolidated Benevolent Association of New York and the Chinese Six Companies headquarters in San Francisco swiftly organized anti-Communist campaigns across the nation to dispel rumors that Chinese Communists had infiltrated the United States. The year 1951 saw the formation in the United States of the Anti-Communist Committee for Free China, which immediately declared its loyalty to America and condemned Communism as un-Chinese. In 1954 the Chinese in New York City organized the All-American Overseas Chinese Anti-Communist League to combat misperceptions that Chinese Americans and Chinese residents in the United States were Communists.

How did McCarthyism intensify Chinese fears of a new era of persecution?

In 1953 Senator **Joseph McCarthy** was selected chair of the U.S. Senate Permanent Subcommittee on Investigations. Before long he would exploit the enormous power of the post to unleash a Red Scare in the United States. Through unsubstantiated accusations of wrongdoing, unidentified informers, and widely publicized hearings, McCarthy pursued any American he cared to classify as a Communist and a subversive. McCarthy's whims destroyed many bright careers.

In this atmosphere of nationalism gone haywire, McCarthy had Americans convinced that Communist infiltrators were all around them, lurking in the shadows or hidden in plain sight, and across the nation vigilant citizens were on guard for signs of espionage and sabotage activities. In late 1955 the American consul general in Hong Kong, **Everett F. Drumwright,** warned Washington that Communist Chinese agents were infiltrating the United States by utilizing fraudulent citizenship papers to obtain American passports. In response, the U.S. Immigration and Naturalization Service began investigating in early 1956 thousands of "suspect" Chinese in the United States, a good number of them paper sons, and raiding Chinatowns on both coasts in hopes of taking Communist Chinese infiltrators into custody. The Chinese community in America was shrouded in fear, and most Chinese, and especially paper sons and others who had entered the United States and established their citizenship status by fraudulent means, worried that the paper past would come back to haunt them or their relatives.

How did World War II and the Cold War lead to a change in U.S. immigration policies?

America's desire to emerge from World War II and the Cold War as the leader of the free world led the country in the 1950s to rethink its domestic policies, including those related to Asian immigration and naturalization, which had stirred so much trouble in the past. In 1952 the U.S. Congress enacted the McCarran-Walter Act (otherwise known as the Immigration and Nationality Act), which eliminated racial and ethnic barriers to naturalization, allowing Asian immigrants to become naturalized U.S. citizens for the first time in history. At the same time, the act preserved and extended the race-based National Origins Quota System, creating an Asia-Pacific restrictive zone and allotting each of the nineteen countries in the zone a quota of two thousand immigrants.

Congress passed the McCarran-Walter Act over the veto of President **Harry S. Truman,** who believed that the race-based National Origins Quota System should have been completely abolished. After the passage of the McCarran-Walter Act, President Truman appointed a Special Commission on Immigration and Naturalization to study the U.S. immigration system. The commission's report, issued in 1953, urged that the National Origins Quota System be replaced with a system of allocating visas without regard to national origin, race, creed, or color. Although President **Dwight D. Eisenhower,** who took office in 1953, endorsed the findings of the report, he was unable to eliminate the quota system.

What was the Confession Program?

In 1955, three years after the McCarran-Walter Act was passed, the U.S. government, which was in hot pursuit of Communist Chinese spies it believed had infiltrated the United States, put in place a mechanism, known as the Confession Program, to allow those Chinese who had entered the country illegally, such as paper sons, to confess their illegal status in exchange for assistance in adjusting it. Confessors were required to expose their paper trails of false documentation and divulge the names of family members and friends who had aided them or were also in the United States illegally. As it turned out, the majority of illegal Chinese aliens were too distrustful of the FBI and the U.S. Immigration and Naturalization Service (INS) to step from the shadows. They knew all too well that the FBI and the INS were engaged in gathering information from confessions, intelligence reports, and loyalty tests to deport or exclude Chinese people who allegedly sympathized with Red China. Others refused to implicate family members and friends, a phenomenon that generated much tension and confusion in the community.

Still, tens of thousands of Chinese, some members of whole paper families, chose to confess in order to regularize their status; 92 percent of confessors had their immigration status adjusted to legal resident alien or naturalized citizen. In 1957 the Confession Program became the Act of

September 11. The act allowed those Chinese who had secured entry visas by fraud or misrepresentation to avoid deportation if they had a spouse, child, or parent who was a permanent resident alien or an American citizen.

STEPS TOWARD EQUALITY

What was the Immigration Act of 1965?

On October 3, 1965, President **Lyndon B. Johnson** signed the Immigration Act (also known as the Hart-Celler Reform Act), which was meant to reunify families separated by World War II and bring skilled workers and professionals into the country to ensure an adequate labor supply for the various sectors of the economy. The Immigration Act abolished over a three-year period the National Origins Quota System established in 1924 and put in its place annual quotas for immigration from each hemisphere. Specifically, it provided for the annual admission of 120,000 immigrants from the Western Hemisphere and 170,000 immigrants from the Eastern Hemisphere, with 20,000 slots per Eastern Hemisphere country. The act also established a preference system, which essentially exempted from the quotas certain classes of immigrants, namely, spouses, children and parents of American citizens and those whose skills were needed in the United States. The new law was by no means designed to create a radical change in the complexion of future immigrants. In fact, its proponents were certain that European immigration would predominate as before. In a statement designed to reassure his colleagues, U.S. Congressman **Emmanuel Celler** of New York declared at the time: "Since the people of . . . Asia have very few relatives here, comparatively few could immigrate from those countries because they have no family ties in the U.S."

History proved Emmanuel Celler wrong. The passage of the Immigration Act of 1965 marked the beginning of a new era in Asian immigration to the United States, as the number of Asian immigrants entering the country soared in ensuing decades. In the years 1961 to 1970, approximately 445,300 Asians immigrated to the United States. This figure more than tripled to 1.6 million between 1971 and 1980, and between 1981 and 1990 an all-time high of 2.8 million Asian immigrants reached American shores. Large numbers of these Asian newcomers were Chinese *san yi man*, or "new immigrants," as these post-1965 arrivals are called. Approximately 711,000 *san yi man* made their way to the United States between 1965 and 1990, nearly double the number of Chinese who reached America's shores in the decades spanning the California gold rush of 1849 and 1930.

How did the Chinese-American community change radically after 1965?

While the Chinese who ventured to America from 1849 until after World War II (that is, the *lo wa kiu*, meaning "old overseas Chinese") were generally poorly educated peasants from rural areas of China, the *san yi man* have been mostly blue-collar and white-collar workers from urban areas who speak Mandarin or Cantonese. Nearly half of all Chinese immigrants who came to America between 1966 and 1975 were professionals, managers, and technical workers.

Like *lo wa kiu* before them, a good number of *san yi man* have fled political upheaval in China. Before the normalization of relations between the United States and China in 1979, many *san yi man* escaping the persecution of the Cultural Revolution found their way from mainland China to Hong Kong or Taiwan, and then on to the United States. Unlike the early Chinese bachelor sojourners, who were cut off from their families and dreamed of getting rich quick and going home, *san yi man* men and women have come to the United States with their children in tow and with the intention of making it in America. Fearless before the U.S. government, they have taken the bull by the horns and have fought for social reforms in Chinatowns, for much-needed legal aid, long-overdue funds for housing, and for essential educational programs.

San yi man white-collar and blue-collar workers have created a dichotomized Chinese-American community. *San yi man* professionals, shocked by the unemployment, poverty, and crowded conditions in America's Chinatowns, have swelled the ranks of upwardly mobile Chinese Americans. They assimilate swiftly into the mainstream and leave Chinatowns behind for middle- and upper-middle-class neighborhoods and suburbs. At the same time, *san yi man* blue-collar workers have settled in the Chinatowns, where the men secure low-paying jobs as dishwashers and cooks in restaurants, and the women slave away as seamstresses in the garment industry. These *san yi man* work hard, pressure their children to excel in school, and dream of owning their own businesses and one day leaving Chinatown for the middle-class suburbs. Yet the future looks rather dim for most of these workers. More than half are trapped in the Chinese ethnic economy due to their lack of English-language fluency and education. Many earn less than minimum wage, have no health benefits or job security, and live below the poverty line.

This dichotomy in the Chinese-American community is readily apparent in New York City, where the "Uptown Chinese," wealthy professionals and business owners who have totally acculturated, rarely rub elbows with the "Downtown Chinese," who toil at low-paying jobs in Chinatown. Still, both sides of the Chinese-American community help preserve the vitality of the Chinatowns. Blue-collar workers in need of cheap housing and social programs supply the service sector, which in turn attracts upwardly mobile Chinese Americans to Chinatowns to shop, dine, and do business, and thus lend financial stability to a way of life that is a step closer to China.

What are the "new" Chinatowns of the 1980s, 1990s, and the new millennium?

In the 1980s wealthy Chinese from Taiwan and Hong Kong became increasingly concerned about the impending transfer in 1997 of Hong Kong, then still a British colony, to the People's Republic of China and the economic turmoil that might result despite promises from Beijing that China and Hong Kong would operate as "one country, two systems." The Taiwanese also feared the reversion of Hong Kong to Chinese rule because it represented a first step toward possible reabsorption of Taiwan by China, a vision Chinese Communists had nurtured ever since their victory in a bitter civil war that forced Chinese Nationalists to set up a rival government in Taiwan in 1949. If China were to reclaim Taiwan, it would take control of Taiwanese investments. To protect their interests, the people of Taiwan and Hong Kong began shifting their capital to Monterey Park, California. Before the 1980s were over, the Chinese had become the largest ethnic minority in Monterey Park, and the city had elected **Lily Lee Chen** its first Chinese mayor and the first Chinese-American woman mayor of a U.S. city. For two decades now, the Chinese have been such a presence in Monterey Park that the city, essentially an upscale Chinatown, has earned the titles "Chinese Beverly Hills" and "Little Taipei."

At the same time that Monterey Park was being transformed into a Chinatown, Chinese big business from Taiwan and Hong Kong was buying up Manhattan's Chinatown, setting off a real estate boom there and attracting large amounts of capital. As a result of the influx of Hong Kong and Taiwan investors, Manhattan's Chinatown doubled in size between 1980 and 1990, incorporating parts of Little Italy and the Jewish Lower East Side, and professional and business service companies, including law offices, accounting practices, advertising agencies, and real estate agencies, set up shop there.

Thus, since the days that they first sprang up on the

American landscape, Chinatowns have continually evolved to suit the needs of their inhabitants and visitors. As **Eric Liu,** a Chinese American, writes in *The Accidental Asian: Notes of a Native Speaker* (1998): "There are more Chinatowns than we can identify. Gangster Chinatown, Dim Sum Chinatown, Bootstraps Chinatown, Welfare Chinatown, Hipster Chinatown, Oldster Chinatown, Bay Bridge Chinatown, Manhattan Chinatown, Flushing Chinatown, Chinese Chinatown, pan-Asian Chinatown, Chinatown the ghetto, Chinatown the gateway. There are now suburban Chinatowns, like Monterey Park outside Los Angeles, places built of free choice, not necessity."

How many people of Chinese ancestry were counted by Census 2000, and where do they live?

The U.S. Bureau of the Census counted 2,734,841 million people of Chinese descent (not including Taiwanese) in the United States in 2000. Of that number, 2,314,537 were Chinese only, 130,826 were Chinese and one or more other Asian ethnicities, and 289,478 were Chinese and at least one other race. Persons of Chinese ancestry constituted the largest Asian-American subgroup in 2000, comprising over 20 percent of the approximately 11.9 million people who declared themselves Asian (alone or in combination with one or more other races) on 2000 U.S. census forms. The five states with the largest Chinese population in 2000 were California with 1,122,187, New York with 451,859, Hawaii with 170,803, Texas with 121,588, and New Jersey with 110,263. Chinese Americans remained the largest Asian-American group in New York City in 2000, at 357,243 (excluding Taiwanese) strong. As for U.S. residents of Taiwanese descent, Census 2000 counted 144,795 in the year 2000.

FIGHTING CULTURAL STEREOTYPES AND FORGING CULTURAL HERITAGE

Who killed Vincent Chin, and why were his murderers given probation?

On the evening of June 19, 1982, a twenty-seven-year-old Chinese-American draftsman named **Vincent Chin** was attending a bachelor party that his friends had thrown for him at the Fancy Pants strip club in Highland Park, Michigan, in celebration of his upcoming wedding. In those days the U.S. automobile industry was gripped by recession, which many outraged Americans attributed to unfair Japanese competition. Two white auto workers, **Ronald Ebens** and his stepson, **Michael Nitz,** who had recently been laid off, were also at the Fancy Pants that fateful evening. They mistook Chin for Japanese and began hurling racial epithets at him, blaming him for the American auto industry's plight. A fight broke out, and both sides were asked to leave the bar. Later that night, Ebens and Nitz spotted Vincent Chin at a nearby fast-food restaurant. The two men brutally attacked Chin, and he died four days later from the injuries he had sustained. Ebens and Nitz were charged with second-degree murder but were permitted to enter a plea bargain of guilty to the lesser charge of manslaughter. At sentencing, Wayne County Circuit Judge **Charles Kaufman** merely fined Ebens and Nitz $3,000 plus $780 in fees each and gave them three years' probation.

The Chinese-American community reacted to the light sentence with disbelief and outrage and formed the Justice for Vincent Chin Committee to see that justice would prevail. The federal government stepped in to investigate the case and indicted Ebens in 1984 for allegedly committing a racially motivated crime and, therefore, depriving Vincent Chin of his civil rights. A federal jury found Ronald Ebens guilty, and he was sentenced to twenty-five years in prison. However, citing judicial errors, an appellate court reversed the conviction on May 1, 1987. In July of that year, in a civil suit filed against Ronald Ebens by **Lily Chin,** Vincent Chin's mother, Ebens was ordered to pay $1.5 million to Vincent Chin's estate. However, Ebens proceeded to dispose of his assets and to flee the state. Neither he nor Michael Nitz spent even one night behind bars for the brutal murder they had committed.

The Oscar-nominated feature-length documentary film *Who Killed Vincent Chin?* (1988) by filmmakers **Christine Choy** (who is of Chinese and Korean ancestry) and **Renee Tajima-Peña** deftly chronicles the events surrounding Vincent Chin's tragic death by weaving interviews with many of the participants in the events, including the killers, news footage, and music. It serves as a reminder of how far Chinese Americans still had to go to secure their equal rights as recently as the late 1980s.

Who are the Chinese Americans in the political arena?

Since the latter half of the twentieth century, Chinese Americans have achieved prominence in American politics. In 1959 **Hiram Leong Fong,** whose father was an indentured worker on a Hawaiian sugar cane plantation, made history as the first Chinese American elected to the U.S. Senate. During his three terms representing Hawaii on the floor of the Senate, Fong encouraged trade and goodwill between the United States and the Pacific Rim nations. In 1966 **March Kong Fong Eu** earned the distinction of being the first Asian-American assemblywoman when she was elected to the California State Assembly, and in 1974 she became the first woman elected secretary of state of California. She served at that post until 1994, when President **Bill Clinton** appointed her U.S. ambassador to Micronesia. In 1976 Democrat **Daniel K. Akaka,** a Native Hawaiian and a Chinese American, was elected to the U.S. House of Representatives by voters in Hawaii's Second Congressional District. He served in the House until April 1990, when he was appointed to the U.S. Senate to fill a vacancy that arose with the death of Senator **Spark M. Matsunaga.** In November 1990 Akaka won a special election to complete Senator Matsunaga's four-year term. He was reelected to his Senate seat in 1994 and 2000. In 1984 **S. B. Woo,** a Chinese-American physicist, captured the lieutenant governorship of Delaware, proving that an Asian could compete for an elected post in a state with a small Asian-American population.

More recently, **Gary Locke,** a Democrat, became the first Chinese-American governor in U.S. history when he was elected governor of Washington in 1996. In 2000 Governor Locke, whose grandfather worked as a houseboy in Olympia, Washington, at the turn of the twentieth century, before returning to China, was reelected to a second term. In 1998 **David Wu** (D-OR) was elected to represent Oregon's First Congressional District, making him the first person born in Taiwan and the third Chinese American to serve in the U.S. House of Representatives. In 2000 Wu—who immigrated to the United States from Taiwan with his family in 1961—won reelection to the House as its sole Chinese-American member. Congressman Wu's legislative priorities include improving the quality of education, passing a real Patients' Bill of Rights, and enhancing public safety. Congressman Wu has also addressed issues of importance to Asian Americans, including racial profiling, an issue that hit close to home in 2001, when he was barred from entering the Department of Energy, despite showing his Congressional identification badge, and was asked to prove his U.S. citizenship.

Secretary of Labor **Elaine L. Chao,** who emigrated from Taiwan to the United States with her family when she was eight years old, is the first Asian-American woman in U.S. history to serve in a president's cabinet. Chao, whose previous posts in government include deputy secretary at the U.S. Department of Transportation, chairman of the Federal Maritime Commission, and deputy maritime administrator in the Department of Transportation, was nominated by President

George W. Bush in 2000 and confirmed by the U.S. Senate on January 29, 2001. Since then she has worked hard to protect the interests of the American workforce in a post–September 11 world and to ensure that all Americans have equal access to opportunity.

Who is Fu Manchu?

The fictional fiend Dr. Fu Manchu is the creation of English mystery writer **Sax Rohmer,** who was born **Arthur Henry Ward** in 1883 to Irish immigrants who had settled in England. Rohmer penned thirteen Fu Manchu novels in all. They have been translated into more than a dozen languages and Braille. In the 1920s a series of British silent films starring **Harry Agar** was made based on the Fu Manchu novels. Over the next six decades, more Fu Manchu movies were made, beginning in 1929 with the Paramount talkie *The Mysterious Dr. Fu Manchu,* starring the Swedish actor **Warner Oland,** and ending in 1980 with the release of the **Peter Sellers** comedy *The Fiendish Plot of Dr. Fu Manchu. The Adventures of Fu Manchu,* a television series starring white actor **Glen Gordon** as the Chinese villain, also aired in 1955 and 1956.

Dr. Fu Manchu, the Chinese master criminal at the head of a secret society at Limehouse in London's East End, first appeared on the scene in *The Mystery of Dr. Fu Manchu,* which was serialized in a magazine in 1912 and 1913 and was published as a novel in 1913. In each of the Fu Manchu novels, the villainous Dr. Fu Manchu plots to conquer the world and resorts to kidnapping, mind control, and extortion to achieve his dastardly ends. Fu Manchu is the perfect embodiment of the "Yellow Peril," a fact spelled out explicitly in hero Nayland Smith's description of the diabolical fiend in *The Mystery of Dr. Fu Manchu:* "a person, tall, lean and feline, high-shouldered, with a brow like Shakespeare and a face like Satan, a close-shaven skull, and long magnetic eyes of the true cat-green . . . the yellow peril incarnate in one man." For this reason, Fu

Manchu has been the object over the decades of much criticism on the part of the Asian-American community and all fair-minded people.

Who is Charlie Chan, and why is he so unpopular among most Asian Americans?

Charlie Chan, the good-natured Chinese detective, is the brainchild of American novelist and playwright **Earl Derr Biggers,** who got his inspiration for the character from a real-life detective named **Chang Apana.** Between 1925 and 1932 Biggers wrote a total of six Charlie Chan novels; all were serialized in the *Saturday Evening Post,* and several were translated into as many as ten foreign languages. In 1925 Charlie Chan, who readers learn was born in China around 1880 and moved as a child to Honolulu, where he never quite mastered the English language, made his debut on the silver screen as a minor character in the silent film *The House Without a Key.*

Two more minor big screen appearances followed, and then in 1931 the Charlie Chan sensation began with the films *The Black Camel* and *Charlie Chan Carries On.* Before it ended with *The Sky Dragon* in 1949, the Chinese detective would be the centerpiece of forty-four Hollywood motion pictures. The pudgy sleuth delighted American audiences as he trotted the globe solving crime puzzles, as in *Charlie Chan in Reno* (1939) and *Charlie Chan in Panama* (1940). Charlie Chan was played by **Warner Oland** (who also played in Fu Manchu movies) from 1931 to 1938, by the non-Asian-American actor **Sidney Toler** from 1938 to 1947, and by another non-Asian-American actor, **Roland Winters,** from 1947 to 1949, but filmgoers didn't seem to mind, and Earl Biggers made a huge profit from Hollywood's adaptations and book sales. In the 1950s, television tried to get in on the act, resurrecting Charlie Chan in a half-hour series starring **J. Carrol Naish,** but the show bombed. Universal's efforts to revive Chan in 1971 in the pilot film *Happiness Is a Warm Clue* were just as futile. In 1981

Tinseltown attempted one last time to reignite interest in Charlie Chan with the release of *Charlie Chan and the Curse of the Dragon Queen,* but audiences and critics gave the film a thumbs-down.

According to **John Stone,** producer of the first Chan film, the Chan books were made into movies "as a refutation of the unfortunate Fu Manchu characterization of the Chinese, and partly as a demonstration of [the] idea that any minority group could be sympathetically portrayed on the screen with the right story and approach." Many Asian Americans refute this notion that the affable Charlie Chan is the perfect antidote to the evil Fu Manchu. At first glance, he appears so. He roams the exotic streets of Chinatown and other international locales, solving murder mysteries and aiding white men in their fight against crime. But a closer look reveals that Charlie Chan walks daintily and in "fortune cookie English" spouts "Confucius-say" aphorisms, supposed nuggets of Chinese wisdom, such as "Woman's intuition like feather on arrow. May help flight to truth." From the perspective of many Asian Americans, Charlie Chan is in essence an effeminate, wimpy, nerdy, inscrutable Asian male who helped plant the seed of the pervasive racist stereotype of Asian Americans as the "model minority." Even kung fu superman **Bruce Lee** was not able to abolish this stereotype decades later.

What is the dragon lady/lotus blossom dichotomy?

This term was coined by film director, screenwriter, and producer **Renee Tajima-Peña,** whose credits include the Academy Award–nominated documentary *Who Killed Vincent Chin?* (1988), to describe the two stock images of Asian women on the silver screen: the cunning and deceitful temptress and the innocent girl who is always ready to please. For instance, in the 1931 Fu Manchu thriller *Daughter of the Dragon,* Chinese-American actress **Anna May Wong** plays the deceptive dragon lady and sexual temptress. By contrast, Suzie, the Hong Kong prostitute played by Hong Kong actress **Nancy Kwan** in the 1961 film adaptation of **Richard Mason**'s bestselling novel *The World of Suzie Wong*, epitomizes the "naive innocent Asian girl" stereotype when she falls in love with a struggling American artist, played by **William Holden,** and tells him in typical good-girl fashion: "I not important," and "I'll be with you until you say—Suzie, go away."

Who are the leading Chinese-American fiction writers?

In the first half of the twentieth century, non-Chinese-American writers perpetuating anti-Asian stereotypes shaped the mainstream's views of Chinese America, while the works of Chinese-American writers went unnoticed. Few heard of **Edith Maude Eaton** (1865–1914), the first Chinese American to transform the Chinese experience in the United States into English prose, who was born to an English father and a Chinese mother and wrote under the Chinese pen name Sui Sin Far. And few heard of her full-length collection of short stories, *Mrs. Spring Fragrance* (1912), which examines the injustices that the Chinese suffered on American shores. After her death in 1914, Edith Eaton and her works were all but forgotten. Only in 1995, when a new version of *Mrs. Spring Fragrance* was published, did Eaton take her rightful place in American history.

The situation had not changed radically in terms of Chinese-American writers' exposure by the time the 1950s rolled around. Still, Chinese-American writer **Chin Yang Lee** did manage to garner some notice with his witty first novel, *Flower Drum Song* (1957), which legendary songwriters **Richard Rogers** and **Oscar Hammerstein II** adapted into a hit Broadway musical in 1958—the first about Asian Americans—and which Hollywood made into a film in 1961. The year 1961 also saw the publication of **Louis Chu**'s humorous novel *Eat a Bowl of Tea,* considered the first novel about Chinatowns by a Chinese-American writer. The book, which was made into a film of the same name and directed by **Wayne Wang** in 1989, examines how the largely bachelor community in New York's Chinatown adjusted to the arrival of significant numbers of women and children after 1943, thanks to the repeal of the Chinese Exclusion Act.

With her bestselling and award-winning *The Woman Warrior: Memoirs of a Girlhood Among Ghosts* (1976), which reflects on the negative impact of sexism in Chinese America by weaving folktales, fantasies, family experiences, and memories, **Maxine Hong Kingston** broke new ground for Chinese-American and feminist writers. Many of her later works, including *China Men* (1980) and *Tripmaster Monkey: His Fake Book* (1989), were also bestsellers. Maxine Hong Kingston helped set the stage for the powerful wave of interest in Asian-American writing that was unleashed in 1988. That year Chinese-American playwright **David Henry Hwang** captivated audiences and critics with the Broadway production of his play *M. Butterfly*, which explores the issue of Asian stereotyping by white America. *M. Butterfly* captured the Tony Award for Best Play, the Outer Critics Circle Award for Best Broadway Play, and other awards in 1988, establishing Hwang as a leading playwright. (In 1989 the play was published.) **Amy Tan** also captured the attention of the American readership in 1989 with her runaway bestseller *The Joy Luck Club*, which was made into a hit movie of the same title in 1993. Since then, Tan has published three more novels, all highly successful: *The Kitchen God's Wife* (1991), *The Hundred Secret Senses* (1995), and *The Bonesetter's Daughter* (2001).

Nineteen ninety-one was a banner year for Chinese-American writers. That year **Gus Lee** made a splash on the literary scene with the publication of his semiautobiographical novel *China Boy*, about growing up Chinese in race-sensitive America; **David Wong Louie** won enthusiastic applause for his witty short-story collection *Pangs of Love*; and **Gish Jen** grabbed the critics' attention with her bittersweet *Typical American*, about three young Chinese immigrants who come to embody all the typical American traits they had once criticized. Gus Lee went on to publish three more autobiographical novels, *Honor and Duty* (1994), *Tiger's Tail* (1996), and *No Physical Evidence* (1998), as well as the nonfictional *Chasing Hepburn: A Memoir of Shanghai, Hollywood, and a Chinese Family's Fight for Freedom* (2003). In 2000 David Wong Louie published his first novel, *The Barbarians Are Coming,* a moving account of the alienation endemic to the immigrant experience. And Gish Jen went on to publish a sequel to *Typical American* entitled *Mona in the Promised Land* (1996), as well as a collection of short stories, *Who's Irish?: Stories* (1999).

Who are the great Chinese-American actors and filmmakers?

In the 1920s, 1930s, and 1940s, Hollywood generally depicted the Chinese in America (and elsewhere) as servants, slaves, hatchetmen, treacherous temptresses and prostitutes, villainous Fu Manchu types in opium dens and back rooms, or as sages à la Charlie Chan. One example out of many is the early Vitaphone feature film *Old San Francisco* (1927), in which character actor **Warner Oland** (the star of the Fu Manchu and Charlie Chan films of the period) plays a crime boss with Chinese blood who mistreats the Chinese locals, confines his dwarf Mongolian brother to a cage in the basement, and plans to sell a white woman into slavery. It was not unusual for Caucasian actors, with "slanted" eyes and feigned "Oriental" accents, to play Chinese roles. Actress **Myrna Loy,** for one, landed numerous Chinese parts, including her last one as Fah Lo See, the nymphomaniac with a sadistic streak in *The Mask of Fu Manchu* (1932). In that same film, British actor **Boris Karloff,** of horror movie fame, plays Fu Manchu. Karloff, like Myrna Loy, took many Chinese roles throughout his career. Perhaps his most noteworthy one is that of James Lee Wong, the Chinese sleuth in the six Mr. Wong films that Monogram Pictures released between 1938 and 1940. **Keye Luke,** best known as Charlie Chan's Number One Son, plays Mr. Wong in the sixth Wong picture, *Phantom of Chinatown* (1940). Mr. Wong came into being thanks to the Charlie Chan series, which caused an abiding interest in Asian sleuths among American audiences. The Japanese detective Mr. Moto, played by **Peter Lorre,** the focus of a series of eight films shot between 1937 and 1939, is yet another Chan-inspired sleuth.

The major Chinese-American actors in Hollywood in the 1920s, 1930s, 1940s, and 1950s had a narrow range of parts from which to choose. Chinese-American actress **Anna May Wong,** a legend of the silver screen who landed roles in sixty-eight films between 1919 and 1960, including Technicolor's first two-strip color motion picture, *The Toll of the Sea* (1922), and *Shanghai Express* (1932), costarring **Marlene Dietrich,** often played the Asian heroine, mystery woman, or evildoer—sometimes alongside Caucasian actors filling Asian parts. Had she been able to choose her parts, Anna May Wong—who was born Wong Liu Tsong, meaning "Frosted Yellow Willows," above her father's laundry on Flower Street in Los Angeles's Chinatown on January 5, 1905—would perhaps be widely recognized as one of the greatest actresses of all time.

Called the "Chinese Bardot," **Nancy Kwan,** who was born in Hong Kong on May 19, 1939, to a Chinese father and a Scottish mother (she is not an American citizen but has lived on and off in Los Angeles over the past four decades), also was limited in the kinds of roles she could play early on in her career. She first attracted attention for her role as Suzie, the Hong Kong prostitute, a stereotypical role, in the 1960 film *The World of Suzie Wong.* Kwan went on to play Linda Low, the American-born Chinese nightclub performer in the highly successful film adaptation of **Chin Yang Lee**'s novel *Flower Drum Song,* which was released in 1961. In more recent decades she has appeared in such American television series as *Fantasy Island, Knots Landing,* and *Trapper John, M.D.*

In the 1960s and 1970s, Hollywood presented American audiences with more positive images of Chinese Americans.

Mainstream America was particularly captivated by Chinese-American actor **Bruce Lee,** the renowned master of the Wing Chun branch of kung fu and the founder of his own martial arts style, Jeet Kune Do. Born Lee Hsiao Lung in San Francisco in 1940, Bruce Lee got his start in Hollywood performing small roles. In 1966 and 1967 he played Kato in the television series *The Green Hornet,* which was a success in the United States and a smash hit in Hong Kong. The Hong Kong motion picture industry wasted no time signing Bruce Lee to his first martial arts classic, *The Big Boss* (1971). Tinseltown took notice, and between 1971 and 1973 Bruce Lee starred in four Hollywood feature films: *Fists of Fury* (1971), *The Chinese Connection* (1972), *Enter the Dragon* (1973), and *Return of the Dragon* (1973).

He had filmed only a handful of scenes for his fifth Hollywood motion picture, prophetically entitled *Game of Death,* when Bruce Lee died suddenly at the age of thirty-two in a Hong Kong apartment from cerebral edema attributed to hypersensitivity to medication. Filmgoers and martial arts fans around the globe mourned the passing of the great martial artist. As for Bruce Lee's last film, *Game of Death,* producers finished it using a double for the star, and it was released in 1978. Chinese-American actor **Jackie Chan,** who was born in Hong Kong on April 7, 1954, to parents who were so poor they nearly sold their newborn son to the doctor who delivered him to cover his medical expenses, was at one time groomed as Bruce Lee's replacement. Chan can be seen in nearly one hundred Hong Kong and Hollywood movies. He first attracted widespread attention in the United States with his performance in *Rumble in the Bronx* in 1996.

Chinese Americans in recent decades have contributed to presenting on screen more realistic pictures of Chinese-American life. Chinese-American film director **Wayne Wong** offered mainstream America some of the first celluloid images of Chinese America from the inside looking out with his critically acclaimed films *Chan Is Missing* (1982); *Dim Sum: A Little*

Bit of Heart (1985); *Eat a Bowl of Tea* (1989), a film adaptation of **Louis Chu**'s 1961 novel of the same title; and *The Joy Luck Club* (1993), based on **Amy Tan**'s bestselling novel of the same name. On the theatrical stage, Chinese-American actor **B. D. Wong** won a Tony and an Outer Critics Circle Award in 1988, among other awards, for his performance as the mistress Song Li Ling in *M. Butterfly.* He has acted in numerous other stage and screen productions. On the big screen, Wong has appeared in such motion pictures as *Jurassic Park* (1993) and *Mulan* (1998). Actress **Joan Chen,** who was born **Chen Chong** in the People's Republic of China, where she earned a following as a child film star, and came to the United States in 1981, distinguished herself on the television screen in 1990 as the enigmatic Josie Packard in the series *Twin Peaks* and on the big screen in such motion pictures as *The Last Emperor* (1987), *Heaven and Earth* (1993), *The Joy Luck Club* (1993), and *Golden Gate* (1994). Chen made her directorial debut with *Xiu Xiu: The Sent Down Girl* (1999) and went on to direct *Autumn in New York* (2000), starring **Richard Gere** and **Winona Ryder.**

Lucy Liu, who was born in Queens, New York, to Chinese immigrants, got her big break in 1997, when she landed the role of the irascible attorney Ling Woo on the critically acclaimed TV series *Ally McBeal,* which premiered that year. On the big screen, she has delighted fans with her performances as the dominatrix opposite **Mel Gibson** in the action thriller *Payback* (1999); the kidnapped Princess Pei Pei, who is rescued by Jackie Chan, in the action comedy *Shanghai Noon* (2000); the Angel named Alex in *Charlie's Angels* (2000), the movie version of the campy 1970s television show; and as Alex in the sequel *Charlie's Angels: Full Throttle* (2003), among others.

Jason Scott Lee, who is considered the first Chinese-American sex symbol, has starred in such motion pictures as *Map of the Human Heart* (1992); *Dragon: The Bruce Lee Story* (1993), in which he plays Bruce Lee, whom he is sometimes mistaken for; and *Russell Mulcahy's Tale of the Mummy* (1999), and is the voice of David Kawena in the feature-length cartoon *Lilo & Stitch* (2002). And Chinese-born model and actress **Ziyi Zhang** has caused quite a sensation since 2001, when *People* magazine named her one of the "50 Most Beautiful People," *Teen People* called her one of the "25 Hottest Stars Under 25," and she appeared in the American motion picture *Rush Hour 2.*

Who is Yo-Yo Ma?

Yo-Yo Ma is one of the greatest cellists of all time. Born in 1955 to Chinese parents residing in Paris, he began cello lessons at age four, gave his first public recital at age five, and settled in New York with his family while still a boy. He has since played on every major stage in the world, exhilarating the classical music world with his dynamic stage presence, extraordinary technique, and insightful interpretation. Incidentally, Yo-Yo Ma plays a 1733 Montagnana cello from Venice and a 1712 Davidoff Stradivarius.

Who are some of the leading Chinese-American scientists and medical researchers?

During World War II, nuclear physicist **Chien-Shiung Wu** distinguished herself with her work on the Manhattan Project. Wu, who was born in Shanghai in 1912, came to the United States in 1936, where she earned a Ph.D. from the University of California in 1940. A professor of physics, she received numerous awards and honors, including being appointed the first female president of the American Physical Society. It was a proud moment for Chinese Americans when, in 1957, **Chen Ning Yang** of the Institute for Advanced Study in Princeton, New Jersey, and **Tsung-Dao Lee** of Columbia University became the first Chinese Americans awarded the Nobel Prize in Physics "for their penetrating investigation of the so-called parity laws which has led to important discoveries regarding the elementary particles." Specifically, the two scientists disproved the basic quantum mechanical law of conservation of parity—universally accepted since 1925—which held that two physical systems that are mirror images of each other must behave in the same way.

In 1976 Taiwanese American **Samuel Chao Chung Ting** of MIT shared the Nobel Prize in Physics with fellow physicist **Burton Richter** of the Stanford Linear Accelerator Center "for their pioneering work in the discovery of a heavy elementary particle of a new kind." That new kind of elementary particle is the J/psi particle, which provides concrete evidence that a fourth quark, known as charm, does exist, just as physicists had conjectured. Nowadays, the J/psi particle still occupies a prominent place in experiments in particle physics. A decade later, in 1986, **Yuan Tseh Lee,** who was born in Taiwan, shared the Nobel Prize in Chemistry with **Dudley R. Herschbach** and **John C. Polanyi** for "their contributions concerning the dynamics of chemical elementary processes." The most recent Chinese-American recipient of a Nobel Prize in a scientific field is **Steven Chu** of Stanford University, who was awarded the 1997 Nobel Prize in Physics with **Claude Cohen-Tannoudji** and **William D. Phillips** "for development of methods to cool and trap atoms with laser light."

Chinese Americans have made vast contributions to the field of medicine. One of them is Dr. **David Da-I Ho,** a physician and a leading AIDS researcher who since 1990 has been the scientific director and chief executive officer of the Aaron Diamond AIDS Research Center in New York, the world's largest private HIV/AIDS research center. In 1996 Ho was named *Time* magazine's Man of the Year after he rendered invalid the prevailing view that the HIV virus remains in a state of dormancy in a person for up to a decade before it develops into full-blown AIDS, demonstrating instead that the virus operates at its full capacity right from the start of infection. Ho, who was born in Taiching, Taiwan, in 1952 and came to the

United States when he was twelve, has received a number of awards for his medical breakthroughs, including the Ernst Jung Prize in Medicine and the Squibb Award of the Infectious Diseases Society of America.

Who are some other prominent Chinese Americans?

In the field of education, the late **Chang-Lin Tien,** a mechanical engineer born in Wuhan, China, and educated in Shanghai and Taiwan, became the first Asian American to head a major research university in the United States when he was appointed chancellor of the University of California, Berkeley, in 1990, a post he held until 1997.

One of the most distinguished architects in the United States and the world is Chinese American **I. M. Pei,** who has designed more than fifty structures, among them the glass pyramid in the courtyard of the Louvre Museum in Paris; the John F. Kennedy Library near Boston; the East Building of the National Gallery of Art in Washington, D.C.; the National Center for Atmospheric Research in Boulder, Colorado; the Jacob K. Javits Center in New York City; the Society Hill development in Philadelphia; the Overseas Chinese Banking Corporation Center and Raffles City in Singapore; and the seventy-two-story Bank of China in Hong Kong, one of the world's tallest buildings.

Another Chinese-American architect, **Maya Ying Lin,** has won the admiration of millions of Americans for her designs of the Vietnam Veterans Memorial (1982) in Washington, D.C., the Civil Rights Memorial (1989) in Montgomery, Alabama, and the Langston Hughes Library in Clinton, Tennessee, among others. Her extraordinary design for "the Wall," the polished black stone wall that is the Vietnam Veterans Memorial, took shape in 1981, when still an undergraduate student at Yale University, she submitted the chosen entry in the national design competition for the memorial, which was slated to be built in Washington, D.C. In 2000 Maya Lin published *Boundaries*, a collection of sketches, workbook entries, photographs, and original designs interwoven with text that detail the inspiration behind, and evolution of, her architectural creations and sculptures.

In broadcast journalism, **Connie Chung** belongs to the elite club of women broadcast journalists who occupy the upper echelons of American network news. Highlights of her illustrious career spanning more than thirty years include teaming up with **Dan Rather** to coanchor the *CBS Evening News* in 1993, which made Chung only the second woman to anchor a network news broadcast. (The first was **Barbara Walters,** who in the mid-1970s briefly coanchored with **Harry Reasoner.**) From 2001 to 2003 she anchored CNN's *Connie Chung Tonight*, an hour-long program mixing interviews and investigative reporting that examined the people and the issues at the heart of the day's news.

Chinese Americans, many of them leading researchers at the cutting edge of technology, have also distinguished themselves in business. In 1951 **Dr. An Wang** founded, with just a six-hundred-dollar investment, the billion-dollar company Wang Laboratories, Inc., which began as a leader in calculator technology but gradually emerged as a giant in the computer industry. Dr. Wang was once quoted as saying, "I founded Wang Laboratories to show that Chinese could excel at things other than running laundries and restaurants." In 1976 **Charles B. Wang** founded Computer Associates International, Inc., the third-largest software vendor after Microsoft and Oracle (as of 2003). As the company's CEO from 1976 to 2000 and chairman of the board from 1980 to 2002, Wang, who was born in Shanghai in 1944 and came to the United States in 1952, transformed Computer Associates from a single-product company into an international enterprise offering a whole array of *e*Business solutions.

Dr. Gerald Tsai, Jr., who was born in Shanghai, China, joined American Can Company (which later became Primerica Corporation) in 1982 as its executive vice-president.

He ultimately emerged as Primerica's principal strategist in developing its financial services businesses and, consequently, was selected its chief executive officer and chairman of the board. From 1993 to 1997 Tsai served as chairman, president, and CEO of Delta Life Corporation, a life insurance and annuity company. He currently chairs his own management and consulting company, Tsai Management, Inc.

From 1978 until 1994 Chinese American **Winston H. Chen** served as president, CEO, and chairman of the board of directors of the electronics contract manufacturer Solectron Corporation. He served as Solectron's director until 2002, and since 1993 he has been a director of Intel. In 1984, before the age of thirty, Chinese-American entrepreneur **Gene Lu** founded Advanced Logic Research, which was the industry leader in the design and manufacture of high-performance computer systems before it was acquired by Gateway in 1997. Lu is currently president and CEO of FIA Storage Systems Group. **David Lam** cofounded the multimillion-dollar software company Expert Edge in 1989. He later was an executive at Wyse Technology and Link Technologies and founded Lam Research Corporation.

Taiwanese American **Jerry Yang** created Yahoo!, one of the world's leading global Internet communications, commerce, and media companies, with cofounder **David Filo** in 1994 at Stanford University, where the two were Ph.D. students. Their original intent was merely to keep track of Web sites they found interesting, but before long others were accessing their site, originally named "Jerry's Guide to the World Wide Web." When "Jerry's Guide" got its one millionth hit in the autumn of 1994, Yang and Filo knew there was a business in their future. Old Navy, whose parent company is Gap Inc., was the business in **Jenny J. Ming**'s future. In 1986 she started out with Gap as a buyer. With her intuitive sense for the next trend, Ming, who was born in Macau, worked her way up quickly. In 1999 she was named president of Old Navy, and since then the retailer has been one of the fastest growing in America.

Dr. Henry C. Lee, who was born in China in 1938 and studied police science in Taiwan, is one of the world's leading experts in crime scene investigation and has assisted law enforcement in more than six thousand cases around the globe. He is a familiar face to most Americans, thanks to his invaluable forensics testimony in numerous high-profile criminal and civil cases, including the highly publicized **O. J. Simpson** murder case. In 1998 Dr. Lee founded the Henry C. Lee Institute of Forensic Science at the University of New Haven. Until 2000 he served as commissioner of the Connecticut State Police and director of the Connecticut State Police Crime Laboratory. In addition to being on call as a consultant, he is currently a full professor of forensic science at Yale University. Another prominent Chinese American in law enforcement is **Bill Lann Lee,** the son of Chinese immigrants who ran a laundry business in New York City. In 1997 President **Clinton** appointed Lee assistant attorney general for civil rights, a U.S. Department of Justice post, making him the highest-ranking Asian-American law enforcement official in the country at the time. Lee served at that post until January 2001, when President Clinton's second term in office ended.

Master chef **Martin Yan,** who was born in Guangzhou, China, is the author of a dozen bestselling cookbooks and the colorful host of *The Yan Can Cook Show,* a wildly popular Chinese and Asian cooking series that was launched in 1982 and airs across the United States and in more than seventy other countries. For his work on the show, Chef Yan has been awarded the prestigious James Beard Award twice, for Best Television Cooking Show in 1994 and for Best Television Food Journalism in 1996. In addition to hosting his television series and writing cookbooks, Martin Yan teaches Chinese and Asian cooking at the nation's leading culinary schools, including the Culinary Institute of America, is a food and restaurant consultant, makes frequent radio and television guest appearances, and gives demonstrations and lectures on culinary arts at conventions, trade shows, and other venues.

Who are the world-class Chinese-American athletes?

Among the Chinese-American shining lights in sports is **Michael Chang,** who as a fifteen-year-old, in 1987, astounded the tennis world when he became the youngest tennis player to prevail in a main draw match at the U.S. Open and to advance to a Tour semifinal. This was just the first of Chang's firsts. In 1989, a year after turning pro, he became the youngest player—and the first American male player since **Tony Trabert** in 1955—to win the French Open. In 1989 Chang was also the youngest player in tennis history to rank in the top five in the world. Since then, Michael Chang, who is lauded for his speed and all-court game, has captured myriad singles titles.

In 1996 Chinese-American gymnast **Amy Chow,** who was born in San Jose, California, in 1978, became the first Asian American to make the U.S. Olympic gymnastics team. At the 1996 Olympic Summer Games in Atlanta, she helped the team, known as the "Magnificent Seven," make history as the first U.S. women's Olympic gymnastics team to capture the gold medal. At the 1996 Olympics competition, Chow also took the individual silver medal in the uneven parallel bars, and in 2000 she was U.S. national champion in the balance beam.

A six-time U.S. Champion (1996, 1998–2002) with a record thirty-four 6.0s (perfect scores) in major competitions (as of early 2003) and many other firsts, Chinese-American figure skater **Michelle Kwan** first captivated all the world when she won the silver medal in a dazzling performance in the ladies singles figure skating event at the 1998 Olympic Winter Games in Nagano, Japan. Her bronze-medal performance at the 2002 Winter Olympics in Salt Lake City was one of the Games' most watched. In 1997, Kwan, who was born in

Torrance, California, in 1980, published her autobiography, *Heart of a Champion*, and in 2000 *People* magazine named her one of the "50 Most Beautiful People in the World." Kwan has achieved such celebrity status that she even has her own interactive video game—the first with a figure skating theme—entitled *Michelle Kwan Figure Skating*.

In professional team sports, Chinese American **Eugene Chung** is one of the few Asian Americans to pursue professional football. In 1992 Chung became the first Asian American selected in the first round of the NFL draft, when the New England Patriots picked the offensive line guard.

How has Confucius contributed to both Chinese and Chinese-American society's devotion to order, respect, and patriarchy?

The founder of Confucian philosophy, **K'ung Ch'iu**—known as K'ung Fu-tzu ("Master K'ung"), hence the Latinized name **Confucius**—lived from approximately 551 to 479 B.C. The abuses of China's feudal system led Confucius to develop a social and political philosophy that stresses such ethical precepts as righteousness, benevolent love, decorum, sincerity, and wise leadership. According to Confucius, the individual, the family, society, and government should govern themselves according to these precepts. Thus, for instance, a monarch must rule over his subjects with benevolence and concern, and in turn the monarch's subjects, like a father's children, must show respect, abiding loyalty, and reverence. Confucius's teachings, preserved in the *Analects*, would form the basis of later Chinese thought on the ideal individual and the forms of society and government to which he should belong and have shaped and continue to shape the conduct of the Chinese and Chinese Americans. The Chinese adherence to modesty, civility, decorum, and kindness and devotion to ancestor worship, familial and social obligations, and tradition can all be traced to the teachings of Confucius.

What is Taoism?

Taoism is a philosophy developed in China in the sixth century B.C. by **Lao-tzu,** a contemporary of **Confucius.** Lao-tzu saw a tragic perversity in the human pursuit of superfluous and temporal matters, and consequently he withdrew from society and government service. In his short treatise entitled *Tao-te ching,* or *The Way of Virtue,* he describes in an obscure, poetic style an alternative path that is based not on artificial divisions in society, codes of conduct, and so forth but on the *Tao* (literally, "the Way"). To follow the Tao is to live by "nonaction," or "nonstriving." Nonaction, though, does not mean doing nothing. It means avoiding actions to force events to unfold in a certain way. It means being quiet and tuning in to the natural flow. Contemplation and harmony with this flow—not willfulness—bring contentment, dissolve conflict, and promote peace.

Over time Taoism, like Confucianism and Buddhism, emerged as one of the great religions in China, and in 440 C.E. it was adopted as a state religion. The Communist victory in China in 1949, followed by the Cultural Revolution from 1966 to 1976, ushered in the destruction of much of the country's Taoist heritage. Nowadays Taoism is centered in Taiwan, with small numbers of followers scattered around the globe, including in the United States.

Which variety of Buddhism did the Chinese bring to America, and which religions do they practice nowadays?

Buddhism was founded in India at the end of the sixth century B.C. by **Siddhartha Gautama,** called the Buddha ("the Enlightened One"). Buddhism moved east from India along trade routes, reaching China about the first century A.D. It was not until the fifth and sixth centuries A.D., however, that Buddhism emerged as a popular and established religion in China. The Chinese embraced Mahayana Buddhism in particular, as opposed to the Hinayana, Theravada, and related Buddhist schools. The main philosophical tenets of Mahayana Buddhism—that good deeds lead to a better life in future reincarnations and that the Buddha is but one incarnation in a series—appealed to all layers of Chinese society, including the common people. Buddhism was essentially transformed in China into a religion bringing enlightenment only to the mystic or the learned but capable of bestowing universal salvation on the masses.

Buddhism managed to coexist with a wealth of native religions and philosophies in China by providing insights into salvation rather than being a rigid and monolithic system of absolutes. Certain aspects of Buddhism were already present in Chinese traditions, and these were emphasized. Thus, Buddhist meditation was practiced intensively by the Chinese because of its resemblance to the Taoist *kuan*, or "mystical vision." For Chinese consumption, the Buddhist *dharma*, or "teaching," was likened to the *Tao*, or "the Way," while the Buddhist concept of *nirvana*, or "enlightenment," was equated with the Taoist notion of "nonaction."

Early Chinese immigrants brought Mahayana Buddhism to the United States, erecting numerous temples in California, twenty of which still stand today. Other Chinese immigrants practiced Taoism and Confucianism in the New World, and still others were converted to Christianity by American missionaries who set up social welfare programs in Chinatowns. Chinese Christians, particularly the foreign-born, however, tended to adhere both to the teachings of Christianity and to Buddhist, Taoist, or Confucian practices. To this day, Chinese Americans worship religions brought from China as well as the Christian religions they or their forebears came in contact with in the United States.

How does traditional Chinese medicine differ from Western medicine?

Chinese medicine is based on the fundamental Taoist concepts of yin and yang. Yin emblematizes the passive principle of life, which includes the female, the moon, earth, and water, while yang represents the active principle, the male, the sun, heaven, and fire. Yin and yang do not clash but, in fact, interact in a balanced and all-embracing circle, representing the Tao, the universal harmonizing force of nature. Harmony with the Tao results in good health. When the balance between the forces of yin and yang has been disturbed, illness results. The purpose then of medicine is to restore this balance.

Diagnosis by a traditional Chinese doctor consists of a thorough examination of the pulse and palpitations of the left and right wrists, which give clues as to the condition of internal organs. Over fifty-two kinds of pulses have been recorded, seven of which signify imminent death. Medicinal herbs and substances (such as ginseng, angelica root, and tiger bone), massage, acupuncture, and moxibustion are commonly prescribed to restore the balance of yin and yang in the patient's body. Moxibustion involves burning a stick or cone of plant substances, often mugwort, a spongy herb, on the skin at acupuncture points, that is, spots where acupuncture needles have been withdrawn. The heat released in the process is believed to further stimulate the flow of Qi, the fluid, life-giving energy of the universe; relieve pain; and alleviate weakness and fatigue. Every Chinatown in America has its share of traditional Chinese doctors and apothecaries, and Chinese Americans, particularly those who reside in Chinatowns, are apt to turn to traditional Chinese medicine rather than Western medicine.

What is t'ai chi ch'uan, *and what is kung fu?*

T'ai chi ch'uan ("supreme ultimate fist") is the most popular of the three "internal" or "soft" martial arts of China, the other two being *hsing-i* and *pakua.* At the core of *t'ai chi ch'uan* is form, a meditative sequence of postures and circular actions that flow from one to the next without interruption. The end result is a kind of ballet or slow dance. For this reason, *t'ai chi ch'uan* is one of the most difficult martial arts to master and requires a long apprenticeship. An important aspect of *t'ai chi ch'uan* is *chi,* the universal energy that runs through the body. Chinese medicine strives to keep a person's *chi* in balance to maintain good health. If there is too much or too little *chi* in the body, it must be rebalanced. Chinese physicians regard the study of *t'ai chi ch'uan* as a form of "physical therapy," which, through its tranquil movements, restores balance to the body. Another facet of *t'ai chi ch'uan* is the practice of "push hands," a complex technique of pushing a partner and yielding to a partner's pushes with attention given to balance. Some schools of *t'ai chi ch'uan* have transformed "push hands" into a fighting technique by concentrating *chi* to unleash hard pushes on the opponent.

In contrast to *t'ai chi chuan,* kung fu is an "external," meaning more physical, system of self-defense, similar to karate, but with circular rather than linear movements. It is widely accepted that this system of martial arts was developed in China around 2600 B.C. and that it gained popularity during the Han dynasty. As it developed, kung fu incorporated various fighting styles based on the movements of such animals as the monkey, the white crane, the tiger, and the praying mantis. Monkey-style kung fu is one of the most fascinating. It demands that the student mimic the monkey, adopting its leaps, rolls, and alertness. Praying mantis kung fu was founded by Master **Wong Long** at the Shaolin monastery in China's Honan Province in the seventeenth century. The most striking feature of the praying mantis style is the mantis claw, which entails shaping the fist to imitate the claws that the insect uses to seize prey.

Kung fu caught on in the United States in the 1970s, thanks to **Bruce Lee** and his Hollywood kung fu films, such as *Fists of Fury* (1971) and *Enter the Dragon* (1973), and to two television series that starred **David Carradine** as Kwai Chang Caine, a half-Chinese, half-American Shaolin priest: *Kung Fu* (1972–75) and its sequel, *Kung Fu, The Legend Continues* (1993–97).

Which Chinese holidays do Chinese Americans typically celebrate?

The Chinese New Year, also known as the Spring Festival, is perhaps the Chinese holiday most often observed by Chinese Americans. It begins with the new moon on the first day after the new year, usually between January 21 and February 19, and ends on the full moon fifteen days later, although most Chinese Americans limit their celebrating to the first three days. The Chinese New Year is based on the Chinese calendar, which not only recognizes twelve months in a year but also twelve years in a cycle. In the Han dynasty, each year in the Chinese cycle was matched with a different animal, beginning with the rat, then the ox, tiger, hare, dragon, serpent, horse, ram, monkey, rooster, dog, and pig. Every individual, according to the Chinese, possesses qualities of the animal in whose year he or she was born. Thus, a person born in the Year of the Rat will exhibit persistence, "gnawing away" until a goal is achieved. Chinese New Year celebrations incorporate the "animal of the year."

In Chinatowns across America, Chinese Americans from all walks of life, and tourists too, gather to watch and participate in colorful and noisy New Year's Parades. In San Francisco, a three-hour procession winds down Grant Street, in the heart of Chinatown, while in Lower Manhattan a parade twists and turns through Mott, Pell, and Bayard Streets. Lion dancers, folk dancing, and martial arts demonstrations entertain the crowds, but everyone thrills at the sight of the *gum lung*, the ceremonial golden dragon, often made in Hong Kong and shipped to America expressly for the celebration. This most beneficent creature, a symbol of strength and longevity for the Chinese, floats through the streets held aloft by dozens of dragon-bearers. It bespeaks *Gung hay fat choy!*—Happy New Year!

Another of the many Chinese holidays that Chinese Americans observe is the Mid-Autumn Festival, or Moon Festival, a celebration of the year's harvest and of fertility that dates back to the Tang dynasty in A.D. 618. The Moon Festival takes place on the fifteenth day of the eighth Chinese lunar month, when the full moon, or harvest moon, which is considered a female deity, shines more brightly than at any other time of the year. Family reunions and moon gazing activities are an integral part of the festivities. During the Moon Festival, young girls burn incense in the temple and ask Yueh Lao, the man in the moon, for a vision of their future husbands. No Moon Festival would be complete without moon cakes—rich-tasting pastries with a round shape, symbolizing the moon and family unity, that feature one of an assortment of fillings, such as sweet red bean paste, lotus seed paste and a whole salted egg yolk (the traditional filling), mung bean paste, winter melon paste, ham, mixed nuts, and dried fruits.

What are some of the Chinese delicacies that Chinese Americans enjoy?

A list of the more unusual Chinese delicacies available in America's Chinatowns might include hundred-year eggs—also called thousand-year eggs, century eggs, Ming dynasty eggs, and ancient eggs—which are chicken, duck, or goose eggs preserved in a mixture of lime, salt, and ash for approximately one hundred days until an outer ring of egg white turns black and the yolk turns gray-green. The shell and the black outer coating are removed, and the yellowish egg white and yolk beneath are served as an appetizer, alone or accompanied by minced ginger or soy sauce, or are added to rice gruel. The eggs can be stored in the refrigerator for up to a month or at room temperature (not above 70° F) for up to two weeks.

Shark fins, actually just the cartilage of the shark's dorsal fin, pectoral fin, and a portion of the tail fin, are an expensive Chinese delicacy with a reputation as an aphrodisiac. One of the best known dishes featuring the shark fin is shark's fin soup, which gets its flavor and body from the gelatin released by the cartilage as it simmers. Some Chinese restaurants in America, especially those catering to a Chinese clientele, have shark's fin soup on the menu, but it is not a big seller, as a bowl can cost between $40 and $150. The love affair with the shark fin and shark's fin soup has led to overfishing on a global scale and a subsequent decline in some shark populations. Each year approximately one hundred million sharks are caught. Since shark fins fetch much more in the marketplace than shark fillets, fishermen commonly chop off the fins and toss the sharks overboard to die. In 2001 the United States banning this practice, known as finning.

Birds' nests built by swiftlets, small, sparrowlike birds, in areas of Southeast Asia are also highly prized in China and in Chinese-American communities. The nests, which swiftlets construct in dark caves, are made of seaweed held together with strands of gelatinous condensed saliva that the male swallow secretes from swollen sublingual salivary glands. Nest collectors carry lights into pitch-black caves, climb to the top of bamboo scaffolding, and gently pry the nests from the cave walls. The Chinese go through all this trouble because they believe that birds' nests contain properties that strengthen all the vital organs and increase sex drive. "Raw" birds' nests are tasteless, but like shark fins they impart a delicious flavor when boiled in stocks. Heavy demand for the nests and the hazards of harvesting them mean high prices at the market for the delicacy. Nowadays birds' nests are a multibillion dollar industry. In 2002 Hong Kong, the largest consumer of birds' nests, imported approximately one hundred tons, at a cost of roughly $25 million U.S. The profits are so high that efforts by Western nations to protect the swiftlet—whose numbers are in decline from the overharvesting of nests, the dumping of eggs and chicks that have not yet fledged from their nests, and the destruction of swiftlet habitat—have met only with opposition from Southeast Asian nations.

How did chow mein, chop suey, and the fortune cookie come to America?

Contrary to popular belief, early Chinese immigrants did not bring recipes for chow mein, chop suey, and fortune cookies with them from China. Rather, these popular dishes were invented by Chinese Americans.

Chow mein, a dish comprised of small bits of meat, especially chicken, or shrimp that are stir-fried with vegetables such as bamboo shoots, bean sprouts, water chestnuts, onions, and mushrooms and served over crisp fried noodles, came into existence purely by accident. According to popular lore, a Chinese cook accidentally dropped some noodles into a frying pan filled with fat. Much to his surprise he had invented a tasty dish. Other Chinese cooks toyed with his fried noodles over time by adding various combinations of stir-fried meat, shrimp, and vegetables. Voilà, chow mein.

Chop suey, which is Cantonese for "odds and ends," consists of little pieces of beef, chicken, or shrimp that are stir-fried with an assortment of vegetables that usually includes onions, celery, bean sprouts, water chestnuts, and mushrooms. The dish is served over white rice. Theories abound as to the origins of chop suey. A popular explanation is that Chinese Americans invented the recipe in the nineteenth century to please a Chinese viceroy visiting the United States as the Chinese emperor's emissary. Apparently Viceroy **Li Hung-chang** suffered from indigestion during his visit and requested vegetables cooked with a little bit of meat. The dish was concocted and quickly coined "chop suey." According to another theory, Chinese workers building the transcontinental railroad across America invented the dish. Chop suey became so embedded in American culture that American realist painter **Edward Hopper** made it the subject of his oil on canvas *Chop Suey* (1929), which depicts four diners seemingly suspended in time in a Chinese restaurant.

Many theories abound as to the origins of the fortune cookie. According to one popular theory, the fortune cookie was one outcome of a campaign, devised in the early 1900s, to transform San Francisco's Chinatown from a ghetto of "inassimilable" and "undesirable" Chinamen into a "quaint" tourist attraction. Advertisements for Chinatown lured tourists with promises of an "Oriental experience" in the Occident, a tour of Canton and the distant and magnificent land of Cathay. Exoticism was essential to attract tourists, and so Chinese pageantry, architectural styles, and decoration were promoted. When San Francisco's Chinatown was destroyed by the 1906 earthquake, it was rebuilt and, though modern, was designed to retain its "Oriental charm and attractiveness," as the *San Francisco Chronicle* put it in 1917. By the 1930s the enclave was attracting bus loads of tourists. As the theory goes, tourists flocking to Chinatown restaurants that decade were disappointed by the lack of a dessert course, and the fortune cookie was designed to satisfy their expectations. Apparently a worker in San Francisco's Kay Heong Noodle Factory invented a plain, flat cookie that, while still warm, was folded around a little slip of paper on which a prediction or pearl of wisdom had been written. Incidentally, the fortune cookie reached China's shores only in 1992.

POPULAR FEATURE FILMS WITH AN ASIAN/ ASIAN-AMERICAN THEME*
(*Directed by and/or starring Asian Americans)

Chan Is Missing (1982, directed by Wayne Wang)

The Killing Fields (1984, starring Haing S. Ngor)

The Karate Kid (1984, starring Noriyuki "Pat" Morita)

Dim Sum: A Little Bit of Heart (1985, directed by Wayne Wang)

The Karate Kid Part II (1986, starring Noriyuki "Pat" Morita)

A Great Wall (1986, directed by and starring Peter Wang)

China Girl (1987, with a largely Asian-American cast)

The Last Emperor (1987, starring Joan Chen)

True Believer (1988, starring Yuji Okumoto)

The Karate Kid III (1989, starring Noriyuki "Pat" Morita)

Eat a Bowl of Tea (1989, directed by Wayne Wang)

Come See The Paradise (1990, predominantly Japanese-American cast)

Lonely in America (1991, starring Ranjit Chowdhry)

Iron Maze (1991, directed by Hiroaki Yoshida)

Thousand Pieces of Gold (1991, directed by Nancy Kelly and Kenji Yamamoto)

Mississippi Masala (1992, directed by Mira Nair)

The Joy Luck Club (1993, directed by Wayne Wang, with an Asian-American cast)

Combination Platter (1993, directed by Tony Chan)

Picture Bride (1994, directed by Kayo Hatta with a Japanese-American cast)

Catfish in Black Bean Sauce (2000, directed by Chi-Muoi Lo, starring Chi Muoi Lo and Lauren Tom)

TWO

Japanese Americans

Why are Japanese Americans called Issei, Nisei, Kibei, Sansei, and Yonsei?

When did the first Japanese find their way to Hawaii?

Why did the Japanese begin to venture to Hawaii in significant numbers?

How did the Japanese laborers in Hawaii fare compared to other ethnic minorities?

What is a "picture bride"?

Were Japanese women laboring in Hawaii paid a living wage?

Where did the first Japanese colony spring up in the United States, and what was its fate?

When did the Japanese begin arriving in the United States in significant numbers, and where did they settle?

Just how severe was discrimination against the Japanese in California in the 1890s and the early decades of the twentieth century?

What was the Gentlemen's Agreement?

Why were laws passed forbidding the Japanese from owning or leasing land?

What was the Immigration Act of 1924?

What was the Japanese American Citizens League?

Why was Pearl Harbor called a "lifetime of infamy" for Japanese Americans?

How were the Japanese in the United States treated after the Empire of Japan bombed American forces at Pearl Harbor?

What was Executive Order 9066?

How was Executive Order 9066 implemented?

When did the actual evacuation of Japanese Americans and permanent residents begin?

How did the Japanese react to the evacuation orders?

Why were Hawaiians of Japanese descent not evacuated and interned?

What did the evacuation cost the Japanese community in America?

How were the evacuees organized, and what were conditions like in the assembly centers and internment camps?

Were the internees forced to take loyalty tests, and who were the No-No boys?

Did the Nisei volunteer to serve in the U.S. military during World War II?

How did the 442nd Regimental Combat Team perform?

Did the Nisei also serve in the Military Intelligence Service?

Were the Nisei ever drafted?

Who was Tokyo Rose?

Other than fighting men and women, were any other Japanese Americans permitted to leave the camps during the years of internment?

Who is Mitsuye Endo, and why was she a true World War II hero?

When were the internment camps finally emptied?

Did the U.S. government provide redress to Japanese Americans and resident aliens interned during World War II?

When did life improve for the Japanese community in America?

Why did relatively few numbers of Japanese immigrate to the United States with the passage of the Immigration Act of 1965?

Have the Sansei and Yonsei managed to fulfill the American dream despite the setbacks their forebears faced?

Why was anti-Japanese discrimination rampant in the United States in the 1980s and early 1990s?

How many Japanese Americans are there, and where do they live?

Who are some prominent Japanese-American politicians?

Who are the leading Japanese-American actors?

Who are some world-class Japanese-American musicians?

Who are some renowned Japanese Americans in the world of art and architecture?

Who are some other prominent Japanese Americans?

Who are some great Japanese-American athletes?

Which religions do Japanese Americans observe?

What is Zen Buddhism?

What are the more popular Japanese systems of martial arts?

What are some major Japanese-American festivals?

What foods are popular among Japanese Americans?

Japanese Americans have inherited a history in the New World that stretches back nearly a century and a half and embodies the relentless human struggle from persecution to acceptance. Generations of Japanese in America suffered decade after decade of overt discrimination—which even took the form of years of forced internment in the aftermath of Japan's surprise attack on American military forces at Pearl Harbor on December 7, 1941. Against the odds, Japanese Americans have emerged as one of the most successful minority groups in the United States and as an integral part of a society in which sushi and Toyota are as American as apple pie and Chevrolet. The Japanese-American success story is nothing short of remarkable.

Why are Japanese Americans called Issei, Nisei, Kibei, Sansei, and Yonsei?

Japanese Americans, known collectively as the Nikkei, meaning "of Japanese lineage," are perhaps the only ethnic group in the United States that couches its history and evolution on American shores in terms of generational groups. This phenomenon is largely due to the fact that the bulk of Japanese immigration to Hawaii and the United States took place between 1885 and 1924, and since then the Japanese-American community has been largely comprised of the offspring of those immigrants. The immigrants who arrived in Hawaii and the United States between 1885 (or rather 1868 in the case of the Japanese venturing to Hawaii) and 1924 are known as the Issei. Many Issei never became American citizens, as the Japanese were ineligible for naturalized U.S. citizenship until the passage of the McCarran-Walter Act in 1952. The Issei generation has largely passed away. The offspring of the Issei, that is, American-born Japanese of the second generation, are known as Nisei. Kibei are Nisei who received their education in Japan. For the most part, the Nisei, whose ages fall within a wide range (since their parents immigrated to the United States over four decades), spent part of their youth or adult years in the internment camps set up for Japanese Americans and permanent resident aliens during World War II. The younger Nisei are now in their golden years. The Sansei are the children of the Nisei, or third-generation Japanese Americans. Finally, there are the Yonsei, fourth-generation Japanese Americans, the progeny of Sansei.

Since the postwar period, Japanese Americans have been joined by newcomers from Japan, but their numbers have been quite small due to economic prosperity and political stability at home. With their small numbers, the newcomers have complemented but have not significantly altered the Japanese community in America.

When did the first Japanese find their way to Hawaii?

With the exception of a few shipwrecked sailors and students and diplomats abroad, the first Japanese to land on Hawaiian shores were approximately 150 farm laborers who were recruited and shipped to Hawaii in 1868 by **Eugene M. Van Reed,** Hawaii's consul general in Japan, to work as contract laborers on sugar plantations. As it turned out, Van Reed's recruits were treated poorly by plantation owners and most found the work detestable (they were urban dwellers from Tokyo and Yokohama and were unaccustomed to farm labor). When reports of their maltreatment reached Japan, an alarmed Japanese government arranged for the return to Japan of forty of the workers at Hawaii's expense, and for the next seventeen years it prohibited its citizens from working in Hawaii as contract laborers.

Why did the Japanese begin to venture to Hawaii in significant numbers?

Japanese citizens ventured first to Hawaii before setting their sights on the United States. After Hawaii and the United States signed the 1875 Reciprocity Treaty, which allowed for the duty-free importation of Hawaiian sugar into the United States, the Hawaiian sugar industry needed workers to keep up with demand. Hawaii's sugar plantation owners looked to Japan as a potential source of cheap labor. Japanese emigration companies, which had no trouble recruiting young Japanese men in rural areas and thus stood to make a good profit, entered into contracts with Hawaiian sugar plantations to supply workers. In the years 1891 to 1908 alone, they provided Hawaiian sugar plantations with more than 124,000 Japanese laborers. The Japanese recruits were eager to sail to Hawaii and take the jobs that had opened up in the sugar industry because their financial situation in Japan was abominable. In 1868 the newly restored Emperor **Meiji** had begun to levy high taxes to fund the industrialization and militarization campaign the Japanese government had mounted to stave off potential colonization by Western powers, whose presence in China was perceived as an imperialist encroachment toward Japan. Japanese farmers bore the brunt of the government's new taxation program. Many were unable to handle the tax burden and lost their land. Work in Hawaii seemed like one possible way out of the economic morass.

A large percentage of the Japanese who ventured to Hawaii in the last two decades of the nineteenth century and the first decade of the twentieth century were *dekasegi-nin*, or sojourners intent on working abroad temporarily and then returning to Japan with enough money saved to pay off family debts or regain lost farmland. This is precisely the dream that impelled Senator **Daniel K. Inouye**'s grandfather, **Asakichi Inouye,** to venture to Hawaii with his wife and son in 1899, a year after the island chain had been annexed by the United States, to work on the sugar plantations. Like many Japanese immigrants of the time period, however, Asakichi Inouye ultimately chose to make Hawaii his permanent home. Later, some Japanese in Hawaii, which in 1900 became a U.S. territory, found their way to the mainland United States. Thus, Hawaii was first a magnet for emigration from rural Japan, and later a springboard for migration to North America.

How did the Japanese laborers in Hawaii fare compared to other ethnic minorities?

Due to labor shortages and other pitfalls on the way to prosperity, Hawaiian businesses actively recruited cheap labor from China, Portugal, Puerto Rico, Korea, and the Philippines, as well as from Japan. While the diversity of the labor pool bred a climate of tolerance in Hawaii, which worked in favor of the Japanese during World War II, initially this diversity was an absolute liability for Japanese workers. Hawaiian businesses tied laborers' earning power to their ethnicity, with the Japanese receiving the lowest wages. For the length of their labor contracts, usually a period of three years, the Japanese had to work long hours at backbreaking tasks and had to turn a chunk of their earnings over to the Japanese emigration companies who had arranged and funded their passage from Japan to Hawaii. Thus, their work on the sugar plantations amounted to indentured servitude.

After the laws of the United States took effect in Hawaii with the passage of the Organic Act of 1900, on the heels of the transfer of Hawaii's sovereignty to the United States in 1900, the contract system was abolished, as it smacked of slavery to Americans. Still, the plantation owners managed to retain their hold on the Japanese laborers by fixing wages. The Japanese fought back, combating discrimination in labor practices with the 1909 Plantation Strike. It began on May 9, 1909, when Japanese laborers at the Aiea Plantation walked off the job to protest the fact that they were paid only $18.00 a month, while Portuguese laborers took home $22.50 a month. By June 1909, seven thousand Japanese laborers in Oahu had followed suit. The strike did not end until August 1909, and while it lasted, Japanese communities throughout Hawaii rallied in support of the striking laborers with food, money, and free medical care. The 1909 Plantation Strike was worrisome for plantation owners, who realized that they could no longer exploit Japanese laborers so readily. After the strike ended, they launched a massive campaign to import Filipino workers, who were easier to control. Many Japanese dealt with the inequity of the plantations by fulfilling their contracts and then leaving plantation work. Some returned to Japan, while others moved on to Honolulu or the West Coast of the United States.

What is a "picture bride"?

Until the twentieth century, marriage in Japan was strictly an issue of compatibility and joining family lines, not individuals, and, therefore, romance and courtship—individualistic notions—mattered little. Marriage was so serious, in fact, that elders frequently sought the aid of a kind of matchmaker in arranging meetings between their sons and daughters that would hopefully end in matrimony, a practice that survives to this day. When it happened that a man and a woman lived too far apart to meet one another in person, the two parties resorted to exchanging pictures and information to get acquainted. Around the turn of the twentieth century, eligible Japanese bachelors in Hawaii (and later in the United States)—most of whom desired to marry Japanese women but were too far from home to meet their future wives—came to rely on the "picture bride" method of matrimony. Japanese women willing to sail to the Hawaiian Islands were not all that numerous, and so the willing were swamped with marriage offers from Japanese men abroad.

Before a picture bride set sail from Japan to Hawaii, she took part in a traditional wedding ceremony with a curious twist: She exchanged vows with a proxy standing in for her husband. Then, armed with a picture of her newly betrothed, the picture bride departed Japan. Many picture brides were rather dismayed when they finally set eyes on their husbands and new homes. It wasn't uncommon for Japanese men working abroad to mislead Japanese women at home about their lowly status by sending them pictures of themselves dressed in nice clothes that they had rented. Still, rather than risk shaming their families by complaining, most picture brides overcame their initial disappointment over their new husbands and forged a married life.

The Japanese government encouraged picture brides to venture to Hawaii (and later to the United States) in an effort to avoid the problems plaguing the Chinese immigrant community in America with its surplus of bachelors—namely, prostitution and gambling. Picture brides were not the only Japanese women who went to Hawaii. In the late nineteenth century, the Japanese government made it a policy to educate its female citizens and to allow them to enter the labor force as a way to hasten the country's economic development. Japanese women increasingly found employment in the construction industry, textile mills, and coal mines, and by 1900 they constituted 60 percent of Japan's industrial workforce. By this time they were also permitted to immigrate to Hawaii as laborers, where they gradually altered the islands' Japanese bachelor community.

Were Japanese women laboring in Hawaii paid a living wage?

Most Japanese families in Hawaii depended on women's wages for their survival, and so large numbers of Japanese women entered the workforce. Some provided domestic services, such as cooking, sewing and cleaning, to the many single male Japanese laborers in Hawaii. (In 1910 women constituted just 33 percent of Hawaii's Japanese community.) Others went to work on the Hawaiian sugar plantations. Sugar plantation owners happily hired Japanese women to work in the fields, convinced that they increased male workers' sense of well-being and responsibility and, thus, raised overall productivity. In 1910 one-third of all employed Japanese women in Hawaii labored on the sugar plantations. Even though Issei women performed the same strenuous fieldwork as men, such as hoeing, irrigating, and harvesting, and were critical for morale, they were paid much less than male workers. Lower wages forced many Issei women to work extra jobs, ironing and cooking for the bachelor laborers on the plantations.

Given that the great preponderance of Japanese women had to perform physical labor outside of the home to keep their families afloat and that women's employers generally did not provide paid maternity leave or cover the cost of day care, the birthrate in Hawaii's Japanese community was rather low. Japanese women devised strategies to cope with the heavy physical and financial burdens of child rearing, such as staying on the job until their last month of pregnancy, taking their babies along to the fields by strapping them on their backs or carrying them in crude cribs, and placing them in the care of other women. Before long they began to demand equal pay for equal work and improved conditions, especially with regard to child care. They made their demands known through their participation in labor strikes against plantation owners. For instance, in the 1909 Plantation Strike, Japanese women called for, among other things, paid maternity leave before and after pregnancy.

The sugar plantation remained the most important employer for Issei women in Hawaii until 1920, when a good number turned to domestic and personal services or branched out into the pineapple canneries and garment factories. Nisei women would return in significant numbers to the sugar plantations during the Great Depression, but they stayed out of the fields, finding less physically demanding work in plantation stores and offices.

Where did the first Japanese colony spring up in the United States, and what was its fate?

In 1869 a German merchant named **John Henry Schnell,** who had been in Japan during the Meiji struggle to overthrow the Tokugawa shogun, smuggled approximately thirty Japanese citizens out of Japan and took them to California. There the Japanese and John Schnell established a colony, christened the Wakamatsu Tea and Silk Farm Colony, at Granger ranch in Gold Hill, north of San Francisco. The colonists had high hopes of turning a profit from the cultivation of mulberries (perhaps for silkworm production), tangerines, grapes, and tea, but an inhospitable climate and financial trouble plagued their efforts. Resigned to defeat, Schnell abandoned the colony, and the Japanese immigrants dispersed, leaving little trace. While twenty-two of the fifty-five Japanese counted in the 1870 U.S. Census dwelled in Gold Hill, the records of only three have been unearthed. One was a woman named **Okei,** probably the nanny of Schnell's children, who some speculate was the first Japanese woman to die on American soil when she succumbed to a fever in 1871.

When did the Japanese begin arriving in the United States in significant numbers, and where did they settle?

The Japanese, mostly young, unmarried male sojourners who dreamed of making money and returning home to Japan, began venturing from Japan and Hawaii to the United States in significant numbers in the 1890s. While just 149 Japanese came to the United States between 1871 and 1880 (which was fewer than the 186 who arrived in the country between 1861 and 1870), and only 2,270 ventured to American shores in the years 1881 to 1890, between 1891 and 1900, 25,942 Japanese citizens entered the United States. Japanese immigration reached its peak in the years 1901 to 1910, when 129,797 Japanese citizens arrived in America. The Japanese sojourners who came to the United States in these early years entered the country through ports of entry in California, Oregon, and Washington, such as Seattle and San Francisco. The majority lived a migrant life in these three states, where they found abundant work in agriculture, on the railroads, in small businesses, in domestic service, at lumber mills and salmon canneries, and in mining, due in part to the virtual halt in the immigration of Chinese workers to the United States brought about by the Chinese Exclusion Act of 1882, which remained in effect until 1943. Little by little, the Japanese workers gravitated to agriculture, and by 1910 more agricultural workers in California were Japanese than any other ethnicity.

San Francisco was a popular West Coast destination for the Japanese, who found jobs there as unskilled laborers and a sense of security and camaraderie in the ethnic enclave that formed in the city. As the Issei enclave in San Francisco grew, many Japanese established small businesses, such as supply stores, restaurants, barbershops, boardinghouses, ice cream parlors, and banks, to meet its needs. Still, others found employment as domestic workers, schoolteachers, tailors, physicians, and dentists. The Issei also established mutual aid organizations to help members of the enclave gain a financial foothold. After the devastating 1906 earthquake leveled San Francisco, many Japanese immigrants opted to settle in Little Tokyos in other parts of California, particularly in Los Angeles County, where they worked in farming, on the railroad, and in small businesses. According to reports, only thirty-six Japanese resided in Los Angeles County in 1890, but by 1910 that number had grown to 8,641. Like the Chinese, a percentage of Japanese immigrants eventually moved inward away from the West Coast, settling in such states as Utah, Wyoming, and Colorado, where they were primarily engaged in work on the railroad, in the coal mines, and in the sugar beet industry.

Until 1894 the Japanese government strictly regulated which Japanese workers would be permitted to go abroad in an effort to safeguard the country's reputation. Japanese authorities meticulously screened out lowly, illiterate workers and other undesirables, who could potentially jeopardize Japan's high standing in the eyes of the world. Only literate, healthy, strong, and relatively well educated Japanese, who would enhance Japan's standing, made the grade for emigration. The Japanese government also screened its citizens going abroad to minimize the possibility that the U.S. government would bar Japan's subjects from entering the United States in the way it had Chinese citizens with the Chinese Exclusion Act of 1882. Concerned also that its citizens might receive the same maltreatment at the hands of the Americans as Chinese laborers had been subjected to, the Japanese government monitored the treatment of Japanese abroad well into the twentieth century.

Just how severe was discrimination against the Japanese in California in the 1890s and the early decades of the twentieth century?

Anglo-Saxon Americans, who since the 1850s had subjected Chinese immigrants to discriminatory practices, verbal abuse, and even physical violence, in part because they deemed the Chinese as unwanted competition in the workplace, were no more friendly to the Japanese, whom they often mistook for Chinese. San Francisco workers dealt with the perceived threat from Chinese and Japanese labor by forming the Asiatic Exclusion League in 1905, a time when Japanese immigration to the United States had risen significantly, which called for a severe reduction or end to "the immigration of Asiatics to America." Unwilling to wait for Washington to alter the nation's immigration policy, members of the Asiatic Exclusion League lashed out at the Issei, verbally harassing them, picketing their businesses, destroying their property, and even beating them up. Early in 1905, the *San Francisco Chronicle* got on the anti-Japanese, nativist bandwagon, fanning the flames of hatred by publishing a series of inflammatory articles on the "yellow peril," that is, the threat that the rising number of Japanese immigrants posed to the United States. The articles depicted the Japanese as spies, as massive hordes (even though they were a small percentage of the general population) plotting to take over the country, and as criminals who preyed on white women. Some of the more frenzied headlines read: "The Yellow Peril—How Japanese Crowd Out the White Race" and "Brown Artisans Steal Brains of Whites."

Members of the Asiatic Exclusion League and other nativist San Franciscans were especially troubled by the fact that Japanese boys and men who were trying to master English had been placed in classrooms with American-born little children whose skill level was the same. In 1906 the San Francisco school board demanded that all Japanese be forced to attend a special school that had been set up for children of "Chinese or Mongolian descent," claiming that white schoolchildren, especially girls, were at risk of being attacked, sexually or otherwise, by Japanese men and adolescents in their classrooms—even though not a single immoral or disorderly act by a Japanese pupil had been reported. The school board's efforts to segregate the Japanese in a separate school were undermined when it was determined that the Japanese were not Mongolian and, therefore, should be permitted to attend regular schools alongside white students. The San Francisco school board managed to establish that the Japanese were, indeed, "Mongolian," and on October 11, 1906, it ordered the Japanese to attend the Chinese school.

The news that Japanese students in San Francisco were being forced out of the city's schools quickly got back to the Japanese government, which denounced the mistreatment of its citizens and called on Washington to take immediate action to rectify the situation. Acutely aware of Japan's military prowess, as evidenced by its relatively easy defeat of Imperial Russia in the Russo-Japanese War of 1904–05, President **Theodore Roosevelt** was concerned that the infuriated Japanese government would strike back in some way. President Roosevelt sent **Victor H. Metcalf,** his secretary of commerce and labor at the time, to intervene. San Francisco school officials defended their actions, making the case to Secretary Metcalf that the Japanese posed a clear threat to the younger white girls in their classes. Secretary Metcalf recommended that the school board remedy the situation by setting age limits for each grade level rather than segregating students. He also advised that students with poor language skills be sent to separate schools to learn English and later returned to regular classrooms. The U.S. attorney general filed two suits against the San Francisco school board, which caused enough concern among school officials that they rescinded their order that Japanese pupils attend the Chinese school. The matter resolved satisfactorily, the U.S. government dropped its lawsuits.

What was the Gentlemen's Agreement?

By resolving the San Francisco school board crisis swiftly and decisively, President **Roosevelt** reassured the Japanese government that the Japanese in the United States were being treated well. However, he wanted to settle the immigration problem once and for all. He came up with a seemingly ingenious solution, the Gentlemen's Agreement, which would placate exclusionists on the West Coast while at the same time assuring Japan that its national honor and its citizens were respected. Signed by the United States and Japan in 1908, the Gentlemen's Agreement stipulated that Japan could issue passports only to Japanese nonlaborers and to three classes of laborers—namely, "former residents," "parents, wives or children of residents," and "settled agriculturalists"—and obligated the United States to block legislation designed to harass Japanese on its territory. In keeping with the Gentlemen's Agreement, Japan also had to contain the flow of its citizens to Hawaii in a similar fashion. At the same time, President Roosevelt ordered that the migration of Japanese from Hawaii to the United States be halted. This order took effect in the summer of 1908.

Although the Gentlemen's Agreement was designed to stem the tide of emigration from Japan to the United States, it turned out to have the opposite effect. With parents, wives, and children of Japanese already in residence in the United States granted the right to immigrate, the number of Japanese entering the United States remained quite steady: While between 1901 and 1910, 129,797 Japanese had entered the United States, in the years 1911 to 1920, 83,837 Japanese citizens came to American shores. Not surprisingly, Japanese immigration went from being predominantly male to female, as thousands of women were reunited with their husbands or met them for the first time as picture brides. Had it not been for the Gentlemen's Agreement, the Japanese community in the United States would have continued to be overwhelmingly male for decades to come, and many of the Nisei generation probably would not have been born. Instead, by 1924 the sexes were evenly represented among the Japanese in America.

Why were laws passed forbidding the Japanese from owning or leasing land?

The industrialization of the United States in the late nineteenth century created enormous demands for fresh produce in the country's urban centers. This, coupled with the development of an improved irrigation system in California (which made intensive agricultural production feasible) and refrigeration in trains, led to a boom in farming in that state. Some job opportunities for the Japanese had begun to open up outside of agriculture, but small-scale farming remained the most viable way of life for the majority of Issei, and they took advantage of American consumers' demand for fresh vegetables and fruit.

The Japanese laborers knew that they were nobody until they owned their own farms, and often several members of the same *ken,* or clan, pooled their resources in order to lease or purchase land. Thanks to these efforts, in 1909 Issei and Nisei owned 16,449 acres of land in California and leased another 137,233 acres. While this may seem like a lot, in reality the Japanese owned or leased less than 2 percent of all the farmland in California. Nonetheless, white landowners in California and other western states grew increasingly concerned over competition from Japanese farmers, and in an effort to squelch it, they called for strict limits on land ownership by the Japanese. In response to the white landowners' concerns over Japanese competition, the California state legislature passed the Alien Land Act in 1913, prohibiting the ownership of property by "aliens ineligible for citizenship," which included Japanese residents in the United States. The Alien Land Act also barred the Japanese and other aliens in California from leasing agricultural land for more than three years and from bequeathing any land they owned. By 1920 thirteen other western states followed suit with their own alien land laws, some of which remained in effect until 1947.

The Japanese looked for ways to circumvent the grossly unfair Alien Land Act. They discovered one particularly useful loophole: Nowhere in the law was it written that the American-born children of Japanese residents were barred from leasing and purchasing land. Thus, Japanese farmers purchased or leased land in the names of their sons born in the United States, and as their sons' legal guardians, they oversaw this land. This maneuver infuriated white farmers in California, who subsequently pressured the California state legislature to pass alien land legislation in 1920 and 1923 that deprived the Japanese of the right to lease or purchase land on behalf of minors. The Issei managed to get around this legislation and continue in small-scale agriculture by making lease or tenancy arrangements with white landowners, which required little capital investment. The Issei then realized a profit by cultivating intensive crops with unpaid family labor and long days in the field. In 1940 the Issei and Nisei leased 70 percent of the farms they operated in California, but they grew between 30 and 35 percent of the state's truck crops.

What was the Immigration Act of 1924?

Nativists in the United States were outraged when the Gentlemen's Agreement did not achieve the desired effect of stemming Japanese immigration to the United States. However, nativists failed (deliberately) to put the actual numbers of Japanese immigrants in perspective. The reality is that Japanese immigration had always been quite limited compared to European immigration. For instance, between July 1, 1913, and June 30, 1914, approximately 283,000 Italians entered the United States, while in the entire period of Japanese immigration from the 1860s until 1924, only about 275,000 Japanese came to America. This mattered not to the nativists, and once again their cries for an end to Japanese immigration echoed across the nation. The nativists' renewed demands for a stricter U.S. immigration policy vis-à-vis the Japanese culminated in the passage of the Immigration Act of 1924, which excluded aliens ineligible for citizenship from entering the United States and, thereby, brought immigration from most of Asia (not the Philippines) to a virtual standstill until after World War II. With the Immigration Act of 1924 in place, only about 7,000 Japanese entered the United States between 1925 and 1941.

What was the Japanese American Citizens League?

In 1929, a group of educated and assimilated Nisei founded the Japanese American Citizen's League (JACL), the oldest and largest Asian-American civil rights organization in the nation, to address the discrimination against persons of Japanese ancestry in the United States and to fight for their human and civil rights. The JACL—which as of 2003 boasted 112 chapters nationwide, five regional offices, and a membership of 24,000—was popular from the start: From 1930 to 1940, it spawned fifty chapters and membership ballooned to 5,600. Making U.S. citizenship a requirement for membership, the JACL encouraged the Nisei to sever their ties to Japan and its traditions and to embrace the American way as a means to find their niche in society and to eliminate anti-Japanese discrimination and racism. JACL members' trust in the American way would be sorely tested after bombs rained down on Pearl Harbor on December 7, 1941, "a date which will live in infamy," and the United States was plunged into World War II.

Why was Pearl Harbor called a "lifetime of infamy" for Japanese Americans?

The Japanese in America were horrified when the Empire of Japan signed a military pact with Germany and Italy in 1940.

They knew that anti-Japanese hostility, which had been part of the Japanese experience in the United States since the Japanese first set foot on American soil, would only intensify if war between the Japanese empire and the United States broke out. Their worst fears were realized on December 7, 1941, when Japanese air and naval forces dropped bombs on the U.S. Pacific Fleet moored at Pearl Harbor, on the island of Oahu, in an unprovoked act of aggression. The Japanese in America were overcome with shock and shame—and with dread for what lay ahead.

The Japanese in the United States were right to feel enormous apprehension. On December 8, 1941, the day after the bombing raid on Pearl Harbor, President **Franklin Delano Roosevelt** declared war on the Empire of Japan. U.S. Navy Secretary **Frank Knox** was immediately dispatched to Hawaii to assess the damage and investigate the circumstances surrounding the attack. Interestingly, Knox had once been general manager of the Hearst newspapers, which were famous for their fierce anti-Japanese stance. In Knox's assessment, Japanese residents of Hawaii were involved in sabotage and espionage operations in Oahu, and he recommended that they be evacuated to another Hawaiian island. Many government officials, including **J. Edgar Hoover** of the FBI and Lieutenant General **Delos Emmons,** disagreed with Knox's findings. In a radio announcement, General Emmons reassured the Japanese community in Hawaii that the U.S. government had no intention or desire "to operate mass concentration camps . . . we must remember that this is America and we must do things the American Way."

How were the Japanese in the United States treated after the Empire of Japan bombed American forces at Pearl Harbor?

The U.S. government feared that Pearl Harbor was just the initial phase in a planned Japanese invasion of the United

States. It was conjectured that Japan might next target the West Coast of the United States—with the aid of the sizable Japanese community in that region, which, since it had not assimilated into the American mainstream, was deemed tightly bound to Japan by ties of culture, race, custom, and religion. To supposedly preempt another act of aggression on the part of the Japanese empire, Washington immediately took security measures, such as rounding up and interrogating thousands of Issei, or "alien enemies," as they were called, including Buddhist priests, Japanese language teachers, business leaders, and senior citizens. Some Nisei were also interrogated. Many thousands of Issei were arrested and held for a few days and sometimes weeks, and about eight thousand were actually officially interned—in facilities that were more fit to live in than those that would soon be constructed to imprison nearly the entire Japanese community in America.

American newspapers, such as those belonging to **William Randolf Hearst,** promulgated the notion that the Japanese enemy had infiltrated the country. For instance, on December 8, 1941, the *Los Angeles Times* commented: "We have thousands of Japanese here. . . . Some, perhaps many . . . are good Americans. What the rest may be we do not know, nor can we take a chance in the light of yesterday's demonstration that treachery and double dealing are major Japanese weapons." Many newspaper columnists in the ensuing months went so far as to demand the evacuation to points in the country's interior of all Japanese in the western United States, who they commonly called "Nips," "Japs," and "yellow vermin." One such columnist was **Henry McLemore,** of the Hearst papers, who wrote on January 29, 1942: "I am for the immediate removal of every Japanese on the West Coast to a point deep in the interior . . . let 'em be pinched, hurt, hungry. Personally, I hate Japanese." Even the popular American columnist **Walter Lippman** wrote articles in favor of a Japanese evacuation. Times were bad for the Japanese in the United States.

What was Executive Order 9066?

On March 31, 1941, the U.S. House of Representatives passed a resolution to continue the work of the House Select Committee to Investigate Interstate Migration of Destitute Citizens under the title of the House Select Committee Investigating National Defense Migration because the committee had become aware of the large-scale migration of workers to manufacturing centers, which offered jobs in the defense industries. From June 1941 to September 1942, the committee held public hearings in various places around the nation. Hearings scheduled for February and March 1942 were supposed to determine whether an evacuation of persons of Japanese descent in the western states—where the vast majority of Japanese Americans resided—was a military necessity. However, on February 19, 1942, President **Franklin Roosevelt** signed Executive Order 9066, authorizing the secretary of war to evacuate (relocate) approximately 110,000 persons of Japanese ancestry residing in the western United States, nearly two-thirds of whom were American citizens. Thus, when the House Select Committee Investigating National Defense Migration held its hearings on the West Coast in February and March 1942, it discussed the problems intrinsic to the evacuation policy.

At the hearings, JACL leaders agreed to cooperate with the evacuation, even though they knew that the evacuees would not be entitled to individual hearings, in violation of the guarantees of the Bill of Rights and particularly the guarantee of due process of law. They chose to go along with government orders above all because they wanted to assert the Japanese community's unbending loyalty to the United States. They feared that resistance would be misinterpreted as evidence of the community's disloyalty, or worse, as an act of aggression, and that it would eventuate in a forcible evacuation and even bloodshed. The alternatives bleak, JACL leaders urged Japanese Americans and permanent residents to cooperate with the government and the military in the impending evacuation, and they even lashed out at the few in the community who resisted.

How was Executive Order 9066 implemented?

Disinclined to sifting through the entire Japanese population in the western United States to find alleged spies, Lieutenant General **John L. DeWitt,** the U.S. military commander in charge of carrying out Executive Order 9066, proposed, in the name of national security, that all individuals of Japanese descent in Washington, California, Oregon, and other western states be evacuated. Lieutenant General DeWitt also advocated searching Japanese homes and businesses, without obtaining search warrants, to confiscate all weapons or cameras, which it was believed could be used in subversive activities. Reports of the seizure of 2,592 guns, 199,000 rounds of ammunition, 1,652 sticks of dynamite, 1,458 radio receivers, and 2,012 cameras belonging to Japanese in the western states were met with widespread public approval. These reports were misleading because they failed to mention that an appreciable proportion of the objects seized came from a gun shop and a warehouse for a general store, both of which were fully licensed and legitimate.

On March 2, 1942, Lieutenant General DeWitt announced Public Proclamation No. 1, the first in a series of proclamations related to Executive Order 9066 that led to the evacuation of all persons of Japanese ancestry in the western United States. In keeping with Public Proclamation No. 1, the western halves of Washington, Oregon, and California and the southern region of Arizona were designated Military Area No. 1, the area at greatest risk of invasion by enemy forces, while the eastern halves of the Pacific Coast states and the northern region of Arizona were designated Military Area No. 2, an area deemed at a lesser risk of invasion. Public Proclamation No. 1 also included a recommendation that Japanese Americans and permanent residents in Military

Areas Nos. 1 and 2 move inland to avoid forced relocation. Many Japanese (Americans) living in these military areas refused to move: They feared the unknown and more intense hostility inland or simply did not have the financial wherewithal to pack up their homes and businesses and start over in a new place. Only 4,889 of the 107,500 Japanese (Americans) in Military Area No. 1 resettled in inland areas. They endured severe hostility and rejection in their new homes as anticipated, and some, fearing for their lives, simply moved back to the West Coast.

On March 16, Lieutenant General DeWitt issued Public Proclamation No. 2, which designated the states of Idaho, Montana, Nevada, and Utah, and hundreds of other small zones, as Military Areas Nos. 3, 4, 5, and 6. Lieutenant General DeWitt sought to evacuate Japanese (Americans) in these military areas as well, but the War Department opposed him. On March 21, President **Roosevelt** signed a bill granting U.S. military forces the power to govern and monitor the six military areas. On March 24, Lieutenant General DeWitt issued Public Proclamation No. 3, which restricted all "enemy" aliens and individuals of Japanese ancestry to their workplaces, their homes, and an area around their homes five miles in circumference during the daytime, and exclusively to their homes between the hours of eight p.m. and six a.m. Then, on March 27, Public Proclamation No. 4, which prohibited all persons of Japanese ancestry from voluntarily moving out of Military Area No. 1, was issued. Now even those in that area who wished to move inland were no longer permitted to do so.

When did the actual evacuation of Japanese Americans and permanent residents begin?

The actual evacuation of Japanese Americans and permanent resident aliens from the six designated military areas in the western United States began on March 24, 1942, as stipulated by Civil Exclusion Order No. 34. Contingent after contingent of internees were sent to temporary assembly centers and then on to the internment camps until the evacuation was finally complete on August 7, 1942, a little over five months after it began. However, it took until November 3, 1942, for the last internees to be transferred from the assembly centers to the camps. It should be noted that the few thousand Japanese Americans and permanent residents in the continental United States who resided somewhere other than in the six military areas were neither evacuated nor interned, which belies the U.S. government's argument that the Japanese in the United States posed a serious threat to national security and suggests that the **Roosevelt** administration had buckled under intense pressure from panicking military commanders, politicians, and the media on the West Coast to combat the Japanese "enemy" in their midst.

All in all, in what was the largest forced relocation in American history, about 110,000 Japanese-American citizens (whom the army referred to as "non-aliens") and permanent resident aliens in the western United States were uprooted from their homes, businesses, and communities, and were placed in one of ten "Relocation Centers," a palatable euphemism for internment camps or concentration camps. The Relocation Centers were located in Jerome and Rohwer, Arkansas; Gila River and Poston, Arizona (on Indian reservations); Manzanar and Tule Lake, California; Minidoka, Idaho; Topaz, Utah; Amache, Colorado; and Heart Mountain, Wyoming—all remote, uninhabited areas with harsh terrain (from swamps to deserts) and extreme weather conditions. (Once the camps closed, these places were completely deserted and remain uninhabited to this day.) The evacuees, some of whose families were split up and placed in different camps, were incarcerated behind barbed wire and watchtowers for up to almost four years, until the aftermath of World War II.

How did the Japanese react to the evacuation orders?

Most Japanese Americans and permanent resident aliens cooperated fully with the evacuation, perhaps due to their self-proclaimed character trait of *gaman,* meaning "stoical perseverance." A small number of Japanese Americans, however, refused to obey the evacuation orders on the justifiable grounds that their civil rights were being violated. One such resister was **Gordon K. Hirabayashi,** a Nisei student enrolled at the University of Washington who violated both Lieutenant General **DeWitt**'s curfew orders and the evacuation orders. He was consequently arrested, convicted in a local federal court, and sentenced to six months in prison. Hirabayashi appealed his case to the U.S. Supreme Court, which, on June 21, 1943, upheld his conviction for curfew violations in a unanimous decision. In *Hirabayashi v. United States,* the Supreme Court did not rule on the legality of the evacuation order itself; it ruled only that the curfew imposed by the U.S. military to limit Japanese Americans' movement was legal.

Another resister was **Minoru Yasui,** a Nisei who had graduated from the University of Oregon Law School and was a U.S. Army reserve officer, a practicing attorney, and an active member of the JACL. Yasui violated the curfew imposed on Japanese Americans and aliens in order to challenge, in court, the U.S. military's jurisdiction over civilians in such a manner. Yasui's case was heard in a federal court presided over by Judge **James Alger Fee,** who held that Public Proclamation No. 3—which restricted all individuals of Japanese ancestry to their workplaces, their homes, and an area around their homes five miles in circumference during the day, and to their homes at night—was unconstitutional. However, Judge Fee determined that Yasui had given up his U.S. citizenship when he became employed at the Japanese consulate and, thus, was an "enemy alien." Hence, the curfew was legal as it applied to him. Minoru Yasui was fined five thousand dollars and was sentenced to one year in prison. He appealed his case to the U.S. Supreme Court, which ruled on June 21, 1943, the same day of the Hirabayashi ruling, that the curfew was legal and that Yasui was, indeed, guilty of violating it. However, the Court disagreed with Judge Fee that Yasui had relinquished his U.S. citizenship when he went to work at the Japanese Consulate. Once again, however, the Court avoided the issue of evacuation and ruled only on the constitutionality of the curfew order.

A third resister was **Fred Toyosaburo Korematsu,** a Nisei from Oakland, California, who violated Civil Exclusion Order No. 34 by going underground and assuming a Mexican name to avoid internment. Korematsu was working as a welder for the war effort when FBI agents tracked him down. In September 1942, a federal district court in San Francisco found Korematsu guilty of disobeying the evacuation orders and sentenced him to five years' probation. In accordance with Civil Exclusion Order No. 34, he was also evacuated to a relocation center. The civil rights lawyer representing Korematsu appealed on the grounds that the evacuation order itself was unconstitutional. In December 1944, the U.S. Supreme Court upheld in *Korematsu v. United States* the constitutionality of the evacuation order. However, it was not unanimous in its decision.

Why were Hawaiians of Japanese descent not evacuated and interned?

Hawaii was a wartime paradox. Geographically closer to Japan than California and once attacked by the Japanese empire, Hawaii was more vulnerable to ambush than the United States. Nevertheless, all but 1,444 Japanese Hawaiians escaped evacuation and internment during World War II. The reasons for this are simple. In the early 1940s, the Japanese in Hawaii numbered about 150,000, or more than one-third of the island chain's population, and, thus, represented a large chunk of the labor force. Their mass evacuation and internment would have undermined the Hawaiian economy. In addition, the Hawaiian Islands had a diverse population, which meant that Hawaii's Japanese were generally accepted and, therefore, not easily demonized. Also the Hawaiian military had little impetus to harass law-abiding citizens for no apparent reason. Most importantly, the military governor of Hawaii, Lieutenant General **Delos C. Emmons,** opposed internment. He did not want to expend the Hawaiian military's limited resources on relocating and incarcerating a large part of the population. Emmons did face some opposition from U.S. Secretary of the Navy **Frank Knox,** who pushed for the internment of Japanese Hawaiians on the island of Molokai, and from the U.S. Army, which wanted Japanese Hawaiians interned on the U.S. mainland. Nonetheless, plans to evacuate Japanese Hawaiians never got off the ground.

What did the evacuation cost the Japanese community in America?

Evacuation was costly from a financial standpoint for Japanese Americans and permanent residents. Evacuees were given little time to sell their real estate holdings, close down their businesses or find someone else to run them, and to store or sell all of their worldly possessions—except for the few suitcases of clothing, bedding and personal items they were permitted to carry with them into internment. Those who had the opportunity stored their possessions with non-Japanese neighbors or friends. The majority had to sell their belongings at what became known as evacuation sales. Most were able to recoup only a fraction of the true value of their possessions. Even in these desperate times, some put their dignity before profits on the sale of property. In *Farewell to Manzanar: A True Story of* [*the*] *Japanese American Experience During and After the World War II Internment* (1973), **Jeanne Wakatsuki Houston** and **James D. Houston** tell how the mother of the former threw the family's china set worth more than two hundred dollars, one dish at a time, at a greedy dealer who had made a meager offer of seventeen dollars.

Aside from financial losses, evacuation took a heavy psychological toll on Japanese Americans and permanent residents, who felt doubly betrayed: first by the Empire of Japan for ruining their reputation with the attack on Pearl Harbor and then by the United States for subjecting them to the humiliation of forced relocation and incarceration. The evacuees also felt enormous uncertainty about what the future might hold. They did not know where they were going, how long they would be detained, whether their families would be split up, or what the conditions would be in the camps.

How were the evacuees organized, and what were conditions like in the assembly centers and internment camps?

The War Relocation Authority (WRA), which was established on March 18, 1942, in keeping with Presidential Executive Order No. 9102, bore the responsibility of constructing and running the internment camps for Japanese evacuees. By June 5, 1942, the WRA had selected sites on which to construct the ten internment camps in Arizona, Idaho, Colorado, and Wyoming, as well as in Arkansas, California, and Utah, and under the army's direction, the camps were hastily constructed, though at a staggeringly high cost of $56,482,638.

With the camps under construction, the army began to post "instructions to all persons of Japanese ancestry" living in the various military areas to report to control centers, where they were registered and given numbered tags in preparation for internment. With the tags attached to their bags and coat lapels, evacuees were organized not by surname but by number. From the control centers, they reported to local assembly centers before moving on to one of the ten permanent internment camps. Located at fairgrounds and racetracks, most assembly centers consisted of filthy stables for livestock that had been hastily converted, if at all, into temporary living quarters with primitive kitchens and toilet facilities. One evacuee described the situation as "a family of three thousand people camped out in a barn." Still, these minimal facilities cost American taxpayers $10,701,636.

The evacuees did not find conditions much improved once they reached the internment camps. The camps, which were surrounded by barbed-wire fences and watchtowers, housed between seven thousand and nineteen thousand people each in overcrowded conditions. Most featured thirty-six blocks of wood and tar-paper barracks, with each barrack measuring about 20 by 120 feet and partitioned into approximately six rooms, impersonal mess halls, latrines with unpartitioned toilets, communal showers, laundries, and administration and recreation buildings. The construction of the buildings throughout was substandard, and given that the camps were located in regions with extreme temperatures in summer and winter and dangerous wildlife, this posed a severe health threat. Inadequate medical care, nutrition, clothing, and footwear, and a lack of privacy added to the dire conditions. The internees did what they could to improve their living conditions. For instance, they planted vegetable gardens and bred and raised livestock to supplement their diet.

Some internees worked as cooks, dishwashers, and pot scrubbers in the mess halls, or as seamstresses or janitors. Those who had been physicians, nurses, dentists, and teachers in their old lives often worked as the same in the camps. (Even though they had no classroom materials and there were few credentialed Japanese teachers among them because the Japanese had been shut out of pedagogy in America, the Nisei did the best they could to educate the roughly 30,000 school-age children in the camps.) Others were employed as librarians, administrators, agricultural supervisors, or as directors of warehouse supply distribution. The evacuees had a great deal of free time in the camps, which they filled with adult classes in such subjects as American history, bookkeeping, and Japanese flower arrangement. In addition, they organized makeshift libraries, entertaining and educating themselves with whatever books they could collect. The great American photographer **Ansel Adams** perhaps best captured the contours of life for the internees when, in 1943, he photographed those incarcerated in the Manzanar War Relocation Center. His photographs include scenes of work, sports and recreational activities, and agricultural endeavors, as well as portraits, and a selection of them was published along with a text by Adams in 1944 in a book entitled *Born Free and Equal,* which garnered positive reviews. In 2001 the book was reprinted.

Were the internees forced to take loyalty tests, and who were the No-No boys?

All internees over the age of seventeen had to fill out a questionnaire designed to test their loyalty to the United States. The questionnaire contained such questions as: "Are you willing to serve in the Armed Forces of the United States on combat duty, wherever ordered?" and "Will you swear unqualified allegiance to the United States of America and faithfully defend the United States from any or all attack by foreign or domestic forces, and forswear any form of allegiance to the Japanese emperor, to any other foreign government, power or organization?" Sixty-five thousand evacuees answered "yes" to both questions, hoping that these answers would hasten their release from the camps. The U.S. government considered most who answered "yes" loyal. Those who answered "no," on the other hand, were labeled disloyal and branded the "No-No boys." Many No-No boys were removed to the Tule Lake camp in California, which was reserved for those individuals whom the government found especially suspicious.

Did the Nisei volunteer to serve in the U.S. military during World War II?

The Selective Training and Service Act of 1940 ensured that those who registered in the U.S. armed forces would not be discriminated against on the basis of race, creed, color, or membership or activity in any labor, political, religious, or other organization. At the time of the attack on Pearl Harbor, about thirty-five hundred Nisei were enlisted in the U.S. military. In the aftermath of Pearl Harbor, the U.S. armed forces refused to retain Nisei, with their suspect ancestral ties, in their ranks and categorized all Japanese Americans as 4C, nondraftable. Those Nisei previously inducted were transferred to the enlisted reserve or discharged from active duty. However, in February 1943 the War Department experienced a change of heart, thanks in part to intervention by the Japanese American Citizens League, and organized Nisei from the Hawaiian Islands and the mainland United States into two segregated military units, the U.S. Army's 442nd Regimental Combat Team and the 100th Infantry Battalion, an action approved by President **Franklin D. Roosevelt.**

When the U.S. military launched a recruitment campaign in the internment camps, many Nisei men, and some Nisei women, jumped at the opportunity to wear the uniform and prove their loyalty to the United States. In addition to the usual Application for Voluntary Induction, Japanese Americans wishing to enlist had to fill out a special form, the Statement of United States Citizen of Japanese Ancestry, listing all their political, religious, and social affiliations, as well as the newspapers and magazines that they customarily read. They were also required to provide five references from individuals other than employers, indicate their willingness to serve on combat duty anywhere ordered, swear unqualified allegiance to the United States, and forswear any allegiance to Japan. All told, approximately thirty-three thousand Japanese Americans served in World War II and helped the Allies achieve victory.

How did the 442nd Regimental Combat Team perform?

The 442nd Regimental Combat Team (442nd RCT), a segregated army combat unit of Nisei from Hawaii and the western United States, was organized on March 23, 1943. (One of the soldiers of the 442nd was **Daniel K. Inouye,** the future senator from Hawaii.) The unit's battle cry was "Go for broke," and its boys did just that, serving with enormous bravery and self-sacrifice. After training at Fort Shelby in Mississippi for a little over a year, the 442nd arrived in Italy on May 1, 1944, and over the course of the next twelve months fought courageously in Italy's mountainous terrain, engaged the enemy in the Vosges campaign in northeastern France, and then returned to Italy to break through—in a single day—the German Gothic Line, which had blocked the Allied advance for half a year, before forcing the German army to retreat north and finally surrender on May 2, 1945. Among the 442nd RCT's most heroic accomplishments was saving 211 soldiers, mostly Texans, from the "Texas Lost Battalion" of the 141st Infantry Regiment, who were surrounded by the German enemy in France. The rescued men of the Texas Lost Battalion later presented the 442nd with a silver plaque engraved with words of gratitude.

At the end of the war, the 442nd RCT, which suffered 9,486 casualties, was recognized for its heroic deeds. In July 1946 President **Harry S. Truman** held a special ceremony at the White House for the surviving soldiers of the 442nd, praising them for having "fought not only the enemy, but prejudice—and you have won." As a team, the 442nd, one of the most decorated units in the history of the U.S. Army, earned such honors as forty-three Division Commendations, thirteen Army Commendations, two Meritorious Service Unit Plaques, and seven Presidential Distinguished Unit Citations. Between them its members received fifty-two Distinguished Service Crosses, a Distinguished Service Medal, ninety-five hundred Purple

Hearts, about six hundred Silver Stars, and some four thousand Bronze Star Medals. Still, intolerance ran deep and only one member of the unit, Private First Class **Sadao S. Munemuri,** received the military's highest award for valor in action, the Congressional Medal of Honor, at the end of World War II. P.F.C. Munemori risked his life above and beyond the call of duty on April 5, 1945, near Seravezza, Italy, when he threw himself on top of an unexploded grenade to smother the blast, saving the lives of two of his comrades and losing his own.

Half a century later, on June 21, 2000, the United States finally recognized the extraordinary deeds of self-sacrifice and bravery that distinguished some Nisei from their comrades on the battlefields of World War II. On that day, President **Clinton** awarded the Medal of Honor to twenty Japanese-American World War II veterans, thirteen of them posthumously. Among the seven surviving veterans who received the Medal of Honor that day was Hawaii Senator Daniel K. Inouye. The Go For Broke Monument, which was unveiled in Little Tokyo in Los Angeles on June 5, 1999, commemorates the efforts of these Medal of Honor recipients and all Japanese Americans who served their country with gallantry and intrepidity during World War II.

Did the Nisei also serve in the Military Intelligence Service?

Ironically, while the American public was fiercely contesting the Japanese community's loyalty to the United States and the U.S. government deemed Japanese Americans a threat to national security, they were carrying out some of the nation's most top secret work from the very first days of U.S. involvement in World War II to the very last campaign. Operating covertly within the Military Intelligence Service (MIS), Japanese Americans were considered a powerful secret weapon in the fight against Japan; U.S. military officials estimated that their efforts shortened the war by two years. By the end of World War II, six thousand Japanese Americans had lent their expertise to the MIS as interpreters, translators, spies, and intelligence specialists. Attached to American and Allied combat units in the theater and also stationed at the various intelligence headquarters, they performed such tasks as intercepting and monitoring Japanese radio transmissions; translating confiscated Japanese maps, orders, battle plans, journals, manuals, letters, and other documents that revealed enemy tactics and operations; interpreting for U.S. military officers; interrogating Japanese POWs; and persuading the Japanese to surrender.

Were the Nisei ever drafted?

The U.S. military drafted about three thousand eligible Nisei men who were incarcerated in the internment camps. Intent on proving their patriotism, most answered the call. However, about three hundred Nisei, organized into a group called the Fair Play Committee, refused to serve Uncle Sam unless their U.S. citizenship and civil rights were restored and their families were released from the internment camps. They were led by **Frank Emi**, a soft-spoken Nisei interned at the Heart Mountain camp in Wyoming. Emi defied the draft and urged others to do the same, arguing that the very democratic ideals of liberty and justice that Americans were fighting to defend overseas were being denied to Japanese Americans. The U.S. government had no patience for Emi and other Nisei draft resisters, no matter if their civil rights were being denied. It convicted 315 Nisei of violating the Selective Service Act and sent them to federal prison, where they remained behind bars for up to two or three years. (In December 1947 President **Truman** pardoned the Nisei draft resisters.)

Those who bucked the draft got no better reception in the Japanese internment camps: They were taunted and shunned by their fellow internees, who felt that the resisters' actions betrayed the community, since its very survival depended on proving its unwavering loyalty to the United States. After they returned home, the draft resisters lived in the shadows, fearing that the community would lash out at them and their families. Mostly they were met by a wall of silence. In recent decades, as younger generations of Japanese Americans have uncovered the story of the Nisei draft resisters, the community has been forced to face the wounds of the past. Most have come to recognize the courage of those interned Nisei who refused induction orders and chose to battle oppression and racism at home.

Who was Tokyo Rose?

Tokyo Rose was another victim of war hysteria. In the years 1943 to 1945, American troops fighting in the South Pacific pinned the nickname "Tokyo Rose" on all the English-speaking women broadcasters of Radio Tokyo who announced popular music programs and Japanese war propaganda. Most American GIs developed an affection for these American-sounding women, who offered them the music they liked to hear. American journalists after a scoop caught Tokyo Rose fever in 1944 and created the myth of one Tokyo Rose, a seductive and vicious teaser who undermined the morale of U.S. fighting men. With the press fueling the myth, Tokyo Rose's celebrity spread like wildfire among the GIs, who had few amusements and a lot of battle fatigue. She essentially became a pinup girl of the radio waves who lived in the imaginations of American soldiers and journalists. Exploiting the news value of Tokyo Rose, journalists constantly speculated on her identity. The most fantastic rumor was that she was **Amelia Earhart,** the pioneering American aviator who had disappeared over the Pacific in 1937 during an attempt to become the first woman to fly around the world.

Then, in 1945, the myth fell on a Japanese-American woman from Los Angeles named **Iva Ikuko Toguri,** whose father had emigrated from Japan to the United States in 1899. In July 1941, about a year and a half after graduating from UCLA, Iva Toguri traveled to Japan, without a U.S. passport, to visit a critically ill aunt and to study medicine. She was dissatisfied with Japanese life in general and complained about the poor Japanese diet, which had caused her to suffer from bouts of scurvy and beriberi. Longing to return home, Iva presented herself to the United States vice consul in Japan to secure her U.S. passport. Before it was issued, war broke out between the United States and Japan, leaving Iva Toguri trapped in Japan. With bills to pay, she took a job at Radio Tokyo, first as a typist and then as a broadcaster of Japanese propaganda and music, a post she filled until the Japanese surrender.

American reporters hoping to cash in on the Tokyo Rose story followed a few "leads" that in 1945 took them to Iva Toguri. They offered her two thousand dollars for an interview about her alias, Tokyo Rose, promising that if she agreed to answer questions, reporters would stop hounding her. Delighted with the U.S. victory in the war and caught up in the carnivalesque search for Tokyo Rose, Toguri foolishly did the interview and signed a contract saying that she was Tokyo Rose. Now at the center of the massive Tokyo Rose witch hunt, she was before long taken into custody by U.S. military police and spent time in and out of prisons in Japan until August 26, 1948, when the U.S. government presented her with a formal arrest warrant and transferred her to San Francisco. In a San Francisco courtroom, Toguri was tried for "treasonable conduct against the United States during World War II." During the trial, which commenced on July 5, 1949, the prosecution presented falsified evidence to build its case against Toguri. In an egregious miscarriage of justice, the all-white jury reached a verdict of guilty, and on October 6, 1949, Iva Toguri was sentenced to ten years imprisonment and fined $100,000 for the crime of treason. After serving about six years of her sentence, she was released on January 28, 1956. Months later, the U.S. Immigration and Naturalization Service, arguing that her conviction made her a stateless person, issued Toguri a formal order to leave the country or face deportation. She contested the order, and in 1958 the U.S. government canceled deportation proceedings but refused to restore her American citizenship.

During her trial and long after, the Japanese-American community distanced itself from Iva Toguri, whose indictment was viewed with shame. Japanese Americans began to rally around her in the early 1970s, when reports surfaced that her prosecution had been based on testimony that the U.S. Department of Justice knew was false. Dr. **Clifford I. Uyeda,** a retired San Francisco pediatrician who was convinced that Iva Toguri had been terribly wronged, led the campaign for her pardon. Although requests had been denied by both the **Eisenhower** and **Johnson** administrations, on January 19, 1977, his last day in office, President **Gerald Ford** granted Iva Toguri a presidential pardon.

Other than fighting men and women, were any other Japanese Americans permitted to leave the camps during the years of internment?

Two other groups of internees were permitted to leave the internment camps as early as the summer of 1942: workers who pledged to contribute to the American war effort by joining the labor force and college students.

When Japanese Americans were removed from college and university campuses before the 1941–42 academic year had ended, astute educators grew concerned for their future. As a way of minimizing the impact of this interruption on graduating Japanese-American seniors, some educators, such as **Robert Gordon Sproul,** the president of the University of California, awarded them their diplomas in absentia. (**Lee Paul Sieg,** the president of the University of Washington, actually held a special commencement for his Japanese-American seniors at the assembly center in Puyallup, Washington.) More importantly, these educators banded together with church leaders and representatives of the YMCA and YWCA and other national organizations to form in May 1942 the National Japanese American Student Relocation Council, whose aim was to assist the WRA in accommodating the education needs of Nisei college students deemed loyal.

The National Japanese American Student Relocation Council negotiated a plan with the War Department and other government agencies for releasing prospective college students from internment camps so that they could attend colleges and universities. In addition to providing proof of acceptance to a college or university located away from the Western Defense Command, interned prospective college students also had to undergo an FBI security check and have a public official testify on their behalf that they posed no threat to the nation's security in order to obtain clearance to leave the camps. Those students who were cleared faced yet another obstacle: financing their education. The U.S. Office of Education did not help subsidize the students' tuition costs, and the WRA was only able to provide a travel allowance and a grant of approximately twenty-five dollars per student. The students had to depend solely on private scholarships and their families (who in most instances could provide no support because they had no income while interned), at least until the National Japanese American Student Relocation Council was able to drum up some financial assistance for the students.

The council also launched an aggressive campaign to convince colleges and universities to accept Nisei students. Japanese-American students were strictly forbidden from attending educational institutions located near military facilities and strategically sensitive areas or engaged in training and research on behalf of the armed forces. However, many academic institutions that were cleared to accept Japanese Americans refused to admit them. (It was especially difficult to enlist the cooperation of nursing schools, whose administrators were concerned that patients would react negatively to Japanese-American nurses and thus were reluctant to train them.) Other institutions of higher learning did not hesitate to open their doors. According to the records of the National Japanese American Student Relocation Council, by December 15, 1944, 3,593 Nisei had enrolled at about fifty-five institutions of higher learning in forty-six states. It has been estimated that 40 percent of the students were female. Despite the suffocating confines of the camps, embarking on a college career was not an easy decision for these young women. They felt obligated to remain in the camps to care for their elders, and they were also filled with uncertainty about the treatment they would receive in the outside world.

As for those internees who pledged to work for the war effort, they were badly needed during World War II, when droves of American workers left the factories and fields for the battlefields overseas. In May 1942 the first group of internees, fifteen in all, was transferred from an assembly center to a farm in Oregon. When their work was given a seal of approval, more internees were permitted to leave the camps and join the labor force. By the end of 1942, approximately fifteen hundred internees had been released from the camps to work the land in Idaho, Utah, and Montana, and approximately ten thousand had been granted seasonal releases to harvest crops.

The release from internment camps of Japanese-American students and workers and their resettlement in places where they had not traditionally lived, such as Ohio, Idaho, Michigan, Minnesota, New York, and Chicago, the most popular resettlement destination before January 1, 1945, had the effect of spreading the Japanese (American) population throughout the nation. The WRA and President **Roosevelt** applauded the resettlement program. At a press conference conducted on November 21, 1944, Roosevelt stated: "A good deal of progress has been made in scattering them through the country . . .

they are American citizens . . . 75,000 families scattered around the United States is not going to upset anybody."

Who is Mitsuye Endo, and why was she a true World War II hero?

Mitsuye Endo was a Nisei civil servant from Sacramento, California, who in 1942 was dismissed from her job as a stenographer with the California State Highway Commission and then evacuated and confined at the Tule Lake internment camp at Newell, California; all the while her brother, a soldier in the U.S. Army, fought overseas for their country, the United States of America. Although she could have applied for resettlement, since she was clearly employable in the civilian economy, Mitsuye Endo decided instead to challenge her unlawful detention in the courts. In July 1942, **James Purcell,** a civil rights attorney, filed a petition for a writ of habeas corpus on her behalf with the District Court of the United States for the Northern District of California, arguing that her detention was a violation of her civil rights and asking that she be restored to liberty. As in the previous cases challenging the U.S. military's authority to intern Japanese Americans and aliens, the judge denied Endo's petition and upheld the military's right to detain her.

Endo's case was then appealed to the U.S. Supreme Court, which, on December 18, 1944, in a unanimous opinion, held that it was unlawful to detain a law-abiding citizen of the United States and ordered the release of Mitsuye Endo. As the Court stated, "A citizen who is concededly loyal presents no problem of espionage or sabotage. Loyalty is a matter of the heart and mind, not of race, creed or color. He who is loyal is by definition not a spy or a saboteur. When the power to detain is derived from the power to protect the war effort against espionage and sabotage, detention which has no relationship to that objective is unauthorized." The Supreme Court ruled in favor of Mitsuye Endo but against **Fred Kore-**

matsu and **Gordon Hirabayashi** in two prior cases because **Endo** had obeyed the unlawful military order of internment without resistance and then had found the appropriate means to challenge its legality in court.

COPING WITH ADVERSITY

Call it denial, but many Japanese Americans never quite understood that the promise of America was not meant for them. They lived in horse stalls at the Santa Anita racetrack and said the Pledge of Allegiance daily. They rode to Relocation Camps under armed guard, labeled with numbered tags, and sang "The Star-Spangled Banner." They lived in deserts or swamps, ludicrously imprisoned—where would they run if they ever escaped—and formed garden clubs, and yearbook staffs, and citizen town meetings. They even elected beauty queens. . . . Call it adaptive behavior. . . . Get along, work hard, and never quite see the things that can bring you pain. Against the tyranny of nature, of feudal lords, of wartime hysteria, the charm works equally well. And so my parents gave me an American name and hoped that I could pass. They nourished me with the American dream: Opportunity, Will, Transformation.

—Lydia Yuri Minatoya, *Talking to High Monks in the Snow* (1992)

When were the internment camps finally emptied?

On December 17, 1944, the War Department announced that the evacuation orders related to West Coast Japanese Americans and nationals would be rescinded effective January 2, 1945. A day later—the same day the Supreme Court ruled in the Endo case—the WRA announced that all of the relocation centers would be closed before the end of 1945 and that the WRA program would be dissolved on June 30, 1946. By

December 15, 1945, all of the internment camps except for Tule Lake had closed, and most of the fifty thousand internees who remained in the internment camps had been released. (On March 20, 1946, the Tule Lake Relocation Center was finally closed and the last of the internees were liberated.) Upon their departure, the WRA provided internees only basic assistance—twenty-five dollars to individuals and fifty dollars to families, plus transportation costs—despite urging on the part of the JACL that it take on a greater role in helping with the resettlement of Japanese. Upon returning home, the Issei and Nisei were shocked to find their former lives in total ruin. Most of their homes and businesses had been either completely destroyed, vandalized, or neglected by tenants, and their possessions had been picked clean. Some discovered to their great sorrow that family graves had been desecrated. All in all, Japanese Americans and permanent residents suffered staggering financial losses—totaling an estimated $400 million. Many wondered how they could possibly reconstruct their former lives.

The physical toll of forced internment was as devastating as the material impoverishment that resulted from it. The incidence of cardiovascular disease and premature death was two times higher for internees than for Japanese Americans who had not endured internment. The long-term psychological costs were also great. Internees felt intense humiliation, a sense of inferiority, and confusion that lingered for decades to come. Some were unable to openly discuss this painful chapter in their lives with others, even their own children.

Did the U.S. government provide redress to Japanese Americans and resident aliens interned during World War II?

In 1948 the U.S. Congress passed the Evacuation Claims Act, which gave internees token compensation ($38 million in total) for the property losses they suffered due to forced evacuation and internment—about one dime for every dollar lost. The internees chose not to criticize the U.S. government for this lowly sum, what they perceived as yet another act of injustice, because they feared that their grievances would only engender a backlash from xenophobic, nativist Americans. A formal apology from the U.S. government for their evacuation and internment was not so fast in coming. On February 19, 1976, on the thirty-fourth anniversary of President **Franklin D. Roosevelt**'s signing of Executive Order 9066, President **Gerald R. Ford** issued Proclamation 4417, which revoked Executive Order 9066, and declared that "We now know what we should have known then—not only was [the] evacuation wrong, but Japanese-Americans were and are loyal Americans." While this admission did not constitute a formal apology, it was a first step in that direction.

Their hopes for final justice buoyed by the U.S. government's acknowledgment that the internment of persons of Japanese ancestry in the United States during World War II was a national mistake, the JACL and its Sansei-led National Coalition for Redress/Reparations (NCRR) passed a resolution in 1978 seeking twenty-five thousand dollars in reparations payments for each surviving internee. Their efforts at monetary redress were met with opposition not from racist Americans but from JACL members, who echoed past fears that such demands would only drum up resentment for Japanese Americans. Some JACL members also insisted that no sum, and especially one so small, could compensate adequately for the internees' suffering and losses and that monetary restitution simply put a price tag on freedom. Others argued that redress was a form of welfare and a reminder of a past best forgotten. Opposition from within the Japanese-American community motivated the NCRR to support a bill, introduced on August 2, 1979, calling for the appointment of a commission "to determine whether a wrong was committed against those American citizens and permanent residents relocated and/

or interned as a result of Executive Order Number 9066 . . . and to recommend appropriate remedies."

In 1980, during the last days of the **Carter** administration, the U.S. Congress established the Commission on Wartime Relocation and Internment of Civilians (CWRIC) to carry out such an investigation and recommend a remedy. The CWRIC's nine members, one a Japanese American, conducted countless interviews, examined wartime documents, and held public hearings on the internment in 1981, during which they heard testimony from more than 750 witnesses, including internees and officials involved in the relocation program. Opinions were varied. **Abe Fortas,** who, as undersecretary of the interior, had supervised the WRA, testified that the mass evacuation of Japanese Americans and resident aliens "was a tragic error" and that "racial prejudice was its basic ingredient." Others, however, defended the internment. **John J. McCoy,** in defense of his immediate superior, Secretary of War **Henry L. Stimson,** insisted that "the action of the President of the United States and the United States Government in regard to our then Japanese population was reasonably undertaken and thoughtfully and humanely conducted."

In 1983, the CWRIC concluded in its formal report entitled "Personal Justice Denied" that the U.S. government had, indeed, committed a "grave injustice" when it interned loyal Japanese Americans and resident aliens. The CWRIC recommended to Congress that all surviving internees be compensated with a tax-free payment of twenty thousand dollars for financial losses suffered due to the internment and receive a formal apology from the U.S. government. When Congress failed to act on this recommendation, Senator **Spark Masayuki Matsunaga** of Hawaii introduced a bill, the Japanese American Redress Bill, in 1987 that would grant each survivor of evacuation and internment twenty thousand dollars in reparations, the amount that the CWRIC had proposed. In 1988 Congress passed the bill, which became known as the Civil Liberties Act, and on August 10, 1988, President **Ronald**

Reagan signed it into law. In November 1989 President **George Bush** (senior) put his signature on the actual reparations payment program. The first checks, along with a formal letter of apology, were sent in October 1990 to the oldest internees, and the last went out in 1994. The payments totaled $1,639,480,000 and were granted to 81,974 surviving internees. At last, they received what was long overdue.

When did life improve for the Japanese community in America?

Forced internment during World War II left the Issei and Nisei impoverished and disheartened and their communities and social organizations in ruins. Many would never return to their old ethnic enclaves, as the U.S. government encouraged them to spread out across the country as a way to avoid discrimination by white Americans. (In 1915, 30 percent of Issei lived in Japanese enclaves; by 1967 just 4 percent of Nisei resided in Japanese-American communities.) The Issei and Nisei resolved to put their lives back together through hard work, a reliance on familial ties, and deferred gratification. Two events helped them advance in the postwar period. One was the passage of the McCarran-Walter Act of 1952, which abolished racial qualifications for U.S. citizenship, allowing Issei to become naturalized U.S. citizens and, thus, rendering void numerous anti-Japanese state statutes that hinged on the Issei's alien status. Many Issei jumped at the opportunity of citizenship, and by 1965 forty-six thousand had been naturalized. The other event was Hawaii's admission into the Union as the fiftieth state on August 21, 1959, which opened the door for the first Japanese American **(Daniel K. Inouye)** to serve in the U.S. Congress. With the passage of legislation in favor of Japanese in the United States, burgeoning Japanese-American political clout, as well as stories circulating about the heroism of Japanese Americans who fought in World

War II, public opinion of Japanese Americans became much more positive.

As hostility toward the Japanese-American community abated and the United States experienced a postwar boom, barriers to opportunity fell for Japanese Americans. They pursued higher education (while the average Issei had some secondary education, the average Nisei had attended college) and entered white-collar professions in ever-increasing numbers. In 1940 over 25 percent of Japanese Americans and permanent residents (males) were laborers and just 3.8 percent were professionals, but by 1960 only 5 percent were laborers and 15 percent were professionals. In the 1950s and 1960s a good number of Nisei worked in civil service and in banks. The high demand for teachers in postwar America meant that Nisei were able to find jobs in pedagogy, a field largely closed to them before the war. Ironically, many had learned to teach in the camps. By the 1960s Japanese Americans were solidly middle class and had largely assimilated into mainstream American society. According to U.S. Bureau of the Census reports for 1970, Japanese Americans had achieved a higher educational level than any other group, there were more professionals among them than in the general population, and their median family income exceeded the median family income for the general population by four thousand dollars. The war years robbed the Japanese in America of their material wealth and their dignity, but for the most part the community recovered remarkably.

Why did relatively few numbers of Japanese immigrate to the United States with the passage of the Immigration Act of 1965?

The passage of the Immigration Act of 1965 (see *What was the Immigration Act of 1965?*, p. 50) swung open wide the doors to Asian immigration to the United States: 445,300 Asians immigrated to the United States between 1961 and 1970; 1.6 million, between 1971 and 1980; and 2.8 million, between 1981 and 1990. Japanese immigration represented only a minor portion of the total immigration from Asia in these decades. According to the U.S. Immigration and Naturalization Service, 39,988 Japanese immigrated to the United States between 1961 and 1970; 49,775, between 1971 and 1980; and 47,085, between 1981 and 1990. The small size of Japanese immigration in these decades can perhaps be attributed to Japan's postwar economic expansion, which provided both jobs and financial security for Japanese citizens.

Have the Sansei and Yonsei managed to fulfill the American dream despite the setbacks their forebears faced?

Just as the Nisei had hoped, the Sansei and Yonsei enjoyed greater opportunities than their forebears to pursue higher education, and for this reason they are better educated than the Nisei: The average Sansei and Yonsei is a college graduate who has completed some graduate work. With their higher educational attainment, the Sansei and Yonsei have surpassed the Nisei in terms of socioeconomic achievement. While some Nisei were professionals, the majority worked in agriculture, the service industries, and the trades, ran their own small businesses, or were employed in large enterprises, such as banks and state governments. The Sansei and Yonsei, on the other hand, are largely professionals, with many achieving a high degree of success in medicine, engineering, accounting, law, and business. They enjoy a standard of living higher than the national average. The Sansei and Yonsei live predominantly in middle-class suburbs, away from Japan Towns and Little Tokyos.

With this high degree of assimilation into American society has come a diminished sense of ethnic community and allegiance to Japanese values (such as family closeness, humility, and perseverance) among the Sansei, Yonsei, and the children of the Yonsei (fifth-generation Japanese Americans). Fewer than one in ten Nisei intermarried, as compared to five in ten Sansei and Yonsei. Few Sansei speak much more than "kitchen" Japanese. Some of those who can communicate effectively with Japanese speakers actually learned Japanese in college. The Yonsei possess even less Japanese language proficiency. All the same, the Sansei and Yonsei have sought over the decades to preserve Japanese values and customs—with the input of their Nisei elders, for whom they must now care—and remain connected to the ethnic community.

Why was anti-Japanese discrimination rampant in the United States in the 1980s and early 1990s?

Although Japanese Americans experienced tremendous social and economic gains in the decades after World War II, their status still hinged on the United States's relationship with Japan. In the 1980s and early 1990s, Japan's formidable state-guided economy commanded higher growth rates than the freer U.S. economy, and the United States confronted a growing trade deficit with Japan, stimulating dire projections by American politicians, business leaders, and the media that the Land of the Rising Sun would surpass the United States as the world's largest economy, in what amounted to an "economic Pearl Harbor." In an effort to compete, companies in the United States cut the pay and benefits of industrial workers or eliminated their jobs altogether. The workers' anger over their imperiled jobs manifested itself as resentment over Japan's supremacy in the international marketplace.

This resentment quickly spawned incidents of anti-Japanese hostility in the United States. For instance, members of the United Auto Workers protested Japan's dominance in U.S. markets by printing bumper stickers proclaiming "Toyota Datsun Honda = Pearl Harbor" and "Unemployment Made in Japan." And **Bennett E. Bidwell,** Chrysler's executive vice president for sales and marketing, suggested at one point that the most effective way to stem the flow of automobile imports into the United States would be to charter the *Enola Gay*, the B-29 that dropped the first atomic bomb on Hiroshima. Congressman **John D. Dingell,** a Democrat from Michigan, complained on one occasion that American jobs were being taken by "little yellow men." Americans in various corners of the United States lashed out at whomever they perceived to be of Japanese ancestry. Often their victims were not Japanese. One of the most publicized cases of such mistaken identity was that of **Vincent Chin,** a Chinese American who was beaten to death on the night of June 19, 1982, by two white autoworkers who had been laid off due to the downturn in the American automobile industry. The two had mistaken Chin for Japanese.

How many Japanese Americans are there, and where do they live?

The Japanese are the nation's only Asian subgroup to decline in numbers in the decade of the 1990s. The reasons for this decline include a very low rate of Japanese immigration to the United States in the 1990s, Japanese Americans' very high degree of assimilation, their low birthrate, and their high intermarriage rate (which makes their children less likely to view themselves as Japanese). Census 2000 counted 1,148,932 persons of Japanese ancestry in the United States, 796,700 of whom were Japanese alone, 55,537 of whom were Japanese and one or more other Asian ethnicities, and 296,695 of whom were Japanese and at least one other race. The great preponderance of those counted were American citizens. The five states with the greatest number of Japanese Americans (alone) in 2000 were California (288,854), Hawaii (201,764), New York (37,279), Washington (35,985), and Illinois (20,379).

Who are some prominent Japanese-American politicians?

One of the first Japanese Americans to enter the political arena was the Democratic senator from Hawaii, **Daniel K. Inouye,** who was born in Honolulu on September 7, 1924. When the Japanese empire attacked U.S. armed forces at Pearl Harbor on December 7, 1941, a seventeen-year-old Inouye, who had some medical aid training, attended to civilian casualties. In March 1943 he answered his country's call to fight and enlisted in the 442nd Regimental Combat Team, one of the U.S. Army's segregated combat units for Nisei. Inouye fought valiantly in Europe during World War II, losing his right arm on the battlefield in Italy while single-handedly trying to take out an enemy machine-gun nest that had his platoon pinned down. After spending twenty months recovering in army hospitals, Daniel Inouye returned home a decorated hero. But about a half century would go by before he was finally awarded the country's highest honor, the Medal of Honor, for risking his life for his comrades above and beyond the call of duty during World War II. (On June 21, 2000, he was one of twenty Japanese Americans awarded the Medal of Honor belatedly by President **Bill Clinton**.)

Daniel K. Inouye entered politics in 1954, when he was elected to the Hawaii Territorial House of Representatives. In 1956 he was reelected to the Territorial House, and in 1958 he was elected to the Hawaii Territorial Senate. When Hawaii attained statehood on August 21, 1959, Hawaiians chose Inouye at the polls to work on their behalf in the U.S. House of Representatives, making him the first Japanese American to serve in either House of Congress. New York congressman **Leo O'Brien**'s reminiscences of the day that Daniel Inouye took the oath of office in the House are recorded in the *Congressional Record*: " 'Raise your right hand and repeat after me,' intoned Speaker Rayburn. The hush deepened as the young Congressman raised not his right hand but his left and repeated the oath of office. There was no right hand, Mr. Speaker. It had been lost in combat by that young American soldier in World War II. Who can deny that, at that moment, a ton of prejudice slipped quietly to the floor of the House of Representatives."

In 1960 Daniel Inouye was reelected to a full term in the House, and in 1962 he won a seat in the U.S. Senate, where he continues to serve to this day. Over the years, Senator Inouye has garnered respect for his work as a member of the Senate Watergate Committee from 1973 to 1974, as chair of the Iran-Contra Committee from 1987 to 1988, and much more. He is the recipient of numerous honors and awards, including the Spirit of Hope Award (1999), the highest honor of the United Services Organizations; honorary membership in the Class of 1949 of the United States Military Academy (2002); and the United States Doughboy Award in recognition of his outstanding contribution to the United States Army Infantry (2002).

Another Nisei Democrat from Hawaii and World War II veteran (who served in the 100th Infantry Battalion and 442nd Regimental Combat Team) to enter the political arena in 1954 is **Spark Masayuki Matsunaga,** who from 1954 until 1959 worked tirelessly in Hawaii's Territorial House of Representatives alongside Daniel Inouye—at least until the latter was elected to the Hawaii Territorial Senate in 1958. As House majority leader during his last year in the Territorial House, Matsunaga was instrumental in securing Hawaii's statehood. When Daniel Inouye went from the U.S. House of Representatives to the U.S. Senate in 1962, Matsunaga filled his seat in the House, serving from 1963 until January 3, 1977. There he fought to ensure that the rights of immigrants, Japanese Americans, and veterans were protected.

On January 3, 1977, Spark Matsunaga joined Daniel Inouye in the U.S. Senate, where he served until his death on April 15, 1990. He was chief deputy whip for all but two of his years in the Senate and backed such legislation as establishing the United States Institute of Peace, an independent, nonpartisan federal institution funded by Congress to "strengthen the nation's capacity to promote the peaceful resolution of international conflict." Senator Matsunaga also was a driving force behind the Civil Liberties Act of 1988, which extended reparations and an official apology to the survivors of the U.S. internment camps. In honor of Senator Matsunaga and his lifelong commitment to peace, the University of Hawaii founded in 1985 the Matsunaga Institute for Peace, which supports research into nonviolent alternatives to resolving conflicts.

A third Nisei Democrat from Hawaii, **Patsy Takemoto Mink,** not only blazed new trails in politics for Americans of Japanese ancestry but also championed the cause of women. While overcoming gender discrimination herself, she shepherded landmark gender-equity legislation through the U.S. House of Representatives that would ensure that future generations of women would not have to endure the prejudice she faced. Born on December 6, 1927, in Paia, Maui, Mink was denied entry into a number of medical schools in 1948 solely because of her gender and, consequently, shifted her focus to law, gaining entrance to the University of Chicago Law School because its admissions office viewed her as a "foreign" student, despite the fact that Hawaii was a U.S. territory. Before long, she earned the distinction of being Hawaii's first Asian-American woman to practice law.

In 1956 Patsy Mink was elected to the Hawaii Territorial House of Representatives. In the years 1958 to 1959 and 1962 to 1964, she served in the Hawaii Territorial Senate as Hawaii's first woman in the state legislature. Then, in 1964, she earned the distinction of being the first Asian-American woman in the U.S. House of Representatives when she was elected to the House after Hawaii was awarded a second seat. Mink served in the House for six consecutive terms, until 1976, when she relinquished her seat to make a run for the U.S. Senate, losing to Spark Matsunaga in the Democratic primary.

After her unsuccessful Senate bid, Mink was appointed assistant secretary for the Office of Oceans and International Environmental and Scientific Affairs at the Department of State, a post she held for two years during the **Carter** administration.

In September 1990, Patsy Mink returned to the U.S. House of Representatives after emerging the victor in a special election to fill out the term of Congressman **Daniel Akaka,** who had been named to Spark Matsunaga's Senate seat. Until her death on September 28, 2002, she worked tirelessly in the House to open the doors to equal opportunity and fair treatment to women, minorities, children, working people, the poor, and the downtrodden. One of her greatest achievements in her twelve terms in the House was Title IX of the Education Act, which she coauthored in 1972. (Title IX banned gender discrimination in federally funded institutions, making athletics a possibility for girls and women at schools and college campuses across the nation.) At a large memorial service held for her at the State Capitol in Honolulu on October 4, 2002, U.S. Transportation Secretary **Norman Mineta** told gatherers that Patsy Mink "was born into a nation that thought an American of Japanese ancestry was a contradiction in terms. She was born into a nation that far too often barred women not only from achieving their dreams but even from the right to try."

In 1974 **George Ryoichi Ariyoshi** broke new ground as the first Asian American elected governor of a state. Born in Honolulu, Hawaii, on March 12, 1926, Ariyoshi worked as an interpreter in Japan for the U.S. Army's Military Intelligence Service at the end of World War II before serving in Hawaii's Territorial House of Representatives from 1954 to 1958 and in its Territorial and State Senate from 1958 to 1970. From 1970 to 1974 he was lieutenant governor of Hawaii. In 1973 Ariyoshi was also appointed acting governor of Hawaii. He was elected governor of Hawaii in his own right in 1974 and served the state in that capacity for three terms, until 1986.

After leaving public office, Ariyoshi, an accomplished businessman and lawyer, joined the law firm of Ing & Kawabashi.

Japanese-American mainlanders have blazed new political trails as well. **Samuel I. Hayakawa,** a Republican from California, served for one term in the U.S. Senate, from 1977 until 1983. Born to Japanese immigrants in Vancouver, British Columbia, on July 18, 1906, Hayakawa established himself as a leading expert in the field of semantics with the publication of his bestselling book *Language in Action* in 1941; became a U.S. citizen in 1955; taught English and language arts at several American colleges and universities; and was appointed acting president of San Francisco State College in 1968, in the midst of a student strike and rioting. He swiftly restored order on campus, earning a national reputation as an enemy of leftists and a permanent appointment as college president in 1969, a position he held until 1973. After completing one term in the U.S. Senate, Hayakawa did not seek a second but chose instead to become special advisor on East Asia and the Pacific Islands to the secretary of state. He remained at that post until 1990. On February 27, 1992, after a varied and distinguished career, S. I. Hayakawa passed away in Greenbrae, California.

Japanese American **Norman Y. Mineta,** who was born in San Jose, California, on November 12, 1931, spent part of his boyhood behind the barbed wire of a U.S. internment camp during World War II. At the camp he befriended a visiting white Boy Scout by the name of **Alan Simpson,** the future senator from the state of Wyoming. Mineta emerged from internment with his patriotism intact: In 1953 he joined the U.S. Army and over the next three years served as an intelligence officer in Japan and Korea. He entered politics in 1967, when he became the first non-white member of the San Jose City Council. He served at that post until 1971, when he was elected mayor of San Jose, making him the first Asian-American mayor of a major American metropolis. Mineta stepped down as San Jose's mayor in 1974, when he was elected to the U.S. House of Representatives, where he served until his resignation on October 10, 1995. While he chaired numerous committees and was the driving force behind key legislation in the House, Mineta's greatest achievement, in his view, was the Civil Liberties Act of 1988.

In honor of his contributions to advancing civil rights, George Washington University bestowed upon Norman Mineta the Martin Luther King, Jr., Commemorative Medal in 1995. From 1995 until 2000 the former congressman was vice-president of Lockheed-Martin Corporation. Then, on July 20, 2000, during the Clinton administration, Norman Mineta was sworn in as U.S. secretary of commerce, becoming the first Asian American to serve in the Cabinet. With **George W. Bush** in the White House, Mineta was nominated to a second Cabinet post, and on January 25, 2001, he was sworn in as the fourteenth U.S. secretary of transportation and the first to have previously occupied a Cabinet position. As secretary of transportation, Norman Mineta oversees an agency with a $59.3 billion budget and sixty thousand employees (as of 2003).

Congressman **Robert T. Matsui** (D-CA), a Sansei, was just six months old when he and his family were evacuated and interned at the Tule Lake Relocation Center in California in 1942. He went on to get his law degree and founded a law practice in Sacramento in 1967. In 1971 Matsui was elected to the Sacramento City Council. He was reelected to that post in 1975, and in 1977 he became vice mayor of the city. In 1978 the people of Sacramento's Fifth District elected Matsui to represent them in the U.S. House of Representatives, where he has served since. During his many years on the Hill, Congressman Matsui has shown an abiding commitment to promoting free and open international trade, to strengthening the nation's social security program, and to reforming health care, welfare, and the tax system.

Who are the leading Japanese-American actors?

One of the first Japanese actors to enjoy success in Hollywood was **Sessue Hayakawa,** who was born **Kitaro Hayakawa** in Chiba, on the island of Honshu, Japan, in 1889. Hayakawa rose to international stardom in 1915 with his role as the wealthy "Oriental" villain in **Cecil B. DeMille**'s silent film *The Cheat.* When the "talkies" came along in the mid-1920s, Hollywood lost interest in Hayakawa, and the actor went to Europe, where he appeared in such films as the silent French melodrama *J'ai Tué!* (*I Have Killed,* 1924). Hayakawa was back in Hollywood in 1931 starring as Fu Manchu, the Chinese criminal mastermind, in the thriller *Daughter of the Dragon* (see *Who is Fu Manchu?*, p. 58). The film earned a thumbs-down and the actor returned to Europe. Hollywood beckoned again at the end of the 1940s. In 1949 Columbia Pictures cast Hayakawa opposite **Humphrey Bogart** in the melodrama *Tokyo Joe.* Sessue Hayakawa starred in several more films before being nominated for an Academy Award for his performance as Japanese POW camp commander Sato in the 1957 war epic *The Bridge on the River Kwai.* In the mid-1960s the actor retired from the screen and moved to Japan, where he became a Zen priest and taught drama.

Japanese-American actress **Miyoshi Umeki** was born on the island of Hokkaido, Japan, but was raised in the United States. She made her motion picture debut in 1957, starring as a Japanese woman who marries an American serviceman, played by **Red Buttons,** in the romantic drama *Sayonara.* Both actors were honored with Academy Awards for their efforts. Umeki went on to play the part of Mei Li in the Rodgers & Hammerstein Broadway production of *Flower Drum Song* and to act in four more Hollywood films, *Cry for Happy* (1961), *The Horizontal Lieutenant* (1961), *Flower Drum Song* (1961), and *A Girl Named Tamiko* (1962), before retiring from the big screen. Baby boomers might also remember Miyoshi Umeki for her role as Mrs. Livingston, the housekeeper in the ABC sitcom *The Courtship of Eddie's Father*, which aired from 1969 to 1972. Another accomplished Japanese-American actress is **Nobu McCarthy,** who starred in Hollywood films over the course of five decades. In the 1950s she was typecast as the geisha girl in such screen productions as *The Geisha Boy* (1958), *Tokyo After Dark* (1959), *Wake Me When It's Over* (1960), and *Walk Like a Dragon* (1960). In the 1970s and 1980s McCarthy landed less-stereotypical roles in the made-for-TV *Farewell to Manzanar* (1976) and in the motion pictures *The Karate Kid, Part II* (1986) and *The Wash* (1988).

One of the most prolific and talented Japanese-American actors is **Noriyuki "Pat" Morita,** who has starred in dozens of films since first appearing in the **John Wayne–John Huston** collaboration *The Barbarian and the Geisha* in 1958. Morita is perhaps best known for his role as Mr. Miyagi, the karate master in the 1984 hit film *The Karate Kid* and its three sequels, as well as for his principal role in the 1987–89 television detective series *Ohara.* One of his more recent projects was hosting the eighteen-part PBS Pioneer Living Series (2001), which examines the American experience from the immigrant perspective. Few Americans are aware that Pat Morita endured spinal tuberculosis in childhood and incarceration in a World War II internment camp in the United States as a youth.

While he has starred in over thirty feature films and has made many guest-starring appearances on television, **George Hosako Takei** captured the hearts and imaginations of Americans, particularly Trekkies, with his portrayal of Hikaru Sulu, the chief navigator in the seventy-nine episodes of the landmark science-fiction TV series *Star Trek* (1966–69) and in the seven *Star Trek* feature films that the series spawned. Like Pat Morita, George Takei, who was born in Los Angeles, spent part of his childhood behind the barbed wire of World War II internment camps. In 1986 Takei earned the distinction of being the first Japanese American immortalized on Hollywood's Walk of Fame, and in 1988 he was honored with a Grammy Award nomination for Best Spoken Word or Non-Musical

Recording for his reading of *Star Trek IV.* Since the early 1970s, the actor has actively participated in political and civic affairs. In 1973 he ran for a seat in the Los Angeles City Council, losing by a slim margin, and from 1973 to 1984 he served on the board of directors of the Southern California Rapid Transit.

Who are some world-class Japanese-American musicians?

Acclaimed master conductor **Seiji Ozawa** has for decades enjoyed an international following. Ozawa, who was born in Shenyang, China, to Japanese parents in 1935, burst onto the world stage in 1961, when American conductor **Leonard Bernstein** of the New York Philharmonic Orchestra, impressed by his talent, made Ozawa an assistant conductor for the 1961–62 season. Seiji Ozawa was music director of the Toronto Symphony from 1965 to 1969 and the San Francisco Symphony from 1970 to 1976. From 1973 to 2002 he served as music director of the Boston Symphony Orchestra, enhancing its fine reputation with concerts at Boston's Symphony Hall, at Tanglewood, and on tours across the United States and around the world. His twenty-nine-year tenure with the Boston Symphony Orchestra was the second longest in history at a major American orchestra. (**Eugene Ormandy**'s forty-four-year tenure with the Philadelphia Orchestra was the longest.) In 2002 Osawa assumed the music directorship of the Vienna State Opera, after a long association as the company's guest conductor. He has received many honors over the years, including being named a Chevalier de la Légion d'Honneur in 1998 by French president **Jacques Chirac.**

In 1982, when she was just eleven years old, internationally acclaimed violinist **Midori**—who was born in 1971 in Osaka, Japan, and resides in New York City—took the music world by storm with her surprise debut, orchestrated by **Zubin Mehta,** at the New York Philharmonic's traditional New Year's Eve concert. At age fourteen, Midori made headlines around the world when, hampered by two broken strings, she managed to finish a performance with the Boston Symphony Orchestra at Tanglewood. She has since appeared with the most distinguished symphonic ensembles on the great concert stages of Europe, North America, and Asia. Midori plays the 1734 Guarnerius del Gesu "ex-Huberman," which she has on lifetime loan from the Hayashibara Foundation. In 1992 she established Midori & Friends, a foundation committed to bringing free music instruction, workshops, and concerts to thousands of children in New York City, including hospitalized and special needs children, who might otherwise have no exposure to classical music. She has also established a similar organization in Japan.

Who are some renowned Japanese Americans in the world of art and architecture?

Internationally acclaimed painter **Yasuo Kuniyoshi** was born in Japan in 1893 and ventured to Vancouver in 1906, where he worked at menial jobs before moving on to New York for formal art training. By the 1920s Kuniyoshi was an integral part of the New York art scene, regularly exhibiting his works, which fuse American folk art, Renaissance, and modern influences, at the renowned Daniel Gallery in Manhattan. Kuniyoshi was awarded the Temple Gold Medal of the Pennsylvania Academy of Fine Arts in 1934 and first prize in the annual exhibition of American painting at the Carnegie Institute of Art in 1944. In 1948 the Whitney Museum of Art in New York held a major retrospective exhibition of his art, the museum's first solo exhibit of works by a living artist. Although he requested U.S. citizenship, Kuniyoshi never got to enjoy it. At the time of the Japanese attack on Pearl Harbor in 1941, the artist's petition for U.S. citizenship was under review. He was designated an enemy alien but managed to avoid the fate of internment that befell Japanese Americans and permanent resident aliens in the western states during World War II. Still, Kuniyoshi was hampered by travel and financial restrictions in the war years. His U.S. citizenship papers were nearing final approval when the artist died in 1953.

Japanese American **Isamu Noguchi**, one of the twentieth century's greatest sculptors, earned an international reputation for his metal, stone, and marble sculptures; for his furniture, gardens and playgrounds; and for his Akari lamps, which are his most celebrated light sculptures. Noguchi, who was born in Los Angeles in 1904 to a Japanese father and a Caucasian mother, was a fixture in the American art world by 1925, when he was exhibiting his sculptures at the National Academy of Design and the Pennsylvania Academy of Fine Arts. After World War II, the artist began to pay frequent visits to Japan. Soon his art reflected a fusion of East and West, as evidenced by his Akari lamps, which have their origin in the ancient Japanese craft of paper lanterns and yet depart radically from that craft as they are unpainted and asymmetrical, consist of mulberry bark paper on a bamboo spiral frame, and are lit by bulbs instead of candles.

Among Noguchi's other notable creations are the gardens at UNESCO headquarters in Paris (1956–58), the Sunken Garden at Yale University's Beinicke Rare Book and Manuscript Library (1960–64), and the 102-foot stainless-steel sculpture entitled *Bolt of Lightning,* in homage to **Benjamin Franklin,** in Philadelphia (installed in 1984). It should be noted that during most of his artistic life, Noguchi was also committed to American dance: He designed stage sets for **Martha Graham**'s productions and also collaborated with **George Balanchine** and **Merce Cunningham.** For his artistic contributions, Isamu Noguchi was awarded the National Medal of Arts in 1987. A comprehensive collection of the artist's works are on exhibit at the Isamu Noguchi Garden Museum in Queens, New York.

One of the preeminent architects of the twentieth century, **Minoru Yamasaki** made invaluable contributions to the world's cityscapes over the course of several decades. A Nisei, Yamasaki was born in Seattle on December 1, 1912. He experienced poverty and virulent racism in his childhood and youth, but managed to work (at a cannery) his way to a bachelor's degree from the University of Washington, and then to complete his master's at New York University. Minoru Yamasaki is perhaps best known as the chief architect of the ill-fated World Trade Center complex in New York City (1970–77), whose 110-story twin tower buildings altered the Manhattan skyline during their brief twenty-four years and American history forever. The architect's other major projects include the St. Louis Airport Terminal (1951–56), the Woodrow Wilson School of Public and International Affairs at Princeton University (1965), and the Performing Arts Center in Tulsa, Oklahoma (1973–76).

Born into an aristocratic Tokyo family on February 18, 1933, **Yoko Ono,** an artist and musician in her own right, moved with her family to Scarsdale, New York, at age eighteen, when her father was appointed president of a bank in New York City. After dropping out of Sarah Lawrence College, she went to live in Greenwich Village, where she came in contact with avant-garde artists. In the early 1960s Yoko Ono earned a reputation for her "interactive conceptual events," performance art that hinged on the involvement of observers. Her most famous work, staged in 1964, entailed having audience members cut off pieces of her clothing until she was naked, which was meant to signify the shedding of disguises and materialism. In 1966 Ono met her third husband, Beatle **John Lennon,** at a solo exhibition of her art in London. Until Lennon's untimely death by an assassin's bullet in 1980, the pair collaborated on numerous art, film, and music projects, as well as on conceptual events. One of their most publicized conceptual events was their "bed-in" in a hotel room in Amsterdam during their honeymoon, which was staged to promote world peace during the Vietnam War. In the two and a half decades since John Lennon's death, Yoko Ono has continued to express herself artistically, releasing three albums, holding two concert tours, composing two Off-Broadway musicals, and much more.

Who are some other prominent Japanese Americans?

Astronaut **Ellison Shoji Onizuka,** who was born in Kealakekua, Kona, Hawaii, in 1946 and was the grandson of Issei sugar plantation workers, was a pioneer in space travel. On January 24, 1985, Onizuka became the first Asian American in space when the space shuttle *Discovery* was launched from Kennedy Space Center in Florida. A mission specialist, he was in charge of primary payload activities. About one year later, on January 28, 1986, Onizuka was one of seven crew members on the space shuttle *Challenger,* which exploded just one minute and thirteen seconds after launch, costing all on board their lives in what was at the time the worst accident in NASA's history.

Dr. **Paul Terasaki,** currently a professor emeritus at UCLA's School of Medicine, was a pioneer in the development of a test to determine the compatibility of donated organs and recipients. This test was critical to the success of the first heart transplant operation, performed in 1967.

Who are some great Japanese-American athletes?

One of the greatest Japanese-American athletes of all time is **Tamio "Tommy" Kono,** who won gold in weightlifting at the 1952 Olympics in Helsinki and at the 1956 Olympics in Melbourne (after lifting a world-record 385 pounds), and silver at the 1960 Olympics in Rome. What is perhaps most extraordinary is that Kono won these three medals in different weight divisions, a first in Olympic history. Tamio Kono was inducted into the U.S. Olympic Hall of Fame in 1990 and the International Weightlifting Federation Hall of Fame in 1991. Born in Sacramento, California, in 1930, Kono first took up weightlifting when he and his parents and siblings were incarcerated at the Tule Lake Relocation Center along with other West Coast Japanese Americans and permanent residents during World War II.

Three other Japanese-American athletes, swimmers all, collected medals at the 1952 Olympic Games in Helsinki. **Yoshinobu Oyakawa,** who was born on the island of Hawaii, won gold in the one-hundred-meter backstroke, breaking the Olympic record. **Ford Hiroshi Konno** took gold medals in the fifteen-hundred-meter freestyle and the eight-hundred-meter freestyle relay and a silver medal in the four-hundred-meter freestyle. (Konno also captured silver in the eight-hundred-meter freestyle relay in Melbourne in 1956.) And **Evelyn Kawamoto** captured bronze in both the four-hundred-meter freestyle and the four × one-hundred-meter freestyle. It should be noted that Konno, Kawamoto, and other Olympic swimmers were coached by Japanese American **Soichi Sakamoto,** an assistant coach for the U.S. Olympic Swim Team from 1952 to 1956.

Kristi Tsuya Yamaguchi—a Yonsei whose mother was born in an American internment camp during World War II—was America's top female figure skater of the 1990s. Born with club feet on July 12, 1971, in Hayward, California, Yamaguchi began to ice-skate at the age of six, after her condition was corrected with special shoes, braces, and physical therapy—and after she watched on television as America's figure skating sweetheart **Dorothy Hamill** won gold at the 1976 Winter Olympics. Following her win at the nationals in 1992, Yamaguchi captured the gold medal in the ladies singles figure skating competition at the 1992 Olympic Games in Albertville, France. She then outskated the competition at the 1992 World Figure Skating Competition, becoming the first American female figure skater with consecutive international victories since **Peggy Fleming** in 1968. Another world-class Japanese-American figure skater is **Ina Kyoko,** who was born in Japan in 1972 and immigrated to the United States with her parents when she was just a baby. Kyoko and her pairs partner, **John Zimmerman,** have been a force to contend with in the ice skating rink since they joined up in 1998, capturing three U.S. titles (2000–2002), finishing in the top ten at the World Championships on four occasions (1999–2002), and winning the silver medal at 2001 Skate America.

Which religions do Japanese Americans observe?

The Japanese worldview has long been based on several religious traditions. Shinto, the only indigenous faith of the Japanese people, is the cornerstone. It has no founder, no sacred scriptures, and little preaching. The objects of worship in Shinto are the *kami,* or sacred spirits in the form of natural elements, such as the sun, wind, and trees, and abstract entities, such as national heroes, ancestors, and fertility. Confucianism was introduced to Japan from China in the Christian era, and its ethical aspects, particularly its sense of hierarchy and loyalty, eventually fused with Shintoism. Buddhism, which arose in India and was introduced to Japan in the mid-sixth century C.E., brought with it a sense of religious contemplation and a sophisticated culture of arts and temples. While at first Shintoism and Buddhism were in conflict, they gradually came to coexist in harmony and even intermix at certain points, so that the Japanese in large measure came to adhere to both religious denominations—without any sense of conflict. At the onset of the seventeenth century, Christianity, called the "evil religion," was banned in Japan, but soon after the Meiji restoration, anti-Christian fervor diminished. Given the hostile environment in Japan, Christianity never found many converts among the Japanese, but it did later in Japanese America.

Not surprisingly, a large number of Issei brought the dominant religion of Japan, Buddhism—and its major sects, namely Tendai, Shingon, Zen, Shin, Nichiren, and Jodo—with them to America. According to a survey conducted in the early 1930s, 75 percent of Issei considered themselves Buddhists and 20 percent Christians. They erected Buddhist temples in their communities and raised their children to be Buddhists. Decades later, however, half of all Nisei identified themselves as Christians. This is due to the fact that Christianity won converts among the Issei as soon as they began arriving in the United States. Interdenominational missions provided employment opportunities and helped the Issei to navigate in American culture. Eventually segregated branches of the various Protestant churches formed and provided services in both Japanese and English.

Increasingly, Japanese Buddhists in America came to be identified as less assimilated—and, therefore, less American—than their Japanese Christian counterparts. Some Issei chose not to associate openly with Buddhists, fearing that their association with a foreign religion would make them more vulnerable to attack. Their fears were substantiated after the Empire of Japan bombed Pearl Harbor: The FBI wasted no time in rounding up Japanese Buddhist priests for interrogation about their suspect ties to Japan. After World War II, the segregated Japanese churches were abolished, and the Issei and Nisei joined regular congregations. Hostility from the white majority, however, forced the churches to segregate Japanese congregants once again and then to gradually, over decades, integrate them into the regular branches. In more recent times, the Christian church has served a completely different need—teaching Japanese traditions to highly assimilated Japanese Americans.

What is Zen Buddhism?

According to popular belief, Zen Buddhism was founded by **Bodhidharma,** an Indian monk who attained enlightenment after nine years of extreme, grueling asceticism that entailed staring at a blank wall. Zen Buddhism made its way from China to Japan in 1191. Enlightenment is central to the practice of Zen, as are the notions of the connectedness of all to the universe and the illusory nature of material existence. While other sects of Buddhism maintain that enlightenment can be achieved only by study, prayer, and right living after enduring the cycles of reincarnation, Zen Buddhists believe that enlightenment may come in one pure moment of intense meditation. Thus, Zen meditation is designed to bring the mind to the brink of enlightenment by freeing it of all attachments and judgments. This is achieved in part by concentrating on zen *koans*, riddles that on the surface appear absurd and illogical. One popular *koan* is "What is the sound of one hand clapping?" Thanks to the spread of Zen Buddhism from Japan to the United States, Zen monasteries are accessible to all Americans. The Zen Mountain Center near Carmel, California, which boasts luxuriant hot springs conducive to a sense of well-being, is just one of America's many Zen monasteries frequented by Japanese Americans, other Asian Americans, and non-Asians alike.

What are the more popular Japanese systems of martial arts?

The more popular Japanese martial arts are karate, judo, and aikido. It is believed that the Buddhist monk **Bhodidharma,** credited with founding Zen Buddhism, also developed its parallel school of training, kung fu and karate, which he brought to China in the sixth century A.D. It all began when Bhodidharma founded the legendary Shaolin monastery in China's Hunan Province. There Shaolin monks devised a skillful style of fighting that combined unarmed physical combat with the same emphasis on the body's nerve centers and weak points found in Chinese acupuncture. As this fighting style spread, the Chinese modified it to suit their needs: Workers in the rice paddies of the south, with their strong upper torsos, emphasized techniques using the arms, while the horsemen of the northern plains emphasized kicking. The fighting styles that emerged in China were brought to the island of Okinawa, where they were further adapted. When Okinawa came under domination by Japanese with a habit of wearing wooden armor, the Okinawans emphasized techniques utilizing both feet and hands in their fighting so that they could destroy the armor.

In 1917 Japan's Ministry of Education invited **Funakoshi Gichin,** a proponent of the Okinawan style of fighting, to give demonstrations. The Okinawan style soon caught on throughout Japan. Originally called *tang,* which means "Chinese hand," the style was soon renamed karate, meaning "empty hand," due to increasingly anti-China sentiment in Japan in the 1930s, as well as the desire to introduce the Zen concept of "emptiness" to the style. Karate was brought to the United States by American servicemen who had been stationed in Japan after World War II, as well as by Japanese instructors who moved overseas in the late 1960s and early 1970s. Karate now enjoys great popularity in the United States among Japanese Americans and the wider society.

While karate emphasizes punches and kicks, judo relies on throws and sweeps, and aikido, wrist and hand locks. Judo was founded in Japan in the nineteenth century by Dr. **Jigoro Kano.** Called the "way of gentleness," it is based on the principle of least resistance. In keeping with this principle, the objective is to move under an opponent's center of gravity, located below the navel, to knock him or her off balance. Aikido, which is also based on the principle of nonresistance and incorporates elements of ancient martial arts, such as swordsmanship, was founded in Japan in 1942 by **Morihei Uyeshiba,** who worked at its development for two decades. The "ai" in aikido means harmony, the syllable "ki" denotes spirit or energy, and "do" refers to discipline. The aikido practitioner neutralizes attacks by coordinating his or her movements with those of his or her opponent. Thus, if pushed, the aikido practitioner goes along with the push. This strategy of "going with the flow" channels the opponent's force so that he or she is knocked off balance and can then be neutralized with maneuvers aimed at weak points, such as wrist twists or elbow locks. With the correct techniques, the gentle can subdue the strong, and the small, the large.

What are some major Japanese-American festivals?

Japanese Americans celebrate some traditional Japanese festivals, such as Japanese Children's Day and the Obon Festival, a midsummer festival of the dead, which commemorates those who have passed on in the previous year in an amalgam of Buddhist and earlier Japanese beliefs and customs. An integral part of the Obon Festival in America is the *Hatsu-Bon*, a service held at Buddhist temples around the country that centers on remembering the deceased. Obon Festivals in the United States also feature outdoor festivities, including carnival games and *Bon Odori*, folk dances in which dancers circle a *yagura*, a raised platform or tower, to the beat of the *Obon taiko*, a kind of drum, as well as much snacking on traditional Japanese and American fare.

Japanese Americans have also created festivals all their own. One of the largest is the Nisei Week Festival, a celebration of Japanese-American culture, which is held in Little Tokyo in Los Angeles, one of the oldest and most vibrant Japanese-American communities in the continental United States. The first Nisei Week was organized in 1934, in the midst of the Great Depression, to help the struggling economy of Los Angeles's Little Tokyo. It featured essay and poster contests, a fashion show, a variety of cultural exhibits and demonstrations, and a parade. Since then, Nisei Week has been held annually in Los Angeles, except during the period spanning the mass incarceration of Japanese Americans and permanent residents in U.S. internment camps and the year 1949, when the Japanese community in Los Angeles was able to regroup and revive the festival. Events during Nisei Week include traditional Japanese flower arrangement (*ikebana*) and Japanese calligraphy exhibits, Japanese tea ceremony demonstrations, Japanese sword and Kimekomi Doll displays, traditional Japanese dance performances, karate tournaments and demonstrations, the Opening Ceremony and Queen's Tea, the Coronation Ball, and the much-anticipated Nisei Week Grand Parade.

Another major Japanese-American festival is the Cherry Blossom Festival held each April in San Francisco's Japantown to celebrate the coming of spring, a centuries-old Japanese custom, as well as the Bay Area's rich Japanese cultural heritage. The festival, Japantown's largest event of the year, was begun in the late 1960s and grew out of the burgeoning ethnic awareness of Nisei and Sansei. In terms of its events, the Cherry Blossom Festival has much in common with Nisei Week. There are Japanese tea ceremony demonstrations; Japanese dance and music performances; *shigin* (poetry readings); bonsai exhibits; woodcut print, origami, and *ikebana* exhibits and demonstrations; the festival queen pageant; and the Japantown Cherry Blossom Parade, which features the *Taru Mikoshi,* a portable shrine that is carried down Post Street. In 2002 Pasadena, California, seeking to showcase its own Japanese-American community, launched a Cherry Blossom Festival, complete with a parade, Japanese cultural and martial arts demonstrations, and newly planted cherry trees.

What foods are popular among Japanese Americans?

Most Americans of Japanese ancestry are fond of typical American fare, but they also enjoy Japanese cuisine, traditional foods and dishes such as white rice; udon, soba, and ramen noodles; pickled vegetables; miso soup; sukiyaki; gyoza (little savory dumplings filled with pork, tofu, or vegetables); shrimp and vegetable tempura; chicken, fish, or beef teriyaki; yosenabe (a seafood and vegetable stew); sushi; sashimi; and more. Sukiyaki, bite-sized pieces of beef, onions, mushrooms, other vegetables, and occasionally tofu, in a broth of soy sauce and sweet sake, is known in Japan as the "friendship dish" because of its popularity with foreigners. It is one of the relatively few Japanese dishes featuring beef (the Buddhist tradition of vegetarianism and the scarcity of land for grazing in Japan discouraged beef consumption).

Japanese (American) chefs in the United States not only prepare traditional Japanese dishes at Japanese sushi bars and restaurants as well as at Japanese noodle shops (which began to pop up in the 1990s in answer to the craze for steaming hot bowls of ramen, soba, or udon noodles), they also have given sushi a twist in response to the love affair that Americans, Japanese or not, have had with the delicacy since the 1990s. To the repertoire of traditional maki sushi (seaweed-wrapped rolls)—such as tekka maki (tuna roll) and kappa maki (cucumber roll)—sushi chefs have added some unusual Americanized rolls, including the California Roll (crab, avocado, cucumber), and the Philadelphia Roll (fresh or smoked salmon, cream cheese, and avocado). These rolls and the more traditional ones are so popular in mainstream America that they are nowadays a fixture—along with shiitake mushrooms, daikon, miso paste, pickled ginger, and instant wasabi, a fiery horseradish paste that is light green in color—in markets in neighborhoods, mostly upscale, across the United States—and not just in California, where the hybrid sushi craze began. Some supermarkets even have sushi chefs in residence, so that their customers can enjoy rolls fresh from the bamboo sushi mat.

THREE

Korean Americans

When did the first Koreans make their way to the United States?

When did the trickle of Koreans leaving for the United States become a torrent?

When did the movement of Koreans to Hawaii resume?

What was life like for the early Korean laborers in Hawaii, and who were the picture brides?

When did Koreans begin venturing to the continental United States in significant numbers?

What kind of reception did Americans give the Korean immigrants in the early decades of the twentieth century?

Who was Chang In-hwan, and how did he achieve hero status among Koreans in America and around the world in 1908?

What united the Korean community in America after 1910?

What brought Korean immigration to the United States to a screeching halt in 1924?

How did Koreans in America react to the Japanese attack on Pearl Harbor, and why did the U.S. government classify them as "enemy aliens"?

Why did Koreans on the U.S. mainland wear signs during World War II that read "I'm No Jap"?

Did Koreans in America serve during World War II?

How did Korea come to be divided into north and south?

What precipitated the Korean War?

How did the end of the Korean War unleash the second wave of Korean immigration to America?

What piece of legislation stimulated a third wave of Korean immigration to the United States?

What is a kye*, and how did it enable Koreans to establish themselves in America?*

How did Koreans in New York City and elsewhere find success as greengrocers and owners of other small businesses?

Where are America's Koreatowns?

Why did African Americans clash with Koreans in New York City and Los Angeles in the early 1990s?

How many Korean Americans are there, and where do they live?

How are Korean Americans faring?

Who are some Korean Americans in the political and legal arenas?

Who are some prominent Korean-American writers?

Who are some renowned Korean-American musicians and artists?

Who are the celebrated Korean Americans of the stage and screen?

Who are some outstanding Korean-American athletes?

Which religions do Koreans in America observe?

Which Korean holidays do Korean Americans celebrate?

Do Korean Americans rely on traditional Korean medicine?

Which five flavors and five colors are essential in Korean cuisine, and which classic Korean dishes do Korean Americans enjoy?

When did the first Koreans make their way to the United States?

While the first period of recorded Korean history, known as the Period of the Three Kingdoms, commenced in 53 B.C., Koreans did not venture to the United States until about two millennia later, at the close of the nineteenth century. The movement of Koreans to the United States was precipitated by the struggle between China and Japan for dominance over Asia in the eighteenth and nineteenth centuries. Japan emerged the victor in the struggle when it defeated China in the Sino-Japanese War (1894–95) and then invaded the Korean peninsula. The Koreans resisted the Japanese invaders, but to no avail. Korea's Queen **Min** made covert overtures to Russia to intercede on her nation's behalf, and Japanese forces responded by assassinating her on October 8, 1895. Russia did intercede, and for ten years Russian forces, with the help of Korean resistance fighters, called "righteous troops," battled Japan for control of the Korean peninsula. The Japanese again proved mightier, defeating the Russian forces in the

Russo-Japanese War (1904–05). In September 1905, at the Portsmouth Peace Conference marking the end of the conflict, the United States, Britain, and China recognized Japan's prerogatives in Korea.

Its control of the Korean peninsula no longer a matter of dispute, Japan sought to consolidate its hold by forcing the Korean emperor to sign a treaty in November 1905 that rendered Korea a Japanese protectorate. Hoping for intervention from the outside world, the Korean emperor dispatched in 1906 a secret emissary to the international peace conference that was being held at The Hague that year to compel the great powers to challenge the Japanese occupation of the Korean peninsula. The mission was a failure. Korean armed resistance, which took the form of guerrilla warfare, only escalated, spreading to every corner of the peninsula. The Japanese managed to gain the upper hand over the armed resistance (but not to destroy it), and on August 10, 1910, Japan officially annexed Korea "in order to maintain peace and stability in Korea [and] to promote the prosperity and welfare of Koreans," according to Japan's Treaty of Annexation.

Rather than promote the "welfare of Koreans," the Japanese colonial government in Korea then set about to "promote the prosperity" of Japanese by obliterating all trace of the Korean national consciousness, which it pursued by denying the Korean people the right to assembly, free speech, association, and the press; confiscating and burning books on Korean history, culture, and geography (200,000 to 300,000 volumes were destroyed in 1910 alone); and reorganizing Korea's financial and monetary system. The Japanese also overhauled the Korean school system as part of their campaign to destroy the Korean national identity: Classes were conducted in Japanese instead of Korean, and Korean history and culture were expunged from the curriculum. In some areas of the country, Korean schoolchildren were actually denied access to schools so that they remained illiterate. The colonial government also expropriated Korean land; confiscated crops, including rice, for Japanese consumption; and prohibited Koreans from engaging in commerce.

The Japanese invasion and occupation of Korea was a traumatic moment for the citizens of Korea. Still, by the time the nineteenth century came to a close, only a few had sought refuge from the turmoil in the United States. Some scholars estimate that all told, fewer than fifty Koreans arrived in America in the last decades of the nineteenth century.

When did the trickle of Koreans leaving for the United States become a torrent?

This trickle of Koreans venturing to the United States became a torrent when word spread in 1903 that jobs awaited Koreans in the U.S. territory of Hawaii. It seems that in 1902 sugar plantation owners in the Hawaiian Islands, who found themselves in desperate need of cheap labor after the passage of the Chinese Exclusion Act of 1882, which barred Chinese citizens from entering the United States and its territory of Hawaii, turned to Korea as a viable source of workers. Hawaiian sugar planters were especially keen on recruiting Koreans because they could harness Koreans' anti-Japanese sentiment to undercut the increasing threat of strikes by Japanese laborers on Hawaii's plantations, which was jeopardizing productivity and, thus, profits. In 1902 a representative of the Hawaiian Sugar Planters Association (HSPA) met in San Francisco with **Horace N. Allen,** the American ambassador to Korea, to devise a plan for recruiting Korean laborers.

Allen found the perfect recruiter in **David William Deshler,** an American businessman in Korea who owned and operated a steamship service. The HSPA agreed to pay Deshler fifty-five dollars for every Korean that he recruited for work on Hawaii's sugar plantations. Deshler persuaded Koreans to go to Hawaii with promises of high wages, free housing and health care, and loans to cover transportation overseas. American Presbyterian and Methodist missionaries in Korea acted as intermediaries, encouraging Koreans to venture to the Hawaiian Islands with claims that life there would transform them into better Christians and, therefore, they would be blessed with riches. Posters and newspaper advertisements portraying Hawaii as a land of milk and honey, which stood out in dramatic relief in a Korea crippled by drought-induced shortages of rice, gave Koreans even more incentive to hang their hopes on the Hawaiian Islands.

In December 1902, 121 Koreans recruited by the HSPA boarded the SS *Gaelic* for the journey by sea to Honolulu. Nineteen of the recruits failed their medical exams in port and were made to disembark before the ship set sail. On January 13, 1903, the remaining 102 recruits (56 men, 21 women, and 25 children) reached Honolulu Harbor. Over the next two years, they would be joined by about 7,000 other Koreans (mostly male) who dreamed of prosperity in Hawaii and an eventual return to Korea to a comfortable life. In May 1905, the Japanese government, which was by then firmly in control of Korean domestic and foreign affairs, brought Korean emigration to Hawaii to a screeching halt out of concern that too many Koreans were fleeing the peninsula.

When did the movement of Koreans to Hawaii resume?

In 1908 the United States and Japan signed the Gentlemen's Agreement, which was designed to stem the flow of Japanese laborers to the mainland United States and to the U.S. territory of Hawaii, while at the same time alleviating the intense discrimination that Japanese citizens already on American soil were experiencing. In keeping with the Gentlemen's Agreement, Japan could issue passports solely to Japanese nonlaborers and to three classes of laborers: "former residents," "parents, wives or children of residents," and "settled agriculturalists." Since Koreans were under Japanese colonial rule, they were subject to the same restrictions. Many Koreans took advantage of the "parents, wives or children of residents" clause to join loved ones who had already immigrated to Hawaii and to flee Japanese persecution in Korea.

What was life like for the early Korean laborers in Hawaii, and who were the picture brides?

Conditions for laborers on Hawaii's sugar plantations in the early decades of the twentieth century were harsh, and to the Korean recruits, who had largely been urban dwellers in Korea, they seemed even worse. For comfort and guidance, Korean laborers turned to Protestant church activities, which the preachers among them organized upon their arrival in Hawaii. (Catholic mission activity began in Korea in the seventeenth century, while Protestant missionaries, especially Presbyterians and Methodists, poured into Korea beginning in 1884 and were highly successful in their conversion.) Preacher **Yijie Kim** held the very first service for Korean laborers at the Magalia Farm in Hawaii on June 14, 1903.

The very first Korean laborers moved from plantation to plantation in an attempt to improve their lot and then abandoned plantation work altogether as soon as jobs outside of agriculture opened up for them. By 1928, 90 percent of Korean immigrants had left the plantations and had settled for the most part in Hawaii's towns and cities, where they ran restaurants, small shops, and vegetable and fruit stands, worked as tailors, carpenters, and street peddlers, or found other jobs that did not entail planting and harvesting. With the annexation of Korea by Japan in 1910, the Koreans in Hawaii, who left Korea as sojourners, relinquished all hope of returning home and adopted a settlers' mentality. In fact, while approximately half of the Chinese and more than half of the Japanese laboring in Hawaii ultimately returned home, just one-sixth of the Koreans who reached Hawaii before the Japanese halted Korean immigration to the islands in May of 1905 returned to Korea.

As settlers, not sojourners, the Koreans in Hawaii sought by and large to assimilate into the mainstream society, and for this reason, the rate of outmarriage was higher among them than among the Chinese and Japanese. Still, a large percentage of Korean bachelors in Hawaii also strove to maintain racial purity in their families, and to this end, they exchanged pictures and letters with prospective brides in Korea, who were preselected by matchmakers and the bachelors' families back home. When a man and a woman agreed on a match, the groom's family made the union legal by writing the bride's name into the family register. The picture bride then sailed to Hawaii, where she met her husband for the very first time. In the years 1910 to 1924 more than one thousand Korean picture brides ventured to the Hawaiian Islands (and in some cases to the mainland United States). With their arrival, the extremely lopsided male-female ratio of the Korean community in Hawaii was dramatically altered.

When did Koreans begin venturing to the continental United States in significant numbers?

Koreans began reaching America's shores in sizable numbers soon after Hawaii's sugar plantations introduced Korean labor. Of the thirty-three immigrant groups who were recruited to toil on the sugar and pineapple plantations in Hawaii, the Koreans were the first to lay down their tools and migrate to the mainland United States, mainly the West Coast. By 1907 approximately one thousand Koreans made the voyage from Hawaii to the U.S. mainland, entering through the port city of San Francisco. Many settled in the city and its environs. Their employment opportunities were limited mainly to menial jobs as restaurant workers, gardeners, janitors, and domestic help. To promote the welfare of Korean newcomers, Korean intellectual **Ahn Ch'ang Ho** established the Chinmok Hoe (Friendship Society) in San Francisco in 1903, and in 1905 members of that society organized the Kongnip Hyop

Hoe (Mutual Assistance Society), which published the *Kong-nip Sinpo,* the first publication geared to Korean speakers on American soil. Not all Koreans remained in San Francisco. Many worked in agriculture, migrating up and down the Pacific Coast with the crops, while a small number toiled in the copper mines in Utah, the coal mines in Wyoming and Colorado, and on the railroads in Arizona. Eventually some in farming pooled their pay and leased tracts of land, which they farmed intensively. Others made inroads into the hotel business. In 1906 Korean newcomer **Wu Kyong-sik** opened the first Korean-owned hotel in Sacramento, California, and by 1920 more than twenty Korean-owned hotels had sprung up around the country.

On the U.S. mainland, the Korean migrants from Hawaii were joined by Korean political refugees and students who managed to escape from Japanese-occupied Korea. By 1924, 541 Korean political refugees and students had found safe harbor in the continental United States. Among them was **Syngman Rhee,** who later would become the first president of South Korea. Rhee had first come to the United States as a student, eventually earning his doctorate at Princeton University. He then had returned to Korea to protest the Japanese occupation of his country. When his arrest in Korea appeared imminent, he fled back to the United States, where he remained until the conclusion of World War II.

What kind of reception did Americans give the Korean immigrants in the early decades of the twentieth century?

Like the Chinese and Japanese in the United States in the early decades of the twentieth century, the Koreans were designated aliens ineligible for citizenship, and they experienced overt racial discrimination on the part of nativists, who wanted to preserve America for the Anglo-Saxon Americans. White landlords commonly refused to rent to Koreans, and restaurants, shops, and recreational facilities customarily refused them service. Movie theaters ofttimes segregated Koreans from white patrons. In the early days Koreans were apt to blame the Chinese and Japanese for the ill treatment they received in America. In their estimation, the Chinese and Japanese had soured Americans' views of Asians by adhering to the ways of the old country. To reverse the tide of Asian discrimination, Koreans believed they had to prove their willingness to conform to American ways.

Who was Chang In-hwan, and how did he achieve hero status among Koreans in America and around the world in 1908?

Anti-Japanese sentiment in the fledgling Korean community in the United States in the opening decade of the twentieth century ran especially high after Japan declared its hegemony in Korea with the signing of the Treaty of Portsmouth in September 1905, ending the Russo-Japanese War. Koreans in America could not contain their anger when **Durham White Stevens,** an American advisor to the Korean government, in a secret pact with the Japanese Resident General Prince **Ito Hirobumi,** publicly supported Japan's takeover of the Korean peninsula. In March 1908 Stevens made a stopover in San Francisco, where he delivered public statements justifying the Japanese occupation of Korea. The nascent Korean community was in an uproar. On March 22, two representatives, one from the Kongnip Hyop Hoe and another from the Taedong Pogukhoe (Great Eastern Protection Association), another Korean organization in San Francisco, met with Stevens to air their concerns. Stevens only declared his position on Japanese occupation more emphatically, enraging the Koreans. Upon learning that Stevens would depart San Francisco the next day by train, two Korean students, **Chan In-hwan,** a member of the Kongnip Hyop Hoe, and **Chun Myung Un,** who belonged to the Taedong Pogukhoe, resolved to confront him at the train station. On their way to the station, they happened to spot Stevens in front of the Ferry Building. In the angry confrontation that ensued, Chang In-hwan shot Stevens twice, mortally wounding him. A third shot missed its intended target and hit Chun. Korean immigrants in America believed that Durham Stevens had gotten just what he deserved, and they honored Chang In-hwan as a national hero for his deed. In a show of gratitude, Koreans in Hawaii and California sent contributions for In-hwan's legal defense.

What united the Korean community in America after 1910?

The Koreans who left Korea for Hawaii and the mainland United States between 1903 and August 9, 1910, were a people with a homeland. When Japan annexed Korea on August 10, 1910, Koreans abroad suddenly awoke to life as *yumin,* exiles, drifters without a homeland. They were not only troubled about their futures (a good number had planned to return home), they feared for the safety and well-being of relatives and friends back in Korea. For the vast majority of Koreans in America, *kwangbok,* the end of Japanese colonialism in Korea and the restoration of Korea's sovereignty, emerged as their ultimate goal, their rallying cry, and a powerful unifying force. They worked all the harder so that they could contribute more dollars to the fund to liberate Korea, and they grew more determined to bolster the Korean national consciousness by instilling Korean values in their children and ensuring that they received a Korean education.

In 1909 Koreans in San Francisco founded the Korean National Association (KNA), an organization devoted to *kwangbok* and the preservation of Korean national identity. The KNA and the Korean community in America rejoiced when Korean guerrilla resistance to Japanese rule, which had been silenced but not destroyed in 1910, metamorphosed into massive protests by the Korean people in the March First Independence

Movement of 1919. While the movement failed, it did spawn a Korean provisional government, which was installed in Shanghai in April 1919 and elected American-educated **Syngman Rhee** as its president by that September. The KNA was eventually transformed into a Korean government in exile, representing Koreans in talks with the U.S. government. (It would remain in San Francisco until 1937, when it was moved to Los Angeles, which by then had emerged as the Korean hub in America.)

What brought Korean immigration to the United States to a screeching halt in 1924?

The passage of the Immigration Act of 1924 (see *What was the Immigration Act of 1924?*, p. 103), which excluded aliens ineligible for citizenship from entering the United States, brought immigration from Korea (which was treated in the same manner as Japan since it was under Japanese control) to a virtual halt, at least until after World War II, when the second wave of Koreans entered the United States between 1951 and 1964.

How did Koreans in America react to the Japanese attack on Pearl Harbor, and why did the U.S. government classify them as "enemy aliens"?

Koreans in the United States viewed the Japanese empire's attack on the U.S. Pacific Fleet moored at Pearl Harbor, on the island of Oahu, on December 7, 1941, as yet another act of Japanese aggression aimed at Japan's takeover of all of Asia. When the United States declared war on Japan the very next day, Koreans in America felt a sense of hope, convinced that American involvement in World War II would usher in the destruction of the Japanese empire and, hence, the restoration of Korean national independence.

Since Korea, annexed by Japan in 1910, remained under Japanese control during World War II, the Alien Registration

Act, which the U.S. Congress passed on June 29, 1940, classified Koreans in the United States as subjects of Japan. Therefore, when the United States declared war against Japan on December 8, 1941, Koreans, like the Japanese, on U.S. soil were designated "enemy aliens." Naturally, the Korean community in America, which since its first days had fought for an end to Japanese involvement in Korea, was up in arms over this classification. Koreans in Hawaii were even more horrified when they were ordered to wear badges with black borders to signify their restricted category status. Infuriated over being literally blacklisted, Koreans in Hawaii staged numerous protests until finally they were allowed to print on their badges the declaration "I am Korean."

Why did Koreans on the U.S. mainland wear signs during World War II that read "I'm No Jap"?

Koreans in Hawaii were not the only ones who resorted to publicizing their ethnic identity on badges during World War II. Americans in the mainland United States commonly mistook Koreans in their midst for Japanese. To avoid being mistaken for Japanese, America's Koreans took to wearing traditional dress or to attaching signs to their clothing that read "I'm no Jap!" It should be noted that while some in the Korean community sympathized with the plight of the Japanese in the United States during World War II, an appreciable proportion of the community was just as suspicious of them as most Americans. **Kilsoo Haan,** the leader of the Sino-Korean People's League, was right to be suspicious. Apparently he learned before December 7, 1941, that the Korean underground in Korea and Japan had caught wind of Japan's plan to attack American forces stationed at Pearl Harbor sometime before Christmas 1941. Haan divulged what he had learned to **Eric Sevareid** of CBS but was not taken seriously. He then shared his information with Iowa senator **Guy Gillette,** who acted decisively, warning the State Department, army and naval intelligence, and even President **Franklin Roosevelt** of the Japanese empire's intentions. Kilsoo Haan was certain that the thirty-five thousand to fifty thousand Japanese in Hawaii would aid forces of the Japanese empire in the fight against the United States, and in 1942 he called for the forced evacuation of Japanese living on the West Coast as a defensive measure.

Did Koreans in America serve during World War II?

Since they first arrived on American soil, Koreans had devoted themselves to the cause of Korea's liberation, a cause that became more urgent after Japan annexed Korea in 1910 and launched a concerted campaign to assimilate Koreans. After the United States declared war on Japan, the Koreans in America were eager to lend muscle and, for those who possessed it, knowledge of the Japanese language to the U.S. armed forces. The U.S. government employed Koreans with Japanese-language proficiency as language instructors for U.S. troops, interpreters for U.S. military officers, and as translators of confiscated Japanese documents, such as maps, manuals, and letters. Koreans in the service of the U.S. government also monitored and translated Japanese radio transmissions and delivered American propaganda in Japanese to the Japanese enemy as radio broadcasters. Some also signed on to collect intelligence and were embedded as underground agents in parts of Japanese-occupied Asia.

Koreans also actively served the American cause on the homefront. An amazing 20 percent of the Korean population in Los Angeles signed up with the California National Guard, which organized them into a special unit called the Tiger Brigade. The Tiger Brigade drilled regularly for several hours every weekend to prepare for a possible Japanese invasion of California. Even Korean senior citizens contributed to the war effort: The men served as emergency fire wardens and at other posts, and the women worked for the Red Cross.

Koreans also lent their financial support to the war effort; for instance, in the years 1942 and 1943 alone, the Korean community in America, which was only about ten thousand strong, purchased $239,000 worth of U.S. defense bonds.

How did Korea come to be divided into north and south?

On December 1, 1943, the United States, Great Britain, and China issued the Cairo Declaration, which established that Korea would regain its independence "in due course." The vague timetable for Korean independence gravely concerned the Korean provisional government, which, with the fall of Shanghai to the Japanese, had relocated to Chungking in southwestern China, and its leaders turned to the U.S. government for clarification of the wording. Washington declined to answer, further signaling to the Korean provisional government that something was amiss. About two years later, it became clear just what the United States and Great Britain were planning for the Korean peninsula. At the Yalta Conference in February 1945, the historic meeting of President **Franklin D. Roosevelt** and Soviet premier **Joseph Stalin,** Roosevelt proposed that a four-power trusteeship of the United States, Great Britain, the Soviet Union, and China be implemented for Korea.

Stalin agreed in principle, and on August 8, 1945, at the U.S. government's insistence, the Soviet Union entered the war against the Japanese empire, vowing to support independence for Korea. On August 9 Soviet troops, accompanied by a contingent of expatriate Korean Communists, entered northern Korea. Two days later, on August 11, the United States drafted General Order No. 1, which stipulated that Japanese forces situated north of latitude 38° N (the 38th parallel) would surrender to Soviet forces, while those located south of the 38th parallel would surrender to U.S. forces. The Kremlin expressed no opposition to the order, and on September 8 U.S. troops advanced into the southern part of Korea. The very next day, Japanese forces in Korea surrendered in Seoul. By then Soviet forces had already commenced sealing off the northern zone of Korea at the 38th parallel.

In the southern zone, Koreans organized in August 1945 a Committee for the Preparation of Korean Independence, and on September 6 the committee held a national assembly, where delegates proclaimed the People's Republic of Korea. The U.S. military government in the southern zone refused to recognize the republic. Nor did it recognize the Korean provisional government upon its return from exile in China as the legitimate government of Korea. Instead the White House pursued its plan of organizing in Korea a four-power trusteeship of the United States, Great Britain, the Soviet Union, and China, reaching a formal agreement with the nations involved at the Moscow Conference of December 1945. News of the trusteeship infuriated the Koreans, and to quell their anger, the U.S. military government established the Representative Democratic Council, an advisory board comprised of influential Koreans. Its chair was **Syngman Rhee,** the former president of the Korean provisional government.

In the north, the Soviet occupation authorities permitted expatriate Korean Communists to form the Provisional People's Committee for North Korea, a central government modeled on the Soviet political system, with guerrilla leader **Kim Il-sung** as its chairman. After the Joint U.S.-U.S.S.R. Commission, which had been created at the Moscow Conference, made no progress on the issue of Korea's unification, the United States took the matter to the United Nations in September 1947. The UN General Assembly responded by adopting a resolution calling for general elections in Korea to be observed by a UN Temporary Commission on Korea. The south held elections on May 10, 1948, soon adopted a constitution, and elected Syngman Rhee president on July 20. On August 15, 1948, the Republic of Korea was proclaimed, with Seoul the capital, and the U.S. military government in southern Korea ceased to operate. It was altogether a different matter in the north. The Soviet Union prohibited the UN

Temporary Commission on Korea from entering the northern zone. Kim Il-sung was appointed premier (his dictatorship, a veritable cult of personality, lasted until his death in 1994), and on September 9, 1948, the People's Republic of Korea was inaugurated, with Pyongyang as the capital.

What precipitated the Korean War?

By June 1949, the United States had completely withdrawn its troops from South Korea. All that remained behind was a force of about five hundred American servicemen, whose mission was to train the South Korean armed forces. The U.S. government had authorized a substantial military aid package for South Korea, but the U.S. military equipment included in it had not yet arrived in South Korea when North Korean leader **Kim Il-sung,** with his better trained forces, superior equipment, and support from China, mounted an unprovoked, full-scale invasion of South Korea on June 25, 1950, with the intent of overrunning the Korean peninsula.

On June 27, 1950—without a formal congressional declaration of war but with the approval of the UN Security Council—President **Harry S. Truman** committed U.S. air and naval forces to combat in an effort to contain Communist expansion on the Korean peninsula, and the United States entered what would later be called the Korean War. Seoul fell to the North the very next day. On June 30, with the demoralized South Korean army now in a state of collapse, President Truman ordered American ground troops stationed in Japan to move into Korea. The United Nations then approved the formation of a Unified Command (of sixteen member nations), under a commander designated by the United States, to combat the North Korean forces. President Truman appointed U.S. General **Douglas MacArthur**—who had commanded the Southwest Pacific Theater during World War II and had administered Japan during the postwar Allied occupation—commander of the Unified Command. The North Korean armies swiftly drove the UN coalition forces southward to Pusan in southeastern Korea, but in September 1950 General MacArthur launched a successful counteroffensive, Operation Chromite, with a surprise amphibious landing at Inchon, west of Seoul, trapping North Korean troops in the area. By October 1, UN forces had driven the North Koreans back to the 38th parallel and had recaptured Seoul. They then advanced into North Korea, capturing Pyongyang on October 20 and reaching the Manchurian frontier at the Yalu River, North Korea's northern border, on October 26—so that North Korea, at least on a military map, no longer existed as a state. But the war was not over.

In November 1950 the conflict took a surprising turn when massive Chinese forces, allied with the North Koreans, crossed the border into Korea and forced the UN troops to retreat to around Pyongtaek (approximately thirty miles south of Seoul). The UN coalition forces regrouped and launched a counteroffensive in late January 1951, and by March 31 they once again crossed the 38th parallel. Without the sanction of the Truman White House, General MacArthur publicly championed extending the war to China because of the Chinese involvement in Korea. An enraged President Truman dismissed him from all of his duties, replacing him with General **Matthew B. Ridgway.** By late June 1951 a military stalemate had developed, and the 38th parallel once again became the definitive dividing line between the two opposing governments and ideologies on the Korean peninsula.

Negotiations for a cease-fire and armistice commenced in June 1951, but they remained deadlocked until July 27, 1953, when an armistice was signed. The 38th parallel was designated the border between North and South, and a demilitarized zone (DMZ) extending 1.2 miles north and south of the border was established. By the time it ended, the Korean War was one of the costliest U.S. military undertakings of the twentieth century, both financially and in terms of human lives. 33,629 American servicemen, 3,194 UN soldiers, and about

47,000 South Koreans died in action. Another 103,284 Americans were wounded on the battlefield. A staggering 900,000 Chinese and 520,000 North Koreans were killed in combat. Millions of Korean civilians on both sides of the 38th parallel perished or were wounded. Many Korean families were torn apart and never reunited, with members living on either side of the border—with no contact permitted between them—to this very day.

How did the end of the Korean War unleash the second wave of Korean immigration to America?

In the aftermath of World War II, the South Korean government frowned upon Korean emigration and the North Korean government strictly prohibited it, while the United States still excluded aliens ineligible for citizenship, Koreans included, from entering the United States. With restrictions on both sides of the Pacific, only a handful of Korean citizens, mostly women with training as nurses, whose skills were needed, managed to immigrate to the United States.

In the aftermath of the Korean War, more Korean women managed to gain entry to the United States by taking advantage of the War Brides Act of 1945. It seems that a generous number of American GIs who served in the Korean War married Korean women while overseas, and when they went back home, they took with them their Korean wives. Since the U.S. military maintained a presence in South Korea after the Korean War (and to this day, as the border between North and South is one of the most heavily armed in the world), marriages between American GIs and Korean women were not uncommon in the 1950s and 1960s. Between 1951 and 1964, more than 28,000 Korean war brides found a new life in America. In the aftermath of the Korean War, approximately 150,000 Korean orphans, left parentless by the war, also entered the United States, where they were adopted by American families, as did a very small number of Korean professionals and students. (Interestingly the trend in America of adopting South Korean babies continued, on a lesser scale, until the 1990s, when South Korea was accused by the world community of operating "baby mills.")

What piece of legislation stimulated a third wave of Korean immigration to the United States?

A third wave of Korean immigration was stimulated by the Immigration Act of 1965 (see *What was the Immigration Act of 1965?*, p. 50). Koreans took advantage of this relaxation in America's immigration policy and began in the second half of the 1960s to flock to the United States. While only 2,165 Koreans gained admission in 1965, between 1965 and 1980 approximately 299,000 Koreans came to America's shores, and the nation's Korean population grew in leaps and bounds from just 69,130 in 1970 to 354,593 in 1980, a more than fivefold increase. Post-1965 Korean immigration peaked in 1987, when approximately 36,000 Koreans entered the United States. All in all, the Korean community, centered in the Los Angeles area and New York City, more than doubled in size in the decade of the 1980s, reaching 798,849 in 1990. After 1987, Korean immigration to the United States gradually declined and then leveled off, thanks to South Korea's "tiger economy" in the 1980s and early 1990s and to the beginnings of democratic rule in the country in 1992, marked by the election that year of **Kim Yong-sam,** South Korea's first civilian president since **Syngman Rhee.**

What is a kye, *and how did it enable Koreans to establish themselves in America?*

The *kye* is a rotating credit system that ofttimes involves substantial amounts of money. South Korean immigrants in America have depended on this old Korean financial tradition to jump-start their own businesses and to support other community members in their endeavors. In the early decades of Korean immigration, family members and close friends, operating on good faith, pooled their money in a *kye* and then one by one borrowed from it until it had rotated to all *kye* members. Borrowers who drew from the *kye* were obligated to repay the loan, plus interest. Each time the fund rotated, the interest rate decreased so that by the time the last member drew from the *kye*, the loan was interest free. With the tremendous growth of the Korean community after 1965, *kye* members began to include strangers in their groups, which increased the possibility of fraud. To combat fraud, *kye* members introduced to the system promissory notes from borrowers and general managers/creditors, who are not obligated to contribute to the fund but who must make up for losses if another member defaults before every *kye* member has had a turn. Korean Americans are generally reluctant to discuss *kye* rotating credit funds out of fear of IRS scrutiny of unreported interest income derived from their *kye* investments.

How did Koreans in New York City and elsewhere find success as greengrocers and owners of other small businesses?

Korean professionals in the medical field who arrived in the United States in the first decades after the passage of the Immigration Act of 1965 had a much easier time resurrecting their careers than their compatriots in such fields as accounting, engineering, education, and administration, who were often stymied by a lack of English-language proficiency, highly competitive job markets, and racial discrimination. Faced with occupational downgrading, as well as the decrease in manufacturing jobs in America, an appreciable number of these Korean professionals turned to running their own small businesses or to working for Korean small business owners until they gathered enough experience and capital to launch their own businesses. In New York City, Korean entrepreneurs got their first big chance at owning and operating their own businesses in the 1960s and 1970s, when younger generations of Jews and Italians, whose families had dominated the retail produce business, chose more prestigious professions over carrying on the family business, creating a need in the city for greengrocers. In the late 1960s Koreans owned just a handful of greengroceries in New York City, but by the mid-1980s they ran three-quarters of the city's thousands of greengroceries. Nowadays Koreans own an estimated 80 percent of such establishments in the entire New York tristate area, and they also dominate the inner-city grocery business in Atlanta and Washington, D.C. Since the 1980s, Koreans have also owned and operated a large percentage of the dry cleaners, fish markets, bakeries, delicatessens, shoe repair shops, nail salons, discount stores, gift shops, and moving companies in New York City and in and around Los Angeles.

The overwhelming success of Korean greengrocers and other Korean small business owners in New York City, as well as in Los Angeles and other cities, can be attributed to certain key strategies to which they adhere. These include keeping their businesses open around the clock; keeping their businesses small; working long hours alongside family members, who are customarily not paid employees; setting up shop in distressed locations, where the rents are low; introducing innovations that attract customers (such as the self-serve salad bar in Manhattan greengroceries); and utilizing organizations that match Korean merchants with established Korean suppliers, distributors, and other subcontractors. Another key to the Koreans' success is that they bring capital to invest with them to the United States. Those without capital of their own turn to traditional sources in the Korean community for loans—relatives and friends, *kyes,* and Korean-American banks. Many Korean-American banks are affiliated with a parent bank in Korea and are able to check on borrowers' credit histories. As a result, they tend to be more willing than mainstream American banks to lend to Koreans. Koreans also commonly turn to their churches for financial help (and for brainstorming about new joint ventures with fellow churchgoers). By employing these strategies, Korean small business owners have not only lowered their cost of doing business and, therefore, increased their profit margin, they have kept jobs and investments in the Korean community.

Where are America's Koreatowns?

The most visited Koreatowns in the nation are in Los Angeles and New York City. New York City's small but vibrant Koreatown, which came into being only in the early 1980s and which Korean Americans affectionately call K-town, is a largely commercial zone stretching from Thirty-first Street to Thirty-sixth Street between Fifth and Sixth Avenues in midtown Manhattan. The heart of Koreatown lies on Thirty-second Street between Broadway and Fifth Avenue. By the mid-1980s Koreatown had emerged as a shopping and restaurant mecca for the city's Koreans (who, according to census data, numbered 86,473 in 2000) and other Asians and non-Asians alike, as well as an important center of operations for Korean corporations, wholesalers, import-export firms, and three Korean newspapers. Nowadays Koreatown is also a nightlife destination for the younger set, with numerous cafés, karaoke lounges, and bars.

While New York City boasts a thriving, compact Koreatown, the largest Korean enclave in the nation is in Los Angeles, in an area loosely bordered by Beverly Boulevard to the north, Pico Boulevard to the south, Hoover Street to the east, and Crenshaw Avenue to the west, although the folks in Koreatown have different ideas of where the community begins and ends. Most concur that the heart of this sprawling community is Olympic Boulevard. The area first drew Korean businesses in the late 1960s, but the city of Los Angeles did not officially designate it a community until 1980. Los Angeles's Koreatown is both a thriving commercial and residential area and, thus, is the site not only of Korean restaurants, cafés, groceries, retail stores, six Korean banks, an upscale shopping mall (Koreatown Plaza on Western), entertainment centers, and other businesses but also of three Korean radio stations, three Korean television stations, and numerous Korean churches. Los Angeles's Koreatown is not by any means monolithic: Latino markets, *botanicas,* street vendors, and trucks serving Mexican food dot the neighborhood.

Why did African Americans clash with Koreans in New York City and Los Angeles in the early 1990s?

The Korean-American success story has inspired both praise and resentment. In the early 1990s violent conflicts erupted between African Americans and Korean Americans in Flatbush, Brooklyn, and in Los Angeles. The trouble in Flatbush all began in January 1990 when a Haitian customer, **Ghislaine Felissaint,** shopping at **Bong Jae Jang**'s Korean greengrocery claimed that Jang had insulted and physically assaulted her. The store employees told quite a different story, insisting that Felissaint had become enraged when they helped another customer while she dug for money to pay for her purchases, all the while shouting racial slurs against Koreans. African Americans in the neighborhood responded to Felissaint's claims by launching a fourteen-month boycott of Jang's greengrocery, demanding that he sell the store and leave the community. Racial tensions fueled by the boycott at times spilled over to the streets. In one violent episode, on May 13, 1990, a large group of black youths attacked three Vietnamese men with baseball bats, knives, and bottles after mistaking them for Koreans. The boycott and the violence surrounding it were covered closely by the media, and Koreans in America found the national spotlight on them for the first time.

Even though Bong Jae Jang was acquitted in a criminal case of any wrongdoing, he suffered severe financial setbacks from the boycott of his store. On one of his worst days, he sold just three onions for thirty-eight cents. Citing the serious financial harm the boycott was causing him, Jang applied for and was granted a court order limiting demonstrators' proximity to his store entrance to fifty feet. The more than 100,000 Korean Americans and nationals in the New York metropolitan area in 1990, who were known as a quiet, insular minority, came out in droves to rally in support of Bong Jae Jang. In September 1990, 10,000 Korean Americans gathered in front of Mr. Jang's greengrocery to protest the boycott and to call for racial harmony. **David Dinkins,** mayor of New York City at the time, participated in the rally, making a symbolic anti-boycott purchase.

The violence aimed at the Korean-American community in Los Angeles that erupted on April 29, 1992, and raged for three days was touched off when a predominantly white jury returned a "not guilty" verdict in a case involving four white police officers charged with beating African American **Rodney King** in a brutal attack caught on tape that shocked the country. African Americans in South Central Los Angeles, at the intersection of Florence Avenue and Normandie Avenue, were the first to react with violence to the acquittal, but the mayhem spread rapidly to other parts of the city. Koreatown, which lies just to the north of South Central, was directly in the path of the devastation. African Americans struck back at the Koreans because these newcomers had bought up a high percentage of struggling businesses in poorer, mostly African-American and Latino neighborhoods, which created serious tensions and stereotyping. As African Americans looted and set ablaze store after store in Koreatown with little response from the police and fire departments, some Koreans took to the streets armed with guns to try to defend their family businesses. When the smoke finally cleared, approximately 2,100 Korean-owned stores had been looted, burned, and otherwise damaged, and approximately 350 had been completely destroyed—with an estimated loss of about $350 million.

In the aftermath of the devastation, some Koreans simply

threw in the towel and returned to South Korea. Thousands, however, rallied together, marching through the charred streets of Koreatown on May 2 to air their complaints that the L.A. police and fire departments had responded sluggishly, and the national guard not at all, to the frantic calls for help by Koreatown's merchants and to call for harmony between the various ethnic groups of Los Angeles. During and after the rioting, Korean-American attorney and activist **Angela E. Oh** gained the national spotlight by speaking frequently about the violence from the perspective of the Korean community in Los Angeles and, thus, bringing Korean Americans into better focus for a nation that was hitherto barely aware of their existence. (In 2003 she published *Open: One Woman's Journey*, a collection of essays commemorating the ten-year anniversary of the Los Angeles riots that range in subject matter from the riots themselves to September 11, 2001.) A few months after the riots, Koreans in Los Angeles began to rebuild Koreatown—bigger and better than before. Still, the inferno in Koreatown will never be forgotten—just say "4/29" to anyone there.

How many Korean Americans are there, and where do they live?

In 2000 the U.S. Bureau of the Census counted 1,228,427 persons of Korean ancestry in the United States, up from 798,849 in 1990 (but fewer than the Korean community had expected). Of those tallied in 2000, 1,076,872 described themselves as Korean alone, 22,550 as Korean and at least one other Asian ethnicity, and 129,005 as Korean and at least one other race. According to Census 2000 data, the five states with the greatest number of Koreans (alone) in 2000 were California (345,882), New York (119,846), New Jersey (65,349), Illinois (51,453), and Washington (46,880). Most of the 345,882 persons of Korean ancestry in California reside in the five counties in and around Los Angeles (Los Angeles,

Orange, San Bernardino, Riverside, and Ventura counties). Census 2000 data also indicate that Koreans in the 1990s moved to areas where they have not traditionally settled—especially the South, with Georgia the number-one draw (28,745 Korean Americans and nationals lived there in 2000)—most probably to take advantage of employment opportunities.

How are Korean Americans faring?

The majority of post-1965 Korean immigrants are highly educated, and with their skills and initiative they have placed the Korean community in America squarely in the middle class. While many of these Koreans were professionals back in the old country, a large majority have opted to flex their entrepreneurial muscles in the United States. According to Census 2000 data, Korean Americans owned and operated 135,571 American businesses, especially groceries, liquor marts, dry cleaners, gas stations, and garages, across the nation in 2000, employing 333,649 persons and enjoying gross sales and receipts of $46 billion. While their parents pursue the American dream through entrepreneurship, the children of Korean immigrants are more apt to seek upward mobility through the professions.

Tensions between North and South Korea and the trauma of families split by the 38th parallel have been matters of serious concern for Korean Americans and Korean nationals since the end of the Korean War and the division of the Korean peninsula. Since December 2002, when North Korean president **Kim Jong-il** announced plans to reactivate a nuclear reactor, which led President **George W. Bush** to include North Korea in an "axis of evil" alongside Iran and Iraq, the Korean community in America has been especially jittery that tensions may escalate into a nuclear standoff and an international conflict on the Korean peninsula, engulfing South Korea.

Who are some Korean Americans in the political and legal arenas?

The Korean-American experience in the political arena has been quite limited and rocky at times. In 1992 **Jay C. Kim,** who was born on March 27, 1939, broke new ground as the first Korean American and the first Asian-American Republican elected to the U.S. House of Representatives, where he served Los Angeles's Forty-first Congressional District from January 1993 until January 1999. However, Congressman Kim's victory turned bittersweet in 1997, when it came to light that he had accepted more than $250,000 in illegal foreign and corporate contributions, the largest amount ever by a member of Congress, to finance his 1992 primary campaign. In July 1997 the congressman pled guilty in federal court to three misdemeanor violations of federal election campaign laws. On behalf of his campaign committee, he also pled guilty to five felony counts of concealing campaign contributions in reports that the committee submitted to the Federal Election Commission between 1992 and 1997. Congressman Kim faced up to three years in prison for his felonies but was sentenced to two months' home detention, two hundred hours community service, and a $5,000 fine. Called the "convict congressman," Kim was permitted to hold on to his seat in the House and even ran for a fourth term. However, his house arrest made it impossible for him to travel to California to campaign in his district. In 2000 Kim tried to pull his political career from the ashes by campaigning unsuccessfully for the Republican nomination in Los Angeles's Forty-second Congressional District.

In 1971 Korean American **Herbert Y. C. Choy**—who was born in Makaweli, Hawaii, on January 6, 1916, and served as Hawaii's attorney general in 1957 and 1958—became the first Korean American and only the second Asian American appointed to a federal judgeship, when President **Richard Nixon** appointed him to the U.S. Court of Appeals for the Ninth Circuit. Choy served as an active circuit judge until 1984.

Who are some prominent Korean-American writers?

One of the first Korean writers in the United States to enjoy national prominence was **Younghill Kang,** who was born in Song-Dune-Chi, Hamkyong Province, Korea, on May 10, 1903; attended Korean Christian schools organized by American missionaries in Korea; and fled his homeland in 1921 to escape persecution for his political activism, arriving in the United States with just four dollars to his name. In 1931, Kang published his first novel, *The Grass Roof,* which documents life in Korea in the first decades of Japanese occupation and ends with the main protagonist sailing toward America. Two years later, in 1933, he became the first Asian American to receive a Guggenheim Award in Creative Literature. During his lifetime, Kang was also honored with the Louis S. Weiss Memorial Prize for Adult Education from the New School, France's Le Prix Halperine Kaminsky, and an honorary doctorate in literature from Korea University. In 1937 Younghill Kang published *East Goes West: The Making of an Oriental Yankee,* a gripping story about a Korean immigrant's search for identity in America. During his writing career, he also published English-language translations of Korean literary works; a children's book entitled *The Happy Grove* (1933), which is based on *The Grass Roof*; as well as *New York Times* book reviews. Younghill Kang passed away in 1972.

Richard E. Kim, who was born **Kim Eun Kook** on March 13, 1932, in Hamhung City, Korea, and immigrated to the United States in his youth, was the next Korean writer in America to gain widespread attention. His first novel, *The Martyred* (1964)—an examination, against the backdrop of the Korean War, of human suffering and God's relation to humankind in times of war—has been compared to the writings of existentialist **Albert Camus.** Another of Kim's noteworthy contributions is

Lost Names (1970), an account of his first thirteen years of life in Japanese-occupied Korea. Korean-American novelist and artist **Gloria Hahn** (born **Kim Ronyoung** in Los Angeles on March 28, 1926) inherited the mantle from Kim with the publication in 1986 of *Clay Walls*, about Korean immigrants' struggle to assimilate into American society in the period from the early 1920s until the end of World War II. Tragically Gloria Hahn passed away in 1987, but her memory and her works live on in the United States, as well as in South Korea, where a Korean translation of *Clay Walls* has been published.

In the 1990s Korean-American writers began to receive more sustained attention from mainstream readers, thanks in large measure to celebrated Korean-American writer **Chang-rae Lee.** Born on July 29, 1965, in Seoul, Lee immigrated to the United States with his family in 1968, earned his B.A. from Yale University, and worked for a year as an analyst on Wall Street before committing himself full time to fiction. His first novel, *Native Speaker,* about a Korean American who becomes entangled in espionage, appeared in 1995 and earned him the prestigious PEN/Hemingway Award, an American Book Award from the Before Columbus Foundation, and other distinctions. In 1999 Lee published his highly acclaimed second novel, *A Gesture Life,* about a Japanese immigrant of Korean parentage in America who in the days of World War II served as a Japanese army medic and fell in love with a "comfort woman," one of at least 200,000 women and girls (mostly Korean) that Japanese forces enslaved in military brothels. For *A Gesture Life,* Lee was awarded the Anisfeld-Wolf Prize in Fiction, the Asian-American Literary Award for Fiction, and other honors.

Another Korean-American novelist who came to the fore in the 1990s is **Nora Okja Keller,** who was born in Seoul to a German father and a Korean mother, and grew up in Hawaii. In 1995 Keller was awarded the Pushcart Prize for her short story "Mother Tongue," which she later incorporated into her

Comfort Women (1997), a novel chronicling the brutality that a Korean woman endures as a sex slave for Japanese soldiers. For that first novel she received the 1998 American Book Award. Her second novel, *Fox Girl,* a harrowing tale about three alienated young Koreans abandoned in the aftermath of the Korean War who suffer abuse at the hands of American GIs, appeared in 2002.

Other contemporary Korean-American fiction writers now coming into their own include **Heinz Insu Fenkl,** author of the autobiographical novel *Memories of My Ghost Brother* (1996) and coeditor of *Kori: The Beacon Anthology of Korean American Literature* (2001), the first Korean American literary anthology, as well as *Century of the Tiger: One Hundred Years of Korean Culture in America, 1901–2001* (2003); **Gary Pak,** who penned the short-story collection *The Watcher of Waipuna and Other Stories* (1992) and the novel *A Ricepaper Airplane* (1998); **Walter K. Lew,** author of *Treadwinds: Poems and Intermediate Texts* (2002) and editor of the poetry anthology *Premonitions: The Kaya Anthology of New Asian North American Poetry* (1995) and other works; **Patti Kim,** author of the autobiographical novel *A Cab Called Reliable* (1997), for which she was awarded the 1997 Towson University Prize for Literature; novelist **Leonard Chang,** who penned *The Fruit 'N Food* (1996), *Dispatches from the Cold* (1998), and *Over the Shoulder* (2001); and **Susan Choi,** who published her first novel, *The Foreign Student,* in 1998 and received an NEA Award in 2000.

Who are some renowned Korean-American musicians and artists?

The United States is home to a number of preeminent classical musicians and composers of Korean ancestry. Korean American **Earl Kim,** who was born on January 6, 1920, in Dinuba, California, to parents who had emigrated from Korea, garnered wide recognition as, in the words of violinist **Itzhak Perlman** upon Kim's death in 1998, a "composer, devoted teacher, musician extraordinaire." Among his numerous distinctions are commissions from the Fromm, Koussevitzky and Naumberg Foundations, a Prix de Paris, a National Institute of Arts and Letters Award (1965), and a Brandeis Creative Arts Award (1971). Earl Kim is perhaps best known for his musical scores to texts by **Samuel Beckett,** including his chamber music, solo piano pieces, and song cycles to the Beckett-inspired opera *Footfalls.* His works have been performed by some of the twentieth century's greatest musicians, conductors, and orchestras, including Itzhak Perlman, conductors **Zubin Mehta** and **Seiji Osawa,** the New York Philharmonic, the Boston Symphony Orchestra, and the Philadelphia Orchestra. All the while he was composing, Earl Kim also performed as a pianist and enjoyed an illustrious academic career.

Ensemble violinist **Chouhei Min,** who was born in Seoul, was the first in a line of Korean-American violinists to garner worldwide accolades. Min took up the violin at age five and debuted on the concert stage at age nine with the Seoul Philharmonic. After studying at the Boston Conservatory of Music, graduating from the Hartt College of Music in Connecticut, and earning a master's degree from the Yale School of Music, Chouhei Min was named associate concertmaster of the Dallas Symphony Orchestra. In 1974 she joined the Minnesota Orchestra, where she served as associate concertmaster from 1974 to 1990.

The Ahn Trio—the all-sister chamber ensemble featuring violinist **Angella Ahn** and her older twin sisters, pianist **Lucia Ahn** and cellist **Maria Ahn**—has been charming audiences the world over since the late 1980s. Born in Seoul, the three sisters took up their respective instruments at an early age and gave their first joint performance—which was broadcast on Korean television—in Seoul in 1979. In 1981 the Ahn sisters moved with their mother to New York, where they attended the pre-college program at the prestigious Juilliard School. The gifted and dynamic Ahns first caught the attention of the nation in 1987, when *Time* magazine ran a cover story about them entitled "Asian-American Whiz Kids." In 1988 NBC aired a documentary about the threesome during coverage of the Winter Olympics in Seoul. In 1992 the Ahn sisters garnered top prizes at the Alliance Northeast Competition for Chamber Ensembles and the Coleman Chamber Competition. The year 1995 saw the release of their critically acclaimed first recording, *Paris Rio,* showcasing trios by **Maurice Ravel** and **Heitor Villa-Lobos**. Their next recording, featuring trios by **Josef Suk, Antonin Dvořák,** and **Dmitri Shostakovich,** also received rave reviews when it was put out in 1999. In 2000 the sisters released their third recording, *Ahn-Plugged,* which contains their marvelous renditions of works by **Eric Ewazen, Kenji Bunch, Leonard Bernstein, Astor Piazzolla,** and **David Bowie.** *Ahn-Plugged* was followed in 2002 by *Groovebox,* the Ahn Trio's latest creation.

Korean-American violin soloist **Sarah Chang** ranks among the world's finest classical musicians. She has appeared on stages around the globe with most major orchestras. Born in Philadelphia in 1980, Chang, a child prodigy, began to study the violin at age four, and at age eight she auditioned for distinguished conductors **Zubin Mehta** and **Riccardo Muti.** They were so impressed with her talent that she secured immediate engagements with the New York Philharmonic and the Philadelphia Orchestra. When she was nine years old, Sarah Chang recorded her bestselling first album, for EMI Classics, entitled *Debut* (1992), which showcases virtuoso pieces by **Sarasat, Paganini, Prokofiev,** and others, which she played on a quarter-sized violin. She has since released numerous other recordings. In 1997 Chang debuted at Carnegie Hall, and in 1999 she was the recipient of the Avery Fisher Prize, a prestigious award bestowed on instrumentalists.

In the art world, Korean American **Nam June Paik,** a pioneer of video art who was born in Seoul in 1932 and left Korea with his family in 1950 to escape the ravages of the civil war, became associated in the 1960s with performance art and the Fluxus group, an experimental arts movement. (Another influential member of the Fluxus group was **Yoko Ono.**) Paik gained an international following in the early 1970s with his artistic interpretations of television and video, such as his installation *TV Buddha* (1974), in which a Buddha sitting cross-legged stares at its own image on a television screen. One of Paik's most celebrated works of the 1980s is *Tricolor Vidéo* (1982), a video sculpture comprised of television sets arranged to form the French flag, which he created for the Musée national d'art moderne in Paris.

In 1996 Nam June Paik created *Video Flag*, a bank of seventy video monitors that display at split-second intervals the Stars and Stripes, rotating Statues of Liberty, news stills, lines of zeros and ones (the binary language of computers), and a face that morphs from that of President **Harry S. Truman** through all the U.S. presidents up to and including **Bill Clinton**. Paik eventually incorporated laser into his installation art, as in *Modulation in Sync* (2000), his collaboration with **Norman Ballard, Paul Garrin, David Hartnett,** and **Stephen Vitiello.** Nam June Paik's works have been exhibited at the Museum of Modern Art, the Whitney Museum, the Guggenheim Museum, and the Kitchen Museum in New York; the Museum of Contemporary Art in Chicago; and at the Metropolitan Art Museum in Tokyo.

Who are the celebrated Korean Americans of the stage and screen?

On the silver screen, internationally acclaimed Korean-American actor **Philip Ahn,** who was born **Pil Lip Ahn** on March 29, 1905, in Highland Park, California, enjoyed a Hollywood career spanning three decades and more than eighty films. He landed his first role in 1936 in the acclaimed motion picture *Anything Goes,* starring **Ethel Merman** and **Bing Crosby.** During the remainder of the 1930s, Ahn played supporting roles in such popular feature films as *The Good Earth*

(1937), based on **Pearl S. Buck**'s celebrated 1931 novel by the same name, and *Charlie Chan in Honolulu* (1938), and he also had starring roles opposite legendary Chinese-American actress **Anna May Wong** (with whom he fell head over heels in love) in *Daughter of Shanghai* (1937) and *King of Chinatown* (1939). During the World War II years, Philip Ahn played the evildoer in numerous motion pictures that were meant to arouse animosity toward the Japanese enemy and heighten Americans' sense of patriotism, such as *Betrayal from the East* (1944), about an ex-pat ex-GI who is approached by a Japanese spy ring and ends up a counterspy for U.S. Army Intelligence. His performances as villainous Japanese military officers and spies were so convincing that the actor actually received hate mail and death threats and was also physically attacked. Ahn once said that inciting hatred for the Japanese enabled him to do his part for the Korean independence movement, of which his father was a leader.

In the 1970s Philip Ahn captivated a new generation of viewers with his exceptional portrayal of the wise Master Kan, the kung fu leader of the Shaolin Temple, in the hit television series *Kung Fu* (1972–75), which also starred **David Carradine** as a half-Chinese, half-American Shaolin priest. All of Hollywood, generations of fans, and family mourned Philip Ahn's passing on February 28, 1978. On November 14, 1984, a day that Los Angeles mayor **Tom Bradley** declared Philip Ahn Day and Korean Day for the City of Los Angeles, Ahn became the first Asian-American actor to be immortalized with a star on the Hollywood Walk of Fame.

On the stage, Korean-American actor **Randall Duk Kim** gained a national reputation in the 1970s as one of the finest interpreters of the works of **William Shakespeare.** One of Kim's greatest contributions is his co-creation in 1980 and nurturing of the American Players Theatre, a professional classical theater, located just south of Spring Green, Wisconsin, that is committed to staging Shakespeare. Between 1980 and 1991 Kim acted in numerous productions by the American Players Theatre, helping to make it the nation's second most popular outdoor classical theater. In more recent years Randall Duk Kim has captivated audiences with his performances on Broadway in *The King and I* (1996–97), *Golden Child* (1998), *Flower Drum Song* (2002), and in numerous other productions.

A Korean-American actor who has garnered fanfare for his work on the stage and on the small and big screens is **Soon Tek Oh,** who was born in Korea in 1943. A founding member of the theatrical company East-West Players in Los Angeles, Oh also serves as one of its directors, writers, and actors. On television, he has played supporting roles in numerous episodes of leading shows, including *M*A*S*H** and *Cagney & Lacey,* in TV movies, and in miniseries. On the big screen, he has performed in about a dozen feature films, among them the drama *Red Sun Rising* (1994), the comedy *Beverly Hills Ninja* (1997), and Walt Disney's *Mulan* (1998) as the voice of Fa Zhou (Mulan's father).

A Korean American who has brought laughs to both the stage and the screen is comedian **Margaret Cho**, who happens to be one of the most recognizable Asian Americans in the nation. Born in San Francisco on December 5, 1968, Cho started performing stand-up at age sixteen at The Rose & Thistle, a comedy club situated above the bookstore her parents operated. When she was in her early twenties, the comedian set out on the college circuit, performing over three hundred comedy shows in two years. An instant success, Cho was honored for her comedic talents with the American Comedy Award for Female Comedian in 1994, which led to appearances on late-night television with **Arsenio Hall** and on a **Bob Hope** prime-time television special. Cho's antics with Hall and Hope brought her instant celebrity. Before long she landed the starring role on ABC's *All-American Girl,* which aired in 1995 as television's first prime-time sitcom about an Asian-American family.

All-American Girl proved to be a poor showcase for Margaret

Cho's talents. After she quit the show and it was canceled, she appeared in a slew of motion pictures, including director **John Woo**'s action/thriller *Face/Off* (1997), starring **Nicolas Cage** and **John Travolta,** and continued to tickle funny bones at sold-out gigs in comedy clubs and theaters and on college campuses. In 1999 Cho took her Off-Broadway one-woman show, *I'm the One That I Want,* on the road. The touring production made *Entertainment Weekly*'s list of Great Performances of the Year and earned the comedian *New York* magazine's Performance of the Year Award and a Manhattan Association of Cabarets and Clubs (MAC) Award. Cho's performance of *I'm the One That I Want* at The Warfield in San Francisco was taped, and in 2000 it was released as an independent film of the same name. The film received kudos from critics, as did the comedian's next indie, *Notorious C.H.O.* (2002). In addition to her work on the stage and screen, Margaret Cho has also penned a bestselling memoir, *I'm the One That I Want* (2002), which is as hilarious as her stand-up.

Who are some outstanding Korean-American athletes?

Korean American **Sammy Lee,** who was born in 1920 in Fresno, California, to Korean immigrants who had labored on a Hawaiian plantation, distinguished himself in both the world of sports and the world of medicine. As an athlete he earned the distinction of being the first male diver to win gold medals in high diving in consecutive Olympics: He captured gold in ten-meter platform diving at the 1948 Summer Olympics in London and repeated his stellar performance in this event at the 1952 Games in Helsinki, where he also won the bronze medal in three-meter springboard diving. (Sammy Lee is also the first Asian American to win Olympic gold for the United States.) Lee had to overcome a lot of obstacles to emerge a world-class diver. One of the pools he practiced in in Los Angeles, Brookside pool, was open to non-whites only one day a week. Each time minorities swam in the pool, it was drained and then refilled with fresh water. On days that the pool was off-limits, Lee often resorted to practicing his diving by jumping onto a sand pile. Eventually he was taken under the wing of distinguished diving coach **Jim Ryan,** who got the young diver through the door at the Los Angeles Athletic Club, even though it barred minorities. Another obstacle that Lee faced was the cancellation of the Olympics in 1940 and 1944, years when he was at his prime as a diver. By the time 1948 rolled around, Sammy Lee was twenty-eight. He did not let his age stop him then or four years later, when he set another record at the 1952 Olympics, earning the distinction of being the oldest athlete to capture a gold medal in diving.

In 1953 the Amateur Athletic Union bestowed upon Sammy Lee its James E. Sullivan Award, given each year to America's top amateur athlete, and in 1968 the diver was inducted into the International Swimming Hall of Fame. After he retired from world-class competition, Lee turned to coaching. He steered diver **Bob Webster** to Olympic gold medals in both 1960 and 1964, and about a decade later he coached **Greg Louganis,** considered the greatest diver of all time, for the 1976 Summer Olympics in Montreal, where Louganis captured silver in the ten-meter platform diving event. All the while he was diving for gold, Lee was working toward his medical degree from the USC medical school (which he earned in 1947) and serving in the Army Medical Service Corps in Korea (from 1943 to 1955). He later opened a private medical practice in Orange, California, which he ran for many years.

Thanks to his superb fastball, slider, curveball, and change-up, baseball pitcher **Chan Ho Park,** who was born in Kong Ju City, South Korea, on June 30, 1973, debuted in the major leagues with the Los Angeles Dodgers in the 1994 season and has posted a winning record every season since he moved to full-time play in 1996. In the 2001 season, one of his best so far, Park racked up fifteen wins for the Dodgers and led the team in strikeouts (218) and innings (234). That season he was also selected for the All-Star team, a first by a Korean-born player. Traded to the Texas Rangers, Park finished the 2002 season with a 9-8 record, leading the team in wins and strikeouts (121), despite two stints on the bench with injuries.

Which religions do Koreans in America observe?

When Koreans began venturing to American shores around the turn of the twentieth century, Buddhism, which was introduced to the Korean peninsula in the fourth century A.D., had long enjoyed the largest following of all religions in Korea. Still, thanks to the conversion efforts of Catholic missionaries who reached Korea in the seventeenth century and of Protestant missionaries who first set foot on the peninsula in the 1880s, the Protestant churches and the Catholic church also had quite a number of followers in Korea around the time Koreans began venturing to America. These churches gained more and more converts as the twentieth century wore on, due especially to the aid that Catholic and Protestant relief organizations rendered to the Korean people in their darkest moments of Japanese occupation. By 1991, 51 percent of South Koreans identified themselves as Buddhists, 2 percent as Confucianists, 35 percent as Protestants, and 11 percent as Catholic. The majority of Koreans who have immigrated to the United States since 1965 practiced Christianity in their homeland and have continued the tradition in their new home. The disproportionate number of Christians in the Korean immigrant population stems from the fact that post-1965 Korean immigrants have come from urban areas, where Christianity is commonly practiced; that many Christians from North Korea took refuge in South Korea before and during the Korean War and were then more apt than South Koreans to immigrate to America; and that Korean Christians are more likely than Korean Confucianists and Buddhists to immigrate because of Christianity's dominance in the United States.

Which Korean holidays do Korean Americans celebrate?

In addition to strictly religious holidays and the New Year, Koreans in America celebrate *Ch'usok*, the Harvest Moon Festival, which falls sometime in September or October and is the Korean equivalent of Thanksgiving. Large Korean communities around the country hold Harvest Moon Festival celebrations complete with parades. Korean Americans in New York City flock to Manhattan to celebrate the Korean Moon Festival with a parade down Broadway featuring Korean-American beauty queens atop floats, marching bands, Korean-American folkloric groups, official Korean delegations, marchers from Korean-American associations, and floats representing Buddhist temples and Korean churches.

Korean Americans may also observe such traditional Korean festive days as Children's Day, which falls on the fifth of May, and *chanchi'i*, traditional celebrations of the first and sixty-first birthdays. (Infant mortality rates in Korea were once quite high, so children who made it to their first birthday were honored. Similarly, because the average life span was considered to be sixty years, which coincides with the cycle of years in the lunar calendar, a sixty-first birthday also received recognition.) Korean Americans may also observe Korea's Independence Movement Day (March 1) and Hangul Proclamation Day (October 9), a day of tribute to *Hangul*, the Korean alphabet, which is not only a system of orthography but represents freedom from Chinese and Japanese domination and the restoration of sovereignty in Korea.

Do Korean Americans rely on traditional Korean medicine?

The majority of Korean Americans rely both on Western medicine and at least a few aspects of *hanyak*, traditional Korean medicine, which is a blend of Korean folk medicine and traditional Chinese medicine. The basic premise of *hanyak* is that good health depends on harmony between the dual cosmic forces of yin and yang. Illness, then, is associated with disharmony between these forces. The restoration of the proper balance between yin and yang, and, therefore, of good health, entails such procedures as acupuncture, moxibustion, pulse analysis, and deep breathing, as well as the use of medicinal herbs and substances—everything from ginseng, chrysanthemum petals, snake wine, and dried tortoise to deer antlers, dried reptiles, and insects—that are commonly made into teas.

Which five flavors and five colors are essential in Korean cuisine, and which classic Korean dishes do Korean Americans enjoy?

Korean cooks on both sides of the Pacific seek to incorporate five flavors in traditional Korean dishes: salty, sweet, sour, hot, and bitter. Beet sugar, honey, and sweet potatoes sweeten Korean dishes, while table salt, soy sauce, and bean paste add a salty taste. Mustard and dried red chile peppers lend hotness; citron vinegar, sourness; and ginger, bitterness. Koreans also make an effort to choose ingredients that represent all of the five traditional colors of Korea: green, red, yellow, white, and black. (They rely often on cloud ear mushrooms to add a touch of black.)

Korean cuisine, which, in the way of other Asian cuisines, has developed over thousands of years, features myriad dishes. Some of the favorites in Korean America are *bul koki,* Korean barbecue, the preparation of which entails first marinating thin strips of beef, chicken, squid, or octopus in a mixture of soy sauce, sugar, garlic, ginger, and sesame oil, and then cooking the strips to perfection at a table grill fueled by gas jets or the special hardwood charcoal that Koreans favor. The grilled meat is then served with rice or wrapped in lettuce leaves. *Kalbi,* beef short ribs, is another popular Korean grilled dish. Korean Americans also enjoy meat and vegetable dumplings and beef soup. An assortment of side dishes and condiments, such as pickled fish or crab and *kim-chee,* pungent, spicy pickled vegetables (commonly cabbage and white radish), accompany most Korean meals.

Many Koreans and Korean Americans swear by black goat when they need an energy boost, and they often prepare it as a restorative for patients recovering from a serious illness. In Los Angeles, Korean Americans sometimes satisfy their hunger for black goat at a number of Koreantown restaurants, including Chin Go Gae on W. 8th Street, which serves goat grilled at the table or stewed in a rich broth.

FOUR

Filipino Americans

If the Philippines is an Asian nation, why does it have such a European-sounding name?

Why did Spain conquer the Philippines?

Who were the Manilamen?

How did the Filipino rebellion against the Spanish lead to the American domination of the Philippines beginning in 1898?

How did the United States restructure Philippine society?

Who were the pensionados?

Why did Filipinos catch "Hawaiian fever"?

Did all the Filipino agricultural workers head for Hawaii?

What were working conditions like for the Filipinos in America in the 1910s, 1920s, and 1930s?

In what way did Filipinos endure racism from two sides?

Who was one of the first to chronicle the racism that Filipinos endured in the United States?

Why did Filipinos get in a jam when they dated white American women?

What was the Tydings-McDuffie Act of 1934, and why was it bad news for Filipinos?

If Filipinos were legal aliens, why were they ineligible for U.S. citizenship?

Did Filipinos serve in the U.S. armed forces during World War II?

When did Filipinos begin to immigrate to the United States in significant numbers once again?

Why did Filipinos immigrate to the United States in the 1980s and 1990s?

How have Filipinos of the second wave differed from those of the first wave?

How many Filipino Americans are there, and where do they live?

How is the Filipino community in America faring?

Why are there no "Little Manilas" in America, and what impact has this had on Filipinos?

Do Filipino Americans wield political clout?

Who are some other prominent Filipino Americans?

Who are some world-class Filipino-American athletes?

Which holidays do Filipino Americans celebrate?

What are some favorite foods of Filipino Americans?

Filipino Americans have long been a silent, inconspicuous ethnic group in the United States, though their number is actually sizable. In fact, the U.S. Bureau of the Census counted 2,364,815 persons of Filipino ancestry in the United States in 2000, making them the second-largest Asian-American group. Filipino Americans have a unique place among Asian Americans because the history of their ancestral homeland, the Philippines—an archipelago of approximately 7,100 islands and islets situated about five hundred miles off of the Asian continent's southeastern coast—was shaped largely by the United States, at least since 1898, when Spain ceded the Philippines to the United States after American forces defeated the Spanish in the Spanish-American War.

If the Philippines is an Asian nation, why does it have such a European-sounding name?

If you guessed "Spain," then you're familiar with the mighty Spanish Empire, which extended its sphere of influence to Latin America and Asia beginning in the early sixteenth century. For more than three hundred years, from 1521 to 1898, Spain dominated the Philippines. A vestige of that domination is the country's name, which Spanish explorer **Miguel Lopez de Legazpi** gave the archipelago—in honor of King **Philip II** of Spain, who had ascended the Spanish throne in 1556—after he made landfall there in 1565. As the indigenous peoples of the Philippine Islands, who were descendants of the Malays and Indonesians who had ventured to the archipelago long before the Christian era, intermarried and interbred with their conquerors, they, too, inherited Spanish names. Nowadays many of their descendants, from Manila all the way to Los Angeles and New York City, bear distinctly Spanish names—and some speak Spanish in addition to Pilipino, the national language of the Philippines, and English, the second language of that nation's government workers, professionals, and academicians.

Another vestige of many centuries of Spanish occupation of the Philippines is the term "Filipino," which originally referred to a person of Spanish ancestry (either a full-blooded Spaniard or a Spanish mestizo, that is, one with both Spanish and native blood) who was born in the Philippines but now signifies any person born in the archipelago. (While the term "Filipino" applies to both men and women, "Filipina" is used only to describe a person of the female gender who was born in the Philippines.)

Why did Spain conquer the Philippines?

Spanish involvement in the Philippines commenced on March 16, 1521, when Portuguese explorer and navigator

Ferdinand Magellan—who, with the financial backing of the Spanish crown, was circumnavigating the globe in his search for the western route to the Spice Islands through or around South America, a route he was certain existed—made landfall on the island of Cebu. He claimed the lush island chain for Spain and christened it the Archipelago of San Lazaro. The indigenous peoples of San Lazaro were not as excited about Magellan as he was about their islands. Six weeks after the explorer made landfall in the Philippines, which at the time had no centralized government in command of a large territory, the native chief, **Lapu Lapu,** killed him in an act of resistance to Spanish rule and efforts to convert the indigenous peoples of San Lazaro to Catholicism. Spain refrained from retaliating full force.

In fact, the Spanish did not flex their muscles much in the archipelago until **Philip II,** "the most Catholic of kings," ascended the Spanish throne in 1556, vowing to increase the might of his empire and defend the Catholic Church. In 1565 he sent **Miguel Lopez de Legazpi** to the Archipelago of San Lazaro. Legazpi implemented a vigorous campaign of colonization, renaming the island chain after Philip II of Spain and establishing in 1565 the first Spanish settlement, in Cebu. Nevertheless, it took Spanish colonizers until 1571 to subdue the native peoples of the Philippines, which they never did completely. The Spanish found it particularly difficult to gain control of the Muslims in the archipelago, whom they called *Moros,* or Moors, after the North African Muslims who had conquered Spain and then had been driven out of the country by King **Ferdinand** and Queen **Isabella** during the Catholic reconquest of Spain, which was completed in 1492, when the Spanish captured Granada. While the Spanish could not wipe out Islam in the Philippines altogether and while their domination of the archipelago was never absolute, the strong centralized government that Spain installed there proved mighty, lasting until the Spanish-American War of 1898, and missionaries were enormously successful in their efforts to convert the indigenous population to Roman Catholicism.

Who were the Manilamen?

During the reign of **Philip II** of Spain, ambitious Spanish merchants swarmed the Philippines, intent on making their fortune. The merchants claimed exclusive trading rights in the islands and transformed Manila into a major commercial port and trading center. The Spanish, who didn't want to give anyone else a piece of the pie, treated the Filipinos unjustly, stripping them of all privileges. Only the *ilustrados*—those born in the Philippines of mixed race—were given access to education, land, and high positions in the government. The Spanish forced a great proportion of the Philippine population to labor as slaves in the Philippines or as deckhands on Spanish galleons plying the trade routes linking Manila and Mexico. A significant number of Filipinos escaped the brutality of the galleon trade by jumping ship at Acapulco, then a major port. In 1763 some made their way north to the Louisiana Territory—which France had ceded to Spain in February of that year—where they settled in the fishing village of St. Malo, Louisiana, and forged a life as fishermen and hunters. These Filipinos, the first on what would be American soil, and their descendants became known as Manilamen. In 1893 a hurricane demolished St. Malo, killing most of its inhabitants, who lived virtually unprotected in huts perched above the swamps. Four years later, in 1897, a Filipino sailor named **Quintin de la Cruz** founded Manila Village, a fishing port in Barataria Bay, forty miles south of New Orleans. Manila Village thrived: By 1933 the Filipinos of the port, who supported themselves by fishing, shrimping, and hunting muskrats, numbered fifteen hundred.

How did the Filipino rebellion against the Spanish lead to the American domination of the Philippines beginning in 1898?

From the moment that Portuguese explorer **Ferdinand Magellan** set foot in the Philippine Islands in 1521, the Filipinos never ceased in their efforts to rid their homeland of Spanish domination. The most critical uprisings against Spanish rule occurred from 1896 to 1898, when Filipino nationalists, under the command of Filipino rebel **Emilio Aguinaldo,** fought for their independence in what was called the Philippine Revolution, waging all-out war against the Spanish to regain control of their country. Aguinaldo allied himself and the Filipino independence movement with the United States, which had expressed sympathy for the cause and whose military might he was certain would bring Spain, a dwindling empire, to its knees.

Tensions between the United States and Spain mounted in 1898, when the United States—which for most of the nineteenth century had envisioned gaining control of Cuba, a Spanish colony—promised to aid the Caribbean island in its push for liberation from Spanish domination. On April 11, 1898, President **William McKinley** asked the U.S. Congress "to authorize and empower the President to take measures to secure a full and final termination of hostilities between the Government of Spain and the people of Cuba. . . ." Two weeks later, on April 25, 1898, the United States declared war on Spain. It wasted no time targeting Spain's other colonies, including the Philippines, halfway around the world from Cuba. On May 1, 1898, a squadron of U.S. warships led by naval commander **George Dewey** attacked the Spanish fleet anchored in Manila Bay, defeating it the very same day.

As Emilio Aguinaldo had predicted, the United States emerged the victor in the Spanish-American War of 1898 and swiftly ousted the Spanish from power in the Philippines. On

June 12, 1898, Aguinaldo declared independence for the Philippines, and in January 1899 a new government was put in place, of which he was named president. However, contrary to Aguinaldo's vision for the future, the U.S. government did not restore sovereignty to the archipelago. Instead, under the Treaty of Paris signed on December 10, 1898, which formally ended the war, Spain ceded the Philippines (as well as its other remaining colonies, that is, Cuba, Puerto Rico, Wake Island, and Guam) to the United States, and the archipelago was declared a U.S. commonwealth, not a sovereign nation. That same year the United States, now a major world power, established its first three military bases in the Philippine Islands, and the U.S. Navy began to enlist Filipinos as mess boys and stewards. By 1930 the U.S. Navy would have about twenty-five thousand Filipinos in its ranks.

As a "protector," the United States would retain control of the Philippines until it judged the island nation fit to govern itself, that is, until it was no longer in the interest of American imperialists to control the archipelago. Outraged that they had traded one colonizer for another, Filipino nationalists—peasants, workers and members of the intelligentsia among them—rebelled against U.S. hegemony, taking on the approximately 100,000 American soldiers stationed in the Philippines to ensure a smooth transfer of power from Spain to the United States. The nationalists' attacks on U.S. armed forces escalated in 1899 into the Philippine-American War, what the United States dubbed an "insurrection" in an effort to downplay the bloodshed. U.S. forces employed brutal tactics to subdue the peoples of the Philippines during the war. In Samar and Batangas Provinces, for instance, they burned villages and ruthlessly slaughtered all Filipinos suspected of being guerrillas. Even though U.S. forces captured Aguinaldo on March 23, 1901, and he called on his fellow Filipinos to accept U.S. control of the Philippine archipelago, the Philippine-American War stretched on until 1902. And, even after the

U.S. government declared officially on July 4, 1902, that it had regained control of the archipelago, Filipino Muslim guerrilla fighters continued to rebel sporadically against American domination—at least until 1913, when they were finally defeated.

How did the United States restructure Philippine society?

Despite the Filipinos' resistance to foreign domination, the United States went to work "uplifting" a people whom it referred to as "scarcely more than savages," "our little brown brothers," and "yellow bellies." The U.S. colonial government in the Philippines, which was declared temporary, sought to improve the country's infrastructure and quality of life, building roads, bridges, and railroads on the islands, and introducing a health care program to eradicate tropical diseases. The United States's key objective in its administration of the Philippines was to lay the groundwork for the creation of a free and democratic government based on the American model. Toward this end, the U.S. colonial government introduced a party system, a legislative assembly in 1907, the separation of church and state, and a free secular education system in 1901 that was fashioned after the American one, in which English, not Tagalog or Spanish, was the language of instruction. American teachers, called Thomasites because they arrived in the archipelago on board the vessel the *St. Thomas,* were recruited to "civilize" the native population of the Philippines by teaching students about the history, heroes, and values of the United States. The American colonization of the Philippines had an enormous impact on the country's future. For one, it paved the way for the first wave of Filipino immigration to Hawaii (declared a U.S. territory in 1900) and to the mainland United States, a wave that began around 1906 in response to the demand for cheap labor.

Who were the pensionados?

The *pensionados* have been mistakenly called the first Filipino immigrants in the United States. They were, in fact, neither immigrants nor even sojourners, but rather Filipino students who received a free university education in the United States in the years 1903 to 1910. The U.S. colonial government handpicked the *pensionados*, who were given the nickname "fountain-pen boys," from among the Filipino best and brightest and arranged their free schooling in the United States in an effort to create a pool of highly educated civil servants in the Philippines who embraced American values. After completing their studies at American colleges and universities, the majority of *pensionados* returned home, as the U.S. colonial government had banked on, and secured positions of high status in the colonial bureaucracy, agriculture, business, education, and medicine.

The U.S. colonial government lent financial backing to the *pensionado* program only until 1910, but Filipino students, seeking the better employment opportunities and prestige that the *pensionados* enjoyed, continued to go to the United States to expand their horizons, financing their education themselves. Some Filipino families even mortgaged their houses to raise funds to send their children to college in America, hoping that their investment would pay off in the end. Ofttimes the money ran out, and students were forced to drop out of school and take jobs as unskilled laborers, a far cry from the elite posts they had envisioned for themselves back home. Some beat the odds: They completed their studies and returned to the Philippines to assume high-ranking positions alongside the *pensionados*.

Why did Filipinos catch "Hawaiian fever"?

With the virtual halt in the flow of Chinese laborers to Hawaii and the United States brought about by the Chinese

Exclusion Act of 1882, which remained in effect until 1943, as well as the limited flow of Japanese laborers to both destinations, thanks to the 1908 Gentlemen's Agreement, desperate Hawaiian sugar plantation owners eyed Filipinos as a source of efficient and cheap labor. The Hawaiian Sugar Planters Association deployed recruiters to the Philippines, in particular to Vigan, Cebu, and Ilocos Sur, to sign on Filipino laborers for the sugar plantations. Despite tough economic times at home, Filipinos were initially hesitant about going to a faraway land. In 1906 the first group of Filipino laborers, just fifteen in all, arrived in Hawaii, which by then was a U.S. territory. As stories of their success in Hawaii began to circulate in the Philippines, Filipinos came down with "Hawaiian fever," fantasies of making it rich in the Hawaiian Islands and returning home to a comfortable life, unleashing the first wave of Filipino immigration to the United States and its territories. While in 1909, 639 Filipinos were employed as plantation labor in Hawaii, by 1910 that figure had risen to 2,915. All told, between 1909 and 1934, some 119,470 Filipino sojourners ventured to the Hawaiian Islands to toil on sugar and pineapple plantations. By the 1930s they constituted the largest ethnic group of plantation workers there. The recruits were overwhelmingly male, since most Filipinas thought it unsavory to travel to Hawaii to work the land. Hence, in the years 1920 to 1929, the ratio of Filipinos to Filipinas in Hawaii was 100 to 7.

The Filipinos' Hawaiian success stories were greatly exaggerated, of course. Hawaii's higher prices rapidly depleted the Filipinos' earnings from their work on Hawaiian sugar plantations. And for the pittance that they managed to save, the Filipino laborers in Hawaii endured the grueling tasks of planting, hoeing, and harvesting the cane; a long workday with few breaks; harsh living conditions; and abuse from the plantation foremen and the plantation police. The Filipinos quickly organized to contest their unfair pay and treatment and to promote the welfare of members of the community.

Filipino labor leader **Pablo Manlapit** organized the Filipino Federation of Labor in 1911 and the Filipino Unemployed Association in 1913. And in 1919 members of both organizations established the Higher Wages Association to fight for fair wages and benefits.

When the sugar planters did not bend to their demands, Filipino laborers resorted to labor agitation. They took an active part in the first major interethnic strike against the sugar planters, which began on June 19, 1920, and lasted for seven months. Then in April 1924 approximately thirty-one thousand Filipino laborers organized a bloody eight-month strike that brought operations to a halt on half of Hawaii's plantations. After Pablo Manlapit was placed under arrest in September of that year, Filipino workers organized large protests in Hanapepe plantation, Kauai. Sixteen were killed and many others were wounded when police opened fire on the protesters. As for Manlapit, he was finally freed in 1927 on condition that he leave Hawaii and never return. He returned defiantly in 1932 and resurrected the Filipino Federation of Labor with the aid of **Epifanio Taok** and **Manuel Fagel,** only to be rearrested and deported. In 1937 Fagel staged the last strictly Filipino strike in Hawaii.

Did all the Filipino agricultural workers head for Hawaii?

Around the same time that Filipino laborers were venturing to the U.S. territory of Hawaii to work the sugar and pineapple plantations, some of their fellow countrymen, who also envisioned getting rich abroad and returning home, were setting their sights on the mainland United States—but in much smaller numbers. In 1910 only 406 Filipinos lived in the United States, mostly in California. The trickle became a flow after the passage of the Immigration Act of 1924, which barred the entry into the United States of "aliens ineligible for citizenship," a group consisting of most non-white peoples of the world. (Since they were officially U.S. nationals with American passports, and not aliens, Filipinos, unlike other Asians, were not hampered by restrictions on entry into the United States, at least in the early years of Filipino immigration.) While in 1920 the Filipino population of the United States was 5,603, with 2,674 of those counted living in California, by 1930 the number of Filipinos in the country had risen to 45,208, with 30,470, about two-thirds, in California. More than half of the Filipinos who toiled in the Golden State in the 1920s came via Hawaii, where they had fulfilled or broken their plantation contracts. The Filipinos in California worked for low wages in agriculture, domestic service, and the hotel and restaurant industries, essentially dominating the migrant labor force, particularly in the Central Valley. Those outside of California found employment in the fishing and fish-canning industries in Alaska or on farms in Arizona, Colorado, Utah, North Dakota, and Montana. Some even ventured all the way to New York in search of seasonal work.

The few Filipinas who were part of the first wave of immigration made their way to the United States for a variety of reasons, including to join husbands or fiancés who had already secured jobs as laborers, to pursue educational opportunities or professional training, and to find employment. Unlike Filipinos, many Filipinas in America were able to secure jobs outside of agricultural and manual labor. Those with the qualifications were even able to land semiprofessional and professional jobs in medicine, education, and business.

What were working conditions like for the Filipinos in America in the 1910s, 1920s, and 1930s?

On the U.S. mainland in the 1910s, 1920s, and 1930s, Filipinos found the same low-paying, sweaty jobs as in Hawaii. Life was miserable for the Filipino farmworkers in California, who called themselves *pinoys.* While Filipino agricultural laborers in Hawaii remained on the plantations, in California they moved from farm to farm, constantly migrating with the crops, such as asparagus, lettuce, tomatoes, melons, grapes, apricots, and citrus. They engaged in punishing stoop labor, bending over the crops six days a week from dawn to dusk, sometimes in temperatures that reached well above one hundred degrees. If that were not bad enough, dust from the fields mixed with the workers' sweat, causing them to itch unbearably. The crowded makeshift shelters, akin to chicken coops, and the inedible food that their cruel employers provided them offered little relief after hours for the *pinoys.*

Filipinos who found work unloading, cleaning, cutting, and packing fish, especially salmon, in Alaska's fish-canning industry were also victimized by ruthless employers. The fish canneries themselves were dank, dark, and dismal, and the workers were subjected to serious health hazards during their long, exhausting shifts. **Carlos Bulosan,** a Filipino immigrant who came to the United States in 1930, recounts a harrowing incident in an Alaskan fish cannery in the 1930s in *America Is in the Heart* (1946), his fictionalized autobiography and one of the first works to chronicle the early Filipino experience in America: "I was working in a section called 'wash lye.' Actually a certain amount of lye was diluted in the water where I washed the beheaded fish that came down on a small escalator. One afternoon a cutter above me, working in the poor light, slashed off his right arm with the cutting machine. It happened so swiftly he did not cry out. I saw his arm floating down the water among the fish heads." Not only did Filipinos in the fish canneries face extraordinary perils on the job, they were paid less for their hardship than non-Asian employees. To make matters worse, the cannery owners withheld wages from the Filipinos' paychecks to cover "room and board" and other so-called expenses, so that in the end they earned very little for their grueling labor.

Filipino laborers in the mainland United States were swift to organize. In 1933, after the American Federation of Labor refused to help their cause, thousands of Filipino lettuce pickers in Salinas and Stockton, California, organized the Filipino Labor Union (FLU). A year later the FLU and another labor union, the Vegetable Packers Association, merged and staged a strike in Monterey County, California. The FLU was forced to end the strike when farm owners resorted to such draconian measures as burning down their camps.

In what way did Filipinos endure racism from two sides?

While their long exposure at home to Western culture and the English language made it easier for Filipinos to adjust to American life in the first decades of the twentieth century as compared to other Asian immigrants, such as the Chinese and the Japanese, who knew little of the New World before stepping foot in it, and while, as U.S. nationals (at least until 1934), not aliens, Filipinos were exempt from the discriminatory laws that hampered Asian immigration to the United States, they were ineligible for U.S. citizenship and, thus, could not enjoy its privileges, such as the right to vote or own land. Perhaps most importantly, their status as U.S. nationals did not shield them from the institutionalized racism and persecution that all Asians suffered in the nineteenth century and well into the twentieth at the hands of the white majority in America, which was extremely concerned that Asians, Filipinos included, who as a group were willing to work for rock-bottom wages, were taking their jobs and destroying their way of life.

Even worse, xenophobic, racist Americans considered Filipinos savage, violent, unscrupulous, and ignorant—the lowliest of all Asians. They, therefore, subjected Filipinos to particularly brutal treatment, which went far beyond "No Dogs or Filipinos Allowed" signs and the refusal of service in restaurants, stores, barbershops, and movie theaters as late as 1946. Between 1929 and 1939, Filipino laborers in California endured a string of violent attacks. In one particularly brutal incident, which lasted for four days in January 1930, a white mob beat up forty-six Filipinos and killed one, **Fermin Tobera,** in Watsonville, California. The six whites accused of the crime pleaded guilty but were sentenced only to probation or a couple of days behind bars.

Fellow Asian immigrants were just as unkind to Filipinos. For a long period other Asians in America viewed the Filipinos as uncivilized and filthy, and their habits strange, particularly their taste for wild weeds and grass, and their penchant for smoking and *sabong*, or cockfighting, in which prize roosters fought to the death and spectators invariably ended up in a brawl. Asians in America generally believed rumors that all Filipinos wielded switchblades and were a threat to public safety. Such negative stereotypes greatly hindered Filipinos' advancement in America.

Who was one of the first to chronicle the racism that Filipinos endured in the United States?

Carlos Bulosan is considered the voice for Filipinos in the United States. Born in the town of Binalonan, Pangasinan, Philippines, on November 24, 1913, Bulosan grew up under American colonialism. The U.S. presence was clearly evident in Binalonan: American entrepreneurs pursuing business ventures in the region took up residence in the large houses around town, and American tourists hungrily snapped photos of Filipinos, a people they considered savage and primitive.

Inspired by the example of **Abraham Lincoln,** who rose from abject poverty to the American presidency, Bulosan sailed with high hopes to Seattle in 1930, a time when the Great Depression gripped America. His hopes soon turned to anguish, when with empty pockets he signed up to work in a fish cannery in Alaska. After surviving a season in the Dickensian canneries with little pay to show for it, he became a migrant farm worker, harvesting fruits and vegetables from Washington State to Southern California. As he crisscrossed America, Bulosan experienced firsthand the blatant prejudice and racist violence aimed at Filipinos, something he was completely unprepared for, and his American dream swiftly became a nightmare. In *America Is in the Heart* (1946), his best known work, he writes:

> I came to know afterward that in many ways it was a crime to be a Filipino in California. I came to know that the public streets were not free to my people: we were stopped each time these vigilant patrolmen saw us driving a car. We were suspect each time we were seen with a white woman. And perhaps it was this narrowing of our life into an island, into a filthy segment of American society, that had driven Filipinos like Doro inward, hating everyone and despising all positive urgencies toward freedom.

For Carlos Bulosan, writing served as an escape from the harsh reality of American life. Even though he had had just three years of formal education and barely spoke English when he arrived in the United States, he emerged as one of the country's first Filipino writers writing in English. In addition to *America Is in the Heart,* Bulosan penned *The Laughter of My Father,* a short-story collection that appeared in 1942, and *The Cry and the Dedication,* a novel that was published posthumously in 1995, among other works. Despite the exploitation, racial prejudice, and inhumanity of his American experience, Carlos Bulosan somehow regained his utopian vision of America as a promised land. As he writes at the very end of *America Is in the Heart:* ". . . no man—no one at all—could destroy my faith in America again. It was something that had grown out of my defeats and successes, something shaped by my struggles for a place in this vast land, digging my hands into the rich soil here and there . . ."

Carlos Bulosan participated in America's betterment without enjoying the privilege of U.S. citizenship, much in the same way as Filipino national **O. J. Santa Maria,** who risked his life and limb fighting in the war to liberate Iraq in 2003 and was sworn in on April 11, 2003, as a U.S. citizen—in the presence of President **George W. Bush** and First Lady **Laura Bush**—*after* he was wounded on the battlefield and lay in a U.S. military hospital bed. Carlos Bulosan never did obtain U.S. citizenship. He died in Seattle on September 11, 1956, and was buried in a cemetery in a section of the city known as Queen Anne Hill. In 1984 the Asian-American community in Seattle raised funds to replace the modest marker at Bulosan's gravesite with a polished black granite headstone.

Why did Filipinos get in a jam when they dated white American women?

The great majority of Filipino immigrants of the first wave were single men. The absence of Filipinas drove many Filipinos to seek female companions outside of their enclaves. This caused the Filipinos no angst: They had long been exposed to other ethnic groups and had witnessed Spanish-Filipino marriages in their homeland as a result of colonialism. In this way the Filipino immigrant experience was dramatically different from that of Japanese male immigrants, who seldom socialized with non-Japanese women and awaited the arrival of picture brides, who were essentially wives they imported from Japan. While discriminatory laws on the American books forbidding interracial marriage contributed to the social practices of Japanese immigrants, they were mainly governed by an intense desire to preserve ethnic purity. This was true for the early waves of Chinese and Korean immigrants as well.

The Filipinos' interest in white women scandalized xenophobic American nativists, who clamored for Filipino exclusion from the United States. Despite such widespread condemnation from Anglo-Saxon America, Filipino men continued to seek the companionship of white women. (In the 1920s and 1930s, dance halls in which young white women were hired to dance with male customers were a popular venue for Filipinos looking for love.) Those who found white female companionship essentially stepped on a hornets' nest. Filipino-white couples endured society's scorn, gossip, and cruel remarks and acts, which placed an immense strain on their relationships.

Interracial couples also faced legal barriers with the passage of antimiscegenation legislation. Initially Filipinos were able to marry white women, since antimiscegenation laws on the books barred only marriages between whites and persons with African, mulatto, or Mongolian blood. Since Filipinos are descendants of the Malay, they were able to bypass these laws and legally marry white women. However, racism ruled the day, and some state legislators quickly revised their statutes to ban marriages between whites and those of the Malay race. In 1933 the California Court of Appeals, in *Roldan v. Los Angeles County*, ruled that Malays, like "Negroes, mulattoes, and Mongolians," were barred from marrying white people. By 1936 Nevada, Oregon, and Washington had passed laws banning marriages between Filipinos and whites. Thus, Filipinos in these four states who wanted to marry white women had to travel to states where such interracial marriages were not prohibited. Even after obtaining marriage certificates, these couples faced further legal challenges as legislators sought to suspend the white women's privilege of U.S. citizenship as punishment for breaking social strictures. It was not until 1948, when the California Supreme Court ruled in *Perez v. Sharp* that antimiscegenation laws violated individual civil rights, that Filipinos were finally permitted to marry the persons of their choosing without having to confront legal barriers.

Due to the difficulties inherent in marrying white women and the absence of laws prohibiting marriage between Filipinos and Mexicans, Filipino men fraternized and exchanged marriage vows with Mexican women with some frequency. Filipino men were also drawn to Mexican women because of their shared Spanish colonial history and their knowledge of the Spanish language in some instances.

What was the Tydings-McDuffie Act of 1934, and why was it bad news for Filipinos?

From the very beginning of Filipino migration to the United States, Filipinos, as U.S. nationals, had been exempt from the legislation limiting or barring the immigration of Chinese, Japanese, and eventually all persons of the Mongolian race to the United States. This did not stop American exclusionists from searching for some way to bring an end to Filipino immigration. One solution they proposed was to bestow upon the Philippines its independence so that its citizens would belong to an independent country and, thus, could be excluded from entering the United States along with other "undesirable" immigrants. This solution became the basis of the Tydings-McDuffie Act, enacted on March 24, 1934, which put in place a transitional government in the Philippines and promised the archipelago its independence in ten years, while at the same time limiting Filipino immigration to the United States to just fifty persons per year, restricting Filipinos in Hawaii from migrating to the U.S. mainland, and changing the classification of Filipinos from U.S. nationals to legal aliens. (After successful lobbying, the Hawaiian Sugar Planters Association convinced Congress to allow more Filipinos to immigrate to Hawaii, where cheap labor was needed.) Senator **Millard Tydings,** a cosponsor of the Tydings-McDuffie Act, defended using the carrot of independence for the Philippines to bring to a screeching halt Filipino immigration to the United States by declaring that "It is absolutely illogical to have an immigration policy to exclude Japanese and Chinese and permit Filipinos en masse to come into the country. . . ."

Some exclusionist Americans wanted to go beyond prohibiting Filipino immigration and clamored for the deportation of those Filipinos already in the United States. In response to such demands, the U.S. Congress passed yet another piece of anti-Filipino legislation, the Filipino Repatriation Act of 1935, which allowed for the allotment of funds for the transportation back to the Philippines of all Filipinos who desired to return to their homeland. The vast majority of Filipinos declined the offer, believing that the racial climate in the United States was more bearable than the economic morass in the Philippines. In the end, the Repatriation Act of 1935 stimulated the relocation of just 2,190 Filipinos from the United States to the Philippine Islands, a major disappointment for American exclusionists.

The Great Depression was a time of immense hardship for the people of the United States. Between 1930 and 1933 the number of unemployed Americans soared from four million to more than fourteen million. Wages plummeted from thirty-five cents an hour to fifteen cents an hour. Desperate over the shortage of jobs across the nation, nativist Americans lashed out with renewed intensity at what they perceived as unfair competition in the workforce from Filipinos and other immigrant groups, who were willing to work for low wages. The nativists' vociferous cries of outrage and protest turned increasingly to mob violence at Filipino workplaces in the Depression years. Conditions grew even more dire for unemployed Filipinos who were barely making ends meet on public assistance. In 1937, in the midst of the Great Depression, the U.S. Congress passed the Relief Appropriation Act, which gave preference for relief assistance first to U.S. citizens and then to aliens who were eligible for U.S. citizenship. Filipinos were by this time aliens ineligible for citizenship, and so their public assistance was terminated. Out of work and penniless, many had no choice but to return to the Philippines.

If Filipinos were legal aliens, why were they ineligible for U.S. citizenship?

Although they were first categorized as U.S. nationals and then as legal aliens, Filipinos were by and large ineligible for U.S. citizenship before 1946. The laws governing citizenship in effect until that year extended naturalization rights only to white and black immigrants. Legislation passed in 1925 made an exception for those Filipinos who had served in the U.S. armed forces for at least three years and had received an honorable discharge. Although most Filipinos were little more than mess stewards in the military (they were barred from training for other posts), they were granted the right to apply for U.S. citizenship. With naturalization papers in hand, these Filipinos could no longer be legally excluded from the benefits and privileges afforded U.S. citizens. They were also spared the humiliation that their fellow Filipinos experienced in 1940, when they were forced to register with the authorities and have their fingerprints taken. Still, Filipino naturalized U.S. citizens were not protected from racial prejudice and harassment.

Did Filipinos serve in the U.S. armed forces during World War II?

At the onset of World War II, Filipinos in the United States, whose classification had changed from U.S. nationals to legal aliens with the passage of the Tydings-McDuffie Act in 1934, were prohibited from enlisting in the U.S. armed forces or working in the defense industry. However, on the heels of the Japanese invasion of the Philippines on December 8, 1941, Secretary of War **Henry Stimson** opened the door for Filipinos to serve in the U.S. Army by organizing them, much in the way that Japanese Americans were, into a segregated army regiment, the all-volunteer First Filipino Infantry Battalion, which was activated on April 1, 1942. In July of that year, the battalion was reorganized as the First Filipino Regiment. (A few weeks later, President **Franklin D. Roosevelt** issued an executive order that made it possible for Filipino civilians to work in the U.S. government and in the defense industry. Filipino plantation laborers in Hawaii provided some of the manpower that the defense industry so desperately needed.) On February 20, 1943, one thousand Filipinos of the First Filipino

Infantry Battalion were granted U.S. citizenship in a ceremony held on the parade grounds of Camp Beale, near Marysville, California. Some months before, in October 1942, a second Filipino army unit, the Second Filipino Infantry Battalion, had been organized. Both the First Filipino Infantry Battalion and the Second Filipino Infantry Battalion fought with bravery in New Guinea and then in the Philippines.

Filipinos in the U.S. Navy were not afforded the same opportunity to display their courage under fire. While the U.S. Navy had begun recruiting Filipinos in the Philippines before the ink was barely dry on the Treaty of Paris ending the Spanish-American War of 1898 and permitted Filipinos in the Philippines, Hawaii and the U.S. mainland to serve during World War I, they were relegated to the entry-level post of mess steward. During World War II the navy barred Filipinos from new assignments, keeping them in the galleys.

There is a group of Filipinos who fought to defend the United States and the cause of freedom during World War II that has largely been forgotten. At the beginning of the war, President Roosevelt issued an executive order calling the military forces of the Philippines into the American armed forces, promising those Filipinos who served veterans benefits. Approximately 142,000 Filipinos, who were American nationals at the time, heeded Roosevelt's call and were placed under the command of General **Douglas MacArthur.** The Filipinos fought alongside American citizen soldiers in the Philippines against the invading Japanese in the battles of Bataan and Corregidor, and in smaller fights that hampered the Japanese in their campaign to conquer the Western Pacific. Thousands of them died defending both the Philippines and the American flag. And yet, in 1946, after the war was won, the U.S. Congress passed the Recision Act, which dramatically reduced veterans benefits for Filipino veterans but not for any other allied nationals who served under the American command. Nearly half a century passed before the Filipino veterans received any recognition from the U.S.

government for their contributions in World War II. In 1990 Congress granted U.S. citizenship to those Filipino veterans who could prove they had served as members of the U.S. armed forces during World War II. With citizenship papers in hand, approximately 26,000 of the Filipino veterans, many of them disabled, immigrated to the United States in the 1990s. However, to this day they have not been afforded the full medical and retirement benefits enjoyed by other American veterans.

During World War II, the American public warmed to the Filipinos in the Philippines and those in their midst because of their invaluable contributions to the outcome of the war. In recognition of these efforts, on the eve of granting the Philippines its sovereignty—which was delayed until July 4, 1946, due to the Japanese invasion and subsequent occupation of the Philippine archipelago, which lasted until September 3, 1945—the U.S. Congress passed the Filipino Immigration and Naturalization Act, which extended naturalization rights to Filipino residents in the United States who entered the country prior to March 24, 1943. Nearly ten thousand Filipinos seized the opportunity to become naturalized citizens of the United States.

When did Filipinos begin to immigrate to the United States in significant numbers once again?

Filipino immigration to the United States began to pick up after World War II, thanks largely to the arrival of Filipinas (and their children), who circumvented the quotas on Filipino immigration dictated by the Tydings-McDuffie Act of 1934 by taking advantage of the 1945 War Brides Act, which permitted Asian women married to American servicemen who fought during World War II to enter the United States. Due in large measure to the influx of Filipina war brides in the aftermath of the war, the Filipino community in America, which had been predominantly male since the early days of Filipino immigration, underwent a decisive shift in its male-female ratio. By 1960, 37.1 percent of the 176,310 persons of Filipino descent in the United States (according to U.S. Bureau of the Census figures) were female. These Filipinas were largely responsible for the strides their ethnic community made toward assimilation into the American mainstream in the postwar era. They found employment in the larger Anglo society, which exposed them to American customs and practices, and started families, passing their knowledge of America on to their children. At the same time, they played a vital part in bolstering their community's solidarity and cohesiveness.

The passage of the Immigration Act of 1965 (see *What was the Immigration Act of 1965?*, p. 50) unleashed a second wave of Filipino immigration to the United States. This second wave, which continues to this day, was initially comprised in large measure of Filipinos seeking to be reunited with their families and to escape the widespread corruption and disorder of the regime of **Ferdinand E. Marcos,** who assumed the presidency of the Philippines in 1965 and ruled until 1986, when he was ousted from power by a civilian-military uprising. The second wave of Filipino immigration soon made Filipinos in America one of the country's largest ethnic groups: 343,060 were counted in the 1970 U.S. census, roughly double the number tallied in 1960, and a decade later, in 1980, 774,652 were counted, more than double the tally for 1970.

Why did Filipinos immigrate to the United States in the 1980s and 1990s?

The civilian-military forces who drove the regime of **Ferdinand Marcos** from power installed **Corazon C. Aquino,** the widow of the prominent Filipino politician **Benigno Aquino,** as president of the Philippines on February 25, 1986. (Benigno Aquino had lost to Marcos in rigged presidential elections in 1978, had gone into exile in the United States in 1980, and was assassinated in 1983 upon his return to the Philippines.) Despite her popularity both at home and abroad, Corazon Aquino was ill-equipped to revive the country's ailing economy, combat its huge foreign debt, and contend with Communist and Muslim insurgents, daunting challenges that fueled the second wave of Filipino emigration to the United States. Ultimately her administration was beset by accusations of corruption and human rights abuses, and she chose not to run in the presidential election held in May 1992. **Fidel Ramos,** army chief of staff and presidential advisor during the Aquino presidency, emerged the victor of the 1992 election, garnering just 24 percent of the vote in a seven-way race.

Fidel Ramos inherited a nation plagued by grinding poverty (more than half of all Filipinos were severely impoverished), a debilitating energy crisis, a decaying infrastructure, an enormous foreign debt, and Communist and Muslim insurgencies. While the Ramos government achieved some success in squelching the insurgencies, it was ineffective at alleviating the nation's poverty, leaving the way open for **Joseph Ejercito Estrada,** who pledged to work on behalf of the impoverished masses, to win the presidential election held in May 1998 with overwhelming support. However, rather than giving to the poor, Estrada gave to himself, illegally amassing a huge fortune, about $80 million. Charged with corruption, he was deposed in a constitutional coup in February 2001, and his vice president, **Gloria Macapagal-Arroyo,** was installed in his place. In her few years in office, she has made little progress in tackling the Philippines' longstanding ills, as she acknowledged in January 2003: "[The Philippines is] now closer to the category of backward countries, wherein powerful, selfish interests are able to exploit poverty and ignorance." With ever-worsening economic conditions, political oppression, and deepening poverty and despair in the Philippines, Filipino emigration to the United States remained steady in the 1990s and into the first decade of the twenty-first century.

How have Filipinos of the second wave differed from those of the first wave?

While Filipinos of the first wave of immigration were primarily unskilled workers who had to settle for low-paying, back-breaking work in the western United States and Hawaii, the majority of second-wave Filipinos, in what amounts to a brain drain, have been skilled workers, intellectuals, and highly educated professionals—including physicians and nurses, accountants, engineers, and teachers—who have settled on the East Coast, particularly in New York and New Jersey, as well as on the West Coast. Given more stringent U.S. certification requirements, many of these professionals have been barred over the years from practicing in their fields of specialization until they received further training. Those who have had neither the time nor resources for such training have had to settle for jobs below their capabilities.

While the vast majority of first-wave Filipino immigrants ventured to America alone, those of the second wave have generally arrived with their spouses and children or have sent for them once they have established a foothold in American society. As a result of this influx of spouses and children, by 1980 the Filipino community was 51.7 percent female.

How many Filipino Americans are there, and where do they live?

The U.S. Bureau of the Census counted 2,364,815 persons of Filipino ancestry (either Filipino alone or in combination with at least one other race or Asian ethnicity) residing in the United States in 2000, up from 1,406,770 in 1990. Of those tallied in Census 2000, 1,850,314 described themselves as Filipino alone, while 456,690 categorized themselves as Filipino and at least one other race, and 57,811 as Filipino and at least one other Asian ethnicity. Filipino-American community leaders argue that if Filipinos who entered the United States illegally are taken into consideration then the actual size of the Filipino population in the United States in 2000 was 3 million. At nearly 2.4 million strong (or possibly more), Americans and nationals of Filipino descent constitute the second-largest Asian-American subgroup in the United States, comprising 18.1 percent of the Asian-American population.

According to Census 2000 data, the five states with the largest Filipino (alone) population in 2000 were California (918,678), Hawaii (170,635), Illinois (86,298), New Jersey (85,245), and New York (81,681). These figures reflect only those individuals who described themselves as Filipino alone. Most of the 918,678 persons with Filipino roots counted in California call San Francisco and Los Angeles home.

How is the Filipino community in America faring?

Most of the persons of Filipino ancestry counted in Census 2000 are immigrants who entered the United States in the years since 1980. A large majority of these immigrants went on to become naturalized U.S. citizens. According to the Immigration and Naturalization Service, 65.4 percent of those Filipinos who entered the United States in 1982 had become naturalized citizens by 1997, making Filipinos the immigrant group with the second-highest rate of naturalization in the nation.

Those Filipinos who have immigrated to the United States in recent decades are for the most part educated professionals with some proficiency in English. While they have encountered difficulties related to licensure in the United States, most have persevered and have succeeded in restarting their professional careers and acculturating to the United States. Filipino Americans born in the United States, who are called Fil-Ams by some, are generally not as well educated as these foreign-born Filipinos, and for this reason, the Filipino-American community as a whole has not enjoyed the same degree of success in the labor market as Chinese and Japanese Americans.

Ever since the Bush administration opened up a second front in the Philippines in its war against terrorism after drawing a connection between the Philippine Muslim separatist group Abu Sayyaf and al-Qaeda, the terrorist organization responsible for the attacks on the World Trade Center and the Pentagon on September 11, 2001, Filipino Americans and Filipino nationals in the United States have had to fight the insidious belief that they harbor hordes of terrorists and have been subjected to indiscriminate acts of violence, racial profiling, and even detention. The obvious truth of the matter is that Filipino Americans are by and large patriotic, hardworking Americans, who have contributed to making the United States the great nation that it is.

Why are there no "Little Manilas" in America, and what impact has this had on Filipinos?

Centuries of Spanish colonial rule in the Philippines, followed by nearly a half century of U.S. colonial tutelage, or Americanization, had the effect of diluting Filipinos' sense of cultural cohesiveness. One consequence of this is that since the end of World War II, new Filipino immigrants have exhibited a greater affinity for American culture and, conversely, a weaker attachment to the concept of ethnic community than other new Asian immigrants. While the Chinese, Japanese, Korean, Vietnamese, and other Asian subgroups in the United States found security in close-knit ethnic enclaves, centers of social and economic activity that bind the generations together, which thrive to this day—such as Chinatowns, Little Tokyos, Koreatowns, and Little Saigons—the Filipinos, despite their large numbers in relation to most other Asian subgroups, mainly established communities, called Little Manilas, that were fleeting in nature. This is not to say that Filipinos in the United States have never stuck together; they just have not done so with the same intensity and duration as other Asian subgroups.

This lack of cultural cohesiveness has made it difficult for Filipino Americans born in the United States, many of whom speak only a few words of Pilipino or of a Philippine dialect, to learn about their cultural heritage, which in turn fosters their invisibility in American society, as evidenced by the scant attention the American public education system, the media, and the book publishing world pay to Filipino Americans in comparison to Americans of Chinese, Japanese, Korean, and Vietnamese ancestry. Invisibility has in turn engendered a collective identity crisis and a tendency for self-deprecation among Filipino Americans. (Self-deprecation runs so deep that younger Filipino Americans even began in the 1980s to refer to themselves by the acronym FLIP, which stands for "funny little island people" or "flippin' little island people.")

In recent decades, Filipino Americans have established a number of organizations to combat the Filipino community's silence and invisibility in the United States and to promote its welfare. One is the Filipino American National Historical Society, which was formed in Seattle in 1982 "to promote understanding, education, enlightenment, appreciation and enrichment through the identification, gathering, preservation and dissemination of the history and culture of Filipino Americans." Another is the National Federation of Filipino American Associations, which was organized in Washington, D.C., in 1997. It is committed to promoting Filipino Americans' active participation in civic and national affairs and an awareness of their contributions to American life, to "securing social justice, equal opportunity and fair treatment of Filipino Americans through advocacy and legislative and policy initiatives at all levels of government," to bolstering institutions dedicated to Filipinos' cultural heritage, and to eradicating "prejudices, stereotypes, and ignorance of Filipino Americans."

FILIPINO INVISIBILITY

Despite the media barrage of information, the ordinary citizen in suburbia cannot say whether the Malay is a Mongolian; whether the Filipino is an African, Chinese, Japanese, or what. Even today, because of the shape of my eyes and nose, I am mistaken for being a Japanese or Chinese at the university, in the desolate malls of New England, along small-town streets of the Midwest and the South, almost everywhere. And when I tell the curious observer I am from the Philippines (an original, as they say, "born in the islands"), indeed, the image of an island in the Caribbean immediately flashes in their minds, especially because my name (and those of most Filipinos) is Spanish in origin.

—E. San Juan Jr., *From Exile to Diaspora: Versions of the Filipino Experience in the United States* (1998)

Do Filipino Americans wield political clout?

Persons of Filipino descent in America have been underrepresented in government since the early days of Filipino immigration. While Filipinos have been quiet in the political arena, they have not been silent: A fair number have held elected office at the local and state level, mainly in Hawaii, and a handful have served in federal government.

Filipino Americans were first elected to public office in Hawaii, where the Asian majority provided support to Filipino-American candidates. The first Filipino American elected official was **Peter Aduja,** who was born in Ilocos Sur, Philippines, and immigrated to the United States at age eight. In 1955 Aduja was elected to the Hawaii House of Representatives. After losing his bid for a second term, he was appointed deputy attorney general by Hawaii governor **Samuel B. King.** Then, in 1966, Aduja was elected once more to the Hawaii House, this time serving for three consecutive terms. Another Filipino American, **Bernaldo D. Bicoy,** was elected to the Hawaii House of Representatives in 1958. After Hawaii was granted statehood in 1959, Bicoy ran for a seat in the new State Senate but was defeated. In 1968 voters returned him to the Hawaii House, where he served for one term. In 1958 **Pedro de la Cruz,** a Philippine-born immigrant from Hawaii, joined Bicoy in the Hawaii House of Representatives, where he worked on behalf of Hawaiians for sixteen years, until his defeat in 1974.

Other notable Filipinos who held public office in Hawaii include **Alfred Lareta,** who in 1962 became the first Filipino American named to a state cabinet position in the United States, when Hawaii governor **John A. Burns** appointed him director of the state's Department of Labor and Industrial Relations. **Eduardo E. Malapit** earned the distinction of being the first Filipino-American mayor in the United States when he was elected to steer Kauai in 1975. And in 1994 **Benjamin Cayetano,** who had previously served in the Hawaii legislature and as the state's lieutenant governor, was elected governor of Hawaii, making him the first and only Filipino-American governor in U.S. history.

As far as the rest of the nation is concerned, Filipina American **Thelma Garcia Buchholdt** achieved a political first in 1974, when she was elected to represent a predominantly white district in the Alaska House of Representatives, a post she occupied until 1983. And, in 1991 **Gene Canque Liddell** became the first Filipina-American mayor of an American city when she was elected to lead Lacey City, Washington. The sole Filipino American elected to the U.S. House of Representatives is Democratic congressman **Robert Cortez Scott,** who currently represents Virginia's Third Congressional District, which is home to a significant Filipino-American community. Scott, whose maternal grandfather was of Filipino descent and who also has African-American roots, joined the House in 1993, after serving in the Virginia House of Delegates from 1978 to 1983 and in the Virginia State Senate from 1983 to early 1993. Over the years Congressman Scott has consistently backed legislation geared toward bolstering the nation's health care, education, employment, economic development, and social services.

Who are some other prominent Filipino Americans?

There are far too many prominent Filipino Americans to mention, but here are a few. Artist **Eulalio Buena Silva,** who was born in Baguio City, Philippines, in 1941, attained international recognition beginning in the 1980s for his portraits, landscapes, still lifes, and figurative compositions, which hang in public and private art collections and institutions around the world. Among his most renowned works are his portraits of Pope **Paul VI** and Pope **John Paul II,** which are housed in the Vatican Art Collection, Vatican City, Italy, and his life-size paintings of President **Ronald Reagan** and California senator **Dianne Feinstein.**

Illustrator **José Espiritu Aruego,** who was born in Manila on August 9, 1932, and came to the United States in the 1950s to study at the Parsons School of Design in New York City, derives inspiration for his work from his childhood experiences in the Philippines. Aruego first became known for his cartoons, which appeared in such leading magazines as the *Saturday Evening Post, Look,* and *The New Yorker.* In 1969 he turned to illustrating children's books, publishing his first, *The King and His Friends,* that year. His delightful *Whose Mouse Are You?* (1970) was selected as an American Library Association Notable Book, and his *Juan and the Asuangs* (1970) captured the *New York Times* Outstanding Picture Book of the Year Award. All told, José Aruego has illustrated over sixty books, ten of which he wrote.

Journalist, novelist, and activist **Ninotchka Rosca** left the Philippines in the 1970s after she was imprisoned for protesting President **Ferdinand Marcos**'s declaration of martial law. Since coming to the United States, Rosca has authored five works, including two critically acclaimed novels, *State of War*

(1988), a novel within a novel, and *Twice Blessed*, which garnered her the American Book Award for excellence in literature in 1993. Rosca is a cofounder of GABRIELA Network, a Philippine-U.S. women's solidarity organization established in 1989 to address issues impacting the women and children of the Philippines. Since its inception, the organization has focused on the Philippine mail-order-bride industry, forced labor migration, and prostitution. (More than half a million Filipinos leave the Philippines annually to work abroad for low pay as domestic servants and prostitutes.)

Another distinguished writer is **Jessica Tarahata Hagedorn,** who was born in the Philippines in 1949 and immigrated to the United States with her family at age fourteen. She caught the attention of readers and critics with the publication in 1990 of her debut novel, *Dogeaters,* which she has described as "a love letter to my motherland: a fact and fiction borne of rage, shame, pride. . . ." In 1990 *Dogeaters*—whose title makes reference to one of the racial epithets Americans once hurled at Filipinos—was nominated for the National Book Award and won the American Book Award from the Before Columbus Foundation. The year 1993 saw the publication of Hagedorn's much-discussed work *Danger and Beauty*—a collection of poems, prose pieces, cultural commentary, and performance text—as well as a work that she edited, the groundbreaking collection *Charlie Chan Is Dead: An Anthology of Contemporary Asian American Fiction.* In 1996 Jessica Hagedorn published her second novel, *The Gangster of Love,* about a Filipina growing up in post-1965, neoconservative America.

Another Filipina-American writer is **Cecilia Manguerra Brainard,** who was born in Cebu City on the island of Cebu, Philippines, in 1947 and immigrated to the United States in 1969 to study film at the University of California, Los Angeles, and to escape the dictatorial regime of Ferdinand Marcos. Brainard is the author of the novel *When the Rainbow Goddess Wept* (1994), which chronicles a family's flight during the Japanese occupation of the Philippines; several short-story collections, including *Woman With Horns and Other Stories* (1988) and *Acapulco at Sunset and Other Stories* (1995); and essay collections, among them *Journey of 100 Years: Reflections on the Centennial of Philippine Independence* (1999), which she coedited with **Edmundo F. Litton.**

Singer **Jocelyn Enriquez,** the "Queen of Freestyle," who was born to Filipino immigrant parents in San Francisco and received formal training with the San Francisco Girls Chorus and the San Francisco Opera Company, is the first Filipino American to make a splash in the mainstream American music industry. It all began in 1997, when Tommy Boy Records released her second album, *Jocelyn,* with its hit singles "Do You Miss Me?" and "A Little Bit of Ecstasy," which brought her fame overnight. The singer went on to collaborate with **Amber** and **Ultra Nate** on the remake of the song "If You Could Read My Mind" for the soundtrack to the motion picture *54* (1998) and with **Thunderpuss** on the song "So Fabulous, So Fierce" for the soundtrack to Disney's classic canine sequel *102 Dalmations* (2000), starring **Glenn Close.** Jocelyn Enriquez released her second album, *All My Life,* in 2003. A single from the album, "No Way No How," soared to number eighteen on the Billboard Club Dance Music/Club Play Chart by spring 2003.

On the big screen, **Lou Diamond Phillips,** who was born **Lou Upchurch** in the Philippines on February 17, 1962, grew up in Flour Bluff, Texas, and has described himself as part Filipino, Hawaiian, Cherokee, and Scots-Irish, won instant recognition in 1987 with his starring role as **Ritchie Valens**—the Mexican-American rock star who perished in a plane crash in 1959, just as his career was taking off—in the motion picture *La Bamba.* A year later the actor won enthusiastic applause for his performances in *Stand and Deliver* (1988) and *Young Guns* (1988). In 1995 he took the stage as King Mongkut in a critically acclaimed production of **Rodgers** & **Hammerstein**'s *The King and I,* which garnered six Tony Award nominations, including one for Best Actor for Phillips. Phillips was back on the silver screen in 1996 in *Courage Under Fire.* Since then he has played starring and supporting roles in fifteen films, including the satirical comedy *Picking Up the Pieces* (2000), starring **Woody Allen,** and *Hollywood Homicide* (2003), starring **Harrison Ford.**

Hawaiian-born actress-model **Tia Carrere,** who was born **Althea Dujenio Janairo** in Honolulu on January 2, 1967, and is of Filipino, Spanish, and Chinese ancestry, first caught the attention of American audiences with her role as Jade Soong on the ABC daytime drama *General Hospital.* Since 1988 she has starred in a number of motion pictures, including the 1992 comedy *Wayne's World,* which made her an overnight Hollywood sensation, its sequel *Wayne's World 2* (1993), the action comedy *True Lies* (1994), and Disney Pictures' animated comedy *Lilo and Stitch* (2002). Actor-screenwriter **Rob Schneider,** who was born on October 31, 1963, in San Francisco to a Filipina mother and a Jewish father, was a writer and actor for *Saturday Night Live* from 1991 to 1994, when he left the show to pursue a big-screen career. Since then he has landed roles in televison series and motion pictures, mainly comedies, including the box-office smashes *The Waterboy* (1998) and *Big Daddy* (1999), and *Deuce Bigalow: Male Gigolo* (1999), in which he played the lead.

In ballet, Filipina **Maniya Barredo,** who left the Philippines for New York City at the age of eighteen to attend a summer workshop at the prestigious Joffrey Ballet School and has resided in the United States ever since (but remains a Filipino citizen), was selected by the legendary ballerina and choreographer **Alicia Alonso** to represent Canada at the International Ballet Festival in 1976, which was held in Cuba. In ensuing years Barredo worked with **Mikhail Baryshnikov, Maya Plisetskaya,** and **Burton Taylor;** earned the title, bestowed by Dame **Margot Fonteyn,** of "Prima Ballerina of the Philippines" for her stellar performances in *Swan Lake* and *Giselle* on the world's stages; and danced for nearly two decades beginning in 1977 with the Atlanta Ballet, one of America's most prestigious dance companies. After she retired from the stage, Maniya Barredo served as an artistic consultant to the Ballethnic Dance Company, Atlanta's first and only professional black ballet company, and to the Cultural Attache to the Philippines, and as artistic director of the Atlanta School of Ballet Performing Ensemble. She is nowadays director and CEO of the Metropolitan Ballet Theater, a dance school that was established in 1998 in Roswell, Georgia.

In journalism, Filipino Americans **Byron Acohido** (who also has Korean roots) and **Alex Tizon,** journalists with the *Seattle Times,* were awarded the Pulitzer Prize in 1997, one of the field's highest honors, for their fine reporting. In fashion, **Josie Cruz Natori,** who was born in Manila in 1947 and went to New York in 1964 to study, founded Natori Co., her luxury lingerie label, in 1977. Her products, which are known for their bold patterns, vibrant colors, embroidery, and detailing, and express both Asian and American aesthetics, are sold at fine department stores.

Who are some world-class Filipino-American athletes?

The many Filipino-American world-class athletes include boxer **Pancho Villa,** who is considered the greatest Asian boxer of all time. Born **Francisco Guilledo** in Ilog, Negros Occidental, Philippines, on August 1, 1901, Villa proved by age eighteen to be a formidable boxer with an unrelenting style and attracted the attention of a manager/promoter of Filipino fighters by the name of **Frank Churchill,** who invited him to box in the United States in 1922. On September 14, 1922, about three months after he arrived in America, Villa knocked out former bantamweight champion **John Lesky** (who was known in the world of boxing as Johnny Buff) in the eleventh round to capture the American flyweight title. After successfully defending his title in his next eight bouts in 1922 and 1923, Villa lost it to the quick-footed **Frankie Genaro** on March 1, 1923, in a controversial fifteen-round decision.

Since the fight was so close and Villa was deemed a better draw, he was chosen to box the Welsh boxing great **Jimmy Wilde,** the "Mighty Atom," for the world flyweight title in a match held in New York City on June 18, 1923. Villa outlasted Wilde in the ring and went on to defend his title in several fights. On July 4, 1925, he battled **Jimmy McLarnin** in Oakland, California, in a non-title bout even though he was in pain from a recent wisdom tooth extraction. A subsequent visit to the dentist uncovered an infection, and Villa was advised to rest and come back for a follow-up visit. The boxer ignored the advice, and on July 14, 1925, succumbed to the infection, which had spread to his throat cavity. With 73 career victories in 105 bouts and 22 career knockouts, Pancho Villa was inducted into *The Ring* magazine's Boxing Hall of Fame in 1961 and into the International Boxing Hall of Fame in 1994.

Another Filipino powerhouse in the boxing ring was **Salvador "Dado" Marino,** who was born in Olowalu, Maui, and turned pro in 1941. On August 1, 1950, Marino clinched the world flyweight title when he defeated defending flyweight champion **Terry Allen** of England in a bout in Honolulu Stadium. Soon after losing the title to Japan's **Yoshio Shirai** in Tokyo in 1952, Marino retired from boxing with a career record of 57-14-3. He later moved to California, where he died in Gardena in 1989. In 2003 cnnsi.com, a CNN and *Sports Illustrated* Web site, ranked Marino among its "50 Greatest Sports Figures."

The first Filipino American in Major League Baseball was outfielder **Bobby Balcena,** who was born in San Pedro, California, on August 1, 1925. After numerous seasons of spectacular minor league play with the Seattle Rainiers of the Pacific Coast League, Balcena enjoyed just seven games and two official at-bats in the majors after he was called up to the Cincinnati Reds late in the 1956 season. In 1998 outfielder **Benny Agbayani,** who hails from Hawaii and is known as a clutch hitter, hit fourteen home runs in just 276 at-bats for the New

York Mets. It was Agbayani's dramatic home run in the thirteenth inning of Game Three against the San Francisco Giants in the 2000 National League Championship that clinched the Mets' victory. The slugger played another season with the Mets before he was traded to the Colorado Rockies prior to the 2002 season. In August 2002 the Boston Red Sox claimed Agbayani off waivers from the Rockies, and he started the 2003 season as a reserve Red Sox outfielder.

NFL player **Roman Gabriel,** one of few Filipino Americans to play professional football, got off to a stellar start when, as an All-American quarterback for North Carolina State University, he was the Los Angeles Rams' first-round pick in the 1962 AFL draft. He played for the Rams for a decade, the highlight of which was being named the NFL Most Valuable Player and NFL Player of the Year in 1969, after throwing twenty-four touchdown passes and only seven interceptions. In 1973 Gabriel signed on with the Philadelphia Eagles. Suffering from chronic injuries, he retired from football in 1977, having amassed 201 touchdowns and 29,444 yards in his sixteen playing seasons as a pro.

One of the first Filipina-American athletes to earn recognition is **Victoria Manalo Draves,** who made history at the XIV Olympic Games in London in 1948 as the first woman to win Olympic gold in both the women's platform and springboard diving events. Of Filipino and English descent, the swimmer used her mother's maiden name, Draves, while training at swim clubs in California out of concern that she would be barred from entering if it were known that she was Filipina. After capturing Olympic gold medals in 1948, Victoria Manalo Draves retired from swimming, and in 1969 she was inducted into the International Swimming Hall of Fame.

Filipina-American ice skater **Tai Babylonia** and her partner **Randy Gardner** won the pairs competition at the U.S. Nationals five consecutive times between 1976 and 1980 and also captured the pairs event at the World Championships in 1979, ending the nearly decade-and-a-half-long Soviet domination of pairs skating. Babylonia and Gardner were favored to win the pairs skating competition at the Winter Olympics in Lake Placid in 1980; sadly, their hopes for gold were shattered when Randy Gardner fell during a warm-up session due to a groin injury he had sustained earlier and the pair had to withdraw from the competition. After the 1980 Olympics they skated professionally for almost two decades, until 1996. In 1992 Tai Babylonia and Randy Gardner were inducted into the United States Figure Skating Hall of Fame in Colorado Springs, Colorado.

SOME IMPORTANT WORKS BY ASIAN AMERICANS

Carlos Bulosan, *America Is in the Heart* (1946)

Lin Yutang, *Chinatown Family* (1948)

Hisaye Yamamoto, "The Legend of Miss Sasagawara" (short story, 1950)

Jade Snow Wong, *Fifth Chinese Daughter* (1950)

Monica Sone, *Nisei Daughter* (1953)

Chin Yang Lee, *Flower Drum Song* (1957)

John Okada, *No-No Boy* (1957)

Louis Chu, *Eat a Bowl of Tea* (1961)

Richard E. Kim, *Lost Names: Scenes from a Korean Boyhood* (1970)

Frank Chin, *The Year of the Dragon* (1974)

Maxine Hong Kingston, *The Woman Warrior: Memoirs of a Girlhood Among Ghosts* (1976)

Shawn Hsu Wong, *Homebase* (1979)

Kim Ronyoung, *Clay Walls* (1987)

Yoshiko Uchida, *Picture Bride* (1987)

Cynthia Kadohata, *The Floating World* (1989)

Amy Tan, *The Joy Luck Club* (1989)

The Kitchen God's Wife (1991)

The Bonesetter's Daughter (2001)

Jessica Hagedorn, *Dogeaters* (1990)

Gish Jen, *Typical American* (1991)

Mona in the Promised Land (1996)

Gus Lee, *China Boy* (1991)

David Wong Louie, *Pangs of Love* (1991)

Lydia Yuriko Minatoya, *Talking to High Monks in the Snow* (1992)

Garrett Hongo, ed., *The Open Boat: Poems from Asian America* (1993)

Nina Vida, *Goodbye, Saigon* (1994)

Julie Shigekuni, *A Bridge Between Us* (1995)

Lan Cao, *Monkey Bridge* (1997)

Lydia Yuriko Minatoya, *The Strangeness of Beauty* (1999)

Which holidays do Filipino Americans celebrate?

Holy Week (*Mahal na Araw*), Easter (*Pasko ng Pagkabuhay*), and Christmas (*Pasko*) are the most important holidays for Filipino Americans, the overwhelming majority of whom are Roman Catholic. Christmas festivities begin in mid-December for most Filipino Americans, who typically attend daily mass in the early morning from December 16 to December 24. The climax of the week is the midnight Christmas Eve Mass and *noche buena,* the Christmas Eve feast. Before the mass there is a traditional procession through the streets that reenacts the story of Christ's birth, ending at the church. The birth of Christ is also the focal point of the fiesta season in January, ten days of daily mass in honor of the Christ child, meant to highlight the values of charity and understanding. The holiday ends with the Feast of El Niño, during which a procession brings the Christ child to the church.

As a way to preserve cultural traditions, many Filipino communities in America celebrate their own fiestas as well as Philippine national holidays, such as Philippine Independence Day on June 12 and Rizal Day on December 30, which commemorates the life of Dr. **José Rizal.** Rizal, the national hero of the Philippines, worked for a peaceful liberation of the Philippines from Spanish rule, which led to his arrest, conviction of sedition, and execution by a firing squad on December 30, 1896. At the various fiestas, the *rondalla,* or string band, provides traditional Filipino music, and celebrants perform traditional folk dances, such as the *fandango saw ila,* which demands dexterity, since each dancer must balance an oil lamp on top of his or her head and in each hand. *Tinikling* dancers also perform intricate dances over and around bamboo poles. Beauty pageants are another common feature of Filipino American fiestas.

What are some favorite foods of Filipino Americans?

Filipino Americans are fans of both "American" cooking and the distinctive cuisine of the Philippines. East meets West in the Filipino kitchen, as in the culture, and Malayan, Chinese, Japanese, Spanish, and American culinary influences are readily apparent. The popular cooking methods of *adobado* (marinading) and *guisado* (sauteeing) and such dishes as *arroz valenciana* (a chicken and rice stew), *menudo* (pork stew), *empanadas* (flaky beef or chicken turnovers), and *leche flan* (custard) reflect centuries of Spanish dominance. Asian influences are readily apparent in such dishes as *pancit Canton* (fried noodles, which are Chinese in origin) and *lumpia* (fried egg rolls), which are filled with pork and vegetables, and in the abundance of steamed rice at the Filipino table. An indication of Western influences, Filipino cuisine is characterized by mild seasoning, with garlic, palm vinegar, green tamarind, coconut milk, and the *calamansi*, a tiny lime, figuring prominently. Filipinos also flavor their food with native sauces, such as *patis* and *bagoong*, both with a fermented fish base.

Filipinos are particularly fond of barbecued and fried meats and fish. In fact *sinangag* (fried rice) is often served for breakfast with a side of *longanisa* (pan-fried marinated pork patties), *tapa* (thinly sliced pan-fried marinated beef), or *tocino* (thinly sliced pan-fried marinated pork). A popular drink among Filipino Americans is *salabat*, a sweet and fragrant hot tea made with fresh ginger root and sugar. *Salabat* is the drink of choice when Filipino Americans need an energy boost. Another popular drink is *halo-halo*, a milkshake usually concocted from about ten ingredients, including jackfruit, sweet red beans, coconut, egg custard, red gelatin, and milk, and sometimes served with a scoop of ice cream.

FIVE

South Asian Americans

ASIAN-INDIAN AMERICANS

What were Asian Indians in America called in the early days and later?

How did scholarship bring Asian Indians to America at the dawn of the twentieth century?

When did Asian-Indian laborers first make their way to the United States?

Were Asian Indians treated better than other Asian immigrant laborers in the first decades of the twentieth century?

Who was Bhagat Singh Thind, and how did Asian Indians in the United States "change color" in 1923?

How else were Asian Indians affected by the U.S. Supreme Court's decision in United States v. Bhagat Singh Thind*?*

What were the Pacific Coast Hindustani Association and the Gadar Party?

Did many Asian-Indian women come to the United States between the 1890s and World War II?

How did Asian-Indian Sikhs, Muslims, and Hindus maintain their religious practices in America in the first half of the twentieth century?

Which changes in U.S. immigration and naturalization policy in the post-war era impacted Asian Indians?

How did Asian-Indian immigration change after 1965?

What motivated Asian Indians to come to the United States after 1965, and how successful have they been?

Have Asian Indians encountered rampant discrimination and racism in America since 1965?

Have Asian Indians formed organizations to counter racism and xenophobia in American society?

Who are some distinguished Asian-Indian Americans in the music, literary, and film worlds?

Who are some prominent Asian-Indian Americans in science, medicine, and business?

Who was Dalip Singh Saund?

Where do America's Hindus, Sikhs, and Muslims with roots in India worship nowadays?

Which secular and religious holidays do Asian Indians in America observe?

What is Ayurveda?

Who is Deepak Chopra?

What foods are found on the Asian-Indian American table?

PAKISTANI AMERICANS

What brought Pakistanis to the United States?

How many Pakistani Americans are there, and where do they live?

How did the tragedy of September 11, 2001, impact Pakistanis in the United States?

THE OTHER AMERICANS OF SOUTH ASIAN DESCENT

What brought Bangladeshis to America's shores, and where do they live?

How many Sri Lankans live in the United States, and where have they settled?

What about Nepalese in the United States?

And what of the Bhutanese?

South Asian Americans have roots in India, Pakistan, Bangladesh, Sri Lanka, Nepal, and Bhutan. While the historical record indicates that a traveler from Madras visited the United States as early as 1790, and small numbers of South Asians began arriving on America's shores around the turn of the twentieth century, it would not be until the last quarter of that century that South Asian immigration to the United States would mushroom. Asian-Indian Americans are by far the largest of the South Asian subgroups in the United States, and they are the third-largest Asian subgroup in America, after Chinese Americans and Filipino Americans. Pakistanis are the second-largest South Asian subgroup in America, but Asian Indians far exceed them in number. A small number of South Asians in the United States hail from Bangladesh, Sri Lanka, Nepal, and Bhutan.

ASIAN-INDIAN AMERICANS

What were Asian Indians in America called in the early days and later?

Britain's defeat of Mogol and French forces in Bengal in 1757 marked the beginning of its gradual domination of the entire region. By 1858, when the British government assumed direct control over India in place of the British East India Company, it had consolidated its rule over much of the Indian subcontinent. Until 1947 Great Britain would rule over India, a country that then encompassed not only present-day, largely Hindu India but also what would later become largely Muslim Pakistan (which itself would be divided in 1971 into Pakistan and Bangladesh). Thus, all mention of Asian-Indian immigration to the United States until the year 1947 refers to immigration from British-controlled India (the territory of the future India, Pakistan, and Bangladesh).

When the first individuals from British-controlled India, mainly traders, stepped foot in the United States in the 1820s (just nine arrived between 1820 and 1830), they were called East Indians, since Americans reserved the term "Indian" for Native Americans. Later they were referred to as Hindus, in reference to Hindustan, another name for the subcontinent of India. Since a Hindu is also an adherent of Hinduism, this term caused a degree of confusion, as among the "Hindus" were Muslims and Sikhs (adherents of Sikhism, a monotheistic religion of India founded around 1500 and marked by a rejection of caste and idolatry). "Asian Indian" is nowadays the preferred term.

How did scholarship bring Asian Indians to America at the dawn of the twentieth century?

In the nineteenth century few Asian Indians, mainly merchants, miners, and religious leaders, made their way to America. Between 1820 and 1900 just 696 Asian Indians entered the country as immigrants. Beginning in 1901, a small number of Asian-Indian students, mostly young men from all corners of British-controlled India, went to the United States to take advantage of opportunities to pursue degrees in engineering, medicine, agriculture, and manufacturing at institutions of higher learning throughout the country, from the

University of Washington to Harvard and Columbia. Most, however, enrolled at universities on the West Coast, especially the University of California, Berkeley, where tuition and living costs were manageable, and students had ample opportunity to work their way through college. (Some Asian-Indian students at Berkeley took jobs in agriculture in the summer months or sold Indian goods.)

When did Asian-Indian laborers first make their way to the United States?

Asian-Indian laborers, most of whom came from the Indian state of Punjab, began venturing to America's shores in a steady trickle at around the same time as the students, that is, in the twentieth century's first decade. The years 1907 to 1910 saw the greatest number of arrivals: More than thirty-eight hundred Asian Indians came to America in that period. By 1912 the number of arrivals had diminished, and from that year until 1962, annual Asian-Indian immigration would reach the five hundred mark just once due to restrictions on immigration and virulent discrimination. In the early years most of the newcomers were sojourners, intent on staying only until they had earned enough money to buy a plot of land or pay off a debt back in the home country. Approximately 85 percent of these early arrivals were Sikhs, while 10 percent were Muslims, and just a handful were Hindus. Most made their way to America by traveling by steamship from Calcutta to Hong Kong, and then from Hong Kong to Canada or the western United States, a journey that took about one month in all. A high proportion borrowed money from relatives or mortgaged land in order to cover the cost of the voyage.

Once in America, the Punjabis, who were generally skilled farmers, found work in agriculture in California, as well as in the lumber mills of Oregon, in factories, and on the Western Pacific Railroad. Many who were recruited to labor on the

Canadian Pacific Railway later headed south across the U.S.-Canada border in search of work.

Were Asian Indians treated better than other Asian immigrant laborers in the first decades of the twentieth century?

In the way of other Asian laborers in the first decades of the twentieth century and after, including Chinese, Japanese, Filipinos, and Koreans, Asian-Indian laborers encountered rampant exploitation by employers. For instance, California fruit growers lured Asian-Indian laborers to their farms with promises of competitive wages. As it turned out, the fruit growers paid the Asian Indians significantly less per day than they did Japanese laborers and also pitted them against the Japanese to discourage labor unrest. After a time, some of the Punjabis managed to escape the exploitation and poor living and working conditions by pooling their earnings until they had collected enough money to lease or purchase farmland. By 1920 Asian Indians in California owned about 2,100 acres and leased 86,340 more. They cultivated cash crops, such as rice and cotton, as well as almonds, grapes, peaches, pears, apricots, potatoes, beans, peas, corn, celery, asparagus, and lettuce.

Asian Indians were treated no better by white laborers, who resented them for making the job market more competitive and for driving down wages with their willingness to work for a pittance. Hostility turned to violence on the night of September 4, 1907, when some four hundred to five hundred white workers—angry over "unfair" competition from Asian Indians and egged on by San Francisco's racist Asian Exclusion League—stormed into the Asian-Indian enclave in Bellingham, Washington, beating up its inhabitants and driving them out of town, in what became known as the Anti-Hindu riot. (Similar riots targeting Asian-Indian enclaves erupted across California in ensuing months.)

After the Anti-Hindu riot, members of the Asiatic Exclusion League campaigned fervently for an end to Asian-Indian immigration, citing "the undesirability of the Hindus, their lack of cleanliness, disregard of sanitary laws, petty pilfering, especially of chickens, and insolence to women." They were not the only exclusionists to disparage the Asian Indians: In 1908 **Samuel Gompers,** then president of the American Federation of Labor, expressed typical American racist sentiments about Asian Indians, and other Asians, when he declared that "[s]ixty years' contact with the Chinese, and twenty-five years' experience with the Japanese and two or three years' acquaintance with Hindus should be sufficient to convince any ordinarily intelligent person that they have no standards . . . by which a Caucasian may judge them."

The U.S. Congress responded to the anti-Asian exclusionist fervor spreading across the land by passing the Immigration Act of 1917, which prohibited immigration from what was called the "Asiatic Barred Zone," to which India belonged, and imposed literacy tests on immigrants so that only those who could read and write would be admitted. Immigration from India, already a trickle, slowed even more. Some, however, got around the restrictive immigration laws by going to Mexico and then crossing the U.S.-Mexico border illegally with the aid of smugglers, who charged a lower fee for their services if an Asian Indian shaved his beard and mustache and removed his turban so as to be more inconspicuous. Other Asian Indians who were already in United States left in the face of American xenophobia. In the years 1911 to 1930 about forty-five hundred Asian Indians abandoned the United States.

Who was Bhagat Singh Thind, and how did Asian Indians in the United States "change color" in 1923?

At the beginning of the twentieth century, Asian Indians were categorized as Caucasians because they share a common ancestor with Scandinavians. Theoretically, then, foreign-born Asian Indians in the United States should have been granted naturalization rights, a privilege reserved solely for Caucasians in accordance with the 1790 naturalization law. Realizing that Asian Indians could use the Caucasian argument to try to obtain U.S. citizenship, U.S. attorney general **Charles J. Bonaparte** declared in 1907 that "under no construction of the law can natives of British India be regarded as white persons." His words did not stop Asian Indians from applying for citizenship. In 1920 a Punjabi immigrant by the name of **Bhagat Singh Thind**—who had come to the United States in 1913, had labored in an Oregon lumber mill, worked his way through the University of California, Berkeley, and had served briefly in the U.S. Army—submitted an application for U.S. citizenship. The U.S. district court approved his application, but the Bureau of Naturalization appealed. The case made it all the way to the U.S. Supreme Court. In 1923 the Court ruled in a unanimous decision in *United States v. Bhagat Singh Thind* that Thind could not obtain citizenship due to the fact that "Caucasian" was synonymous with "white" and Asian Indians were not white. In response to the *Thind* decision, federal authorities nullified in many instances the U.S. citizenship rights that lower courts had previously granted to Asian Indians. (The U.S. Supreme Court's 1927 ruling in *United States v. Sakaram Ganesh Pandit* brought such denaturalization proceedings to a halt.)

How else were Asian Indians affected by the U.S. Supreme Court's decision in United States v. Bhagat Singh Thind*?*

With the *Thind* decision, the alien land laws in place in certain states, which prohibited "aliens ineligible for citizenship" from owning property, were applied to Asian Indians, and consequently some who owned property lost it. (Within weeks of the Supreme Court's decision, California attorney general

Webb began nullifying land purchases made by Asian Indians.) Asian Indians got around alien land laws by purchasing or leasing property in the names of Americans they could trust. When in 1933 this practice was challenged in the courts, Asian Indians turned to buying and leasing land in the names of their American-born children (who naturally had U.S. citizenship), a strategy also practiced by the Japanese in America when they were barred from owning property.

The Supreme Court's decision in *United States v. Bhagat Singh Thind* also meant that antimiscegenation laws could be applied to Asian Indians. Furthermore, as aliens ineligible for U.S. citizenship, Asian Indians could not take advantage of certain federal relief programs during the Great Depression. For the next twenty-three years, Asian Indians and Asian-Indian organizations, such as the Indian Welfare League, which was formed in 1938 by **Mubarak Ali Khan,** a prosperous Asian-Indian farmer in Arizona, would fight to have their right to naturalization restored.

What were the Pacific Coast Hindustani Association and the Gadar Party?

In the first decades of the twentieth century, an appreciable proportion of Asian Indians in America, especially students and intellectuals, were as passionate about the political situation in India—that is, about ending British rule of their homeland—as they were about their status in America. In 1912 **Har Dayal,** an Asian Indian who taught Indian philosophy at Stanford University, organized with other nationalists the Pacific Coast Hindustani Association, which would come to be called the Gadar Party. The organization printed articles related to India's struggle for independence from Britain in a newsletter entitled *Hindustan Gadar,* the first issue of which appeared on November 1, 1913. An Asian-Indian student at Berkeley, **Kartar Singh Sarabha,** ran the printing presses and was also an active fund-raiser, gathering donations from Asian-Indian farmers in the area. The British soon caught wind of Dayal's incendiary organization and infiltrated it with spies.

In March 1914 Dayal was arrested, and after he was released on bail, he slipped away to Switzerland. **Ram Chandra** took his place as leader of the Gadar Party and began urging Asian Indians up and down the Pacific Coast to return to India to take part in a revolution of liberation that was supposed to erupt in February 1915. Several members of the party, with the aid of Har Dayal, arranged for the shipment of arms to India, with the financial backing of the German government, for use in an armed revolt against the British. After the revolution failed, numerous Asian Indians, mostly Gadar Party members, as well as Germans in California, were arrested for conspiring to mount a military expedition in India in violation of U.S. neutrality (most Americans at the time supported Britain's colonial endeavors in India). In trials held in 1917, fifteen Asian Indians were found guilty of the charges and received prison sentences. The Gadar Party pursued its goal of sovereignty for India, along with other groups, including the Home Rule League (established in 1910), until August 1947, when British India was partitioned into two successor states, one largely Hindu and one largely Muslim: the independent dominions of India and Pakistan.

Did many Asian-Indian women come to the United States between the 1890s and World War II?

Few women were among the Asian-Indian laborers and students in America in the last decade of the nineteenth and the early decades of the twentieth century. Since neither group planned to remain permanently in the United States, they lived for the most part a bachelor's life. Asian-Indian laborers tended to live together in bunkhouses or in dwellings on land they leased or owned. As they grew accustomed to America, some decided to stay and drive roots into the soil. Given severe restrictions on Asian-Indian immigration before 1946, few were able to bring their families, including brides, to America. Consequently, they turned for companionship to the women in their midst. However, antimiscegenation laws on the books in many states made it difficult for Asian-Indian men to marry white women. Thus, most married Mexican women, which did not ruffle American civil authorities, who viewed both parties as the same race—brown. Most of these marriages were lasting, but some dissolved due to cultural differences. For instance, Mexican women were unaccustomed to the habit of cooking and washing for their husbands' unmarried business partners. More Asian-Indian men were able to have strictly Asian-Indian families after the passage in 1946 of the Luce-Celler Act, extending the right of naturalization to Asian Indians and providing for a small quota of one hundred Asian-Indian immigrants annually. This legislation enabled Asian Indians, to a limited degree, to bring their brides, wives, children, and other relatives to the United States. And, when antimiscegenation laws were erased from the books in California in 1948, Asian-Indian men also began marrying white women with greater frequency.

How did Asian-Indian Sikhs, Muslims, and Hindus maintain their religious practices in America in the first half of the twentieth century?

In 1915 the Pacific Coast Khalsa Diwan Society, whose mission was to protect and promote the welfare of Asian-Indian immigrants, played an instrumental role in the construction of a Sikh temple on Grant Street in Stockton, California, the oldest one in the nation and one of the first centers of worship for Asian Indians in America. In the way of the Sikh *gurdwaras*, or temples, in Punjab, the Stockton Sikh Temple served both religious and secular functions. After the 1917 trials of Gadar Party members, the temple became a kind of party headquarters, hosting all manner of political events, including a lecture by **Sarojini Naidu,** one of the most prominent leaders of pre-Independent India, during her 1929 U.S. tour to mobilize support abroad for India's liberation from British rule.

Asian-Indian Muslims did not construct their first mosque in America until 1947 (in Sacramento)—the year that Britain made largely Muslim Pakistan a dominion within the commonwealth, causing Asian-Indian Muslims in America to feel more separate from other immigrants from the Indian subcontinent. Instead, for most of the first half of the twentieth century, they came together for worship in each other's homes and in rented halls. The few Hindus who came to America in the early decades of Asian-Indian immigration also had no temples where they could pray and give offerings before a high-caste Brahmin priest, so they worshiped and read the *Bhagavad Gita* on their own.

Which changes in U.S. immigration and naturalization policy in the post-war era impacted Asian Indians?

The first was the Luce-Celler Act of 1946, extending the right of naturalization to Asian Indians (and Filipinos) and providing for a small quota of 100 Asian-Indian immigrants per year. (The quota for Poland, by contrast, was set at 6,524.) A second piece of immigration legislation that impacted Asian Indians in the postwar period was the McCarran-Walter Act of 1952, which eliminated racial and ethnic constraints on naturalization for all Asians, allowing Asian immigrants for the first time in history to become naturalized U.S. citizens. The loosening of immigration and naturalization restrictions stimulated Asian-Indian immigration to a small degree: Between 1945 and 1965, 6,907 Asian Indians entered the United States, reviving the greatly diminished Asian-Indian community, which had shrunk to just 1,500 by 1950.

How did Asian-Indian immigration change after 1965?

America's doors swung wide open to immigrants from India and the rest of Asia with the passage in 1965 of the Immigration Act, also known as the Hart-Celler Reform Act (see *What was the Immigration Act of 1965?*, p. 50), but Asian-Indian immigration to the United States remained rather modest from 1966 to 1970, averaging just under 5,000 annually. In contradistinction, in the 1970s Asian-Indian immigration surged: By 1980, when the U.S. Bureau of the Census conducted its decennial count, 361,531 Asian Indians lived in the United States. In the 1980s Asian Indians continued to come to America in a steady stream. In 1990 the U.S. Bureau of the Census counted 815,447 Asian Indians in the United States, more than double the number in 1980. The 1990s also saw substantial Asian-Indian immigration to the United States. In 2000, the U.S. Bureau of the Census counted 1,899,599 persons of Asian-Indian descent in the United States, an increase of 106 percent since 1990. Of that number, 1,678,765 were Asian Indian alone, while 180,821 were Asian Indian and at least one other race, and 40,013 were Asian Indian and at least one other Asian ethnicity.

Not all of the Asian Indians who were admitted to the United States after the passage of the 1965 Immigration Act came directly from India. Some came by way of the United Kingdom, East Africa, the Caribbean, and Canada, which are also home to the South Indian diaspora first created by British colonial pursuits in South Asia. Asian Indians have also entered the United States through illegal channels. (In 1986 they were the largest non-Latino group to cross the U.S.-Mexico border into the United States illegally.) According to U.S. Immigration and Naturalization Service estimates, in 1996, 33,000 Asian-Indian illegal aliens lived in the United States.

In terms of where they have settled, Asian Indians favor

California—314,819 Asian Indians (alone) called the state home in 2000—just as they did a century ago. Still, they have also spread out across the country, which sets them apart from other South Asian subgroups. According to Census 2000 data, the next four states with the highest Asian-Indian (alone) population in 2000 were New York (251,724), New Jersey (169,180), Texas (129,365), and Illinois (124,723), but Florida, Pennsylvania, Michigan, Maryland, and Virginia all boasted Asian-Indian populations in excess of 48,000 in 2000.

What motivated Asian Indians to come to the United States after 1965, and how successful have they been?

While most of the early Asian-Indian immigrants were West Coast farmers, those who have entered the United States since 1965 have been for the most part India's best educated and most highly trained citizens—mainly professionals in the fields of medicine, science, high tech, and business who hail from India's major urban areas. Some newcomers are also students who apply for permanent residency once they have entered the country. Since 1965 high unemployment in India, especially for scientists, physicians, and engineers, and shortages of medical and other personnel in the United States have been motivating factors behind what essentially amounts to a "brain drain" from India.

With their high degrees of education attainment and training, Asian Indians have for decades enjoyed the highest rate of employment as professionals of all Asian Americans. It should be noted that Asian Indians have also put their entrepreneurial spirit to work in America, owning and operating small businesses, predominantly hotels, motels, convenience stores, and gas stations. Whether professionals or entrepreneurs, Asian Indians have achieved high average socioeconomic levels—higher than any other foreign-born group in America. Generous numbers of Asian Indians in the United States send payments, called remittances, back home to help family members. For this reason, Indian emigrants working abroad are a large source of foreign exchange revenue in India. With high achievers for parents, Asian-Indian youths have excelled in school. In 1990 they had the lowest dropout rate and the highest mean grade-point average of all the Asian-American subgroups.

Have Asian Indians encountered rampant discrimination and racism in America since 1965?

Discrimination and hatred aimed at Asian Indians in America have subsided since the passage of the Immigration Act of 1965, which brought relatively large numbers of Asian Indians to America's shores, increasing their visibility, but they have in no way disappeared altogether. The Asian-Indian community in the Northeast went through a very fearful period in the late 1980s. In September 1987 a group made up of blacks, whites, Puerto Ricans, and even other Asians and calling itself the "dotbusters," in reference to the *bindi*, the decorative red dot some Asian-Indian women wear between their eyebrows to indicate their married status or just to make a fashion statement, sent a letter to a daily newspaper in the largely immigrant city of Jersey City, New Jersey, threatening to "go to any extreme to get Indians to move out of Jersey City." The group was motivated not by racism and xenophobia but by resentment of Asian Indians' high socioeconomic status.

Three weeks later, three white men armed with baseball bats attacked an Asian-Indian doctor, **Kaushal Sharan,** in a respectable working-class neighborhood of Jersey City, beating him so badly that later he could not remember the details of the attack that would have put the offenders behind bars. Three days after Dr. Sharan was assaulted, a gang of eleven Latinos in Hoboken beat to death an Asian-Indian man, **Navroze Mody,** who had just walked out of a café. According to witnesses at the scene, the gang members shouted "Hindu, Hindu!" as they pummeled Mody. After that the "dotbusters" warned that they would identify and harass more victims by searching phone books for the common Indian name Patel. The dotbusters' attacks emboldened regular neighborhood thugs, who began vandalizing Asian-Indian property and committing other bias crimes. With time the violence diminished, along with the fear in New Jersey's Asian-Indian communities.

Asian Indians continue to endure episodes of hatred and violence, owing to a general misperception that they are elitist, clannish, dishonest, self-serving, or just plain "foreign," or to confusion over their race (due to the dark coloring of some Asian Indians, who are mistaken for blacks or Latinos) and their religions. In the days and weeks after the terrorist attacks on the World Trade Center and the Pentagon, hate crimes against Asian Indians spiked. To this day they are frequently the victims of attacks, vandalism (of cars, homes, business establishments, and temples), and of racist comments and curses (since 2001, individuals have often been called bin Laden). Asian Indians are also frequently denied services or entry to schools and other public places if they refuse to remove their turbans. In one case, **Amric Singh,** a Sikh police officer with the New York Police Department, was terminated in 2001, after he refused to remove his turban and trim his beard, both religious requirements. Thanks to a greater awareness of Asian-Indian contributions to America, greater Asian-Indian visibility, and the high-profile, celebrity status of such Asian Indians as **Deepak Chopra, Zubin Mehta,** and **Ismail Merchant,** American perceptions of Asian Indians are gradually becoming more favorable.

Have Asian Indians formed organizations to counter racism and xenophobia in American society?

Asian Indians have formed organizations to counter racism on the national, regional, and local level. One of the largest and oldest national Asian-Indian organizations is the Association of Indians in America (AIA), which was founded on August 20, 1967, in Princeton, New Jersey, to promote the social welfare and assimilation into the American mainstream of Asian Indians in the United States, to "facilitate participation by the members of the AIA and others in the development and progress of India," and to facilitate Asian Indians' involvement in "American community life through charitable, cultural and educational activities." The AIA has chapters all across the United States. Among its many accomplishments, the organization fought for the classification of East Indians as Asian Americans in the 1980 U.S. census so that they would be eligible for affirmative action programs. In addition, Asian-Indian Hindus, Sikhs, and Muslims each have their own organizations whose missions are to protect the civil and human rights of, and advocate social justice for, their communities.

Who are some distinguished Asian-Indian Americans in the music, literary, and film worlds?

One of the most recognized Asian-Indian Americans and one of the greatest orchestral and operatic conductors of all time is **Zubin Mehta.** Born in Bombay, India, on April 29, 1936, Mehta grew up hearing classical music all around him: His father, **Mehli Mehta,** made a career of music, founding the Bombay Symphony. From 1962 to 1967 Zubin Mehta served as music director of the Montreal Symphony Orchestra. In 1962 he also became the youngest conductor appointed music director of a major American orchestra when he was selected for that post by the Los Angeles Philharmonic Orchestra. He remained with the Los Angeles Philharmonic until 1978, when he was appointed music director of the New York Philharmonic Orchestra. During his tenure with the New York Philharmonic, which lasted until 1991, Mehta conducted more than a thousand concerts and fostered such young talents as violinist **Midori.** Since 1969 he has also conducted more than sixteen hundred concerts with the Israel Philharmonic Orchestra, which named him music advisor in 1969, music director in 1977, and music director for life in 1981. And, since 1986, Mehta has also served as music advisor and chief conductor of the Maggio Musicale Fiorentino, the summer festival in Florence, Italy. In September 1998 he began a five-year tenure as general music director of the Bavarian State Opera in Munich. Over the decades Zubin Mehta has won numerous awards and honors and has made a number of recordings with major labels.

Award-winning author **Bharati Mukherjee,** who frequently summons the theme of the upheaval and transformational power of exile and immigration in her works, is the first naturalized American citizen to receive the National Book Critics' Circle Award for Best Fiction, for her short-story collection *The Middleman and Other Stories* (1988). Born on July 27, 1940, into an upper-middle-class Hindu Brahmin family in Calcutta, India, Mukherjee lived in England with her family for several years in her youth. She went on to earn an M.F.A. in 1963 and a Ph.D. in 1969, both from the University of Iowa, and immigrated to Canada in 1968. Filled with a sense of cultural isolation in Canada, Mukherjee moved to the United States in 1980, where, finally feeling integrated, she became a naturalized citizen. Bharati Mukherjee is the author of half a dozen novels, *The Tiger's Daughter* (1971), *Wife* (1975), *Jasmine* (1989), *The Holder of the World* (1993), *Leave It to Me* (1997), and *Desirable Daughters* (2002), and two short-story collections, *Darkness* (1985) and *The Middleman and Other Stories* (1988), as well as works of nonfiction.

Film producer **Ismail Merchant** is known throughout the world for the cinematic masterpieces he has made with director **James Ivory** and screenwriter **Ruth Prawer Jhabvala** in what is the longest artistic collaboration in independent filmmaking. Born **Ismail Noormohamed Abdul Rehman** in Bombay on December 25, 1936, Ismail Merchant knew early on that he wanted to devote his life to filmmaking, as he explains in his autobiographical work, *My Passage from India: A Filmmaker's*

Journey from Bombay to Hollywood and Beyond (2002): "I was thirteen years old and had been invited by Nimmi, one of the upcoming stars of the Bombay film industry, to accompany her to the premiere of her first film, *Barsaat.* As we drove toward the cinema in her green Cadillac convertible—quite an impressive car in India at that time—a shower of marigolds began to rain down on us. It seemed so magical—like the movies themselves—that I can remember thinking, 'if this is what the film world is, I want to be part of it.' "

In 1958 Merchant made his way to New York City, where he found a job in advertising but never forgot his life's ambition. In 1961 his first short film, *Creation of Woman,* was an entry from the United States in the Cannes Film Festival and was also nominated for an Academy Award. In April of that year Merchant launched Merchant Ivory Productions with director James Ivory after the two met at a screening of Ivory's documentary on Indian miniature painting, *The Sword and the Flute* (1958), and later that same evening discussed the idea of making English-language motion pictures in India for international audiences. For nearly twenty years Merchant Ivory Productions made films set in present-day India. Ivory was in charge of directing, while Merchant devoted himself to the funding of their projects. Their first feature-length collaboration was *The Householder* (1963), based on the novel of the same name by Ruth Prawer Jhabvala (who has over the last forty years written most of their screenplays). It was the first Indian motion picture distributed globally by a major American company.

Merchant and Ivory gained an international following with their period adaptations. Their first film adaptation of a literary masterpiece was *The Europeans* (1979), based on the **Henry James** novel of the same name. Their cinematic gem *A Room with a View* (1985), a celluloid rendering of the **E. M. Forster** novel, won rave reviews from both critics and moviegoers, garnering them a wide audience for the first time, and captured three Academy Awards—for Best Screenplay, Art

Direction, and Costumes. Their next work of genius was *Howards End* (1992), an adaptation of another Forster novel, which was honored with three Oscars, for Best Actress **(Emma Thompson),** Screenplay, and Art Direction. Then came their adaptation *The Remains of the Day* (1993), which was followed by five more Merchant-Ivory projects: *Jefferson in Paris* (1995), *Surviving Picasso* (1996), *A Soldier's Daughter Never Cries* (1998), *The Golden Bowl* (2000), and *Le Divorce* (2003). Ismail Merchant has also spent time in the director's chair during his long career. For the big screen he directed *In Custody* (1993), *The Proprietor* (1996), *Cotton Mary* (1999), and *The Mystic Masseur* (2002). In addition to his autobiography, Ismail Merchant has penned several cookbooks and *Hullabaloo in Old Jeypore* (1988), about the making of the motion picture *The Deceivers* in 1988.

Who are some prominent Asian-Indian Americans in science, medicine, and business?

Subrahmanyan Chandrasekhar, one of the greatest astrophysicists of the twentieth century, distinguished himself with his work in the field of stellar evolution. In the early 1930s he was the first scientist to conjecture that not all stars ultimately become white dwarf stars: Those retaining a mass above a certain limit—nowadays called Chandrasekhar's limit—experience a further collapse. While his theory was initially greeted with skepticism, it eventually became the foundation of the theory of black holes. In 1983 Subrahmanyan Chandrasekhar shared the Nobel Prize in Physics (with **William Alfred Fowler**) "for his theoretical studies of the physical processes of importance to the structure and evolution of the stars." In the course of his career, he also devised important theorems on the stability of cosmic masses when exposed to gravitation, rotation, and magnetic fields, which would later be critical to comprehending galaxies' spiral structure. Chandrasekhar, who was known as Chandra, which means "moon" or "luminous" in Sanskrit, was born in Lahore, India, on October 19, 1910, immigrated to the United States in 1937, and became an American citizen in 1953. In January 1937 he joined the faculty of the University of Chicago, where he remained until his death on August 21, 1995. In honor of the late Nobel laureate, NASA named its premier x-ray observatory the Chandra X-Ray Observatory.

Dr. Yellapragada Subba Row, called "one of the most eminent medical minds of the century" in a 1948 tribute by the *New York Herald Tribune*, is credited with developing the folic acid vitamin (for anemia), the world's first antibiotic (Gramicidin), Hetrazan (for filariasis and eosinophilia), Aminopterin (for leukemia), and other disease-fighting drugs that have extended the lives of an untold number of people around the globe, as well as with contributing to the production of other medicines, such as Tetracycline and Aureomycin. Subba Row was born into a poor family on January 12, 1895, near Bheemvaram, Andhra Pradesh, India. His schooling was haphazard until he moved to Madras, where he completed studies at the Hindu High School, the Presidency College, and the Madras Medical College. After the death of his two brothers to tropical diseases in the course of just days, Subba Row knew his future lay in medical research, and he applied to the School of Tropical Medicine at Harvard University.

Harvard did not offer him a scholarship, and so he had the arduous task of keeping up his studies while working as a night porter at a hospital to cover his expenses. After he was awarded his diploma in 1928, Subba Row worked with **Cyrus Hartwell Fiske** on developing a colorimetric method for calculating phosphorus in the body tissues and fluids, a method now known as Fiske-Subba Row. This work, as well as his contributions to muscle chemistry, garnered Yellapragada Subba Row a Ph.D. from Harvard in 1930. In 1940 he became associate director of research at the Lederle Laboratories at Pearle River, New York, where he would conduct most of his work in the development of drugs. Due to restrictions in U.S. immigration, Subba Row had to wait to become an American citizen until the passage of the Luce-Celler Act in 1946. He had little time to enjoy his new citizenship: On August 8, 1948, Yellapragada Subba Row passed away in his sleep.

Asian-Indian entrepreneur, political activist, and philanthropist **Gobindram Jhamandas Watumull** met with enormous success in the retail business in Honolulu. With his brother **Jhamandas Watumull,** G. J. Watumull set to work in 1917 transforming a small retail store in downtown Honolulu into a flourishing department store. By 1957 the Watumull brothers' business had blossomed into ten major department stores and numerous other commercial properties. In 1942 G. J. Watumull launched the Watumull Foundation, an organization dedicated to improving conditions in India, fostering U.S.-India relations, and contributing to philanthropic, educational, and cultural projects in Hawaii. In 1944 the Watumull Foundation established the Watumull Prize, which was awarded triennially (and at times biennially) to the best work on the history of India published in the United States. Between 1945 and 1982, when the prize was terminated, twenty-five works were selected for the prize.

Who was Dalip Singh Saund?

In 1956 Asian Indian **Dalip Singh Saund** made history by becoming the first Asian American to win a seat in the U.S. Congress. Born in the village of Chhajalwadi, Punjab, India, in 1899, Saund came to the United States in 1920 to study at the University of California, Berkeley, where he earned an M.A. in 1922 and a Ph.D. in mathematics in 1924. Were he Anglo-Saxon, he might have gone straight into teaching and conducting research in his field. Instead, he pursued the only avenue open to Asian Indians in California at the time: He became a lettuce farmer in the Imperial Valley of California and then worked from 1930 to 1953 as a chemical fertilizer distributor. In his autobiography, *Congressman from India* (1960), Dalip Singh

Saund attributed the insurmountable barrier to the professions that he faced in America to Asian Indians' ineligibility for U.S. citizenship until 1946: "I saw that the bars of citizenship were shut tight against me. I knew if these bars were lifted I would see much wider gates of opportunity open to me, opportunity as existed for everybody else in the United States of America." Discriminatory laws related to U.S. citizenship for Asian Indians affected Saund beyond his career choices. His wife, **Marian Kosa,** an American citizen, had to relinquish her U.S. citizenship when they married in 1928.

In the 1940s Saund turned formidable obstacles into activism, establishing the Indian Association of America, which was devoted to attaining U.S. citizenship rights for Asian Indians in the United States. On December 16, 1949, some three years after President **Truman** signed the Luce-Celler Act extending the right of naturalization to Asian Indians and Filipinos, Dalip Singh Saund finally became a U.S. citizen. The very next year he was elected to a judgeship in Westmorland, California, but was informed he could not serve because he had not been a U.S. citizen for an entire year before the election. Refusing to give up, he ran again in 1952 and was again elected judge of Westmorland, serving at that post until voters from California's Twenty-ninth District (encompassing Riverside County and Imperial County) sent him to the U.S. House of Representatives in 1956. The victory was truly astonishing as Saund was a Democrat and the Twenty-ninth District had always gone Republican. Saund represented the district in the House for three terms. While campaigning for a fourth term, he suffered a debilitating stroke, which brought an end to his political life. Dalip Singh Saund died on April 22, 1973, in Hollywood, California.

ASIAN-AMERICAN HEARTTHROBS

Tia Carrere

Hawaiian-born actress-model Tia Carrere, who is of Filipino, Spanish, and Chinese descent, first achieved heartthrob status as Nurse Jade Soong on the ABC soap opera *General Hospital.* Since 1988 she has starred in a number of motion pictures, including the comedy *Wayne's World* (1992), which brought her Hollywood fame overnight; its sequel, *Wayne's World 2* (1993); the action comedy *True Lies* (1994); and Disney Pictures' feature-length animated comedy *Lilo and Stitch* (2002).

Michael Chang

In 1987, a fifteen-year-old Michael Chang, who is of Chinese descent, stunned tennis fans around the globe by becoming the youngest tennis player to prevail in a U.S. Open main draw match and to advance to a Tour semifinal. Then, in 1989, a year after turning pro, Chang became the youngest player, as well as the first American male player since Tony Trabert in 1955, to capture the French Open. In 1989 Chang was also the youngest player ever to rank in the top five in the world. Michael Chang has since won a slew of singles titles.

Joan Chen

Actress Joan Chen, who was a child film star in the People's Republic of China before she came to the United States in 1981, has delighted audiences with her role in 1990 as Josie Packard in the television series *Twin Peaks* and with her performances in such motion pictures as *The Last Emperor* (1987), *Heaven and Earth* (1993), *The Joy Luck Club* (1993), and *Golden Gate* (1994). Chen made her directorial debut with *Xiu Xiu: The Sent Down Girl* (1999) and the following year directed *Autumn in New York* (2000).

Michelle Kwan

Chinese-American figure skater Michelle Kwan, a six-time U.S. Champion (1996, 1998–2002) and sheer elegance on ice, first captured the national and international spotlight with her silver-medal performance in the ladies singles figure skating competition at the 1998 Olympic Winter Games in Nagano, Japan. Four years later she skated for the bronze at the 2002 Winter Olympics in Salt Lake City in one of the Games' most watched events.

Jason Scott Lee

Called the first Chinese-American sex symbol, Jason Scott Lee has performed in such Hollywood films as *Map of the Human Heart* (1992), *Dragon: The Bruce Lee Story* (1993, as Bruce Lee), and *Russell Mulcahy's Tale of the Mummy* (1999). He is also the voice of David Kawena in the feature-length animated comedy *Lilo & Stitch* (2002).

Dustin Nguyen

Vietnamese-American actor Dustin Nguyen—who fled South Vietnam with his family when it fell to the Communists in April 1975—first gained recognition in America for playing Officer Harry T. Ioki, an undercover police officer, from 1987 to 1990 in the television crime drama *21 Jump Street,* which ran from 1987 to 1992. More recently he played Johnny Loh in the action/drama television series *V.I.P.* On the big screen, Nguyen has performed in such films as *Heaven Can Wait* (1993), *3 Ninjas Kick Back* (1994), *Virtuosity* (1995), and *Hundred Percent* (1998).

Russell Wong

Actor Russell Wong—who is of Chinese, Dutch, French, Canadian, and Indian ancestry, and started out as a dancer in music videos—first made a splash with his good looks and charisma in an episode of *21 Jump Street.* He then dazzled a wider audience with his performances on the big screen in *Eat a Bowl of Tea* (1989) and *The Joy Luck Club* (1993). A high-profile role in the television movie *Vanishing Son* (1994) spawned three sequels and a syndicated TV series for Wong. He then went back to the big screen, landing major parts in such motion pictures as *The Tracker* (2000) and *Romeo Must Die* (2000).

Zhang Ziyi

Chinese-born model and actress Zhang Ziyi attracted a lot of attention in 2001, when she made *People* magazine's "50 Most Beautiful People" roster and *Teen People*'s "25 Hottest Stars Under 25" list and appeared on the big screen in her first American movie, *Rush Hour 2.*

Where do America's Hindus, Sikhs, and Muslims with roots in India worship nowadays?

While few Hindus immigrated to America in the early days, the overwhelming majority of Asian-Indian arrivals since 1965 have been Hindus. Nowadays Hindus in the United States have the choice of worshiping at small shrines at home or attending Hindu temples for group services on weekends and holidays. One of the oldest Hindu temples in North America is the Ganesha Temple in Flushing, New York. It was constructed off-site in the southern state of Andhra Pradesh, India, by a hundred skilled craftsmen. In 1976 the twenty-ton granite structure was transported from India to Flushing, where twenty-five of the craftsmen who had worked on the structure carefully reassembled it. Statues of deities from the Hindu pantheon, such as Ganesha, the elephant-headed god; the god Shiva; and Lakshmi, the goddess of wealth, adorn the elaborate temple. For the first five years after it was erected, the Ganesha Temple attracted vandals. The temple made a concerted effort to reach out to neighbors, who were unfamiliar with, and wary of, Hinduism, and the vandalism subsided. Nowadays there are dozens of Hindu temples across the country, from Massachusetts to California. They differ from Hindu temples in India in one fundamental way. Each of the temples in India is dedicated to one Hindu god (although other gods grace the attendant shrines around a temple's central sanctum), while in the United States, Hindu gods "share" temples.

Since 1915, when the first Sikh temple was built in Stockton, California, Sikhs have constructed temples in several states, from the Sikh Temple of North Texas, to the Gurdwara Baba Deep Singh in Las Vegas, to the Gurdwara of Rochester, New York. By far the greatest number of Sikh temples are in California. Since Muslims in America represent a whole host of ethnic groups, mosques tend to be multiethnic as well. Asian-Indian Muslims attend the 1,209 mosques in America (as of 2000) along with other South Asian Muslims (mainly Pakistanis and Bangladeshis), as well as with Arab, African, Southeast Asian, Turkish, and African-American Muslims.

Which secular and religious holidays do Asian Indians in America observe?

Asian-Indian Americans greet Indian Independence Day each August with much fanfare. In New York City, for instance, the Federation of Indian Associations sponsors a parade with marchers from Asian-Indian American organizations representing all the regions of India, as well as Asian-Indian American dance troops, Asian-Indian American beauty queens atop floats, and marching bands. The floats that depict India's independence from Britain are a highlight of the Indian Independence Day Parade. Asian-Indian Americans also celebrate Republic Day on January 26, which commemorates India's adoption of its constitution in 1950, and Gandhi Jayanti on October 2, the birthday of **Mahatma Gandhi,** the father of India.

In terms of holy days and festivals, Hindus in America

(and Sikhs, too) observe *Diwali*, the Hindu New Year and festival of lights, which falls in October. In New York City and elsewhere around the country, *Diwali* celebrations include a procession of floats bedecked with huge shrines decorated with numerous Hindu deities. As part of the celebrations, Hindus light lamps in their houses to guide departed souls in their journey back to earth. Another Hindu festival is *Holi*, a celebration of good over evil. The main event in the celebration is the carnival of colors, when Hindus take to the streets and throw red, orange, green, blue, and purple powders in the air, wet each other with colored water, and color one another with dyes. One of the most holy days for Hindus is *Maha Shivaratri*, in honor of the god Shiva, which is observed in February or March. Hindus fast and pray to Shiva at night and pay a visit to the temple to pay homage to the god. On the ninth day of the ascending moon, sometime between mid-March and mid-April, Hindus celebrate the birth of Rama, one of the ten incarnations of Vishnu, with the festival *Ramnavami*. During *Ramnavami*, Hindus go to the temple with offerings of money, food, and clothing for the Brahmins, monks, and the poor. They also sing songs in honor of Rama; recite the *Ramayana*, the story of Rama's life; and congregate in movie theaters to watch *Ramayana* films.

One of the most sacred days for Sikhs, who celebrate an equally large number of holy days and festivals, is *Baisakhi* Day (also *Vaisakhi*), which falls on April 13 and commemorates Sikhs' initiation into the Khalsa fraternity, which was founded on April 13, 1699. Sikhs celebrate *Baisakhi* Day by attending religious services at Sikh temples that incorporate readings from the *Guru Granth Sahib*, or holy scriptures, and also by helping in the temples' daily chores. *Baisakhi* Day is also a festive day on the Hindu calendar, for it commemorates the Gaga's descent to earth and signifies the beginning of the New Year. Other important Sikh holidays are Guru Arjun Dev Ji's Martyrdom Day (May or June), Guru Tegh Bahadur's Martyrdom Day (November/December), Guru Gobind Singh

Ji's birthday (December/January), and Guru Nanak Dev Ji's birthday (November). (In 2002, the New Jersey State Board of Education included all of these Sikh sacred days, as well as *Baisakhi* Day, on the official school calendar.)

Asian-Indian Muslims observe such holy days as *Id-ul-Zuha,* the commemoration of the sacrifice of Abraham, which is celebrated in March with prayers in mosques, feasts, and an exchange of greetings. *Muharram,* the first month of the Muslim year, is one of the four sacred months in the Muslim calendar. Voluntary fasting is an important facet of the month of *Muharram. Id-ul-Fittr* is celebrated in January and marks the end of *Ramadan,* the Muslim time of fasting. Muslims pray in mosques, exchange greetings, and give presents to children in celebration of *Id-ul-Fittr.*

What is Ayurveda?

The traditional system of medicine in India is known as Ayurveda, literally "Science of Life," from the Sanskrit word *ayus,* meaning "life," and *veda,* meaning "knowledge" or "science." Ayurveda is perhaps the oldest holistic healing system, with roots going back twenty-five hundred to five thousand years to the Himalayas and southern India. It influenced other systems of medicine, from ancient Greek to Chinese medicine. According to Ayurveda, perfect health is synonymous with a balance between the mind, body, soul, senses and all of nature achieved through regimented daily living and yoga, a system of exercises. The Ayurvedic approach to health recognizes that all individuals are different and thus require different regimens to promote and preserve this balance. When an imbalance in the physiology occurs, practitioners of Ayurveda rely on a unique combination of yoga, meditation, lifestyle practices, diet, herbs, color therapy, and cleansing techniques, specifically geared to the individual, to restore health in a gentle, methodic process. Instant cures in the form of a pill are foreign to the Ayurvedic approach.

Who is Deepak Chopra?

"The poet-prophet of alternative medicine" is how *Time* magazine described **Deepak Chopra,** M.D., when it selected him as one of the "Top 100 Icons and Heroes of the Century" in 1999. In the 1980s Chopra, an endocrinologist by training, created his own form of alternative medicine, specifically mind-body techniques that reflect Ayurvedic holistic healing and state-of-the-art Western science and enable practitioners to enhance their ability to achieve fulfillment and success. Deepak Chopra has penned numerous spiritual-motivational books, including *Everyday Immortality: A Concise Course in Spiritual Transformation* (2003), which presents a series of *koans,* or insights, to ponder; *The Deeper Wound: Recovering the Soul from Fear and Suffering* (2001), a spiritual response to the tragedy of September 11, 2001; *How to Know God: The Soul's Journey into the Mystery of Mysteries* (2001); and *Ageless Body, Timeless Mind: The Quantum Alternative to Growing Old* (1998), a *New York Times* bestseller. In addition, he has written several works of fiction, among them a poetry collection entitled *The Soul in Love: Classic Poems of Ecstasy and Exaltation* (2001). He is also the founder and CEO of The Chopra Center for Well Being in La Jolla, California.

What foods are found on the Asian-Indian American table?

It all depends on the particular religious beliefs of Asian-Indian individuals and the region of India from which they or their ancestors hail. In terms of religion, Sikhs and some Hindus adhere to a strict vegetarian diet, while Muslims do not consume pork. In terms of regional differences, those with roots in the wheat-growing northern regions of India might prefer whole wheat breads, such as *chapati* and *paratha,* and *tandoori,* seared meats that are cooked in clay ovens. Those with roots in the subtropical south might opt for a vegetarian diet replete with rice, *dal* (lentils), vegetable curries made with "wet" *masalas*, or "spice blends," and *papadam*, crispy wafers made of *urad dal*. Those who come from the western state of Gujarat, the home of **Mahatma Gandhi** and Jainism, might favor that region's vegetarian cuisine, with its ubiquitous vegetable curries, vegetable fritters, and *dhokla*, or chick-pea flour cake sprinkled with mustard seeds and cilantro.

PAKISTANI AMERICANS

What brought Pakistanis to the United States?

Between 1526 and 1761 the Mogul Empire held sway over most of South Asia, including the region that constitutes present-day Pakistan. In 1757 the British East India Company subdued the Mogul Empire, and after the British government assumed responsibility for the region in 1858, the British consolidated their control of the subcontinent of India. Consequently, what is present-day Muslim Pakistan belonged to largely Hindu, British-controlled India. It was not until the 1930s that the notion of a separate Muslim state in the region took shape. On March 23, 1940, the leader of India's Muslim League, **Muhammad Ali Jinnah,** endorsed the "Lahore Resolution," calling for the formation of a Muslim independent state in those regions of the Indian subcontinent where Muslims were the majority.

In the aftermath of World War II, Britain became committed to granting India its independence, and in June 1947 it gave full dominion status to two successor states, India and Pakistan, the Muslim state that Jinnah had envisioned. The princely states in the Indian subcontinent had the liberty to join either India or Pakistan. As a result, Pakistan ended up a bifurcated Muslim nation, with West Pakistan, which consisted of the contiguous Muslim region of present-day Pakistan, separated by one thousand miles of Indian territory from East Pakistan, which was comprised of the Muslim-dominated eastern part of Bengal. In response to growing Bengali nationalist fervor in East Pakistan, East and West Pakistan before long became engulfed in civil war. With the aid of India and its large army, East Pakistan won the war and achieved independence in 1971, becoming the sovereign nation of Bangladesh. West Pakistan's name was subsequently changed to Pakistan.

Since Pakistan did not exist as a separate state before 1947 and was part of British-controlled India, U.S. immigration data from 1820 through 1946 makes reference only to immigration from British-controlled India. After Great Britain granted full dominion status to Pakistan and India in 1947, separate data was collected for each. Until 1965 Pakistani immigration to the United States was extremely light due to restrictions on Asian immigration put in place with the passage of the 1924 Immigration Act. The 1965 Immigration Act opened the doors to U.S. immigration to Asians, but, nonetheless, the number of Pakistani immigrating to the United States was small in the 1970s, with an average of 3,000 entering the country annually. In the late 1980s and the 1990s, U.S. immigration from Pakistan picked up considerably, reaching the 10,000 and even the 20,000 mark. All told, more than 163,000 Pakistanis immigrated to the United States in the years 1971 to 1996. A sizable number of Pakistanis also crossed illegally into the United States in those years. According to Immigration and Naturalization Service (INS) estimates, about 41,000 undocumented aliens from Pakistan were on American soil in 1996. Pakistanis who came to the United States in the 1970s, 1980s, and 1990s are, like their Asian-Indian counterparts, mostly the best and the brightest. A generous number are highly trained scientists, doctors, academicians, and businesspeople. This continues to be the case in the opening decade of the twenty-first century.

How many Pakistani Americans are there, and where do they live?

According to Census 2000 data, 204,309 persons of Pakistani ancestry resided in the United States in the year 2000; 153,533 were Pakistani alone, 39,681 were Pakistani and at least one other race, and 11,095 were Pakistani and at least one other Asian ethnicity. The five states with the greatest numbers of Pakistanis (alone) in 2000 were New York (32,692), California (20,093), Texas (19,102), Illinois (15,103), and New Jersey (12,112).

How did the tragedy of September 11, 2001, impact Pakistanis in the United States?

In the aftermath of the al-Qaeda terrorist attacks on the World Trade Center and the Pentagon on September 11, 2001, various U.S. law enforcement agencies, including the INS, the Secret Service, the FBI, and the New York Police Department, raided hundreds of residences and businesses in the Pakistani-American community, which, like Pakistan, is primarily Muslim. These agencies detained hundreds of Pakistanis in the first weeks after the attacks, most of whom were taken into custody for immigration violations, not for terrorist activities. Pakistanis contended at the time that they were targeted by American law enforcement because they were Muslims, as other immigrant groups in the United States with a significant percentage of illegal aliens, such as Mexicans, were not subjected to such raids.

In the days after the September 11 attacks, Pakistanis, and other Muslims in the Asian-American community, also endured a rash of hate crimes because of their adherence to Islam. On September 15, 2001, a Pakistani grocer named **Waqar Hassan** was shot to death in Dallas, Texas, in what his family determined was an act of hate. And, a few days later, two Pakistanis also fell victim to hate when they were murdered in Coney Island. On October 23, 2001, a Pakistani father of five children, **Rafiq But,** died of a heart attack in his prison cell in Hudson County, New York. He had sat in jail for nearly six weeks for an immigration violation. His family maintained that he did not have a history of heart problems.

THE OTHER AMERICANS OF SOUTH ASIAN DESCENT

What brought Bangladeshis to America's shores, and where do they live?

Bangladesh is a small coastal country in south-central Asia bordered by the Bay of Bengal to the south, Burma to the southeast, and India to the north and west, with a population that is 98 percent Bengali and 88 percent Muslim. Until 1947 it was a part of Bengal, which in the nineteenth century had become a region of British-controlled India. When British India was partitioned in 1947 into two successor states—the independent dominions of India (largely Hindu) and Pakistan (largely Muslim)—the region of Bengal was divided, with the mostly Muslim eastern part, called East Pakistan, joining the newly independent Muslim state of Pakistan (even though they were separated by a thousand miles of Indian territory) and the predominantly Hindu western half becoming the Indian state of West Bengal. Tensions developed between distant East and West Pakistan due to ethnic, cultural, and linguistic differences and the East's sense of exploitation by the West Pakistan–dominated central government. In response to rising Bengali nationalist sentiment in East Pakistan, **Sheikh Mujibur Rahman** organized the Awami League in 1949 to work toward Bengali autonomy. Rahman, who was designated president of the Awami League, emerged the leader of the Bengali autonomous movement and was arrested in 1966 for his activities.

In 1970 the Awami League captured a majority of seats in the National Assembly. The Pakistani government responded by postponing convening that body, generating massive civil unrest in East Pakistan in 1971. With the outbreak of unrest, Rahman was rearrested and his party banned, and most of his aides went into exile in India, where they formed a provisional government. On March 26, 1971, Bengali nationalists proclaimed an independent People's Republic of Bangladesh. Fighting intensified between the Pakistani army and the Bengali freedom fighters, unleashing an exodus of ten million Bengali refugees, mainly Hindus, to India. The wave of refugees strained India and East Pakistan's already troubled relationship, and in November 1971 India came to the defense of the Bengalis. On December 16, 1971, Pakistani forces surrendered to the invading Indian army and a country, Bangladesh, meaning "Bengal nation," was born. A parliamentary democracy was created in Bangladesh, with Sheikh Mujibur Rahman as prime minister. The 1970s and 1980s brought bloody and bloodless military coups, assassinations of leaders (including Rahman in 1975), martial law, and widespread civil unrest, all of which dissipated by 1990, when Bangladesh had its most free and fair elections to date. Bangladesh is one of the world's poorest, most densely populated nations.

Given that Bangladesh has been an independent nation only since 1971, statistics related to the immigration of Bangladeshis to the United States have only been available since 1973. Before then the Bangladeshi (Bengalis) were counted as Asian Indians. Bangladesh generated very modest U.S. immigration in the 1970s and 1980s, reaching 1,000 annually only in 1985. In the years 1972 to 1996, fewer than 56,000 Bangladeshis made their way to the United States, with most arriving in the 1990s. In the way of Indian and Pakistani immigrants, Bangladeshi immigrants who came to America in the last quarter of the twentieth century represented the cream of the crop and were mostly professionals in medicine, the sciences, education, and business. They came to America's shores seeking opportunities nonexistent in Bangladesh, where most people work in agriculture. A relatively large contingency of Bangladeshi students also pursue higher education in America's colleges and universities. This continues to be the trend.

Census 2000 counted 57,412 Bangladeshi Americans and Bangladeshi nationals, 41,280 of whom were Bangladeshi alone,

10,507 Bangladeshi and at least one other race, and 5,625 Bangladeshi and at least one other Asian ethnicity. The five states with the largest Bangladeshi (alone) population in 2000 were New York (20,269), California (3,044), Texas (2,438), New Jersey (2,056), and Virginia (1,786). In 2000, 19,148 Bangladeshis in New York called New York City home according to Census 2000 data. And, in the decade of the 1990s, they constituted the fastest-growing Asian subgroup in the city, with a population increase of more than 285 percent between 1990 and 2000.

How many Sri Lankans live in the United States, and where have they settled?

In 2000 the U.S. Bureau of the Census counted 24,587 persons with roots in the ethnically diverse island nation of Sri Lanka (formerly Ceylon), which is about the size of West Virginia and sits eighteen miles off the southeastern coast of India. The five states with the highest number of Sri Lankans (alone and not in combination with other races and ethnicities) in 2000 were California (5,775), New York (2,692), Maryland (1,226), Texas (1,195), and New Jersey (1,183). Since it achieved independence from Britain on February 4, 1948, Sri Lanka has enjoyed strongly democratic governments and considerable political stability, despite intermittent outbreaks of separatist violence beginning in 1956 between the Sinhalese majority and the Tamil minority and the myriad economic challenges the country has had to meet. Both phenomena drove the limited Sri Lankan immigration to the United States in the last quarter of the twentieth century.

What about Nepalese in the United States?

According to Census 2000 data, 9,399 persons of Nepalese ancestry called the United States home in 2000. In the 1990s, Nepalese came to the United States to escape a violent insurgency, unleashed by the Maoist United People's Front, that subjected the police, politicians, and civilians alike to torture, killings, bombings, kidnappings, and extortion. In 2001 a cease-fire was announced and the violence largely ended. Over the decades the Nepalese have also taken refuge on America's shores from the poverty of Nepal, a landlocked, isolated country sandwiched between India and China, with a per capita income of just $240 (in 2001).

And what of the Bhutanese?

Just 212 persons with roots in the Kingdom of Bhutan—a small, landlocked country in the heart of the Himalayas and bordered by Tibet and India—resided in the United States in 2000.

SIX

Southeast Asian Americans

What's the difference between a refugee and an immigrant?

When did the United States become a beacon for the world's refugees and for those from Southeast Asia in particular?

What are first-asylum and second-asylum countries?

Which organizations have been involved in resettling refugees from Southeast Asia in the United States?

Why were Southeast Asian refugees dispersed across the country when they first began arriving in the United States?

What is the 1.5 generation?

VIETNAMESE AMERICANS

Which events in Vietnamese history led up to the mass exodus of Vietnamese to the United States beginning in 1975?

Who was Ho Chi Minh?

Why in the aftermath of World War II did some Vietnamese view the United States as yet another foreign intruder into Vietnam's affairs?

How was Vietnam divided into North and South Vietnam?

When did fighting erupt between North and South Vietnam, and how did the United States get involved in it?

What was the Tet Offensive of 1968?

Besides the hippies, Jane Fonda, and others active in the American antiwar movement, who else opposed the Vietnam War?

When did the Vietnam War finally end?

When did the first wave of South Vietnamese refugees fleeing the Vietnamese Communists arrive in America, and how were they resettled?

Who were the "Vietnamese Boat People"?

Who are the Amerasians?

How did the Vietnamese refugees of the various waves adjust to life in the United States?

How many Vietnamese Americans are there, and where do they live?

How serious is the Vietnamese gang problem?

Who are some prominent Vietnamese Americans?

Which religions do the Vietnamese follow in America?

What is the meaning of Tet *for Vietnamese Americans?*

What is Vietnamese cooking like?

LAOTIAN AMERICANS

Who are the Laotians?

Has Laos endured the same invasions that have plagued Vietnam throughout its history?

Why then did hundreds of thousands of Laotians flee

from Laos to Thailand beginning in 1975, and where did they go from there?

How many Laotians have been resettled in the United States, and do they continue to seek refuge in this country?

How difficult has it been for refugees from Laos to adjust to American life?

What is Hmong sudden death syndrome?

Have Laotians had a collective voice in America?

Which religions do Laotians practice?

What kinds of foods do Laotian Americans like?

CAMBODIAN AMERICANS

What is the story behind the arrival of Cambodians in the United States?

What were the Khmer Rouge's "killing fields"?

How exactly did Pol Pot's genocide end?

How many Cambodian refugees have made their way to America, and where have they settled?

How difficult was it for the three waves of Cambodians to acculturate to the American way of life?

Why did more than a hundred Cambodian women in California suddenly go blind in the 1980s?

How are Cambodians faring in the first decade of the new millennium?

Who is Dith Pran?

Who was Haing Ngor?

Do Cambodians celebrate New Years in the same way as the Vietnamese?

What foods are found on the Cambodian-American table?

THAI AMERICANS

What brought Thais to American shores?

How many Thai Americans are there, and where do they live?

Who is both the most prominent American of Thai ancestry and a legend in his own time?

THE OTHER AMERICANS OF SOUTHEAST ASIAN DESCENT

How many Indonesians live in the United States?

How have Malaysians managed to come to America's shores?

How have Burmese been able to come to America?

If Singapore is a thriving nation, what brings Singaporeans to America?

What about Bruneian Americans?

Southeast Asia is a large region encompassing Vietnam, Laos, Cambodia, Thailand, Indonesia, Malaysia, Burma (renamed Myanmar in 1997 by the country's ruling junta, a name change the U.S. government does not recognize), Singapore, and Brunei. Southeast Asians are relative newcomers to America. The overwhelming majority are Vietnamese, Laotians, and Cambodians, who were forced to flee war, Communism, repression, and severe economic hardship (and genocide in the case of the Cambodians) in their homelands for the United States as refugees in the latter third of the twentieth century. A small number of Thai have also settled in the United States over the decades, spurred not by war and oppressive regimes but by Thailand's close military and trade connections with the United States. Relatively few Southeast Asians in America hail from Indonesia, Malaysia, Burma, Singapore, and Brunei.

What's the difference between a refugee and an immigrant?

The fundamental distinctions between refugees and immigrants pertain to the circumstances surrounding their departure from their homeland. Refugees flee their country due to fear of or experiences of violence or persecution based on race, religion, nationality, social class, or political ideology. They usually have little time or means to prepare for their journey, they seldom know where they will finally end up, and their families are often split apart in the long process of resettlement. Most refugees escape to the border regions of neighboring countries, where they may be threatened with return to their homeland or forced to live for years in refugee camps or underground, on the fringes of society. A refugee's exile is resolved in one of three ways: repatriation, assimilation into the country to which they first flee, or permanent resettlement in a third country. Given the unpredictability of refugee life, those who come to America usually are not very well prepared psychologically, financially, and emotionally for resettlement. Immigrants, by contrast, customarily leave their homeland on a voluntary basis, in search of better economic opportunities abroad and a promising future for themselves and their families.

When did the United States become a beacon for the world's refugees and for those from Southeast Asia in particular?

Even before it became a country, the United States was a promised land, providing refuge to the world's citizens who had been displaced by war and violence and persecuted by governments and their own compatriots. In 1783 President **George Washington** proclaimed the nation's commitment to such individuals in need of protection: "[t]he bosom of America is open to receive not only the opulent and respectable stranger, but the oppressed and persecuted of all nations and religions." In keeping with this commitment, the U.S. Congress on myriad occasions has put aside national quotas and permitted hundreds of thousands of refugees to enter the United States on an ad hoc basis. For instance, the 1948 Displaced Persons Act granted 400,000 refugees, primarily from Europe, safe haven on American shores. Similarly, the 1953 Refugee Relief Act swung open America's gates to 2,800 Chinese refugees fleeing **Mao Tse-tung**'s revolution. (Still, flare-ups of nativist, anti-immigration sentiment have on occasion undermined America's commitment to those in dire need. In the 1930s, for example, the United States tragically turned away from its shores thousands of Jews who had escaped from Nazi Germany.)

The United States formalized its commitment to refugees with the passage of the McCarran-Walter Act of 1952 (also known as the Immigration and Nationality Act), which not only liberalized Asian immigration and naturalization but vested in the U.S. attorney general the power to "parole" into the United States any alien for "emergency reasons or for reasons deemed strictly in the public interest." "Parolees" are granted temporary admittance but not resident status. They may, however, seek an adjustment to another status. The Refugee Relief Act of 1953 permitted those seeking refuge from Communism to enter the United States. The attorney general's authority to parole refugees has been used extensively for those fleeing Communist persecution, including Hungarians who fled the Soviet invasion and occupation of their country in 1956, Chinese terrorized in the 1959 Communist takeover of mainland China, and Cubans who fled **Fidel Castro**'s revolutionary regime beginning in 1959. The 1965 Immigration Act afforded entry to the United States to refugees fleeing Communist-dominated regions of the Middle East and also reasserted the U.S. attorney general's power to grant asylum to parolees facing emergency circumstances.

The North Vietnamese and Vietcong advances in the Vietnam War and the Communist Khmer Rouge advances in Cambodia's civil war, both in 1975, which presaged Communist victories in those countries, imperiled the lives of hundreds of thousands of Vietnamese and Cambodians. In response to the crisis, the U.S. attorney general paroled many in danger into the United States: Between April and December 1975, 130,400 Vietnamese and Cambodian refugees were admitted as parolees. The refugee crisis intensified after the Communists completed their takeovers of Vietnam, Laos, and Cambodia in 1975, stimulating the U.S. Congress, which was dissatisfied with its prior policy of ad hoc admission, to pass in March of 1980 the Refugee Act, lauded as the first comprehensive refugee legislation in U.S. history. The Refugee Act eliminated the parole program and established a refugee quota of 50,000 per year through 1983. The president was granted the power to admit more refugees into the United States, after consulting with Congress, if the need arose. The 1980 Refugee Act also eliminated the ideological preference for refugees from Communist countries, redefining "refugee" as "any person who . . . is unable or unwilling to return to, and is unable or unwilling to avail himself or herself of the protection of [, a] . . . country because of persecution or a well-founded fear of persecution on account of race, religion, nationality, membership in a particular social group, or political opinion." Between 1975 and 1998, 1,342,532 Southeast Asian refugees were admitted to the United States.

The resettlement in the United States of refugees from Vietnam, Laos, and Cambodia continues to this day, although the number of refugees from Laos and Cambodia has sharply declined. In the years 1989 to 2002, 328,052 Vietnamese were resettled in the United States, while just 123 Laotians and 4,313 Cambodians came to America as refugees. Other Southeast Asians, namely, Indonesians and Burmese, who have faced repressive regimes and crippling poverty in their homelands, have also been admitted to the United States as refugees over the last three decades. Their numbers, however, are very small due to the obstacles confronting those who try to flee Indonesia and Burma. Between 1989 and 2002, a mere 37 Indonesians and just 2,256 Burmese were resettled in the United States. It should be noted that in 2002 the number of refugees resettled in the United States, whether from Southeast Asia or elsewhere, fell far below the norm because of concerns over the nation's security that arose in the wake of the September 11, 2001, terrorist attacks on the World Trade Center and the Pentagon.

What are first-asylum and second-asylum countries?

First-asylum countries are nations in the same region as the refugees' homeland that offer some modicum of safety, if only temporarily. In the aftermath of the Southeast Asian refugee crisis that erupted in 1975, Thailand, Malaysia, Hong Kong, the Philippines, and Singapore were designated first-asylum countries for refugees fleeing Vietnam, Laos, and Cambodia en masse. These first-asylum countries, especially Thailand, were overwhelmed by the sheer numbers of refugees—all in need of housing, food, clothing, and medical attention—despite assistance from international organizations, such as the Red Cross and the United Nations. Consequently, Malaysia shut its doors to Vietnamese, Laotian, and Cambodian refugees in 1979, and other countries refused admission to Vietnamese boat people who had begun arriving on unseaworthy boats in 1975. These countries limited their hospitality to fueling the refugees' boats and providing enough food and supplies so they could return to sea in search of another safe haven.

Second-asylum countries are those countries that permanently resettle refugees in their territory strictly on a voluntary basis as a way of easing the burden on first-asylum countries. For the Southeast Asians, the United States has been the leading second-asylum country, although Canada, China, Australia, and France have all shared the burden. Due to its failed foreign policy in Indochina, the United States, perhaps more than any other nation, has felt a moral obligation to alleviate the refugee crisis it helped create.

Which organizations have been involved in resettling refugees from Southeast Asia in the United States?

Various international, national, and private organizations have been involved in helping Vietnamese, Laotian, and Cambodian refugees resettle in the United States. The organization that has assumed the leading role is the Office of the United Nations High Commissioners for Refugees (UNHCR), which was created in 1951. The UNHCR coordinates the efforts of various volunteer agencies and nations around the world working to provide relief to Southeast Asian refugees in camps and has been extensively involved in resettling Southeast Asian refugees in the United States. In 1981 the UNHCR was recognized for its efforts with the Nobel Peace Prize.

On the national level the Office of Refugee Resettlement has been largely responsible for providing information, social services, and cash assistance to new Southeast Asian arrivals. VOLAGs, volunteer agencies under government contract to help resettle refugees through sponsors, have also played a part in the process. These include the United States Catholic Conference, the Lutheran Immigration and Refugee Service, the International Rescue Committee, the Hebrew Immigrant Aid Society, Church World Service, the Tolstoy Foundation, the American Council for Nationalities Services (which became Immigration and Refugee Services of America in 1994), and Travelers' Aid International. VOLAGs have been committed over the decades to finding sponsors for Southeast Asian refugees. These sponsors have tended to be families or church groups, rather than individuals, because of the tremendous effort and cost involved in resettling refugees, such as providing housing, clothing, and other necessities until the newcomers get on their feet and assisting them in such tasks as securing employment, enrolling their children in schools, opening and maintaining bank accounts, and shopping at supermarkets.

Mutual Assistance Associations (MAAs) have also played a significant role in helping Southeast Asian refugees adjust to American life. Created in 1975, MAAs are funded in part by the U.S. government and by private donations from corporations and individuals, and are run by refugees who have assimilated into the American mainstream and are able to volunteer their time to help new arrivals. They show refugees the ropes, offer translation services and English-language classes, and keep new arrivals abreast of services available to them in the community, such as counseling. Many new refugees are more comfortable seeking help from MAAs because the volunteers share their background and language. In addition to providing lessons about America, MAAs also encourage refugees to keep their native traditions alive. They sponsor festivities during holidays that refugees traditionally observed in their homeland.

Why were Southeast Asian refugees dispersed across the country when they first began arriving in the United States?

In 1975, 21 percent of Southeast Asian refugees were settled in California, and the rest were scattered across America, with at least one hundred in every state except Alaska. The rationale behind this approach to resettlement was to minimize the economic impact that a concentration of refugees might have on any one community. Since individuals had to go wherever sponsors could be found, some families were split apart. Cultural isolation and separation from family and friends swiftly bred discontent among the refugees, leading many to relocate after their initial settlement, a process known as secondary migration. By 1980, 45 percent of the first wave of Southeast Asian refugees had moved to ethnic enclaves, mostly in California, Texas, and Louisiana.

What is the 1.5 generation?

Asian immigrants and refugees born abroad but educated in the United States belong to what is known as the 1.5 generation. As the term itself connotes, the 1.5 generation is sandwiched between the old and the new: it looks to the past with nostalgia and is poised for the future. The 1.5ers from Southeast Asia fled their homelands as children, adolescents, or young adults and then swiftly acculturated to American life. This rapid assimilation alienated many 1.5ers from their parents and grandparents. To complicate matters, the 1.5 generation does not fit in entirely with the second generation of Southeast Asians, those born and raised in America.

VIETNAMESE AMERICANS

Which events in Vietnamese history led up to the mass exodus of Vietnamese to the United States beginning in 1975?

Since the beginning of its recorded history, Vietnam—which comprises the eastern coast of the Indochinese Peninsula in Southeast Asia and is bordered by China to the north, Laos and Cambodia to the west, and the Gulf of Tonkin and the South China Sea to the east and south—has endured long periods of foreign conquest and internal instability. From 207 B.C., the year the Kingdom of Nam Viet was formed, until A.D. 939, when the Vietnamese took advantage of China's preoccupation with the degeneration of the T'ang dynasty to establish an independent state, they were mostly under Chinese domination. In 1407 the Chinese reconquered the Vietnamese state, at that time called Dai Viet, but in 1427 the Vietnamese again expelled the Chinese from their lands. (In the seventeenth century they would even dispose of the Chinese ideographs that comprised the Vietnamese writing system and adopt French Jesuit **Alexandre de Rhode**'s transliteration of the traditional Vietnamese alphabet into the roman alphabet.) The Vietnamese then embarked on a period of expansion, advancing southward until they seized the Mekong Delta from Kampuchea in the mid-eighteenth century. Vietnam remained independent, for the most part, until French forces under the command of Emperor **Napoleon III** invaded in 1857, incited by the persecution of Catholic missionaries and converts there, captured Saigon in 1859, and forced Vietnam to cede three of its provinces in the Mekong Delta to France in 1862. In 1867 the French took over the rest of the delta.

In 1883 France was designated a protectorate over the north and central parts of Vietnam, essentially dividing the country into three: the protectorates of Tonkin (northern Vietnam) and Annam (central Vietnam), and the colony of Cochin China (southern Vietnam). In the late 1880s France combined these with the protectorate it had established over Kampuchea (Cambodia) and the one it had formed over Laos and renamed the entire region *Indochine*, or Indochina, to reflect the dual influences of China and India in the three colonized countries. The French colonial administration successfully developed three major industries in Vietnam, rubber, tea and coal, filling France's coffers. The Vietnamese, with the exception of a small elite, gained very little from this newfound prosperity. For many decades to come, they would attempt through uprisings and rebellions to overthrow the French colonial regime.

Who was Ho Chi Minh?

Ho Chi Minh was a Vietnamese revolutionary, nationalist, and Communist. Born **Nguyen Sinh Cung** in a village in rural Vietnam in 1890, Ho Chi Minh set sail as a galley boy for France in 1911, where he worked as a photo retoucher and then joined the French Communist Party. Before long he was working as a secret agent for the Russians, going under cover in Asia's cities, from Canton to Calcutta. In 1929 Ho Chi Minh began mobilizing militants in Hong Kong under a new party, the Indochinese Communist Party (ICP). After the Vichy French government collaborated with the Japanese in their occupation of Vietnam (and the rest of Indochina) in 1940, Ho Chi Minh returned to Vietnam for the first time in thirty years and urged his followers to rebel against both the French and the Japanese occupiers. In a remote camp he organized a Communist-led united front, or guerrilla force, called the League for the Independence of Vietnam, or Viet Minh, which had a strong support base in northern Vietnam. He also gave himself the name Ho Chi Minh, meaning "Bringer of Light."

Two days after Imperial Japan surrendered to the Allies on August 15, 1945, at the end of World War II, the Viet Minh, under Ho Chi Minh's command, launched the August Revolution to free Vietnam from the French. Within two weeks they had seized control of all of Vietnam. On September 2, 1945, Ho Chi Minh, with Communists and other nationalists supporting him, proclaimed an independent government and established the Democratic Republic of Vietnam (DRV), with himself as president. President **Harry S. Truman** refused to recognize the DRV and Ho Chi Minh's presidency, even though during World War II the U.S. Office of Strategic Services (OSS), the CIA's wartime predecessor, had trained Ho Chi Minh's forces in the jungles of Vietnam and an OSS officer, Major **Archimedes L. A. Patti,** had helped Ho Chi Minh formulate the Vietnamese Declaration of Independence. The Truman White House mistrusted the career Communist and his allies, the Soviet Union and Communist China.

Why in the aftermath of World War II did some Vietnamese view the United States as yet another foreign intruder into Vietnam's affairs?

France sought to reimpose its colonial administration on Vietnam, and in March 1946 the French and the Vietnamese reached a preliminary agreement outlining the creation of a Vietnamese free state within the French Union. In July of that year, however, formal negotiations collapsed; efforts to revive them in ensuing months proved fruitless. Then, in November 1946, fighting erupted between the French and Viet Minh forces, igniting the First Indochina War. The U.S.

government, motivated by concern that Vietnam would fall to the Communists, lent France economic assistance to fight the war in exchange for its pledge that it would eventually grant Vietnam full independence. As it turned out, Washington ended up financing 85 percent of the French campaign to recolonize Vietnam—a whopping $2.5 billion by 1954.

The First Indochina War lasted until 1954, when **Ho Chi Minh** and his Viet Minh troops, who were backed by the Soviet Union and the People's Republic of China, defeated the French at Dien Bien Phu, a city in northeastern Vietnam. Ironically, a young U.S. senator by the name of **Lyndon B. Johnson**—who later, as president of the United States, would bear the burden of the Vietnam War—and other key members of the Senate prevented the U.S. military from providing crucial reinforcements to the French at Dien Bien Phu. It seems that the U.S. military command had agreed to a plan, code-named Operation Vulture, that would allow sixty American B-29 bombers based in the Philippines, together with fighter planes of the U.S. Seventh Fleet, to conduct night raids against the Viet Minh at Dien Bien Phu. President **Dwight D. Eisenhower,** however, insisted that Congress had to approve Operation Vulture before it was put into action. When the plan was brought before the Senate, Senator Lyndon B. Johnson, then the leader of the Democratic minority in that body, along with others, vehemently opposed it.

How was Vietnam divided into North and South Vietnam?

After the decisive Viet Minh victory at Dien Bien Phu, an international conference convened in Geneva in the summer of 1954 to negotiate a cease-fire. In an effort to separate the warring parties, members of the conference determined that the French and the Vietnamese allied to the French would move south of the 17th parallel, the designated military demarcation line, while the Communist-led Viet Minh, with **Ho Chi**

Minh as leader, would move north of it. The Vietnamese people were given three hundred days to decide where to live. In keeping with the Geneva Accords, which were signed on July 21, 1954, a national referendum with the aim of reuniting Vietnam was to be held in 1956.

When did fighting erupt between North and South Vietnam, and how did the United States get involved in it?

In October 1954 French armed forces withdrew from Vietnam, and President **Eisenhower** proceeded to begin lending weapons, equipment, and U.S. military advisors to the anti-Communist government, led by Prime Minister **Ngo Dinh Diem,** that took shape in the southern zone of Vietnam, helping that government to establish in 1955 the independent state of South Vietnam, officially named the Republic of Viet Nam (RVN). This was accomplished in part through the creation in September 1954 of the Southeast Asia Treaty Organization (SEATO), an alliance of several western nations, the Philippines, Pakistan, and Thailand whose main function until it disbanded in 1977 was to prevent the spread of Communism in Southeast Asia. Concerned that the Communists would win the 1956 elections on the issue of the reunification of Vietnam's two zones, Ngo Dinh Diem refused to comply with the Geneva Accords' call for a referendum. The Soviet-backed northern zone of Vietnam, or North Vietnam, which was bent on supplanting the non-Communist government in Saigon with a regime that would consent to unification with the Communist government in Hanoi, responded by initiating terrorist acts in the South in 1957. Initially North Vietnam relied on Communist rebels and arms caches the Viet Minh had left behind in the South when they withdrew in 1954, but in 1958 it began to move guerrilla fighters into the South, who joined up with those who stayed behind in 1954 to form a force called the Vietcong, meaning "Vietnamese Communists."

The ranks of the Vietcong swelled as more guerrilla fighters from the North infiltrated South Vietnam and as South Vietnamese were coaxed with propaganda, coerced, and terrorized into joining. By 1961 the Vietcong posed a serious threat to the survival of South Vietnam.

Alarmed that South Vietnam—and then the rest of Asia and beyond—might fall to the Communists in accordance with the geopolitical concept of falling dominoes that governed U.S. strategy during the Cold War, President **John F. Kennedy** sent more U.S. military advisory personnel and supplies to South Vietnam. By November 1963, the month he was assassinated, President Kennedy had increased the number of military advisors stationed in South Vietnam to 16,000. November 1963 also saw the execution of Ngo Dinh Diem, who tried to flee during a coup but was captured and killed by his South Vietnamese bodyguard on November 2, 1963, just weeks before President Kennedy was gunned down in Dallas. The summer of 1964 saw two watershed events in the U.S. military commitment in Vietnam. On August 2 and August 4, 1964, North Vietnamese patrol boats fired on the U.S. destroyer *Maddox* in international waters in the Gulf of Tonkin. In response, the U.S. Congress passed the Tonkin Gulf Resolution that very month, authorizing President **Lyndon B. Johnson** to take all measures "to repel any armed attack against the forces of the United States and to prevent further aggression." (It later came to light that the attacks might have been pure fabrication.)

President Johnson soon began what would be a long, drawn out large-scale military buildup in Vietnam, slowly escalating the war. While at the end of 1964 there were just 23,000 American servicemen in Vietnam, by 1968 the Johnson administration had committed over half a million. (The number of U.S. troops in the country peaked at 543,400 in April 1969.) The financial cost of waging war increased exponentially, too, from $5.8 billion per year in 1965 to $28.8 billion per year from 1966 to 1969, partly because the United States had begun in early 1965 a bombing campaign in the skies of North Vietnam to try to force the North Vietnamese to the negotiating table. The bombing campaign was not massive and, thus, did not have a devastating effect on the North Vietnamese, who consequently refused to negotiate, and the United States sunk further into the quagmire called the Vietnam War.

What was the Tet Offensive of 1968?

Before daybreak on January 30, 1968—in violation of the Vietnamese New Year (*Tet*) truce they had pledged to observe—approximately 84,000 North Vietnamese launched an offensive in South Vietnam that would forever after be known as the Tet Offensive. Their attacks did not target fortifications in the countryside, but rather towns and cities. Saigon was hit hard during the Tet Offensive, and one of its main targets was the United States embassy. Nineteen Vietcong commandos were assigned to attack the U.S. embassy, and in preparation they smuggled arms into Saigon, storing them in an auto repair shop. In the early morning hours of January 31, 1968, the commandos pulled in front of the embassy in a taxicab, and within five minutes they had slaughtered four U.S. soldiers guarding the compound.

Thanks to a communications satellite that just a few months before had been placed over the Pacific Ocean, allowing for the instantaneous transmission of information by a global hookup, horrifying images of the attack were beamed right into America's living rooms—the first time in history that people sitting in their armchairs were truly exposed to warfare and experienced the sensation of being in the thick of it. Those images of U.S. soldiers in Saigon scrambling to secure the U.S. embassy as Vietcong lay dead in the courtyard were burned into American minds. Although the Tet Offensive did not stimulate a popular uprising in South Vietnam as the Vietcong had hoped, it did cast a gnawing doubt on the reassuring war reports released by the **Johnson** White House that victory was right around the corner. The Tet Offensive also caused Americans to associate *Tet,* the Vietnamese New Year, with chaos and bloodshed.

Besides the hippies, Jane Fonda, and others active in the American antiwar movement, who else opposed the Vietnam War?

Vietnamese students and spiritual leaders, among them Catholics, Buddhists, and representatives of indigenous Vietnamese religious groups, such as the Hot Hao sect, led the antiwar movement in South Vietnam. Their opposition to the Vietnam War was motivated by a variety of reasons. Some maintained that U.S. involvement in the war constituted interference in Vietnam's domestic affairs and domination of a Third World country. Others opposed the war because they felt that U.S. military tactics—such as the use of napalm and agent orange and the forcible relocation of rural villagers in supposedly secure "strategic hamlets," that is, fortified settlements, which demolished the rural economy and the cohesive peasant social unit—showed a callous, racist disregard for Vietnamese lives. Still others objected to the war because the Americans had supported French colonialism in Indochina.

It should be noted that while the majority of South Vietnamese were convinced that Communism was a far greater evil than the U.S. presence and, therefore, had no qualms about their government allying itself with the United States to defeat the Communist Vietcong, their optimism did wane as Washington made no progress in the war, despite the massive U.S. combat participation in it. The South Vietnamese generally attributed this failure to the critical tactical errors the Americans were making because they refused to seriously weigh the advice of South Vietnamese military officers. Of course, many other factors were also at play, including the fact that the U.S. government had no senior diplomats well versed in Vietnamese history and culture upon which to rely, underestimated the resolve of the North Vietnamese and the Vietcong, and failed to build a coalition of multinational forces. Furthermore, the U.S. military was not prepared as well as it should have been for unconventional warfare, and America's politicians, and not the Pentagon, directed the war and opted for a gradual escalation rather than a massive, brutal attack on the North at the very onset of the war to bring about the complete destruction of the North Vietnamese regime, which was certainly within the capability of the U.S. military.

Had the military brass been handed total control of the theater, they may have opted for an initial campaign in the North akin to "shock and awe," the massive air attack on Baghdad by U.S. forces that opened the Iraq War of 2003, that is, overwhelming force in the opening days of the conflict to paralyze the enemy. Of course, it was believed at the time that such a strategy would incite North Vietnam's mightiest socialist allies, China and the Soviet Union, and stimulate their massive intervention in the war—just as Chinese "volunteers" had come to the defense of the North Koreans during the Korean War. Finally, a massive, unrelenting attack on North Vietnam would have involved sending in U.S. ground troops, who would have been met by fierce North Vietnamese resistance, costing the lives of untold numbers of both civilians and soldiers.

When did the Vietnam War finally end?

In May 1968 direct talks between the United States and North Vietnam commenced in Paris but did not advance toward a political settlement of the conflict. President **Richard M. Nixon**'s presidential inauguration in January 1969 ushered in a sea change in the U.S. strategy in Vietnam. Despite the stalemated peace talks with the North Vietnamese, in 1970 President Nixon began to scale down U.S. ground operations in Vietnam as part of his policy of Vietnamization, that is, turning responsibility for ground combat and the direction of the war over to the South Vietnamese. In 1970, 150,000 American servicemen were withdrawn from Vietnam, and in 1971 another 100,000. By mid-1971 President Nixon, who by then recognized that an American victory in Vietnam was impossible, had almost completely halted the U.S. ground defense there (although U.S. bombing continued to try to force the North Vietnamese into a settlement of the conflict), and by August 1972 he had withdrawn all U.S. ground troops. At the same time, President Nixon bolstered the South Vietnamese government with financial and material assistance in hopes that it would remain standing long enough, for what was called "a decent interval," after the U.S. withdrawal that the United States would not bear the blame for the defeat in Vietnam.

The so-called Christmas bombing—the most intensive U.S. bombing campaign of the Vietnam War, which began on December 18, 1972, and lasted a fortnight—forced the North Vietnamese and South Vietnamese Communist forces to the negotiating table with South Vietnam and the United States, and on January 27, 1973, the parties managed to hammer out a peace agreement. According to the terms of the Paris Peace Agreement, a cease-fire would go into effect the next morning; the United States would withdraw all of its armed forces from South Vietnam (by the end of 1973, few remained in the South); all prisoners of war would be released; an international peacekeeping force made up of 1,160 troops would preserve the peace; the South Vietnamese would have the right to self-determination; and North Vietnamese troops could remain in the South but could not be reinforced. With the Paris Peace Agreement, U.S. involvement in the Vietnam War, a whopping $200 billion "investment," officially came to an end, not with a victory but with what President Nixon called "peace with honor." In August 1973 the U.S. Congress prohibited any resumption of U.S. military action in Indochina.

To the South Vietnamese, the Paris Peace Agreement was no peace at all. They became quite worried when at the bargaining table it was agreed that North Vietnam would not have to withdraw its troops from the South in the way of the Geneva Accords of 1954, which had required the Viet Minh to regroup north of the 17th parallel. The South Vietnamese rightly feared that the North Vietnamese would not honor the cease-fire or South Vietnam's right to determine its own future and that the fighting would intensify just as soon as they signed on the dotted line and U.S. military operations ceased. However, the South Vietnamese government had no choice but to sign the Paris Peace Agreement, as President Nixon had warned that if it rejected the agreement the United States would enter into a separate agreement with North Vietnam and cut off all aid to South Vietnam. President Nixon also threw the South Vietnamese a bone, pledging to petition Congress energetically for aid to South Vietnam if they signed the agreement.

In spite of the cease-fire and the withdrawal of U.S. armed forces, fighting quickly resumed within Vietnam, just as the South Vietnamese predicted. In March 1975 the North Vietnamese launched a large-scale offensive, attacking Ban Me Thuot in the Central Highlands. President **Nguyen Van Thieu** of South Vietnam ordered a withdrawal of all South Vietnamese forces from the Central Highlands as well as from the country's two northernmost provinces, igniting panic in the streets. The South Vietnamese forces began to unravel, and on April 21 President Thieu stepped down and flew to Taiwan. The remnants of the South Vietnamese government surrendered unconditionally on April 30, and that very same day the Vietcong captured, without a major battle, South Vietnam's capital, Saigon, which would soon be renamed Ho Chi Minh City. (**Ho Chi Minh** had died of a heart attack in Hanoi about six years earlier, on September 2, 1969, and although he wished to be cremated, the North Vietnamese leadership embalmed his body and put it on exhibit in a granite mausoleum, a replica of the Lenin Mausoleum on Red Square in Moscow.) The North Vietnamese installed a military government in the South, and on July 2, 1976, Vietnam was reunified as the Socialist Republic of Vietnam, with Hanoi as its capital city. There had been no "decent interval."

During the Vietnam War, a total of 57,605 American servicemen lost their lives in combat, and 303,700 were wounded. A great number came home with psychological scars that would haunt them for decades to come and cause some to even take their lives. South Vietnam sustained even more casualties: 220,357 South Vietnamese troops were killed in action, and nearly half a million were wounded. The North Vietnamese suffered the greatest losses, with 900,000 troops KIA and an unknown number wounded. The Vietnam War also cost more than one million North and South Vietnamese civilians their lives. Great numbers were also wounded during the long conflict. And approximately half a million South Vietnamese had become refugees by the time North Vietnam declared victory.

When did the first wave of South Vietnamese refugees fleeing the Vietnamese Communists arrive in America, and how were they resettled?

The first wave of Vietnamese refugees was evacuated from Vietnam and resettled in the United States between April and December 1975. In the last days of April, as a Communist victory in the Vietnam War appeared imminent, Vietnamese who feared that their religious beliefs, social class, or work on behalf of the South Vietnamese government or military or the United States would make them prime targets of the new Communist regime jammed the American embassy in Saigon, trying to prove that they had some connection, however tenuous, to the U.S. government or the South Vietnamese government, so as to be included in the American evacuation program. The U.S. government initially planned to evacuate only the approximately 17,600 Americans in South Vietnam, but when it realized that the lives of many Vietnamese were in peril, it expanded its evacuation to include Vietnamese ex-military and government officials, Vietnamese orphans, and others. All told, about 86,000 Vietnamese fled South Vietnam at the end of April, some cramming into helicopters that lifted off the roof of the American embassy and others on the few remaining planes departing from Saigon's Tan Son Nhut Airport. Between April and December of 1975, the U.S. government permitted 125,000 Vietnamese refugees, mostly well-educated urbanites, to enter the United States. These refugees constituted the first sizable group of Vietnamese on American soil, as prior to 1975 only scant numbers of Vietnamese, mostly students, teachers, and diplomats whose stays overseas were temporary, had ventured to American shores. In 1964 there were reportedly only 603 Vietnamese in America.

Upon their arrival in the United States, the Vietnamese refugees of the first wave were flown in U.S. military aircraft to reception centers at Camp Pendleton in Southern California, which opened on April 29, 1975, and later at Fort Chaffee in Arkansas, Eglin Air Base in Florida, and Fort Indiantown Gap in Pennsylvania. At these reception centers, which were under the direction of the Interagency Task Force (composed of representatives from a variety of federal agencies) and the U.S. military, the refugees underwent interviews and physical examinations, received identification numbers, and registered with national volunteer agencies in charge of resettlement that were on contract with the U.S. Department of State. All of their basic needs were met, and they also received lessons on American culture and the English language. Once sponsorships were arranged for the refugees to support themselves until they got on their feet, most left the reception centers.

Who were the "Vietnamese Boat People"?

Many Vietnamese desperate to leave Vietnam in the wake of the Communist takeover of the country were unable to do so through American channels. Either they lacked the connections that would entitle them to a spot on an American plane, there was no space for them on the planes, or they had no money to buy a seat when one became available. For most, the only other way to flee, and a perilous one at that, was by boat. And so a second wave of refugees left Vietnam on little, rickety, overcrowded boats vulnerable to attacks by pirates on the South China Sea. In the first weeks after the Communists seized Saigon, between forty thousand and sixty thousand Vietnamese took to the sea in boats. Many of these first Vietnamese boat people were rescued by U.S. naval ships, which transported them to Guam and the Philippines, where they awaited resettlement.

Other Vietnamese resolved to stay in their homeland, certain that peace would prevail in Vietnam after the Communist victory. However, when the new government instituted in 1979 such oppressive measures as the collectivization of agriculture, the expropriation of private businesses in the South, the "reeducation" of those associated with the Saigon government, restrictions on the press, and the relocation of urban populations to "New Economic Zones," a third wave of refugees abandoned Vietnam, again surreptitiously, by boat, from 1979 until the early 1980s. An appreciable proportion of the third-wave boat people were Vietnamese fishermen and farmers and their families, while about 40 percent were Sino-Vietnamese—that is, Vietnamese of Chinese ancestry, whom the Socialist Republic of Vietnam targeted for persecution, especially after border disputes between Vietnam and China flared up in 1979 and many ethnic Chinese businesses in what was South Vietnam were nationalized. (Although the Sino-Vietnamese constituted just 7 percent of the population in Vietnam in the 1970s, they owned or controlled 80 percent of the retail trade—at least until the Communist takeover.)

The Vietnamese refugees of the third wave often prepared for their escape over many months, slowly gathering supplies such as food, water, and gasoline. Once they left the shore, they had to face the rigors of an ocean voyage and outwit government officials and ubiquitous Thai pirates, and fend off starvation. They also had to find a country that would grant them asylum—not an easy task. Not surprisingly, scores of boat people, some scholars estimate as many as half, perished at sea. A large percentage of the survivors made landfall in Thailand and in other first-asylum countries, where they were given shelter in crowded, squalid refugee camps. Some lived in such squalor for years before they were resettled in the United States and other countries. By the mid-1980s the resettlement program was being phased out, which led to a decrease in the number of Vietnamese fleeing the Socialist Republic of Vietnam.

Who are the Amerasians?

The Amerasians are children born of Asian mothers (mostly Vietnamese) and U.S. servicemen stationed in Southeast Asia during the Vietnam War. When their fathers left Vietnam (in most cases by August 1972), most Amerasian children were left behind in the care of their mothers. They were often discriminated against by the Vietnamese people and by the government, which branded them *bui doi,* "the dust of life," because they were of mixed blood and were reminders of the U.S. presence in Vietnam. Concerned about the Amerasians' plight, the U.S. Congress passed the Amerasian Homecoming Act of 1987 to facilitate the transfer of Amerasians born between January 1962 and January 1977 to American soil as immigrants, not refugees. Between 1987 and 1993 more than 75,000 Amerasians and accompanying family members, mostly from Vietnam, began new lives in the United States. They belong to the fourth wave of Vietnamese to enter the United States, a wave that also includes political prisoners—that is, South Vietnamese troops and government officials who were sent to "reeducation camps" in Vietnam in the wake of the fall of Saigon to Communist forces. For more than a decade, the U.S. Department of State had urged the Hanoi government to release the prisoners and to permit them to emigrate. In 1988 Hanoi finally reached an agreement on the matter with the State Department, allowing a large percentage of the political prisoners, some 100,000, to leave Vietnam through the Orderly Departure Program.

How did the Vietnamese refugees of the various waves adjust to life in the United States?

The Vietnamese who arrived in America as part of the first through fourth waves have adapted to life in the United States with a general degree of success. Members of the first wave of Vietnamese refugees—professionals, technicians, and other educated folk of the upper and middle classes—have assimilated to American life with greater ease than subsequent waves. The first-wave refugees had long been exposed to Western culture and values and had some knowledge of English before stepping foot on American soil, and, hence, they were more prepared for life in the United States than later arrivals. Still, despite their skills and education, many in the first wave experienced occupational downgrading in the United States; for example, the results of a 1978 study indicate that 30 percent of Vietnamese refugees in the United States at the time had been professionals in Vietnam, but after twenty-seven months in America, only 7 percent had managed to maintain their status. The study also indicates that of the 15 percent who had been managers in Vietnam, only 2 percent had found equivalent employment in the United States.

Vietnamese refugees of the second and third waves tend to be much less educated, less skilled, and, consequently, less employable than the earlier arrivals. Most arrived with no English skills, a major obstacle to success in America. As a result, this pool of refugees remained on welfare well beyond the average period of adjustment to the United States and has suffered from a high rate of unemployment. Despite the obstacles they have encountered, a good many second- and third-wave refugees succeeded in starting small businesses. However, a sizable number remain trapped in low-paying jobs, isolated from the mainstream by language and cultural barriers, and from the more established Vietnamese community by economic and regional differences.

How many Vietnamese Americans are there, and where do they live?

The 1990s brought relatively large numbers of Vietnamese immigrants to American shores, anywhere from about 41,000 to 78,000 annually between 1990 and 1996. A large number of Vietnamese refugees were also admitted to the United States in this period: Between 1989 and 2002, 328,502 entered the country. Census 2000 tallied 1,223,736 persons of Vietnamese ancestry in the United States in 2000, up from 614,547 in 1990 and 261,729 in 1980 (the first year that the U.S. Census Bureau counted Vietnamese). Of those counted in 2000, 1,122,528 were Vietnamese alone, just 47,144 were Vietnamese and at least one other Asian ethnicity, and only 54,064 were Vietnamese and at least one other race. According to Census 2000 figures, the five states with the greatest number of Vietnamese (alone) in 2000 were California (447,032), Texas (134,961), Washington (46,149), Virginia (37,309), and Massachusetts (33,962). The vast majority call California home because a significant number of Vietnamese refugees passed through Camp Pendleton in Oceanside, California (just north of San Diego), and the majority of them settled in and around Westminster in Orange County, not far from Oceanside. While the federal government tried to disperse the Vietnamese refugees throughout the nation to lessen the social and fiscal strain on any one community, many found their way to Westminster.

By 1988 so many Vietnamese businesses had cropped up along a two-mile stretch of Bolsa Avenue in the heart of Westminster that the city was officially named "Little Saigon."

In Little Saigon, the sound of Vietnamese is far more prevalent than English in the more than fifteen hundred restaurants, cafés, grocery stores, and shops catering to the tight-knit Vietnamese-American community. Westminster's Little Saigon enjoys political as well as economic clout. It is home to **Tony Lam,** who became the first Vietnamese American to serve in elected office when the city chose him as councilman. Since then Little Saigon has frequently been a stop on the campaign trail for all kinds of candidates. Nowadays Little Saigon and the surrounding area are home to about 350,000 Vietnamese. The second-largest Vietnamese community in California is in San Jose, in the heart of Silicon Valley (in the northern part of the state). Just under 100,000 Vietnamese reside there.

How serious is the Vietnamese gang problem?

Since the Vietnamese first began arriving in the United States in significant numbers in the 1970s, they have been confronted with a confounding, insidious problem, Vietnamese gangs. The "first generation" of Vietnamese gang members in the United States entered the country as unaccompanied minors with no knowledge of English or American culture and belong to what is known as the lost generation. Despite the passage of time, Vietnamese gangs have persisted and continue to inspire fear in Vietnamese communities across the nation, in part because Vietnamese gang members, called *bui doi,* the "dust of life," are less preoccupied than most ethnic gangs with staying put and defending their "turf" and tend instead to case Vietnamese neighborhoods looking for innocent Vietnamese to rob. The tendency among Vietnamese refugee families to hoard their money at home rather than deposit it in banks has made them particularly susceptible to ransacking by gang members. Some gangs travel far and wide searching for victims, whom they find by consulting either the

"Nguyen" page in the local telephone book or undesirables in town who know which houses are the best to hit.

Who are some prominent Vietnamese Americans?

Vietnamese-American writer and humanitarian **Le Ly Hayslip** captured the attention of the media and the public with the release in 1993 of *Heaven and Earth,* the Hollywood motion picture based on her autobiographical accounts of life in Vietnam and America: *When Heaven and Earth Changed Places: A Vietnamese Woman's Journey from War to Peace* (1989) and *Child of War, Woman of Peace* (1993). The first work (written with **Jay Wurts**) chronicles the harrowing experiences of a young peasant girl who finds herself trapped in the violence of the Vietnam War, while the second (written with **James Hayslip**) is a rumination on the refugee experience in the United States. Born in Ky La, a village in central Vietnam, on December 19, 1949, Le Ly Hayslip was in her youth tortured and raped by South Vietnamese soldiers. Filled with shame, she fled to Saigon with her mother, where she worked as a servant in a wealthy household. Made pregnant by the master of the house, she was let go and went next to Da Nang, where she sold American goods on the black market to survive. In 1970 she married an American and came to the United States. In 1986 Le Ly Hayslip journeyed back to Vietnam to visit her family. The anguish that she witnessed in Vietnam inspired her to launch the East Meets West Foundation in 1988, an organization devoted to repairing the devastation wrought in Vietnam and promoting peace between that country and the United States.

Vietnamese-American actress **Kieu Chinh** first captivated American audiences and critics with her outstanding performance in the 1993 box-office hit *The Joy Luck Club,* based on the novel of the same name by Chinese-American writer **Amy Tan.** Her own life is a screenplay waiting to be written. Kieu Chinh was born in Hanoi in 1937 and enjoyed a comfortable family life, though without her mother, who died in 1942, until the Battle of Dien Bien Phu in 1954. After Vietnam was divided into North and South, Chinh, along with her father, brother, and other members of her family, hurriedly prepared to leave Hanoi. The night before they were to go to the airport to fly to safety, her brother vanished into the jungle to join a leftist student militia. Kieu Chinh and her father, **Nguyen Cuu,** who had been a deputy economic minister under the French administration, nonetheless headed for the airport, where they huddled on the runway for two days waiting for a plane. When they were boarding a cargo plane, Kieu Chinh's father instructed her to go on alone while he stayed in Hanoi to search for her brother. She managed to reach Saigon by plane, but she would never again see her father. (In 1960 Nguyen Cuu was imprisoned at the Hoa Lo Prison, which American POWs called the Hanoi Hilton, after a café waiter claimed he had criticized the Communist leadership. After five years Cuu was released, but with his prison record, he could not get a job and was forced to beg. At age sixty-nine he died of dysentery. Kieu Chinh's brother also spent time in Hoa Lo Prison for the crime of playing politically incorrect music on an accordion.)

Once in Saigon, Chinh landed a part in one of the nascent Vietnamese film industry's first efforts. She went on to act in films all over Asia and even starred in the Hollywood productions *A Yank in Vietnam* (1964) and *Operation C.I.A.* (1965). By the end of the 1960s, Kieu Chinh was a household name throughout Southeast Asia. Her career on the Asian big screen came to an abrupt end with the Communist takeover of Saigon on April 30, 1975, which made her a refugee for a second time. As Saigon fell, she boarded a plane to freedom with nothing other than $20,000 in worthless South Vietnamese currency and an address book. Chinh ended up in Toronto, where a refugee agency found her a job cleaning chicken coops with a hose for $2 an hour. Desperate, she called friends in Hollywood and was finally able to reach **Tippi He-**

dren, the lead actress in Alfred Hitchcock's thriller *The Birds*. Hedren promised to help, and Chinh found her way to Southern California. She was intent on pursuing acting in America, and in 1989 her big break came when she landed a part in *Welcome Home* (1989). She went on to act in *Vietnam, Texas* (1990), *The Joy Luck Club* (1993), *Riot* (1996), *Catfish in Black Bean Sauce* (1999), *Green Dragon* (2001), and *Face* (2002). Kieu Chinh has done much on behalf of Vietnamese on America's shores and in Vietnam, such as counseling Vietnamese refugees when they first arrive in America. And, in 1993 Chinh, prominent Vietnam veteran **Lewis B. Puller, Jr.,** who lost both legs and most of both hands during the Vietnam War, and distinguished journalist **Terry Anderson,** a marine who was a prisoner of war in Beirut for six years, established the Vietnam Children's Fund, whose mission is to "create a 'living memorial'—a network of elementary schools throughout Vietnam."

Dat Nguyen, the son of Vietnamese refugees, is the first Vietnamese American to play NFL football. He managed to rise to the top in his sport despite persistent claims that he is too small (he's five feet eleven inches and weighed about 221 pounds in 1999). Nguyen had an extraordinary collegiate career as a lineman with Texas A&M. By the end of his senior season in 1998, he had set Aggie career records with fifty-one consecutive starts, 517 career tackles, and an average of 10.7 tackles per game. For his efforts that season, he earned All-America honors from Walter Camp, *The Sporting News,* The Sports Network, Burger King/AFCA, *Football News,* and *College Football News,* was named the national and Big 12 Defensive Player of the Year, and won the Lombardi Trophy, the Chuck Bednarik Award, and other honors. The Dallas Cowboys selected the linebacker in the third round of the 1999 NFL Draft (he was eighty-fifth overall). Dat Nguyen finished his rookie season as the Cowboy's top special teams tackler, and in 2000 the Cowboys designated him the starting middle linebacker. Injuries kept him on the bench for six games in 2000, but Nguyen still managed to finish the season with forty-two tackles, two interceptions, four passes defensed, and four stops behind the line of scrimmage. In 2001 he played the full sixteen-game schedule and racked up ninety-one tackles, and in 2002 he took the field in just eight games but ended the season with forty-four tackles.

Which religions do the Vietnamese follow in America?

The predominant religion of Vietnam is Buddhism, which was introduced by the Chinese and the Indians early on in the country's history. Mahayana Buddhism is practiced primarily in the North, and Theravada Buddhism is practiced in the South. The Vietnamese also follow Christian religions, primarily Catholicism. Many Vietnamese, both in Vietnam and in America, do not practice one religion at the exclusion of all others: They follow two or even more religions at the same time, some combination of Buddhism, Confucianism, Taoism, Catholicism, Protestantism, Hot Hao, Cao Dai, or Lao Tsu. (Confucianism and Taoism are essential elements of Vietnamese culture, and most Vietnamese adopt some aspects of Confucian and Taoist ethics.) They harmonize their religious practice in such a way that conflicts rarely emerge and, when they do, rarely pose a moral dilemma. Thus, a Buddhist in Saigon or in Little Saigon may also be a Taoist and a Catholic. It is not unusual, then, for Vietnamese family members to be baptized and go to church on Sundays and later attend Buddhist services at a pagoda. (This tendency to adhere to different religions at times was certainly a cause for bewilderment among American sponsors of Vietnamese refugees.)

Incidentally, the Vietnamese religion known as Cao Dai is in itself a mixture of religious and secular beliefs and absolutely appeals to Vietnamese eclecticism. Cao Dai was founded by a mystic named **Ngo Van Chieu,** who claimed to commune with the Cao Dai spirit. Among its saints is **Victor Hugo,** in addition to **Jesus, Buddha,** and **Joan of Arc.**

ELEVEN ASIAN-AMERICAN WOMEN WHO HAVE MADE A DIFFERENCE

1. Anna Chan Chennault

Chinese-American political activist Anna Chan Chennault was born in Beijing in 1925, became a U.S. citizen in 1950, and first joined the Republican Party in 1960. During the Nixon presidency, she emerged as one of Washington's leading lobbyists and hostesses. On numerous occasions she has used her political clout to aid Chinese Nationalists in Taiwan. Chennault is vice-chair of the President's Export Council and an avid supporter of Asian-American participation in the political system.

2. Connie Chung

Chinese-American Connie Chung has enjoyed a long career as one of the nation's leading broadcast journalists. Highlights of that career include coanchoring the *CBS Evening News* in 1993 with Dan Rather, which made Chung only the second woman to anchor a network news broadcast. From 2001 to 2003 she anchored CNN's *Connie Chung Tonight*, an hour-long program combining investigative reporting and interviews that examined the people and the issues in the news.

3. Shamita Das Dasgupta

Asian-Indian American Shamita Das Dasgupta, a professor of psychology at Rutgers University, cofounded in 1985 MAN-AVI, the first organization to address the violence perpetrated against South Asian women in the United States. For her activism and research on domestic violence and cultural diversity, she has received numerous honors, including the Woman Leader Award by the YWCA of Central New Jersey in 1992. Shamita Das Dasgupta edited a collection of essays by and about South Asian women in the United States entitled *A Patchwork Shawl: Chronicles of South Asian Women in America*

(1998) and coedited with her daughter, Sayantani Dasgupta, *The Demon Slayers and Other Stories: Bengali Folk Tales* (1998).

4. March Kong Fong Eu

Chinese American March Kong Fong Eu became the first Asian-American assemblywoman in the nation in 1966, when she was elected to the California State Assembly. She served in that body until 1974, when she earned the distinction of being the first woman elected secretary of state of California. She served at that post until 1994, when President Bill Clinton appointed her U.S. ambassador to Micronesia.

5. Maxine Hong Kingston

With the publication of her bestselling and award-winning work *The Woman Warrior: Memoirs of a Girlhood Among Ghosts* (1976), which reflects on the negative impact of sexism in Chinese America by weaving folktales, fantasies, family experiences, and memories, writer and activist Maxine Hong Kingston became one of the first Asian-American writers to achieve national prominence, paving the way for future generations. A number of her later works, including *China Men* (1980) and *Tripmaster Monkey: His Fake Book* (1989), were also bestsellers.

6. Maya Ying Lin

Chinese-American architect Maya Ying Lin garnered resounding applause for her moving designs of the Vietnam Veterans Memorial (1982) in Washington, D.C.; the Civil Rights Memorial (1989) in Montgomery, Alabama; and the Langston Hughes Library (1999) in Clinton, Tennessee, among others. Her design for "the Wall" was selected from a pool of fourteen hundred in a national competition held in 1981, when she was still an undergraduate student at Yale University. In 2000 Maya Lin published *Boundaries*, a work exploring her architectural creations and sculptures.

7. Midori

Internationally acclaimed violinist Midori—who was born in 1971 in Osaka, Japan, and lives in New York City—stunned the classical music world with her surprise debut at the New York Philharmonic's traditional New Year's Eve concert in 1982, when she was just eleven. Since then she has performed with the most distinguished symphonic ensembles on concert stages around the globe. In 1992 she established Midori & Friends, a foundation committed to bringing classical music to New York City's children.

8. Patsy Takemoto Mink

In her long, illustrious career, Japanese-American congresswoman Patsy Takemoto Mink, a Nisei Democrat from Hawaii, not only opened doors in politics for Asian Americans but opened doors everywhere for women by shepherding landmark gender-equity legislation through the U.S. House of Representatives. After serving in both the Hawaii Territorial House of Representatives and the Hawaii Territorial Senate (as Hawaii's first woman in the state legislature) from 1956 to 1964, Mink became in 1964 the first Asian-American woman in the U.S. House of Representatives. She represented Hawaii in the House until 1976 and then again from 1990 until her death on September 28, 2002.

9. Irene Natividad

In 1985 Filipina American Irene Natividad became the first Asian American to head a national political organization when she was selected to chair the bipartisan National Women's Political Caucus, which is dedicated to electing and appointing women to public office. She was reelected to that post in 1987, and in 1994 President Clinton appointed her director of Sallie Mae, the nation's leading provider of student loans. Natividad is currently director of the Global Summit of Women, a forum devoted to fostering women's economic development.

10. Angela Oh

A criminal defense attorney and activist, Angela Oh gained the national spotlight by speaking on behalf of the Korean-American community during the 1992 Los Angeles riot, which erupted after a predominantly white jury returned a "not guilty" verdict in the case against L.A. police officers charged with beating African American Rodney King. The riots quickly engulfed L.A.'s Koreatown, damaging and destroying many Korean businesses, with losses estimated at $350 million. In 2003 Oh published an essay collection entitled *Open: One Woman's Journey.*

11. Amy Tan

Amy Tan first became a household name in America in 1989, the year her bestselling novel *The Joy Luck Club* hit bookstore shelves. The book was so successful that in 1993 it made it to the big screen as a hit motion picture of the same name. Tan is the author of three other novels, all highly acclaimed: *The Kitchen God's Wife* (1991), *The Hundred Secret Senses* (1995), and *The Bonesetter's Daughter* (2001).

What is the meaning of Tet *for Vietnamese Americans?*

For most Americans, *Tet* is synonymous with the Tet Offensive of 1968. For Vietnamese everywhere, *Tet* is the celebration of the Lunar New Year and usually extends for one week sometime between January 19 and February 20. *Tet* is the most important secular holiday on the Vietnamese calendar, and many Vietnamese families save all year long so they may celebrate it as lavishly as possible. *Tet* demands months of preparation, during which houses are thoroughly cleaned, and sometimes even repainted, in order to usher in a brand-new and hopefully lucky year.

Vietnamese *Tet* shares much in common with the Chinese New Year, which occurs at the same time of the year. Both celebrations hinge on a twelve-year cycle represented by a sequence of a dozen animals: the rat, ox, tiger, rabbit, dragon, serpent, horse, ram, monkey, rooster, dog, and pig. The year 2000, for example, was the year of the dragon, and it will not recur until 2012. And, thus, in 2000 the dragon featured prominently in *Tet* and Chinese New Year celebrations. Both celebrations also feature dragon dances and firecrackers to repel evil spirits, and both the Vietnamese and the Chinese give children new money wrapped in bright red envelopes. In the United States, *Tet* celebrations have been modified to fit the American work calendar, with most festivities scheduled for the weekends before and after *Tet.*

What is Vietnamese cooking like?

Sometimes called the nouvelle cuisine of Asia, Vietnamese cooking is a blend of foreign influences and native ingredients and varies from region to region. In the North the preponderance of stir-fried dishes and black pepper betray Chinese influences, while in the South the influence of India is apparent in the use of curry, cocoa, and tamarind. The inclusion of potatoes, asparagus, pâté de foie gras, french breads, and croissants on the Vietnamese table throughout the country, but particularly in the South, point to the impact of French colonialism on Vietnamese culture.

Fresh herbs, including mint, cilantro, and basil, as well as ginger, lemongrass, chile peppers, and garlic lend a distinctive flavor to Vietnamese cooking. Fish and seafood are popular, as is pork. Unlike other Asians, the Vietnamese serve many uncooked or lightly steamed vegetables, and many dishes are accompanied by plates heaped with fresh herbs, lettuce, carrots, cucumbers, and bean sprouts. Favorite dishes include Vietnamese-style "wraps," which consist of grilled meats, lettuce, fresh herbs, and vegetables encased in soft rice wrappers.

Nuoc mam, an all-purpose condiment made of fermented fish sauce, red chile peppers, garlic, sugar and lime juice, is commonly served with the wraps as a dipping sauce. *Cha gio,* Vietnamese spring rolls, which are not fried and are much lighter than their Chinese counterparts, are another popular dish. They are comprised of cellophane noodles, shredded carrot, pork, and scallions, all wrapped in thin rice wrappers. *Cha gio* are also dipped in *nuoc mam.*

Another favorite on the Vietnamese and Vietnamese-American table is *pho,* or noodle soup, which is such an integral part of Vietnamese cuisine that it has been called the unofficial national dish of Vietnam and is so beloved that the Vietnamese even serve it for breakfast. *Pho* comes in many varieties, but *pho bo,* beef and noodle soup, is a classic. Each steaming bowl of *pho* is accompanied by plates of assorted garnishes that may include fresh bean sprouts and green onions; thin slices of hot peppers; sprigs of fresh mint, cilantro, and basil; and lime or lemon wedges, as well as chile-garlic sauce, fish sauce, and sugar. Each person adds garnishes and sauces to taste. In Saigon the chain of Pho 79 restaurants were as popular as McDonald's, and in Little Saigons across the nation Vietnamese Americans have recreated a bit of home and have opened *pho* restaurants of their own, such as Pho Hot, which got its start in California and spawned franchises as far away as Toronto and Falls Church, Virginia.

LAOTIAN AMERICANS

Who are the Laotians?

Laos, the only landlocked country on the Indochinese Peninsula in Southeast Asia, is bordered by Thailand to the south and west (the Mekong River forms the greater part of this western border), Burma to the northwest, China to the north, Vietnam to the east and northeast, and Cambodia to the south. Laos is home to forty-seven distinct ethnic groups, who fit into three categories: the Lao Lum (valley Lao), who speak Tai languages and are in the majority; the Lao Theung (mountainside Lao), who speak Austroasiatic languages; and the Lao Sung (mountaintop Lao), who speak Hmong-Mien or Tibeto-Burman languages. The Lao (also called Lowland Laotians or Lowland Lao), who are mostly Lao Lum, and the Hmong, who are Lao Sung, are the ethnic groups most represented in the Laotian population in the United States. Smaller numbers of Mien, Khmu, and Thai Dam are also among those who have taken refuge in the United States.

Has Laos endured the same invasions that have plagued Vietnam throughout its history?

Much like Vietnam, Laos has endured foreign domination and internal strife ever since the first unified Laotian state, known as the Kingdom of Lan Xang ("Land of a Million Elephants"), was founded in 1353 by **Fa Ngoum.** With the exception of a period of Burmese domination from 1574 to 1637, the powerful Kingdom of Lan Xang ruled Laos until 1713, when internal dissension and mighty neighbors caused it to split into three kingdoms: Vientiane, Champassak, and Luang Prabang. In the eighteenth century, Siam (northern Thailand) largely controlled the three kingdoms. In the nineteenth century, the king of Vientiane tried to free his kingdom from Siamese control by uniting with Vietnam, but the more powerful Siamese simply made Vientiane a Siamese province. Toward the end of the nineteenth century, France seized control of the Siamese lands east of the Mekong River, and in 1893 Laos became a French protectorate.

During World War II, the Vichy French government agreed to indirect Japanese rule over Indochina, but French administrators stayed put in Laos. Faced with imminent defeat by the Allies in World War II, Japan attempted to bar the European nations from reasserting their dominance in Southeast Asia, and in March 1945 the Japanese announced the end of

French control of Laos. In August of that year, the Laotian premier, Prince **Petsarath,** declared the independence of Laos, which was named the Kingdom of Laos, with King **Sisavong Vong** of Luang Prabang the monarch. The struggle for political power that ensued among the heads of aristocratic Lao families ignited a fierce civil conflict, known as the thirty-year struggle (1945–75). One aristocrat, Prince **Souphanouvong,** allied himself with Vietnamese Communists and proclaimed his own government of Pathet Lao, meaning "Lao Nation," which organized a few thousand guerrilla troops with Vietnamese military support and was more a revolutionary movement than a bona fide government. In the spring of 1946, French troops reoccupied Laos, and in 1949 France granted Laos internal autonomy within the French Union.

In 1953 France granted Laos its full independence. Before long, however, the country was embroiled in a civil war waged between the anticommunist monarchy (the Royal Lao government) and its supporters and the Communist-backed Pathet Lao, which gained strength when, under the terms of the Geneva Accords concluding the First Indochina War, it was handed two provinces in northeastern Laos. (These provinces were supposed to rejoin the Kingdom of Laos through a national referendum held within two years.) The Communist Viet Minh, who controlled North Vietnam, supported the Pathet Lao to ensure that the Ho Chi Minh Trail—a network of tracks that ran through southeastern Laos and constituted North Vietnam's main supply line to the Vietcong in South Vietnam and Cambodia—remained intact. The United States, concerned that Laos would fall to Communism in keeping with the domino theory, supported the Laotian monarchy by training and equipping the Royal Lao Army to ensure its success in its near-constant campaigns against the Pathet Lao.

Even though the United States and the Soviet Union agreed to honor Laos's neutrality in July 1962 at a second international conference that had convened in Geneva, the U.S. government decided to fight a clandestine war, a component of which was a massive bombing campaign, against the Communist Vietnamese in Laos in two theaters, in what was essentially an expansion of the Vietnam War. One theater was in northern Laos, where Pathet Lao soldiers and North Vietnamese and Vietcong "volunteers" battled a "secret army" that was trained and equipped by the U.S. Central Intelligence Agency. To man this army, the CIA recruited great numbers of Hmong, who lived in the highlands along the Laos-Vietnam border, and other ethnic minorities in Laos. The other theater was the Ho Chi Minh Trail, where the CIA also employed its secret army of Hmong to stop the advance of North Vietnamese troops following the trail into South Vietnam and Cambodia, to rescue U.S. soldiers taken prisoner or otherwise imperiled, and to gather enemy intelligence. The Americans had no qualms about relegating high-risk operations to the Hmong, and, as a result, approximately fifteen thousand Hmong lost their lives in the fighting.

After Saigon and Cambodia fell to the Communists in 1975, the Pathet Lao seized control of Laos, and on December 2, 1975—after thousands of Royal Lao government officials and troops were imprisoned—the Lao People's Revolutionary Party abolished the six-century-old Lao monarchy and proclaimed the Lao People's Democratic Republic, a Marxist regime closely aligned with Communist Vietnam and the Soviet Union. The Laotian people offered little resistance to the new regime, taking seriously the Pathet Lao's pledge to build a more democratic Laos that adhered to Buddhist rather than Marxist tenets and embraced all citizens.

Why then did hundreds of thousands of Laotians flee from Laos to Thailand beginning in 1975, and where did they go from there?

Reneging on its promises to the people, the Communist Pathet Lao immediately began to implement hard-line socialist reforms—including the nationalization of industry and the collectivization of agriculture—to flagrantly violate citizens' human rights (such as by denying them freedoms of speech, assembly, association, movement, and the press), and to send Laotians to remote "political reeducation camps." In response to such repression, hundreds of thousands of Laotians, among them even those who had backed the Pathet Lao, fled over the Mekong River into Thailand. The Thai authorities permitted some of the Laotians to occupy refugee camps that had been set up but forced others to return to Laos. Even before the Pathet Lao victory, thousands of Hmong and other ethnic minorities had fled the war, sometimes by burrowing farther into mountain regions of the country, where Americans dropped them supplies. By the early 1970s, a high percentage of American aid for Laos was given to such internal refugees. After the Pathet Lao won the war, the new regime targeted the Hmong, who had fought hard on behalf of U.S. and Royal Lao forces, for systematic extermination, and they fled in large numbers to Thailand. Entire Hmong villages, with as many as twelve thousand to sixteen thousand inhabitants each, crossed the border to Thailand, where they remained in refugee camps waiting for help from the United States. (The U.S. government had promised them any assistance they needed if Laos fell into Communist hands.)

All told, 10 percent of the people of Laos, and as much as 30 percent of the country's Hmong population, ran for their lives across the border. As many as 90 percent of those who fled were from the educated and middle classes; this brain drain would have enormous repercussions for Laos's future development. Once in Thailand, the Laotian refugees eked out an existence in large refugee camps as they waited—sometimes languishing for years—to be accepted into resettlement programs in Western countries, mostly the United States, Canada, France, and Australia. Few headed back to Laos: In the 1980s, for example, only about seven thousand Laotian refugees chose that option. The year 1991 found approximately fifty-five thousand Laotian refugees still waiting in the camps for their day of resettlement, which had virtually halted. The UN High Commission for Refugees, at the prodding of Thailand, made greater efforts to repatriate the remaining Laotians, but by 2000 just half of the refugees had gone home. Those who insisted on staying in Thailand were mostly Hmong.

How many Laotians have been resettled in the United States, and do they continue to seek refuge in this country?

Between 1975 and 1996 the United States gave refuge to 250,000 persons from Laos, including Lao, Hmong, Mien, Khmu, and Thai Dam. Although they represented a mere 10 percent of the population of Laos, the Hmong comprise nearly half of the total Laotian refugee population in America. When the U.S. Bureau of the Census began counting the Laotian population in the United States in 1990, it created two categories: Laotian (individuals who identify themselves on census forms as Laotian, Laos, or Lao) and Hmong (those who identify themselves as Hmong, Laohmong, and Mong).

According to 2000 census data,186,310 persons of Hmong ancestry resided in the United States in 2000, up from 90,082 in 1990; 169,428 of those tallied in 2000 were Hmong alone, a mere 5,284 were Hmong and at least one other Asian ethnicity, and 11,598 were Hmong and at least one other race. In 2000, as in the past, the Hmong were concentrated in just a few states. According to Census 2000, 65,095 Hmong (alone) called California, especially the Central Valley, home. The next four states with the highest Hmong (alone) populations in 2000 were Minnesota (41,800), Wisconsin (33,791), North Carolina (7,093), and Michigan (5,383).

As for Laotians, in 2000 the U.S. Bureau of the Census counted 198,203 persons of Laotian descent in the United States, up from 149,014 tallied in 1990; 168,707 of those tallied in 2000 were Laotian alone, 10,396 were Laotian and at least one other Asian ethnicity, and the remaining 19,100 were Laotian and at least one other race. Laotians have dispersed to a greater degree than the Hmong in America: Many more states have Laotian populations of 1,000 or more than Hmong populations of the same size. The five states with the greatest number of Laotians (alone) in 2000 were California (55,456), Texas (10,114), Minnesota (9,940), Washington (7,974), and North Carolina (5,313).

In the late 1970s the Laotian government—understanding that it would never be able to mold a socialist state out of such an impoverished, undeveloped nation—moved away from its commitment to the socialist transformation of Laos and began to liberalize the Laotian economy and lift restrictions on religious expression. In August 1991 Laos produced a new liberal constitution, and subsequently its relations with the United States and other Western nations improved. In 1997 Laos became a member of the Association of Southeast Asian Nations, or ASEAN, whose aim is a prosperous, stable, and peaceful Southeast Asia. Despite its turnaround, the Lao People's Revolutionary Party has preserved its monopoly on political power into the twenty-first century and continues to ignore human rights. In the first years of the new millennium, it faced allegations that it had caused the disappearance of approximately 300,000 persons between 1975 and 2001. Still, the number of refugees entering the United States has diminished greatly since 1997. In the years 1998 to 2002, only 123 refugees from Laos were admitted to the United States.

How difficult has it been for refugees from Laos to adjust to American life?

U.S. government agencies have noted that of all Southeast Asian refugees, those from Laos have encountered the most difficulty adjusting to the complex, fast-paced life in the postindustrial, urban United States. The Hmong have experienced the worst culture shock of all Laotians, due to their tribal beliefs, group mentality, and transplantation from a remote and rural region of Laos, where they had no experience at all in urban and modern living. For the Hmong, even simple procedures, such as using an electric stove or a toilet, seem strange. Such tasks as navigating the welfare bureaucracy, dealing with the electric or telephone company, and becoming acquainted with the American school system are downright daunting. To further complicate matters, 70 percent of the Hmong resettled in America are illiterate in their own language. Until 1953, when missionaries arrived in their mountain villages, the Hmong had no written language and relied instead on the oral tradition of folktales to preserve their history. Illiteracy has made the process of learning English doubly taxing for the Hmong.

All of these obstacles have made finding and keeping jobs extremely hard for the Hmong in the United States. Those who find work usually end up making a meager living selling handicrafts, doing housecleaning, or laboring as seasonal migrant workers. Their general maladjustment to American life has left the Hmong feeling isolated, marginalized, and, in numerous cases, homesick and depressed.

What is Hmong sudden death syndrome?

For no apparent reason, a number of Hmong males in the United States who suffered from no physical ailment have met sudden and mysterious deaths in their sleep. The syndrome, called Hmong sudden death syndrome, has tended to strike men aged thirty to fifty who saw combat when they were between the ages of fifteen and twenty. Relatives of victims have described choking and breathlessness as two symptoms that signaled the onset of sudden death syndrome. Nerve gas, which was used in the fighting in Laos in the 1970s, has been ruled out as a cause. Some medical experts contend that severe depression brought on by war trauma and the stress of acculturating to American life is the trigger for Hmong sudden death syndrome.

Have Laotians had a collective voice in America?

Only recently have Laotians created a collective voice in America: 2000 saw the formation of the Laotian American National Alliance (LANA), the nation's first nonprofit organization committed to promoting the economic and social advancement of all people of Laotian ancestry in the United States. At LANA's launch in Berkeley, California, on December 9, 2000, **Puongpun Sananikone,** president and CEO of PacMar, Inc., an international management consulting firm based in Hawaii, summed up what Laotians in America need to accomplish and the purpose of LANA: "To be able to participate productively in, and not be marginalized by, the increasingly globalized American economy, Laotian Americans must find new ways to free themselves from the crippling grip of outdated cold-war issues and mind set, which has divided and paralyzed many Laotian communities in the U.S. and around the world for the past two decades. LANA is an important building block; a new, nonpartisan catalyst to promote cooperation among Laotians of all ethnic origins. . . ."

Which religions do Laotians practice?

Most Laotians in the United States are adherents of Theravada Buddhism, which was founded in the fourteenth century by **Fa Ngoum** (who established the Kingdom of Lan Xang). At the same time they practice Buddhism, most Hmong also follow the cult of *phi*, meaning "religious spirits." Rather than causing conflict, Theravada Buddhism and *phi* coexist harmoniously in the Laotian belief system, perhaps because they pertain to separate realms: Buddhism deals with the next realm, while *phi* concerns itself with progress on this plane of action.

What kinds of foods do Laotian Americans like?

Laotians in America enjoy traditional Laotian cooking as well as typical American fare and other Asian cuisines. Rice, fish, fermented fish paste (*padek*), eggs, beef, corn, cassava, sweet potatoes, limes, white radish, cucumbers, mint, and hot peppers are key ingredients in the Laotian kitchen. A popular Laotian dish is *laap*, which consists of beef or fish that is first sauteed and then combined with lime or lemon juice; fish sauce; a little ground rice; minced mint leaves, garlic, parsley, and green onions; and diced hot peppers. Another favorite is salad made with shredded papaya that is flavored with *padek* and hot peppers.

CAMBODIAN AMERICANS

What is the story behind the arrival of Cambodians in the United States?

Cambodia, or the Kingdom of Cambodia, as it is officially known, is situated in the southwestern part of the Indochinese Peninsula in Southeast Asia and is bordered on the northwest and west by Thailand, on the east and southeast by Vietnam, on the northeast by Laos, and on the southwest by the Gulf of Thailand (part of the South China Sea). The ethnic Khmer constitute the major ethnic group in Cambodia, their homeland for more than two millennia. Their language is called Khmer. Cambodia has been shaped by a long history of border struggles and foreign occupation—in the way of Vietnam and Laos—as evidenced by the frequency with which its name has changed. The first Khmer kingdom, called Angkor, meaning "holy city," took shape in what is present-day northwestern Cambodia in 802. Until the Angkor kingdom's demise in 1432, its Khmer forces ranged over Siam (nowadays northern Thailand), Laos, and southern Vietnam, and its people built glorious stone temples that reflect both

Buddhist and Hindu influences—the most famous of which is Angkor Wat, one of the world's largest religious edifices. Ineffectual rulers and the erosion of the state's authority by Buddhism left the Angkor kingdom vulnerable to attack, and in 1432 marauding Thai armies swarmed its capital, forcing the Khmer to flee.

The next four hundred years brought internal and external strife: The Khmer rulers were frequently engaged in armed conflicts with Siam and Vietnam. In 1863 France gained control of Cambodia, and under the terms of a treaty signed that year, the country became a French protectorate. (Its status would not change until 1953, when Cambodia was designated an autonomous state within the French Union.) In the way of the Vietnamese and Laotians, the Khmer fought against French colonialism until World War II, when Japan briefly imposed its rule over the country but left in power Vichy French colonial administrators, who in 1941 installed a nineteen-year-old Khmer prince, **Norodom Sihanouk,** on the throne. Facing certain defeat by the Allied powers, Japan encouraged King Sihanouk to proclaim independence, which he did. But in the aftermath of World War II, the French reclaimed Cambodia. Then, in November 1953, France, which had a lot on its plate with Vietnam, gave Cambodia nominal independence. In keeping with the 1954 Geneva Agreements, Cambodia was granted full independence, and King Sihanouk was named the only legitimate authority in the country.

During the Cold War, which raged in the 1950s, King Sihanouk was committed to a policy of neutrality in an effort to placate the People's Republic of China, the giant to the north, and so he accepted aid from both "the free world" and the Soviet-led Communist bloc. When North Vietnamese forces used the Ho Chi Minh Trail, which ran through eastern Laos and eastern Cambodia, to move military personnel and weapons and found refuge in eastern Cambodia from American troops and bombs, essentially spreading the Vietnam War to Cambodia, King Sihanouk looked the other way, so as not to ruffle the feathers of the Soviet Union and China. In March 1970 a U.S.-backed coup deposed King Sihanouk and put in his place his defense minister (also his prime minister), General **Lon Nol,** who opposed the presence of Vietnamese Communists in Cambodia as well as Sihanouk's "Buddhist socialism."

Once General Lon Nol came to power, he abolished the monarchy and sought to rid the country, which he renamed the Khmer Republic, of Vietnamese Communists and to squelch the small radical Cambodian Communist movement, the Khmer Rouge—with U.S. military and other aid, a sum total of more than $1.5 billion in the five years that the Khmer Republic existed. Meanwhile, the Communist Chinese and North Vietnamese—and the exiled Norodom Sihanouk—lent their support to the Khmer Rouge. Soon after General Nol assumed the presidency of the Khmer Republic, the country was engulfed in civil war, lasting until 1975, between Nol's soldiers and Khmer Rouge forces. Nol permitted American and South Vietnamese forces to support him in the war. An important aspect of that support was Operation Breakfast, the U.S. bombing raids on North Vietnamese depots and supply lines hidden in the Khmer Republic's eastern provinces. (Operation Breakfast was kept from the U.S. Congress and the American people. It became known only later, when American pilots who had taken part in the raids testified in congressional hearings.)

As "collateral damage" from U.S. bombing raids in rural areas of the Khmer Republic mounted, outraged peasants joined the Khmer Rouge. With these new recruits and military backing from the North Vietnamese, the Khmer Rouge's control of the country gradually increased. Shortly before the fall of Saigon on April 30, 1975, it launched a major offensive, storming the capital of the Khmer Republic, Phnom Penh, on April 17, 1975, and seizing the reins of power. The civil war came to an end. A half million people had died in the fighting. The Khmer Rouge renamed the country Democratic

Kampuchea and appointed Norodom Sihanouk head of state. In April 1976 King Sihanouk was ousted, and **Dhien Sanipan** became the first president, with **Pol Pot,** a pseudonym for **Saloth Sar,** as prime minister.

What were the Khmer Rouge's "killing fields"?

Just as soon as it seized power, the Khmer Rouge regime, under **Pol Pot**'s secret and paranoid rule, began to execute a massive social restructuring project to rid Democratic Kampuchea of all remnants of its past and all influence from outsiders and to create a model agrarian society. Pol Pot relied on extreme brutality and genocidal massacres to achieve this new order. His regime outlawed private property and money, suppressed religious expression, and closed schools and hospitals. It also engaged in ethnic cleansing: It expelled approximately 150,000 of the 400,000 ethnic Vietnamese in the country, murdering tens of thousands as they headed to the Cambodia-Vietnam border, and also killed 200,000 ethnic Chinese, mostly through starvation and its accompanying diseases. In addition, the Khmer Rouge engaged in "class" cleansing: Pol Pot's henchmen systematically exterminated educated Cambodians, the upper and middle classes, those who had supported the U.S.-backed government of **Lon Nol,** and all others deemed enemies of the regime.

While it was targeting various groups for persecution and extermination, the regime was also evacuating urban areas, pushing men, women, and children alike into isolated agricultural collectives in the countryside, where they were forced to work in units constructing gargantuan irrigation ditches and dams with their bare hands and growing crops. (In some instances, Khmer Rouge soldiers slashed the tires of those fleeing the cities so that they were forced to go on foot to the collectives.) Children were customarily separated from their parents and were forced to perform agricultural work in mobile working units away from their families. The entire nation was essentially converted into one huge agricultural labor camp, or *gulag archipelago,* and all of its people into agricultural workers.

Cambodians were forced to work long days in the camps on a starvation diet of rice gruel. Any who showed the least resistance were tortured or killed on the spot by Khmer Rouge soldiers. Even foraging for edible plants and insects to ease hunger was deemed stealing from the state and brought harsh punishment, such as being subjected to the excruciatingly painful bites of red ants, or an agonizing death, such as being buried alive. Incalculable numbers of people died from torture, exhaustion, starvation, debilitation, and disease. Those who kept themselves alive suffered from malnutrition and the ailments and diseases that result from it, such as scurvy and beriberi. Before long the Khmer Rouge directed its hideous violence inward, incarcerating some 20,000 Khmer Rouge leaders that a paranoid Pol Pot considered no longer trustworthy and torturing to death all but seven of them. Then, in 1978, the Pol Pot regime rounded up and murdered between 100,000 and 250,000 Khmer Rouge military commanders, cadres, and their relatives. Although exact figures are unknown, by the time Pol Pot's reign of terror came to an end on December 28, 1979, 1.5 to 3 million people had perished in "the killing fields." According to the Cambodian Genocide Program, a project of the Genocide Studies Program at Yale University, 1.7 million people (21 percent of Cambodia's population) died in the Cambodian genocide of 1975–79.

About 34,000 Cambodians did manage to escape the genocide by fleeing across the Cambodia-Thailand border into Thailand. So few made it to safety because the Khmer Rouge maintained strict control over the population's movement, kept the people weak from starvation and illness so they could not mobilize themselves, murdered any found trying to escape, and booby-trapped the escape routes with land mines and walls of sharpened bamboo stakes. Hundreds of Khmer Rouge middle-ranking leaders who opposed Pol Pot's genocidal massacres and torture fled to Vietnam to enlist the aid of the Vietnamese in toppling Pol Pot. The Vietnamese obliged.

How exactly did Pol Pot's genocide end?

Pol Pot's diabolical repression and mass extermination of the Cambodian people ended when Vietnamese troops invaded Democratic Kampuchea on December 25, 1978, mostly in response to Khmer Rouge incursions into Vietnamese territory, and swiftly drove the Khmer Rouge forces into the western back country, where they would wage a second Cambodian civil war for a dozen years. Several days later, the Vietnamese proclaimed the country the People's Republic of Kampuchea and set about installing a client regime made up largely of Khmer Rouge defectors and headed by dissident Khmer Rouge officers **Heng Samrin** and **Hun Sen** (who had both escaped to Vietnam during the Pol Pot years). Once the Vietnamese were in power, the Cambodian people went back to their homes or wandered around the country searching for family members who may have survived. In the late spring to early autumn of 1979, however, approximately 140,000 Cambodian refuge seekers headed for Thailand, the majority on the verge of starvation because an appreciable portion of the 1979 rice crop was not harvested and food aid was not reaching them for myriad reasons, including the fact that the country's severely damaged roads were impassable. In the mass exodus were also Cambodians who refused to live under Communism and the Vietnamese enemy and longed to be resettled in the West.

As for the new socialist government in the People's Republic of Kampuchea, it ran into problems reconstructing the country due to a shortage of skilled workers and professionals and scant foreign aid. Fighting between the Khmer Rouge guerrillas, the client Cambodian government, and Cambodian anticommunist and royalist factions wrought further havoc on the country, which in 1989 was renamed the State of Cambodia. Most of these warring parties signed the UN-brokered Paris Peace Agreement on October 23, 1991, and the civil war ceased. In May 1993 a UN-supervised interim government held free elections in Cambodia. After some controversy, a coalition government, what really amounted to two parallel governments, was set up, and the country was once again renamed, this time the Kingdom of Cambodia. In the mid-1990s the coalition government fell apart, along with the Khmer Rouge. As for Pol Pot, he carried on—and even was able to kill his former defense minister, **Son Sen,** and Son Sen's family in 1997—before he was finally placed under house arrest and died in April 1998. Only two Khmer Rouge leaders were charged in court and sentenced to prison terms for their crimes against humanity. Life in Cambodia for average citizens remains extremely difficult to this day.

How many Cambodian refugees have made their way to America, and where have they settled?

Before 1975 few Cambodians had ventured to the United States. (In the 1950s and 1960s, several hundred had come to pursue education.) In early April 1975, as Khmer Rouge forces were drawing closer to Phnom Penh, the U.S. embassy in the city was authorized to evacuate to the United States one thousand high-ranking Cambodian government officials, military commanders, and individuals who had worked hand in hand with the Americans, all of whom were in danger of being arrested or even killed when the Khmer Rouge seized power. Only eight hundred took the embassy up on the offer, the others confident that peace would be restored. Five thousand Cambodians living abroad were also given the option of entering the United States as refugees. Only forty-six hundred accepted. Both sets of refugees were processed and then airlifted in U.S. military aircraft to reception centers at Camp Pendleton, Eglin Air Base, Fort Chaffee, and Fort Indiantown Gap. From this group of individuals—the first wave of Cambodian refugees—who were educated and multilingual, had experience living abroad in modern societies, and were spared the horror of the killing fields, would come the leaders of the Cambodian community in the United States. Many would abandon their professions to devote their lives to helping their less fortunate compatriots—largely uneducated farmers and fishermen with no English-language skills—who would arrive on American shores as second and third waves.

The second wave of Cambodian refugees consisted of the approximately 34,000 Cambodians who had managed to flee over the border to Thailand during the Khmer Rouge years and were provided for courtesy of the Thai government until they could be resettled in the United States, Australia, France, Canada, and in several other nations. Approximately 10,000 of the 34,000 were given refuge in the United States. The third wave of Cambodian refugees to come to the United States consisted of a little more than 100,000 of the 140,000 Cambodians who had fled starvation for Thailand in 1979, the first 20,000 of whom were selected for resettlement in America in 1981. All told, between 1975 and 1994, when the U.S. government ended its Cambodian refugee admission program, a total of 148,665 Cambodians were admitted to the United States as refugees. In 1990, in its first count of Cambodians, the U.S. Bureau of the Census tallied 147,411 persons of Cambodian ancestry in the United States. Since 1993 about 1,400 Cambodians have immigrated to the United States annually, and between 1989 and 2002, 4,313 were admitted to the United States as refugees. Small numbers have also returned to Cambodia to take part in the country's reconstruction. With the influx of Cambodian immigrants and the high number of births in the Cambodian community in America, in 2000 the U.S. Bureau of the Census tallied 206,052 persons of Cambodian ancestry residing in the United States; 171,937 of those tallied in 2000 were Cambodian alone, while 11,832 were Cambodian and at least one other Asian ethnicity, and 22,283 were Cambodian and at least one other race.

The federal government had a policy of placing the Cambodian refugees in all parts of the United States, wherever it could find sponsors for them, such as local churches. However, many refugees found their new hometowns unsuitable, either due to the climate, few employment opportunities, long distances from relatives, or a lack of support groups and cultural networks. Thus, many Cambodians relocated to places that suited their needs, and for the majority that meant California. According to 2000 census figures, 70,232 Cambodians (alone), the vast majority of the entire Cambodian population in the country, called California home in 2000. Long Beach, California, boasts the largest Cambodian population in America, and the largest Cambodian diasporic community in the world, for that matter. The Long Beach Cambodian community got its start in April 1975, when the few Cambodian residents living there (they had studied at the University of California, Long Beach, in the 1950s and 1960s, had gone home, but then had returned in the 1960s and early 1970s as their country fell into chaos) went to greet the first one thousand Cambodian refugees of the first wave who had arrived at Camp Pendleton. They and university professors in the area sponsored several hundred of the refugees, who then made Long Beach their home. Slowly the community grew with the arrival of second- and third-wave Cambodian refugees. The Cambodians in Long Beach opened small businesses catering to their community, which attracted Cambodia's secondary immigrants. The center of the Long Beach Cambodian community is Little Phnom Penh, which sprouted up on Anaheim Street.

The states next in line with the largest Cambodian (alone) populations in 2000 were Massachusetts (19,696), Washington (13,899), Pennsylvania (8,531), and Texas (6,852). The center of Massachusetts's relatively large Cambodian community is Lowell, a city situated on the outskirts of Boston. With the economic downturn in the textile industry in the 1920s, the economy of Lowell, a nineteenth-century textile and industrial giant founded in 1826, went into a downward spiral. The city was finally revitalized in the early 1980s, thanks to Wang Laboratories, Inc., founded by Chinese American **An Wang,** which had set up its corporate headquarters there, as well as Raytheon and Digital Equipment, which had established electronics assembly plants in the city. The promise of jobs with these companies drew Cambodians to Lowell, and by the late 1980s the city's Cambodian community had grown to about twenty-five thousand strong. The great Cambodian migration to Lowell wrought havoc on a public school system unequipped to meet the special needs of refugee children, causing non-Asians in the city to become disgruntled. When the electronics industry experienced a recession in the early 1990s and non-Asian workers in Lowell were laid off, resentment against the Cambodians in the community turned fierce. Consequently, the steady inflow of Cambodians to Lowell ceased. However, as non-Asians in Lowell came to understand the positive effect the Cambodians had had on the community, tensions diminished and Cambodians began once again to settle in the city.

How difficult was it for the three waves of Cambodians to acculturate to the American way of life?

It was quite difficult for Cambodians to acculturate, for numerous reasons. First, from the perspective of resettled Cambodians, the civil war, followed by the Khmer Rouge's time of terror, stripped them of every remnant of their culture and their past—including family members—leaving them with no way to resurrect their former lives once in America. **Haing Ngor,** a survivor of the Khmer Rouge terror and an award-winning actor who starred in *The Killing Fields* (1984), describes this phenomenon best in his autobiography, entitled *Haing Ngor: A Cambodian Odyssey* (1988):

> [i]n Cambodia a way of life had evolved over many hundreds of years. It was much simpler than America, and that

> was part of its beauty. In Cambodia we didn't have welfare or Social Security. We didn't need them. All we needed were our families and the monks. . . . The system was not perfect, but it worked. Everybody had enough to eat. Cambodian society was stable. For generation after generation we followed our customs, until in 1975 the communists put an end to our way of life. We lost everything, our families, our monks, our villages, our land, all our possessions. Everything. When we came to the United States we couldn't put our old lives back together. We didn't even have the pieces.

Secondly, years of witnessing and enduring unrelenting brutality—torture, executions, hard labor, starvation, and disease—at the hands of **Pol Pot** and the Khmer Rouge left Cambodians with psychological scars, which has made their assimilation process all the more difficult. Many are afflicted with "Pol Pot syndrome," post-traumatic stress disorder, a condition prevalent among survivors of World War II Nazi concentration camps. Its classic symptoms are emotional numbness, depression, withdrawal, recurring nightmares of the ordeal, insomnia, nonspecific pains, palpitations, difficulty breathing, and loss of appetite.

Why did more than a hundred Cambodian women in California suddenly go blind in the 1980s?

Between 1982 and 1989 more than one hundred Cambodian refugee women in California consulted doctors about their blindness, maintaining that their vision became impaired during **Pol Pot**'s reign of terror. One Cambodian woman told of how her vision failed immediately after she bore witness to the execution of her family, while another noted that her world went dark after evidence was found confirming the execution of her brother and his family by the Khmer Rouge. Yet another recalled that she lost her sight for a period of time after watching soldiers beat up a man and then throw him into a fire. One woman suffered from poor vision and painful headaches after witnessing her daughter being bludgeoned to death. Curiously, when the doctors gave the women eye examinations, they could not detect any physical signs of impairment and diagnosed the women's condition as "psychosomatic blindness," also known as hysterical blindness. The women apparently lost their sight because they were so overwhelmed by the horrors of the killing fields. A psychologist who interviewed these women concluded, "Their minds simply closed down; they refused to see anymore."

How are Cambodians faring in the first decade of the new millennium?

The traumas of the past and a lack of education and experience in fast-paced, postindustrial living have been formidable obstacles in the progress of Cambodians in America. Nowadays a little more than half live in crime-ridden inner-city neighborhoods, and a great number of those are dependent on welfare. Their children perform poorly in school and ofttimes drop out for a life of crime or gangs, which perpetuates the cycle of poverty and hopelessness. However, the remaining Cambodians, slightly less than half of the total population, have gotten ahead. Most of these are lower middle class and earn low wages. Still, with two or more wage earners in the family, a good percentage have been able to purchase their own homes and enjoy a comfortable life. The rest, about 5 percent of the total Cambodian community, are middle class. They are professionals educated before the Khmer Rouge years or in the United States and entrepreneurs. Among them are Cambodians in California who, beginning in the late 1970s, did well in the donut industry. One is Cambodian donut pioneer and millionaire **Bun Tek Ngoy**. In 1977 he opened the country's first Cambodian-run donut shop and then expanded his business to a chain of donut shops. Other Cambodians followed suit, hoping to reap a profit in the daily grind of donut making by night and selling by day. However, since the 1990s Cambodians in California have had a harder time getting ahead in the donut business due to the explosion of donut shops in the state and a general decline in donut consumption.

Who is Dith Pran?

A survivor of the Khmer Rouge holocaust, **Dith Pran** was instrumental in documenting the spread of the Vietnam War to Cambodia in the early 1970s and the fall of Phnom Penh to the Khmer Rouge in 1975. Born on September 27, 1942, Pran was hired in 1960 as a Khmer-English interpreter for the United States Military Assistance Group in Cambodia. When Cambodia severed diplomatic relations with the United States in 1965, he found employment as an interpreter for the British film crew that was filming the 1965 motion picture *Lord Jim.* Then Pran was hired as a receptionist at a Cambodia tourist hotel, but when civil war erupted in 1970, tourism dried up. Dith Pran then moved with his wife and children to Phnom Penh, where he went to work as an interpreter and guide for international journalists. From 1972 to April 20, 1975, Pran, by now in his early thirties, served as an assistant to *New York Times* journalist **Sydney H. Schanberg,** who had been covering the drama in Cambodia as a foreign correspondent since 1970. (In mid-1973 the *New York Times* made Pran an official stringer.)

While most American personnel evacuated Phnom Penh before the Khmer Rouge overtook the capital on April 17, 1975, Schanberg remained behind to cover the city's fall. He asked Pran if he wanted to evacuate, but Pran opted to remain and help cover the story. He did, however, evacuate his wife, **Ser Moeun,** and children, who were resettled in San Francisco. It was through Pran's efforts that Schanberg's reports, the only Western eyewitness accounts of the fall of Phnom Penh to the Khmer Rouge, got to the outside world.

Before long Khmer Rouge troops arrested Pran and Schanberg, along with two other journalists. Pran was able to negotiate the release of the three by convincing their captors that they were neutral French journalists. Once they were let go, Schanberg, Pran, and the others took refuge in the French embassy. Sidney Schanberg attempted to falsify a British passport to get Pran out of the country, but the French caught the forgery and refused to accept it, arguing that the Khmer Rouge would retaliate once they saw it. On April 20, 1975, Pran and other Cambodians at the French embassy were forced out the door to fend for themselves.

Pran knew that if the Khmer Rouge uncovered his real identity it would mean certain death, so he disguised himself as a cabdriver and disposed of his American dollars. Along with his fellow countrymen, he was driven to the communes in the countryside, where miraculously he survived four years of brutal torture and near starvation. Malnutrition took a toll on his teeth, and his feet and legs were badly infected from wading in animal manure used to fertilize the rice fields. Sidney Schanberg attempted to no avail to locate Pran through such avenues as the World Health Organization and the American embassies in Bangkok and Singapore. In 1976 he accepted the Pulitzer Prize for international reporting "at great risk" for himself and on behalf of Dith Pran for their work on Cambodia. Having borne witness to the Khmer Rouge's genocidal massacre of the Cambodian people, on October 3, 1979, the eve of the Vietnamese takeover of Cambodia, Pran managed to escape to Thailand. He then made his way, with Sydney Schanberg at his side, to the United States, where he joined his wife and children. About fifty of Pran's family members were not so lucky. His three brothers and one of his sisters perished at the hands of Khmer Rouge soldiers, while his father succumbed to starvation and his mother died later from malnutrition.

Pran was given training as a photographer and then a job in 1980 with the *New York Times* staff photographers. Eventually he became a full staff photographer. Upon receiving an invitation from **Hun Sen,** the prime minister of Cambodia, Dith Pran returned to his homeland for the first time in 1989 as a delegate on the Cambodia Documentation Commission, a group seeking to put the Khmer Rouge on trial in the World Court for the crime of genocide. In Cambodia he was reunited with a sister and a few surviving relatives and friends. To this day Dith Pran continues to travel and lecture widely, working with various organizations devoted to the plight of Cambodian refugees.

Dith Pran's work in Cambodia with Sidney Schanberg and his horrific experiences at the hands of the Khmer Rouge are vividly portrayed in the highly charged motion picture *The Killing Fields* (1984), director **Roland Joffe**'s feature debut. The film won Academy Awards for actor **Haing S. Ngor,** who plays Dith Pran, cinematographer **Chris Menges,** and film editor **Jim Clark.** *The Killing Fields* served an important function of educating the American public about the genocide that had occurred in Cambodia under Pol Pot. To ensure that America's students continue to be educated about the Cambodian genocide, Dith Pran founded the Dith Pran Holocaust Awareness Project, Inc.

Who was Haing Ngor?

Haing Ngor was also a courageous survivor of the Khmer Rouge's killing fields. Though his own particular story of survival is truly remarkable and has garnered widespread attention, Ngor initially gained national and international recognition for his portrayal of **Dith Pran** in the critically acclaimed motion picture *The Killing Fields* (1984). For his stunning debut performance (he had no prior acting experience), the Motion Picture Academy bestowed upon Haing Ngor an Oscar for Best Supporting Actor in 1985, which Ngor dedicated to the family he lost in **Pol Pot**'s genocidal campaign.

Haing Ngor's survival during the Khmer Rouge years closely

parallels that of Dith Pran. Growing up in a village south of Phnom Penh, Ngor aspired to be a doctor. He attended medical school in Phnom Penh, earning his medical degree in 1975, a couple of months before the Khmer Rouge tightened its noose on the Cambodian people. Despite warnings to flee the country, Ngor stayed, certain that Pol Pot's regime would be no worse than **Lon Nol**'s corrupt government and that the Khmer Rouge needed him alive and well because of the shortage of doctors in what was then called Democratic Kampuchea. Ngor continued to practice medicine until one day in April 1975, when Khmer Rouge soldiers burst into his medical office while he was performing surgery. One of the soldiers entered the operating room and demanded to know the whereabouts of the doctor. Sensing danger, Ngor lied about his identity and convinced the soldier that the doctor had already left. Haing Ngor and his wife were soon forced to evacuate Phnom Penh for an agricultural collective in the countryside. Realizing that doctors were among the groups that the Khmer Rouge was targeting for extermination, Ngor took on a new identity as a cabdriver. Even when he witnessed human suffering, he dared not help lest he reveal his medical expertise.

Haing Ngor and his wife suffered from constant hunger, and Ngor was reduced to stealing food to survive. Tragically, his wife, weak and severely malnourished, died during childbirth in 1978, along with their unborn child. Haing Ngor, whose life hung in the balance on several occasions, escaped over the border to Thailand shortly after the Vietnamese takeover in December 1978. He worked as a doctor in Cambodian refugee camps there before moving on to the United States in 1980. Unfortunately, his medical degree was deemed invalid by the American medical profession, and Ngor was barred from practicing medicine in the United States. He had a difficult time mastering English, which prevented him from earning the necessary credentials to resurrect his career. Locked out of medicine, Haing Ngor resorted to working as a security guard while he studied English. Later he landed a job as a caseworker assigned to helping fellow Indochinese refugees.

After the release of *The Killing Fields*, Haing Ngor's life changed considerably. He went on the lecture circuit, recounting the atrocities he witnessed and endured under Pol Pot and calling for peace in his homeland and for improvements in the living conditions of Cambodian refugees. He did whatever he could to help individual Cambodians in America and Cambodians in his homeland, where he supported two medical clinics and a school. He also founded organizations dedicated to helping international refugees and published an autobiography, *Haing Ngor: A Cambodian Odyssey* (1988), which focuses on his ordeal in Cambodia during the Khmer Rouge years. In addition, Ngor played minor parts in other Hollywood motion pictures, namely, *Iron Triangle* (1989), *Vietnam, Texas* (1990), and *My Life* (1993), and a supporting role (as Phung Thi Le Ly's father) in **Oliver Stone**'s *Heaven and Earth* (1993). Very sadly, a forty-five-year-old Haing Ngor, who had survived Pol Pot's killing fields, was gunned down near his home in Los Angeles's Chinatown on February 25, 1996. Upon hearing of Ngor's tragic death, Dith Pran said it was as if he had lost a twin brother: "He was my co-messenger, and now I am alone."

Do Cambodians celebrate New Years in the same way as the Vietnamese?

While Vietnamese *Tet* falls in January or February, the Cambodian New Year occurs in April. Like the Vietnamese, Cambodians celebrate for many days, and even during the entire month. However, Cambodians in America usually celebrate the New Year only on weekends. The New Year is a time for Cambodians in America to make a fresh start, to remember their homeland, and to worship their ancestors. Along with attending cultural performances, they prepare special dishes for the holiday and use it as an opportunity to instruct younger generations about Cambodian culture and history.

What foods are found on the Cambodian-American table?

Traditional Cambodian cuisine is something of a dying art: Most of those well versed in its preparation, that is, members of the elite and middle class, perished at the hands of the Khmer Rouge or endured near famine after the regime fell and then spent time in refugee camps, where there was nothing beyond the basics, such as rice. As a result, Cambodian cooking in Cambodia nowadays more closely resembles Thai. Cambodian-American restaurateur **Longteine De Monteiro,** who was born in Phnom Penh and escaped to France in 1975, as **Pol Pot** unleashed his terror, has almost single-handedly kept classic Cambodian cooking alive. After establishing in France the Western world's first Cambodian restaurant, she moved to the United States in 1990, and the next year opened with her husband her first Cambodian/French restaurant in Boston, The Elephant Walk Restaurant. Before long De Monteiro opened another Cambodian/French restaurant in the Boston area and then one that serves strictly Cambodian fare. In 1998 she published *The Elephant Walk Cookbook*, coauthored with **Katherine Neustadt,** the first cookbook on traditional Cambodian cuisine geared to an American readership.

Traditional Cambodian cuisine blends Chinese, Indian, Vietnamese, and Thai elements with Portuguese, Spanish, and French. It also entails a balance of textures, hues, and flavors, most importantly sour, sweet, salty, and bitter. These flavors are more subtle than in Vietnamese and Thai cooking. Fish, fermented fish paste (called *prahok*), coconut milk, curry leaves, lemongrass, kaffir lime, and galangal (a root that is a member of the ginger family) are essential ingredients. A quintessential Cambodian dish is *nataing*, a creamy dip (dips abound in Cambodian cuisine) made with ground meat, ground peanuts, coconut milk, and fish paste. It is served with rice cakes and French bread for dipping.

THAI AMERICANS

What brought Thais to American shores?

Thailand—which was known as Siam until 1939 and is bordered by the Andaman Sea and the Gulf of Thailand—is distinct from Vietnam, Laos, and Cambodia in that it did not experience European colonization (it's the only country in South and Southeast Asia that did not) and has endured few invasions by other Asian nations. (Burmese armies invaded in 1767 and toppled the Thai kingdom of Ayutthaya, which had ruled for more than four hundred years, and the Japanese occupied Thailand during World II.) A bloodless revolution in Thailand in 1932 eventuated in a constitutional monarchy. Until elections held in 1992, the country, though a constitutional monarchy, was ruled by military governments and knew only brief periods of democracy. The 1992 elections transformed Thailand into a functional democracy, which it has remained ever since. Since the end of World War II, Thailand and the United States have maintained warm diplomatic relations, and over the ensuing decades the two countries developed close trade and military ties. Since 1950 the Thais have received military equipment, assistance in construction, and other aid from the United States. This aid proved vital in the latter half of the twentieth century, when Thailand's neighbors experienced Communist revolutions, and the Thais actively sought to contain the spread of Communism in the region.

The Thai people have never had to flee their homeland for the United States due to internal or external wars, crimes against humanity by their leaders, or severe economic hardship. Trade and military connections are what have motivated

Thai immigration to the United States, which commenced as a significant wave in the 1970s.

How many Thai Americans are there, and where do they live?

According to U.S. Bureau of the Census calculations, 150,293 persons of Thai descent resided in the United States in 2000. The overwhelming majority, 112,989 of those counted, were Thai alone, while 7,929 were Thai and at least one other Asian ethnicity, and 29,365 were Thai and at least one other race. The five states that were home that year to the greatest number of Thai Americans and nationals (Thai alone and not in combination with other races or Asian ethnicities) were California (36,525), Texas (7,384), New York (6,658), Florida (6,233), and Illinois (5,833). More than half of the Thais in California, the majority of whom entered the United States in the 1990s and early 2000s, are dispersed throughout the counties of Los Angeles, Orange, Riverside, and San Bernardino, with high concentrations in Hollywood and the San Fernando Valley. The most prominent Thai enclave in the United States is Thai Town in the East Hollywood section of Los Angeles, where Thais began settling and setting up businesses beginning in the 1960s. This enclave was officially designated the nation's first Thai Town in a ribbon-cutting ceremony held on January 29, 2000. Thai Town is especially lively on the last Sunday in September, when Thais flock to Thai Culture Day, a day of festivities that include a parade of Thai native costumes and Thai kickboxing, mask making, and shadow puppetry demonstrations.

In North Hollywood, not far from Thai Town, is Wat Thai, a center of Thai religious life in Los Angeles and the largest Thai Theravada Buddhist temple (*wat*) in the United States. Other Thai Buddhist temples in America include one in Silver Spring, Maryland, which was completed in 1995 and attracts Thai Buddhists in the Washington, D.C., area. In Thailand, where Buddhism was introduced over a millennium ago, the *wat* is the focal point of the community, and Buddhist monks serve as both spiritual and community leaders and play a strong role in daily life. Given that Thai society in the United States is somewhat more secular than in Thailand, the *wat* and Buddhist monks play a lesser role in daily life. However, the *wat* also performs an added function in the United States: It is not only a center of Buddhism but serves as a cultural and educational center for the Thai community, teaching the next generation about Thai traditions as well as Buddhist practices. Special days on the calendar of Thai Buddhist temples in America include the Songkran Festival, a celebration of the Thai New Year, which falls in April, and Buddha Day, commemorating the birthday of Buddha, his day of enlightenment, and his day of pari-nirvana, or death.

In addition to religious institutions, Thai Americans have established a number of organizations to address the needs of their community and enhance Thai visibility in America. (The vast majority of Americans know nothing about the Thais in their midst: To them "Thai" means the cuisine at the local Thai restaurant, especially in California, where virtually every town has at least one Thai eatery.) In 1994 the Thai Community Development Center was organized in Los Angeles to promote "the rights of Thai Americans as well as advocat[e] for more humane labor and immigration policies," to provide "access to culturally sensitive human and social services," and to develop "leadership among Thai Americans through community service." The year 1998 saw the formation of the Thai American Young Professionals Association, an organization "dedicated to creating a nationwide community of Thai American young professionals."

Who is both the most prominent American of Thai ancestry and a legend in his own time?

Professional golfer **Eldrick "Tiger" Woods** shattered ethnic expectations on the green just as swiftly as he rose to the top of the rankings. One of the greatest golfers of all time, Tiger Woods was born in Cypress, California, on December 30, 1975, to **Earl Woods,** a retired U.S. Army colonel who is African American, and to **Kultida Woods,** who hails from Thailand. By age six months, Tiger delighted in observing his father hit golf balls, and before long he was imitating his swing. At just two years of age, Tiger putted with **Bob Hope** during an appearance on *The Mike Douglas Show,* and at age three the golfing prodigy shot forty-eight for nine holes. *Golf Digest* ran a story on Tiger when he was just five years old, and between the ages of eight and fifteen, the young golfer captured the Optimist International Junior Tournament half a dozen times. As an amateur, Tiger Woods won numerous events and was named Golf Digest Player of the Year in 1991 and 1992, Golfweek National Amateur of the Year in 1992, Golf World Player of the Year in 1992 and 1993, and Golf World Man of the Year in 1994. In 1994 he entered Stanford University and within two years had captured ten collegiate tournaments. For his magnificent play, he earned the Fred Haskins and Jack Nicklaus College Player of the Year awards in 1996.

That same year Tiger Woods turned pro. He lost no time dominating the professional circuit: On June 15, 1997, at age twenty-one years and twenty-four weeks, he earned the distinction of being the youngest No. 1 player in the history of professional golf. By the end of 2002, Tiger Woods had won fifty tournaments, including the 1997, 2001, and 2002 Masters Tournaments, the 1999 and 2000 PGA Championships, the 2000 British Open Championship, and the 2000 and 2002 U.S. Open Championships. Tiger Woods has captured many awards and shattered myriad records in his illustrious career. For instance, in 1996 and 2000 *Sports Illustrated* chose him as Sportsman of the Year, the first athlete ever to earn that distinction more than once. In 1997, 1999, and 2000, the Associated Press selected Woods as the Male Athlete of the Year. In all those years, as well as in 2001, the PGA Tour named him Player of the Year. In 2001, with his second Masters victory,

Tiger Woods became the first golfer ever to hold all four professional major championships at the same time.

THE OTHER AMERICANS OF SOUTHEAST ASIAN DESCENT

Indonesia, Malaysia, Burma (renamed Myanmar in 1997), Singapore, and Brunei have witnessed very limited emigration to the United States due to two diametrically opposed phenomena: economic upheaval (coupled with isolation)—which provides the incentive for emigration but not the opportunity—and economic stability, which gives citizens little impetus to leave their homeland. The first phenomenon applies to Indonesia, Malaysia, and Burma, and the second to oil-rich Brunei and foreign-investment-rich Singapore.

How many Indonesians live in the United States?

The Dutch gradually took control of Indonesia beginning in 1602 and did not grant their rich colonial possession sovereignty until 1949. In 1927 **Sukarno,** who was born in Surabaya in eastern Java in 1901, founded a movement for independence from the Dutch. The Dutch retaliated by imprisoning and exiling Sukarno on numerous occasions in the 1930s. After Japan invaded Indonesia in 1942, Sukarno returned to Jakarta from exile. On August 17, 1945, in the immediate aftermath of Japan's surrender, he and fellow nationalist leader **Muhammad Hatta** declared Indonesia's independence. It was not until December 1949 that the Dutch recognized Indonesia's independence. **Sukarno** emerged a figurehead president with independence and then gradually amassed power. In 1956 he established a "guided democracy," with all political parties represented in the cabinet, and in 1963 he named himself president for life. Under his dictatorial rule, which lasted from 1949 to 1965, the people of Indonesia endured severe economic hardship, which bred popular revolts. Sukarno soon found himself wedged between the army and the Communist Party, both of whom were gaining strength from the chaos.

An attempted Communist coup crushed by the army in 1965 eventuated in the rise to power of General **Suharto.** In 1966 Sukarno's title of president for life was taken from him. He remained under house arrest until his death in 1970. Under Suharto, Indonesia knew political stability and economic growth by the late 1970s and early 1980s. By 1996 the poverty rate had plummeted to 11.8 percent of the total population, down from 60 percent in the early 1970s. However, nepotism, government corruption, and human-rights abuses were the norm of the Suharto regime. (This is especially true in East Timor, which Indonesia annexed in 1975–76 and then occupied until 2002, when East Timor became independent. From 1976 onward, Indonesian forces waged a violent campaign of pacification against the East Timorese, unleashing an East Timor refugee crisis that has still not been resolved completely to this day.) Economic upheaval (the poverty rate rose to 23.5 percent in 1998–99) and popular discontent led to Suharto's resignation in 1998. In presidential elections held in October 1999, **Abdurrahman Wahid** became Indonesia's first democratically elected president, but he was succeeded by Sukarno's daughter, **Megawati Sukarnoputri,** in 2001. By 2002 the poverty rate was down to 16 percent, but in 2003 the number of Indonesians living in poverty began once again to rise due to rampant corruption and a collapsing infrastructure, which were causing business investors to pull out of the country.

Since Indonesia achieved independence from the Dutch, its people have known long periods of poverty so severe that most could not afford the cost of immigrating to the United States if they so chose. In the 1990s the majority of those who overcame the financial burden of leaving Indonesia and went to the United States gained entrance under family preference provisions (relatives in America sponsored them). A very small number of Indonesians entered the United States as refugees in that decade. (Between 1989 and 2002, just

37 Indonesian refugees were admitted to the United States.) Census 2000 tallied 63,073 persons of Indonesian descent in America in 2000. The five states with the highest Indonesian (alone) population in 2000 were California (17,755), New York (2,906), Texas (2,051), Washington (1,369), and Maryland (1,034).

How have Malaysians managed to come to America's shores?

Malaysia has known more than its share of economic calamity, political instability, and violence. By the end of World War II, the country had been occupied by Portugal, Great Britain, and Japan. Until 1966 it was entangled in conflicts with Indonesia. At the same time, Communist guerrilla fighters were creating havoc in northern Malaysia—until a peace treaty was hammered out in 1989. The government also faced a limited Communist revolt in northern Borneo until a peace agreement was reached in 1990. Malaysia has maintained strict control over the movement of its people out of the country. One avenue that has been open since the 1980s to Malaysians seeking to escape the wrenching poverty and violence in their homeland is education. Malaysians represent one of the largest foreign contingencies in American universities and colleges. Some remain legally in America upon the completion of their studies. The U.S. Bureau of the Census counted 18,566 persons of Malaysian ancestry in the United States in 2000, up from 12,243 in 1990. The five states with the highest Malaysian (alone) population in 2000 were California (1,948), New York (1,606), Texas (714), Illinois (455), and Virginia (376).

How have Burmese been able to come to America?

In 1824 the British began to gradually take control of Burma. Upon completing their conquest in 1885, Britain annexed

Burma to India the very same year. In 1948 Burma achieved its independence and formed a government based on equal rights for all the country's ethnic minorities. However, the country was soon engulfed in widespread conflict and internal struggle, which persisted until 1962, when General **Ne Win** seized the reins of power by a coup, did away with the constitution, and installed a military government that brutally persecuted ethnic minorities. The government's socialist economic policies wreaked havoc on Burma's economy, causing it finally to collapse in 1988—an event that ignited protests and cries for democracy by students and the general public in Rangoon in 1988. During mass demonstrations on August 8, 1988, Burma's military lashed out at the demonstrators, slaughtering more than a thousand of them. Then, on September 18, military forces deposed Ne Win's Burmese Socialist Program Party, threw away its constitution, installed a ruling junta known as the State Law and Order Restoration Council, and implemented a campaign to "restore order" in the streets of Burma that cost another three thousand Burmese citizens their lives. In 1990 the junta lost in free elections but refused to acknowledge the results and relinquish power. In 1997 Burma's junta, which maintains a monopoly on power and strict autocratic rule over the citizenry, changed its name to the State Peace and Development Council and renamed the country Myanmar (the country's democratic opposition refuses to recognize the name change, as does the U.S. government).

From their first days in power, Burma's military rulers pledged to develop a market-based economy but instead drove the country into economic quicksand through their mismanagement. They still have not pulled the country out: In the year 2003 the people of Burma subsisted on a per capita annual income of about three hundred dollars. To make matters worse, the junta did little to develop the country's infrastructure, so that to this day large numbers of Burmese have no running water or basic sanitation. As a result of poverty and poor living conditions, Burma has a high infant mortality rate and a short life expectancy. The government's human rights record is not very good either. It has displaced religious and ethnic minorities within the country, and it has continually repressed the democratic opposition, strictly censored information, and used forced labor. The junta has shown no signs of movement toward a political transition or constitutional change. Those who wish to escape Burma's poverty and repressive regime are afforded little opportunity as the junta tightly controls emigration. Over the decades, a small number of Burmese, especially persecuted religious and ethnic minorities, have managed to escape to India, Thailand, and other countries and then have made their way to the United States as refugees. Between 1989 and 2002, 2,256 Burmese were admitted to the United States as refugees. Only about 1,000 Burmese per year are able to immigrate to the United States, many under family reunification provisions. The U.S. Bureau of the Census counted 16,720 Burmese in the United States in 2000.

If Singapore is a thriving nation, what brings Singaporeans to America?

The island city-state of Singapore, which is a little more than three and a half times the size of Washington, D.C., and had a population of approximately 3.8 million in 2000, affords its citizens a comfortable life. Founded as a British trading colony in 1819, Singapore became an independent republic on August 9, 1965, when it broke away from Malaysia, which it had joined in 1963, and set up a parliamentary government with political authority vested in the prime minister and cabinet. In 1965 the government had little in terms of physical resources to work with and a small domestic market, so it cultivated a skilled workforce and embraced a business-friendly, foreign-investment-friendly, export-oriented economic framework. Singapore's strategy has been a resounding success: It has attracted investments from over three thousand multinational corporations in the United States, Europe, and Japan, and from 1960 to 1999 economic growth averaged 8.0 percent. Manufacturing and financial/business services continue to be its strengths.

Singapore's citizens have reaped the benefits of the government's economic prowess and political stability and of their own industriousness. They have experienced long periods of near full employment and enjoy one of the highest standards of living in the world. Consequently, only a scant number choose to immigrate to the United States, about five hundred annually. Given that many Singaporeans grow up speaking English (or at least their version, called Singlish) and all are exposed to English, as it is the language of administration and also is widely used in schools, the professions, and businesses, Singaporeans who come to the United States have a distinct linguistic advantage over most Asian newcomers. However, one disadvantage they face is invisibility, even within the Asian-American community, which stems from their minuscule numbers. In 2000 the U.S. Bureau of the Census counted just 2,394 Singaporeans in the United States.

What about Bruneian Americans?

The Sultanate of Brunei—which is known officially as Brunei Darussalam, is slightly smaller than the state of Delaware, and is bordered by the South China Sea and Malaysia—became a British protectorate in 1888 and achieved its full independence about a century later, on January 1, 1984. Brunei's sultan, or head of state, enjoys full executive authority. His Majesty Sultan **Haji Hassanal Bolkiah Mu'izzaddin Waddaulah,** who ascended the throne on October 5, 1967, has forged a stable economy relying almost solely on exports of crude oil and natural gas. (Brunei is the third-largest oil producer in all of Southeast Asia.) Brunei provides rather well for its citizens: The country boasts one of the finest health care systems in Asia and has a strong education system, and its government subsidizes rice and housing. As a result, very few Bruneians venture to the United States—fewer than twenty-five annually—and consequently, the Brunei community in America is extremely small.

SEVEN

Pacific Islander Americans

When did Pacific Islanders first make their way to the United States, and how many are there nowadays?

HAWAIIANS

Who were the Polynesians, and when did they colonize Hawaii?

How did Captain Cook's "discovery" of Hawaii alter its destiny forever?

What role did the plantation owners play in the annexation of Hawaii by the United States?

What precipitated Hawaii's admission into the Union as the fiftieth state?

How many Native Hawaiians are there, and where do they live?

Is Hawaii the number-one U.S. destination for Pacific Islander immigrants?

SAMOAN AMERICANS

How was Samoa divided, and when did American Samoa become a U.S. territory?

When did Samoans first venture to Hawaii and to the mainland United States?

GUAMANIAN AMERICANS

How did Guam become a U.S. territory?

What triggered Guamanian migration to Hawaii and the U.S. mainland?

TONGAN AMERICANS

Where does the history of Tonga begin?

When and why did Tongans start coming to America?

Pacific Islander Americans and nationals have roots in the islands and island archipelagos—many sovereign nations, some in association with the United States and other countries—that rise from the vast Central and South Pacific Ocean, a region known traditionally as Oceania. Oceania is commonly divided into three geographic areas: Polynesia (many islands), Micronesia (small islands), and Melanesia (black islands). Polynesia, the largest of the three geographic areas, consists of 287 volcanic and coral islands, most notably Hawaii, the Cook Islands, French Polynesia, American Samoa (an unincorporated and unorganized U.S. territory), Western Samoa, Tonga, Niue, Pitcairn Island, Easter Island, Tokelau, Tuvalu, Wallis Island, and Furtuna Island. (Some scholars consider New Zealand part of Polynesia.) Despite the dispersal of the Polynesian islands over a wide expanse of ocean, Polynesians are closely related in terms of culture and language. Micronesia, with its more than 2,000 smaller coral atolls and volcanic islands, includes the Marshall Islands, Guam (an organized, unincorporated U.S. territory), the Northern Mariana Islands (a U.S. commonwealth since 1986), the Federated States of Micronesia, Kiribati, Nauru, and Palau. Melanesia, which is south of Micronesia and close to the Asian and Australian continents, includes New Caledonia, Papua New Guinea, Fiji, Irian Jaya, the Solomon Islands, and Vanuatu.

Given that most islands in the Central and South Pacific have generated negligible immigration to the United States, this discussion will be largely limited to the four largest Pacific Islander subgroups in the United States (in the fifty states and the District of Columbia only and not in U.S. dependencies and possessions) according to U.S. census data: Native Hawaiians (strictly those who classify themselves as predominantly ethnic Hawaiian—that is, as descendants of the original Polynesian inhabitants of the Hawaiian Islands, even though they might be of mixed blood); Samoans (strictly those descended from the indigenous peoples of both Western Samoa and American Samoa); Guamanians/Chamorros (those descended from the original peoples of Guam); and Tongans (strictly those descended from the aboriginal, indigenous peoples of Tonga).

When did Pacific Islanders first make their way to the United States, and how many are there nowadays?

It should be noted that since all Hawaiians, Guamanians, American Samoans, and residents of the Commonwealth of the Northern Mariana Islands are U.S. citizens—no matter if they live in Honolulu, Agana, Pago Pago, or Los Angeles—since Hawaii is the fiftieth state, Guam and American Samoa are U.S. territories, and the Northern Mariana Islands are a U.S. commonwealth, their movement to the fifty United States and the District of Columbia, as well as to all U.S. dependencies and possessions, constitutes migration and not immigration. The movement of all other Pacific Islanders to the fifty United States, including to Hawaii, their number-one destination, and to U.S. dependencies and possessions constitutes immigration.

Before 1950 very few Pacific Islanders ventured to the continental United States. Contact with Americans stationed in the South Pacific during World War II stimulated an interest in the United States and its territories on the part of Pacific Islanders. In the 1950s, as in later decades, economic and educational opportunities, the cultural life and bustle of American metropolises, family reunification (some American servicemen stationed in the Pacific in World War II took Pacific Islanders as their brides), and religion generated Pacific Islanders' (im)migration to the fifty states (forty-nine until Hawaii became the fiftieth in 1959). In 1980 the U.S. Bureau of the Census counted 259,566 Pacific Islanders in the fifty states and the District of Columbia. A decade later that number had risen by 46 percent to 365,024, according to 1990 census data.

In 2000 the U.S. Bureau of the Census tallied 874,414 Pacific Islanders (alone and in combination with at least one other race) in the fifty states and one district. Of those counted, 389,612 identified with one Pacific Islander group only. Among the

Pacific Islanders counted in 2000 were 401,162 Native Hawaiians (alone and in combination with at least one other race), of which 140,652 were Native Hawaiian alone; 133,281 Samoans (alone and in combination with at least one other race), of which 91,029 were Samoans alone; 36,840 Tongans (alone and in combination with at least one other race), of which 27,713 were Tongans alone; 8,796 not specified Polynesians (alone and in combination with at least one other race), of which 3,497 were not specified Polynesians alone; 92,611 Guamanians/Chamorros (alone and in combination with at least one other race), of which 58,240 were Guamanians/Chamorros alone; 9,940 not specified Micronesians (alone and in combination with at least one other race), of which 7,509 were not specified Micronesians alone; 13,581 Fijians (alone and in combination with at least one other race), of which 9,796 were Fijians alone; 315 not specified Melanesians (alone and in combination with at least one other race), of which 147 were not specified Melanesians alone; and 174,912 Other Pacific Islanders (alone and in combination with at least one other race), of which 40,558 were Other Pacific Islanders alone.

According to Census 2000 data, 73 percent of Pacific Islander Americans resided in the West, 14 percent in the South, 7 percent in the Northeast, and 6 percent in the Midwest. Over 58 percent of Pacific Islanders (alone) counted in Census 2000 resided in California (116,961) and Hawaii (113,539). The next five states with the highest Pacific Islander population (of a single race) in 2000 were Washington (23,953), Utah (15,145), Texas (14,434), New York (8,818), and Florida (8,625).

HAWAIIANS

Who were the Polynesians, and when did they colonize Hawaii?

Around fifteen hundred years ago, Polynesian voyagers, mostly from the Marquesas Islands in the South Pacific, found their way in double-hulled sailing canoes to the shores of the Hawaiian Islands. Then, around A.D. 1200, other Polynesian peoples made their way to Hawaii from Tahiti. (A common premise among scholars is that both groups of Polynesian voyagers were originally Southeast Asians who had settled earlier in Tahiti and the Marquesas Islands.) The Polynesians lived in isolation on the Hawaiian Islands for fourteen centuries before the arrival of *haoles*, foreigners, late in Europe's Age of Discovery. European explorers had begun to navigate the Pacific expanse in the sixteenth century, but it was only on January 18, 1778, that they, in the person of English explorer and navigator **James Cook,** finally sighted the Hawaiian Islands. Captain Cook, who was on a quest to find the fabled Northwest Passage, stayed only briefly in the Hawaiian Islands before heading north, naming the island chain the Sandwich Islands, after **John Montague,** the Fourth Earl of Sandwich. After exploring the coastline of Oregon and Alaska and journeying through the Bering Strait, Cook deduced that no Northwest Passage existed and returned to the Hawaiian Islands in January 1779. There, on February 14, Cook met his end when he was stabbed to death by native peoples after an incident involving a boat stolen from one of his ships.

How did Captain Cook's "discovery" of Hawaii alter its destiny forever?

Soon after Captain **Cook** made landfall in Hawaii, the United States, France, and Russia dispatched expeditionary forces to explore the islands. On the heels of the explorers came American missionaries, and by 1820 missionaries from the first New England Congregationalist Church had commenced their efforts not only to convert the Native Hawaiians to Christianity and to replace Hawaiian practices with Christian ones but also to set up schools, hospitals, and other institutions. The Native Hawaiians offered little resistance to the missionaries' campaign to reconstruct Hawaiian society. King **Kamehameha I,** who during his reign had united all the Hawaiian Islands under one rule, died in 1819 and was succeeded by his son, **Liholiho,** christened **Kamehameha II.** During his rule, which ended suddenly when he died of measles in England, Kamehameha II abolished the Native Hawaiian religion with its myriad gods and goddesses, as well as the *kapu* (taboo) system, facilitating the New England Congregationalist Church's conversion efforts. Missionaries and other foreigners in the Hawaiian Islands not only introduced their ways, they also spread infectious diseases, such as syphilis and gonorrhea, to which Pacific Islanders had no natural immunity. By 1858 contact with the outside world and its ailments had caused Hawaii's native population to dwindle from some 300,000 at the time of Captain Cook's arrival to a mere 60,000.

When the European and American newcomers in the Hawaiian Islands realized the potential wealth that lay beneath their feet, in the fertile soil made more valuable by plentiful rainfall and temperatures conducive to year-round growing, they began to pressure the native peoples to sell them acreage for agricultural pursuits, which resulted in the reallocation of land rights in 1848 by an act, signed by Hawaii's ruler, **Kamehameha III,** called the Great Mahele. In keeping with the Great Mahele, millions of acres went to Hawaiian chiefs, the government, and the royal family, and 30,000 acres, a slight percentage of the land, were given to Hawaii's commoners. Since Native Hawaiians had no concept of land ownership, many sold their property to foreigners for a meager sum, believing that the land remained theirs after the sale. In this way, acreage fell in the hands of business-savvy foreign investors, many from the United States, who converted it into plantations that grew Hawaii's signature crops, sugar and pineapple, particularly after the signing in 1875 of the Reciprocity Treaty, which removed duties on Hawaiian trade with the United States.

The demoralizing effect on the Native Hawaiians of losing their land was compounded when sugar and pineapple planters, the new white elite in Hawaii, hired them as cheap labor to work the plantations. When the plantations began to thrive and few additional laborers could be culled from the Hawaiian Islands' dwindling native population (Native Hawaiians succumbed to European diseases for the duration of the nineteenth century, so that in 1890 just 40,000 remained), sugar and pineapple growers stepped up their efforts to recruit cheap labor in faraway lands, namely, in China, Japan, the Philippines, Korea, Portugal, Puerto Rico, and elsewhere, to work the fields. So began the long reign of "King Cane" and a wave of Asian immigration to the Hawaiian Islands that would dramatically alter the makeup of Hawaiian society, transforming it into one of the world's first melting pots and rendering Native Hawaiians an ethnic minority in their own land. Due to the high rate of intermarriage between the various ethnic groups in the Hawaiian Islands, by 1900 Hawaiians of Polynesian ancestry constituted just 24.4 percent of the population.

What role did the plantation owners play in the annexation of Hawaii by the United States?

By the dawn of the 1890s, power in the sovereign Kingdom of Hawaii had become concentrated in the hands of American sugar and pineapple plantation owners. Seeking to curb American involvement in their homeland, Hawaiians installed a staunch nationalist, Queen **Liliuokalani,** on the throne in 1891. When the queen sought to establish a stronger monarchy, American plantation owners grew concerned that her actions would translate into a loss of duty-free status on the importation of their Hawaiian sugar into the United States, cutting their profits. Under the leadership of **Sanford B. Dole,** the "Sugar King" of Hawaii, plantation owners determined that the only way to eliminate the threat of taxation was for the United States to depose Queen Liliuokalani and annex Hawaii. President **Benjamin Harrison**'s administration approved of a takeover of Hawaii and collaborated with **John L. Stevens,** the U.S. minister to Hawaii, in orchestrating a rebellion—supported by sailors from the USS *Boston*—that toppled Queen Liliuokalani on January 17, 1893. (Approximately one hundred years later, on November 23, 1993, President **Bill Clinton** issued a formal apology to Hawaii for the overthrow in 1893 of the Hawaiian monarchy, a legal government, by the United States.)

With Queen Liliuokalani's abdication, Sanford B. Dole assumed the presidency of a provisional government in Hawaii. On July 4, 1894, President Dole declared the Republic of Hawaii and that year urged President **Grover Cleveland** to annex the islands. The Cleveland administration opposed the annexation of Hawaii and attempted to restore Queen Liliuokalani to power. The annexation of the Hawaiian Islands by the United States would not occur until July 6, 1898, when President **William McKinley**—riding a wave of nationalism generated by the Spanish-American War—signed the Newlands Joint Resolution ceding sovereignty over Hawaii to the United States. With the signing of the Organic Act on June 14, 1900, Hawaii officially became a U.S. territory with a territorial government, Sanford B. Dole became its first governor, and all Hawaiians who were citizens of the Republic of Hawaii on August 12, 1898, were declared U.S. citizens but had no right to vote in U.S. elections. Hawaii's statehood would be deferred for more than half a century, due to racist sentiments in American society about its multiethnic population, as well as to arguments that the Hawaiian Islands were much too far away from the continental United States to be a state.

What precipitated Hawaii's admission into the Union as the fiftieth state?

The Japanese empire's surprise bombing raid on the U.S. Pacific Fleet moored at Pearl Harbor, on the island of Oahu, on December 7, 1941, precipitated Hawaii's admission into the

Union. As the Allies sought during World War II to quash Japanese aggression and Imperial Japan's campaign, begun long before the war, to conquer all of Asia, Hawaii emerged as a strategic location in the Pacific zone for the U.S. defense apparatus. The tragedy of Pearl Harbor and Hawaiians' dedication to the war effort generated sympathy and admiration for Hawaii in mainstream America, which worked to erode Americans' racial prejudice against multiethnic Hawaiians, paving the way for Hawaii's admission into the Union as the fiftieth state on March 12, 1959. Interestingly, 1959 also saw the introduction of Boeing 707 airplanes, which were capable of flying from California to Honolulu in a then astounding five hours, shattering all previous speed records by two hours and bringing Hawaii "closer" to the continental United States.

Hawaii's admission into the Union in 1959 provided unprecedented opportunities for Americans with roots in Asia to serve in the upper echelons of the U.S. government. In 1959 voters in Hawaii elected the first Asian American to the U.S. Senate—Chinese American **Hiram Leong Fong** (see *Who are the Chinese Americans in the political arena?*, p. 56). Fong, a Republican, served Hawaii in the Senate until January 3, 1977. In 1959 another Hawaiian, **Daniel K. Inouye** (see *Who are some prominent Japanese-American politicians?*, p. 136), became the first American of Japanese descent to serve in the U.S. House of Representatives. In 1962 Inouye, a Democrat, was elected to the U.S. Senate, where he has served ever since. **Spark Matsunaga,** another Hawaiian Democrat of Japanese ancestry (see *Who are some prominent Japanese-American politicians?*, p. 136), who was instrumental in securing Hawaii's statehood, filled Inouye's seat in the U.S. House of Representatives, working there on behalf of his constituents from 1963 until January 3, 1977, when he joined Inouye in the U.S. Senate. Senator Matsunaga served in the Senate until his death on April 15, 1990.

Another Democrat from Hawaii, **Daniel K. Akaka,** a

Native Hawaiian and Chinese American who served in the U.S. House of Representatives from 1977 to 1990, was appointed to fill the vacancy in the Senate that arose with the death of Senator Matsunaga. Akaka was then elected to the Senate by a special election in November 1990 and continues to serve in that body. In 1964 **Patsy Takemoto Mink,** a Hawaiian Democrat of Japanese ancestry (see *Who are some prominent Japanese-American politicians?*, p. 136), became the first Asian-American woman in the U.S. House of Representatives when she was elected to the House after Hawaii was awarded a second seat. She served in the House for six consecutive terms, until 1976, when she made an unsuccessful run for the U.S. Senate. In September 1990 Mink returned to the U.S. House of Representatives after winning a special election to fill out the term of Congressman Akaka, who had been named to Spark Matsunaga's Senate seat. She served in the House until her death on September 28, 2002. In 1974 **George Ryoichi Ariyoshi,** a Hawaiian of Japanese ancestry (see *Who are some prominent Japanese-American politicians?*, p. 136), became the first Asian-American elected governor of a state when Hawaiians voted him governor of Hawaii, an office he filled for three terms, until 1986.

How many Native Hawaiians are there, and where do they live?

As soon as Hawaii became the fiftieth state, Native Hawaiians, along with Hawaiians of Asian and other ancestries, began flocking to the U.S. mainland, mostly for financial improvement. In the year 2000 the U.S. Bureau of the Census counted 401,162 Native Hawaiians (alone and in combination with at least one other race), of which 140,652 were Native Hawaiian alone. According to Census 2000 data, the five states with the highest Native Hawaiian (alone) population in 2000 were Hawaii (80,137), California (20,571), Washington (4,883), Texas (3,475), and Utah (1,251).

Is Hawaii the number-one U.S. destination for Pacific Islander immigrants?

Hawaii has not only generated a migration of Hawaiians to the U.S. mainland over the decades, it has also attracted Pacific Islander immigrants to its shores. Census 2000 counted 113,539 non–Native Hawaiian Pacific Islanders (alone) in Hawaii, making it the number-two state after California in 2000 for Pacific Islander Americans.

SAMOAN AMERICANS

How was Samoa divided, and when did American Samoa become a U.S. territory?

The volcanic islands of Samoa, situated in the Pacific Ocean about halfway between New Zealand and Hawaii, were first settled by Polynesians who, according to prevailing assumptions, hailed from the East Indies, the Philippines, or the Malay Peninsula. Samoa remained isolated from the West until a Dutchman, **Jacob Roggeveen,** made landfall there in 1722. Life in the Samoan archipelago changed dramatically in 1816 with the arrival of Christian missionaries, who were intent on civilizing the native peoples. Along with the missionaries came eager Europeans and Americans, who viewed Samoa as an excellent location for a coaling station. In 1899 Germany and the United States negotiated a partitioning of the Samoan archipelago. Germany acquired what became known as Western Samoa, which is comprised of two main islands and seven smaller ones, with a total land area of 1,150 square miles. In 1920 Germany handed Western Samoa to New Zealand, which administered the island group until it reestablished sovereignty in 1962. (In 1997 Western Samoa eliminated the word "Western" in its name.) The United States, on the other hand, acquired American (Eastern) Samoa, consisting of five volcanic islands (Tutuila, Aunu'u, Ofu, Olosega, and Ta'u) and two coral atolls (Swains atoll and Rose atoll) distributed over 150 square miles of ocean and with a total land area of 76 square miles. With these islands and atolls, the United States acquired Pago Pago Harbor, the best port in the South Pacific.

The U.S. government formally annexed American Samoa on April 17, 1900. From 1899 to 1951, the U.S. Department of the Navy administered the islands and atolls as a U.S. territory, and American Samoans were accorded the status of U.S. nationals, not citizens. In 1951 American Samoa became an unincorporated territory administered by the U.S. Department of the Interior. To this day, it has never been granted statehood and remains unorganized; that is, it does not enjoy powers of self-government. As U.S. nationals, American Samoans enjoy limited rights. For instance, they may travel freely between American Samoa and the fifty states and other U.S. dependencies and possessions, but they may not vote in U.S. national elections.

When did Samoans first venture to Hawaii and to the mainland United States?

The first Samoans reached Hawaii's shores in significant numbers in 1919—not to work the plantations but to construct a Mormon temple in Laie, Oahu. In 1940 the U.S. Marines transformed the port of Pago Pago in American Samoa into a training and staging area. The marines provided employment for American Samoans, who enlisted during World War II and created a home guard unit, and when the Marines Corp pulled out after the war, the American-Samoan economy nose-dived, sending a wave of American Samoans to Hawaii. (American-Samoan authorities actually encouraged this migration to Hawaii to alleviate some of the tensions caused by the drooping economy and the rapid growth in the American-Samoan population.) Once in Hawaii, many American-Samoan men looked to the U.S. Navy for employment.

In the 1960s American Samoans continued to flock to Hawaii to enlist in the navy for the prestige, adventure, job security, and higher pay it afforded or for other employment. In that decade, they (and Western Samoans alike) began venturing in significant numbers to the continental United States, especially California, also to escape the limited economic opportunities, low wages, and geographic isolation in Western Samoa and American Samoa. These factors continued to stimulate the (im)migration of Samoans to the fifty states in the 1990s. (In 1999, per capita income in American Samoa was $4,357, as compared to $21,587 nationwide.) The top five states for the 91,029 Samoans (single race) that the U.S. Bureau of the Census counted in 2000 were California (37,498), Hawaii (16,166), Washington (8,049), Utah (4,523), and Texas (2,491).

GUAMANIAN AMERICANS

How did Guam become a U.S. territory?

On March 6, 1521, Portuguese navigator **Ferdinand Magellan** made landfall on the island of Guam, the largest and southernmost island in the Mariana Islands archipelago, with a land area about three times larger than Washington, D.C. Magellan named Guam and the rest of the islands in the archipelago *Islas de Ladrones,* or "Islands of Thieves," because the native peoples, the Chamorros, who originated from Southeast Asia, made away with a skiff from his ship. On January 22, 1565, Spanish explorer **Miguel Lopez de Legazpi** declared Guam a Spanish possession and made it a regular port of call for merchants and sailors plying their trade on the route connecting Mexico and Manila. A century later, in 1665, Padre **Diego Luis de San Vitores,** a Jesuit missionary from Spain, stopped in Guam en route to the Philippines. In 1668 he returned to Guam with other Spanish missionaries, who would strive to convert the Chamorros to Christianity. On February 2, 1699, Padre San Vitores established the first Catholic Church in Agana. Then, on April 2, 1672, he and his Filipino assistant, **Pedro Calansor,** were murdered by Chief **Mata'pang** of Tumon for baptizing the chief's infant daughter without his consent but at the mother's request. With Padre San Vitores's murder, the Spanish in Guam launched a fierce campaign to subdue the Chamorros, igniting a native revolt against Spanish domination that lasted until 1695 and nearly wiped out the Chamorro population.

Spanish rule in Guam ended nearly two centuries later. With the Treaty of Paris concluding the Spanish-American War of 1898—a war that the United States waged to end Spain's domination of Cuba and other Spanish colonies in the Pacific and to amass some American colonies of its own—Spain ceded Guam to the United States. Except for a brief period when the Japanese occupied Guam during World War II, the island was administered by the U.S. Department of the Navy until August 1, 1950, when the U.S. Congress passed the Organic Act of Guam, which conferred U.S. citizenship on the inhabitants of the Territory of Guam, established in Guam a civilian administration under the jurisdiction of the U.S. Department of the Interior, and extended control of the local government to the native peoples. In 1970 the governorship of Guam became an elected office rather than one appointed by the president of the United States, giving Guamanians more autonomy. By then, however, Guam had become so Americanized, to the detriment of the indigenous culture, that it had earned the nickname "Guam USA."

What triggered Guamanian migration to Hawaii and the U.S. mainland?

With the passage of the Organic Act of Guam in 1950, Guamanians were granted the right to migrate freely between Guam and the continental United States and all U.S. territories. In ensuing decades, a good number of Guamanian men enlisted in the U.S. armed forces to secure steady employment and escape the isolation of Guam. Other Guamanians migrated to Hawaii and the U.S. mainland to search for economic opportunities. U.S. Immigration and Naturalization Service data indicate that in the years 1963 to 1971, 11,930 Guamanians migrated to Hawaii and the West Coast. On the mainland, most settled in the very ports of entry they had passed through, including San Francisco, Los Angeles, and San Diego, and most found work at naval shipyards. To this day, Guamanians outside of Guam are concentrated in the large port cities of the West Coast. The top five states for the 58,240 Guamanians/Chamorros (single race) tabulated in 2000 were California (20,918), Washington (5,823), Texas (3,641), Florida (2,319), and New York (1,931).

SOME SITES WHERE YOU CAN RELIVE ASIAN-AMERICAN HISTORY

1. **Angel Island** San Francisco Bay, California

Between 1910 and 1940, about 175,000 Chinese aliens and a small number of other Pacific Rim aliens seeking admission to the United States were processed at a special immigration station erected in 1910 on Angel Island in San Francisco Bay. Unlike at Ellis Island, where a would-be immigrant's fate—entry or deportation—was routinely decided in a matter of hours, at Angel Island, aliens were detained in crowded, dirty barracks for two to three weeks on average, and in some cases for up to two years, as immigration authorities scrutinized their documents or subjected them to interrogation.

2. **Chinatown** San Francisco, California

San Francisco's Chinatown took shape in the 1850s around what was then Portsmouth Square after thousands of Chinese laborers in search of opportunity ventured to the city when their work on the transcontinental railroad was completed.

Chinese, seeking a haven from racism and a sense of home amidst Chinatown's Buddhist temples, benevolent societies, and markets, continued to settle in the enclave, and by 1870 it was home to 24 percent of all the Chinese in California and had come to be known as *Dai Fou*, or "Big City." Nowadays Filipinos, Thais, Vietnamese, and Koreans live and work alongside Chinese in San Francisco's Chinatown, adding their own imprint to this overcrowded, bustling, and colorful neighborhood.

3. **Chinatown** Manhattan

The Chinatown in Lower Manhattan, the largest in the nation, began as a very small Chinese neighborhood that sprung up on Doyer's Farm near the Bowery in the years after a Kwangtung merchant named **Wo Kee**, the first Chinese in the neighborhood, took up residence at 8 Mott Street in 1858. While only about fifty Chinese lived there in 1870, in the 1880s the neighborhood was transformed into a self-sufficient Chinatown, thanks to the inflow of Chinese migrants from the western United States beginning in that decade. Chinatown in Lower Manhattan is nowadays a haven both for working-class Chinese immigrants in New York City, who earnestly save their money in hopes of moving one day to middle-class communities in Brooklyn or Queens, and for a smaller number of affluent Chinese from Hong Kong and Taiwan, who beginning in the 1980s made the enclave their center of operations, diversifying the population and sparking heavy investing and a real estate boom.

4. **Tule Lake Japanese Relocation Center** Tule Lake, California

After the Japanese empire bombed U.S. naval forces stationed at Pearl Harbor, Hawaii, during World War II, Japanese Americans and nationals in the western United States were systematically rounded up and incarcerated in ten relocation centers located in remote, uninhabitable areas of Arkansas, Arizona, California, Idaho, Colorado, and Wyoming. Tule Lake was one of those relocation centers. It was hastily constructed on a seventy-four-hundred-acre site in Modoc County, California, thirty-five miles southeast of Klamath Falls, Oregon. The first internees arrived at its gates on May 25, 1942. Thousands of Japanese, as many as 18,789 at the camp's peak occupancy, were confined at Tule Lake until it was completely emptied on March 20, 1946. Nearly thirty years later, on August 20, 1975, the Tule Lake Relocation Center was registered as a State Historical Landmark. A monument commemorating the internment of Japanese at Tule Lake was erected on Highway 139 and dedicated in 1979. The County Fairgrounds Museum and the Lava Beds National Monument maintain small exhibits about the Tule Lake Relocation Center.

5. **Manzanar** Lone Pine, California

Manzanar is another of the ten relocation centers where Japanese Americans and nationals were interned from 1942 to 1946. It was constructed on the remote edge of the desert along the eastern slope of the Sierra Nevada. More than ten thousand Japanese were incarcerated in the harsh confines of Manzanar, most for as long as three and a half years, or until September 1945, when the camp closed. Today the only physical reminder of Manzanar at the site is a graveyard with a single monument commemorating all those who died there. On the last Saturday in April, Japanese Americans make an annual pilgrimage to Manzanar, where they participate in a commemorative ceremony, Japanese folk dancing, and a tour of the Manzanar exhibit at the nearby Eastern California Museum.

6. **Little Tokyo** Los Angeles, California

Little Tokyo in Los Angeles began as a small Japanese community that had formed by the turn of the twentieth century around First and Central Streets in the city's downtown. The community expanded greatly in 1903, when about two thousand Issei from northern California settled there after they were recruited to work on the Pacific Electric Railway, and again in 1906, when a devastating earthquake in San Francisco compelled more northern California Japanese to head to Southern California. After Imperial Japan bombed U.S. forces at Pearl Harbor on December 7, 1941, the U.S. Army uprooted Little Tokyo's Japanese residents and sent them to "relocation centers" along with other Japanese from the western United States. Little Tokyo became a ghost town. African Americans soon moved into the area, but with the end of World War II, a good number of Japanese returned to reclaim their neighborhood. Nowadays visitors can learn about Little Tokyo and Japanese-American history by visiting the Little Tokyo Historic District. A focal point of the district is the Japanese American National Museum, the only museum in the nation devoted to the Japanese-American experience, which is housed in the Nishi Hongwanji Buddhist Temple, the first Buddhist temple in Los Angeles, and opened its doors in 1992.

7. **Koreatown** Los Angeles, California

The largest Korean enclave in the United States is Koreatown in Los Angeles, which is situated in an area loosely bordered by Beverly Boulevard, Pico Boulevard, Hoover Street, and Crenshaw Avenue. The very core of this thriving commercial and residential community is Olympic Boulevard. The area first drew Korean small businesses in the late 1960s, and by 1980, when the city of Los Angeles officially designated it a community, it boasted many Korean restaurants, markets, and shops. In its darkest hour, Koreatown was the site of the riots that raged in Los Angeles for three days beginning on April 29, 1992.

8. **Little Saigon** Westminster, California

The largest Vietnamese enclave in America—and outside of Vietnam—is Little Saigon in Westminster, California. The arrival of the first wave of Vietnamese refugees in the United States soon after the fall of Saigon gave rise to a nascent Little Saigon in 1975. In the early days, it was just a handful of shops situated amid strawberry fields, orange and lemon groves, dilapidated strip malls, and auto repair shops, but by 1988 so many

Vietnamese restaurants, cafés, markets, shops, and professional offices had cropped up along a one-mile stretch of Bolsa Avenue, from Ward to Magnolia Streets, that the enclave was officially named "Little Saigon." Nowadays Little Saigon is poised to become the uncontested capital of international trade with Vietnam, Hong Kong, and other Pacific Rim nations.

TONGAN AMERICANS

Where does the history of Tonga begin?

The Kingdom of Tonga, comprised of 169 islands stretched out over five hundred miles, lies east of Fiji, just to the west of the International Dateline, and a day ahead of Samoa. The prevailing view among scholars is that Polynesians from Samoa settled on the islands of Tonga and lived undisturbed until the arrival of Dutch navigators **Willem Cornelis Schouten** and **James Lemaire** in 1616. More than a century later, English explorer and navigator Captain **James Cook** explored the islands on three occasions, in 1773, 1774, and 1777. He was so impressed with the native peoples' hospitality that he named the isles the Friendly Islands. From 1799 to 1852, the native peoples of Tonga fought a fiery civil war. The missionaries sent to the islands by the London Missionary Society in 1798 got caught in the brewing violence, and after two were killed, the rest fled to Australia. In 1822 the first Wesleyan Methodist missionaries arrived in Tonga from Australia, the Wesleyan Pacific base. They were successful in their efforts to convert a powerful chief, **Taufa'ahau Tupou I,** to Christianity in 1834 and subsequently helped him defeat his rivals in several domestic wars. By 1845 Taufa'ahau Tupou I had united Tonga under his control and had assumed the Christian name King George Tupou I of Tonga. King George Tupou I fell under the heavy influence of a Wesleyan missionary named

Reverend **Shirley Baker,** who ventured to Tonga from Australia in 1860 under the auspices of the Wesleyan Church. Until the British established a protectorate over Tonga in 1889, Baker played a central role in King George Tupou I's government. In an expression of their dominance, the British deported Baker to New Zealand, where he remained for a decade, returning to Tonga in 1900 under the auspices of the Anglican Church. It would not be until 1970 that Tonga gained its independence from Britain.

When and why did Tongans start coming to America?

Thanks to Reverend **Shirley Baker**'s missionary zeal, Tongans have been churchgoing Wesleyans for more than a century. Nonetheless, in the 1960s the Church of Jesus Christ of Latter-day Saints was able to rapidly expand its presence in Tonga, constructing churches, schools, and meetinghouses everywhere on the islands. The conversion of Tongans to Mormonism precipitated a trickle of Tongan immigration to the United States that continues to this day and is encouraged and even funded by the Mormon Church. Since Tongans do not enjoy the right of unrestricted entry into the United States, they depend in part on sponsorship by relatives with U.S. citizenship. Given that the Mormon Church has been a decisive push factor for Tongan immigration to the United States since the 1960s, it is not surprising that Utah, with 6,587 Tongans (alone) counted in 2000, was second only to California, with 12,111 Tongans (alone), as the state with the highest Tongan population in 2000. The next three states with the greatest number of Tongans (alone) in residence in 2000 were Hawaii (3,993), Texas (1,130), and Washington (754).

Selected Readings

GENERAL WORKS

AGUILAR-SAN JUAN, KARIN. *The State of Asian America: Activism and Resistance in the 1990s.* Boston: South End Press, 1994.

Asian Women United of California, eds. *Making Waves: An Anthology of Writings By and About Asian American Women.* Boston: Beacon Press, 1989.

BOW, LESLIE. *Betrayal and Other Acts of Subversion: Feminism, Sexual Politics, Asian American Women's Literature.* Princeton, N.J.: Princeton University Press, 2001.

BROWNSTONE, DAVID M., AND IRENE M. FRANCK. *Facts About American Immigration.* New York: The H. W. Wilson Company, 2001.

CHAN, SUCHENG. *Asian Americans: An Interpretive History.* Boston: Twayne Publishers, 1991.

CHANG, GORDON H., ed. *Asian Americans and Politics: Perspectives, Experiences, Prospects.* Palo Alto, Calif.: Stanford University Press, 2001.

CHEUNG, KING-KOK, ed. *Words Matter: Conversations with Asian American Writers.* Honolulu: University of Hawaii Press, 2000.

CHIN, FRANK. *Bulletproof Buddhists and Other Essays.* Honolulu: University of Hawaii Press, 1998.

CHIU, CHRISTINA. *Lives of Notable Asian Americans: Literature and Education.* New York: Chelsea House, 1996.

CHOW, CLAIRE S. *Leaving Deep Water: Asian American Women at the Crossroads of Two Cultures.* New York: Plume, 1999.

CHU, PATRICIA P. *Assimilating Asians: Gendered Strategies of Authorship in Asian America.* Durham, N.C.: Duke University Press, 2000.

CHUH, KANDICE, AND KAREN SHIMAKAWA, eds., *Orientations: Mapping Studies in the Asian Diaspora.* Durham, N.C.: Duke University Press, 2001.

CIMENT, JAMES, ed. *Encyclopedia of American Immigration.* 4 vols. Armonk, N.Y.: M. E. Sharpe, Inc., 2001.

COHEN, WARREN I. *The Asian American Century.* Cambridge, Mass.: Harvard University Press, 2002.

DANIELS, ROGER. *Asian America: Chinese and Japanese in the United States since 1850.* Seattle: University of Washington Press, 1988.

ESPIRITU, YEN LE. *Asian American Panethnicity: Bridging Institutions and Identities.* Philadelphia: Temple University Press, 1992.

———. *Asian American Women and Men: Labor, Laws, and Love.* Thousand Oaks, Calif.: Sage Publications, 1997.

FENG, PETER X. *Identities in Motion: Asian American Film and Video.* Durham, N.C.: Duke University Press, 2002.

FONER, PHILIP S., and Daniel Rosenberg, eds. *Racism, Dissent, and Asian Americans from 1850 to the Present: A Documentary History.* Westport, Conn.: Greenwood Press, 1993.

GALL, SUSAN B., AND TIMOTHY L. GALL, eds. *Statistical Record of Asian Americans.* Detroit: Gale Research, 1993.

HAGEDORN, JESSICA, ed. *Charlie Chan Is Dead: An Anthology of Contemporary Asian American Fiction.* New York: Penguin, 1993.

HASELTINE, PATRICIA. *East and Southeast Asian Material Culture in North America: Collections, Historical Sites, and Festivals.* New York: Greenwood Press, 1989.

HING, BILL ONG. *Making and Remaking Asian America Through Immigration Policy, 1850–1990.* Stanford, Calif.: Stanford University Press, 1993.

HONG, MARIA, ed. *Growing Up Asian American.* New York: Avon Books, 1993.

HONGO, GARRETT, ed. *The Open Boat: Poems from Asian America.* New York: Doubleday, 1993.

HOYT, EDWIN P. *Asians in the West.* Nashville, Tenn.: Thomas Nelson Inc., Publishers, 1974.

HU-DEHART, EVELYN, ed. *Across the Pacific: Asian Americans and Globalization.* Philadelphia: Temple University Press, 1999.

HUNDLEY, NORRIS, JR., ed. *The Asian American: The Historical Experience: Essays.* Santa Barbara, Calif.: Clio Books, 1976.

HUNE, SHIRLEY, HYUNG-CHAN KIM, STEPHEN S. FUGITA, AND AMY LING, eds. *Asian Americans: Comparative and Global Perspectives.* Pullman: Washington State University Press, 1991.

KARNOW, STANLEY, AND NANCY YOSHIHARA. *Asian Americans in Transition.* New York: The Asia Society, 1992.

KIM, ELAINE H. *Asian American Literature: An Introduction to the Writings and Their Social Context.* Philadelphia: Temple University Press, 1982.

KIM, HYUNG-CHAN, ed. *Dictionary of Asian American History.* New York: Greenwood Press, 1986.

KITANO, HARRY H. L., AND ROGER DANIELS. *Asian Americans: Emerging Minorities.* Englewood Cliffs, N.J.: Prentice Hall, 1988.

KNOLL, TRICIA. *Becoming Americans: Asian Sojourners, Immi-*

grants, and Refugees in the Western United States. Portland, Ore.: Coast to Coast Books, 1982.

LEE, JOANN FAUNG JEAN. *Asian American Actors: Oral Histories from Stage, Screen, and Television.* Jefferson, N.C.: McFarland & Company, 2000.

———. *Asian American Experiences in the United States: Oral Histories of First to Fourth Generation Americans from China, the Philippines, Japan, India, the Pacific Islands, Vietnam and Cambodia.* Jefferson, N.C.: McFarland & Company, 1991.

LEE, RACHEL C. *The Americas of Asian American Literature: Gendered Fiction of Nation and Transnation.* Princeton, N.J.: Princeton University Press, 1999.

LEONARD, GEORGE J., ed. *The Asian Pacific American Heritage: A Companion to Literature and Arts.* New York: Garland, 1999.

LIEN, PEI-TE. *The Making of Asian America Through Political Participation.* Philadelphia: Temple University Press, 2001.

LIM, SHIRLEY GEOK-LIN, AND MAYUMI TSUTAKAWA. *The Forbidden Stitch: An Asian-American Women's Anthology.* Corvallis, Ore.: Calyx Books, 1989.

LYMAN, STANFORD M. *The Asian in the West.* Reno, Nev.: Western Studies Center, Desert Research Institute, 1970.

MA, SHENG-MEI. *The Deathly Embrace: Orientalism and Asian American Identity.* Minneapolis: University of Minnesota Press, 2000.

MANGIAFICO, LUCIANO. *Contemporary American Immigrants: Patterns of Filipino, Korean, and Chinese Settlement in the United States.* New York: Praeger, 1988.

MELENDY, HOWARD BRETT. *Asians in America: Filipinos, Koreans, and East Indians.* New York: Hippocrene Books, 1981.

MIN, PYONG GAP, ed. *Asian Americans: Contemporary Trends and Issues.* Thousand Oaks, Calif.: Sage Publications, 1995.

NG, FRANKLIN, ed. *The Asian American Encyclopedia.* 6 vols. New York: Marshall Cavendish, 1995.

———. *Asian American Women and Gender.* New York: Garland, 1999.

NGUYEN, VIET THANH. *Race & Resistance: Literature & Politics in Asian America.* New York: Oxford University Press, 2002.

NOMURA, GAIL M., RUSSELL ENDO, STEPHEN H. SUMIDA, AND RUSSELL C. LEONG, eds. *Frontiers of Asian American Studies: Writing, Research, and Commentary.* Pullman: Washington State University Press, 1989.

ODO, FRANKLIN SHOICHIRO. *In Movement: A Pictorial History of Asian America.* Los Angeles: Visual Communications, Asian American Studies Central, 1977.

OKIHIRO, GARY Y. *The Columbia Guide to Asian American History.* New York: Columbia University Press, 2001.

———. *Margins and Mainstreams: Asians in American History and Culture.* Seattle: University of Washington Press, 1994.

OKIHIRO, GARY Y., MARILYN ALQUIZOLA, DOROTHY FUJITA RONY, AND K. SCOTT WONG, eds. *Privileging Positions: The Sites of Asian American Studies.* Pullman: Washington State University Press, 1995.

REVILLA, LINDA A., GAIL M. NOMURA, SHAWN WONG, AND SHIRLEY HUNE, eds. *Bearing Dreams, Shaping Visions: Asian Pacific American Perspectives.* Pullman: Washington State University Press, 1993.

SEGAL, UMA A. *A Framework for Immigration: Asians in the United States.* New York: Columbia University Press, 2002.

SUE, STANLEY, AND NATHANIEL N. WAGNER, eds. *Asian-Americans: Psychological Perspectives.* Palo Alto, Calif.: Science & Behavior Books, 1973.

TAKAKI, RONALD. *Spacious Dreams: The First Wave of Asian Immigration.* New York: Chelsea House Publishers, 1994.

———. *Strangers from a Different Shore: A History of Asian Americans.* Boston: Little, Brown and Company, 1989.

THERNSTROM, STEPHAN, ANN ORLOV, AND OSCAR HANDLIN, eds. *Harvard Encyclopedia of American Ethnic Groups.* Cambridge, Mass.: The Belknap Press of Harvard University Press, 1980.

THOMPSON, RICHARD AUSTIN. *The Yellow Peril, 1890–1924.* New York: Arno Press, 1978.

TUAN, MIA. *Forever Foreigners or Honorary Whites? The Asian Ethnic Experience Today.* New Brunswick, N.J.: Rutgers University Press, 1998.

UNO, ROBERTA, ed. *Unbroken Thread: An Anthology of Plays by Asian American Women.* Amherst: University of Massachusetts Press, 1993.

UNTERBURGER, AMY L., ed. *Who's Who among Asian Americans, 1994/95.* Detroit: Gale Research Inc., 1994.

WALKER-MOFFAT, WENDY. *The Other Side of the Asian American Success Story.* San Francisco: Jossey-Bass Publishers, 1995.

WEI, WILLIAM. *The Asian American Movement.* Philadelphia: Temple University Press, 1993.

WHITE-PARKS, ANNETTE, DEBORAH D. BUFFTON, URSULA CHIU, CATHERINE M. CURRIER, CECILIA G. MANRIQUE, AND MARSHA MOMOI PIEHL, eds. *A Gathering of Voices on the Asian American Experience.* Fort Atkinson, Wis.: Highsmith Press, 1994.

WILLIAMS-LEÓN, TERESA, AND CYNTHIA L. NAKASHIMA, eds. *The Sum of Our Parts: Mixed-Heritage Asian Americans.* Philadelphia: Temple University Press, 2001.

WONG, SAU-LING CYNTHIA. *Reading Asian American Literature: From Necessity to Extravagance.* Princeton, N.J.: Princeton University Press, 1993.

WONG, SHAWN, ed. *Asian American Literature: A Brief Introduction and Anthology.* Berkeley: HarperCollins, 1996.

WONG, WILLIAM. *Yellow Journalist: Dispatches from Asian America.* Philadelphia: Temple University Press, 2001.

XING, JUN. *Asian America Through the Lens: History, Representations, and Identity.* Walnut Creek, Calif.: AltaMira Press, 1998.

YU, HENRY. *Thinking Orientals: Migration, Contact, and Exoticism in Modern America.* New York: Oxford University Press, 2001.

ZIA, HELEN. *Asian American Dreams: The Emergence of an American People.* New York: Farrar, Straus and Giroux, 2000.

CHINESE AMERICANS

CHAI, MAY-LEE, AND WINBERG CHAI. *The Girl from Purple Mountain: Love, Honor, War, and One Family's Journey from China to America.* New York: St. Martin's Press, 2001.

CHAN, SUCHENG. *This Bittersweet Soil: The Chinese in California Agriculture, 1860–1910.* Berkeley: University of California Press, 1986.

———, ed. *Entry Denied: Exclusion and the Chinese Community in America, 1882–1943.* Philadelphia: Temple University Press, 1991.

CHANG, PAO-MIN. *Continuity and Change: A Profile of Chinese Americans.* New York: Vantage Press, 1983.

CHEN, HSIANG-SHUI. *Chinatown No More: Taiwan Immigrants in Contemporary New York.* Ithaca, N.Y.: Cornell University Press, 1992.

CHEN, JACK. *The Chinese of America.* San Francisco: Harper & Row, 1980.

CHIN, KO-LIN. *Smuggled Chinese: Clandestine Immigration to the United States.* Philadelphia: Temple University Press, 1999.

CHIN, TUNG POK, WITH WINIFRED C. CHIN. *Paper Son: One Man's Story.* Philadelphia: Temple University Press, 2000.

CHOY, PHILIP P., LORRAINE DONG, AND MARLON K. HOM, eds. *The Coming Man: 19th Century American Perceptions of the Chinese.* Seattle: University of Washington Press, 1995.

CHUN, GLORIA HEYUNG. *Of Orphans and Warriors: Inventing Chinese American Culture and Identity.* New Brunswick, N.J.: Rutgers University Press, 2000.

COOLIDGE, MARY ROBERTS. *Chinese Immigration.* 1909. Reprint, New York: Arno Press, 1969.

DIRLIK, ARIF. *Chinese on the American Frontier.* Lanham, Md.: Rowman & Littlefield, 2001.

DOBIE, CHARLES CALDWELL. *San Francisco's Chinatown.* New York: D. Appleton-Century Company, 1936.

FESSLER, LOREN W. *Chinese in America: Stereotyped Past, Changing Present.* New York: Vantage Press, 1983.

FONG-TORRES, BEN. *The Rice Room: Growing Up Chinese-American—From Number Two Son to Rock 'n' Roll.* New York: Plume, 1995.

HSU, MADELINE YUAN-YIN. *Dreaming of Gold, Dreaming of Home: Transnationalism and Migration Between the United States and South China, 1882–1943.* Stanford, Calif.: Stanford University Press, 2000.

KWONG, PETER. *The New Chinatown.* New York: Hill and Wang, 1987.

LAI, HIM MARK, GENNY LIM, AND JUDY YOUNG. *Island: Poetry and History of Chinese Immigrants on Angel Island, 1910–1940.* 1980. Reprint, Seattle: University of Washington Press, 1991.

LAI, HIM MARK, JOE HUANG, AND DON WONG. *The Chinese of America, 1785–1980: An Illustrated History and Catalog of the Exhibition.* San Francisco: Chinese Culture Foundation, 1980.

LEE, ERIKA. *At America's Gates: Chinese Immigration During the Exclusion Era, 1882–1943.* Chapel Hill: The University of North Carolina Press, 2003.

LING, HUPING. *Surviving on the Gold Mountain: A History of Chinese American Women and Their Lives.* Albany: State University of New York Press, 1998.

LIU, ERIC. *The Accidental Asian: Notes of a Native Speaker.* New York: Vintage Books, 1998.

LOO, CHALSA M. *Chinese America: Mental Health and Quality of Life in the Inner City.* Thousand Oaks, Calif.: Sage Publications, 1998.

LYMAN, STANFORD M. *Chinese Americans.* New York: Random House, 1974.

MARK, DIANE MEI LIN, AND GINGER CHIH. *A Place Called Chinese America.* 2nd ed. Dubuque, Iowa: Kendall-Hunt, 1993.

NEE, VICTOR G., AND BRETT DE BARY NEE. *Longtime Californ': A Documentary Study of an American Chinatown.* 1973. Reprint, Stanford, Calif.: Stanford University Press, 1986.

NG, FRANKLIN. *The Taiwanese Americans.* Westport, Conn.: Greenwood Press, 1998.

STEINER, STAN. *Fusang: The Chinese Who Built America.* New York: Harper & Row, 1979.

SUNG, BETTY LEE. *Mountain of Gold: The Story of the Chinese in America.* New York: Macmillan Company, 1967.

TAKAKI, RONALD. *Ethnic Islands: The Emergence of Urban Chinese America.* New York: Chelsea House Publishers, 1994.

TONG, BENSON. *The Chinese Americans.* Westport, Conn.: Greenwood Press, 2000.

TSAI, SHIH-SHAN HENRY. *China and the Overseas Chinese in the United States, 1868–1911.* Fayetteville: University of Arkansas Press, 1983.

———. *The Chinese Experience in America.* Bloomington: Indiana University Press, 1986.

TUNG, WILLIAM L. *The Chinese in America, 1820–1973: A Chronology & Fact Book.* Dobbs Ferry, N.Y.: Oceana Publications, 1974.

WEISS, MELFORD S. *Valley City: A Chinese Community in America.* Cambridge, Mass.: Schenkman, 1974.

WONG, K. SCOTT, AND SUCHENG CHAN, eds. *Claiming America: Constructing Chinese American Identities during the Exclusion Era.* Philadelphia: Temple University Press, 1998.

WU, CHENG-TSU, ed. *"Chink!": A Documentary History of Anti-Chinese Prejudice in America.* New York: The World Publishing Company, 1972.

YUNG, JUDY. *Chinese Women of America: A Pictorial History.* Seattle: University of Washington Press, 1986.

YUNG, WING. *My Life in China and America.* New York: H. Holt and Company, 1909.

ZHAO, XIAOJIAN. *Remaking Chinese America: Immigration, Family, and Community, 1940–1965.* New Brunswick, N.J.: Rutgers University Press, 2002.

JAPANESE AMERICANS

ADLER, SUSAN MATOBA. *Mothering, Education, and Ethnicity: The Transformation of Japanese American Culture.* New York: Garland, 1998.

Andoh, Elizabeth. *At Home with Japanese Cooking.* New York: Alfred A. Knopf, 1980.

Armor, John, and Peter Wright. *Manzanar.* New York: Times Books, 1988.

Boddy, Elias Manchester. *Japanese in America.* 1921. Reprint, San Francisco: R and E Research Associates, 1970.

Chalfen, Richard. *Turning Leaves: The Photograph Collections of Two Japanese American Families.* Albuquerque: University of New Mexico Press, 1991.

Conrat, Maisie, and Richard Conrat. *Executive Order 9066: The Internment of 110,000 Japanese Americans.*1972. Reprint, Los Angeles: University of California Asian Studies Center, 1992.

Conroy, Hilary, and T. Scott Miyakawa. *East Across the Pacific: Historical & Sociological Studies of Japanese Immigration & Assimilation.* Santa Barbara, Calif.: ABC-CLIO, 1972.

Daniels, Roger. *Prisoners Without Trial: Japanese Americans in World War II.* New York: Hill and Wang, 1993.

Daniels, Roger, Sandra C. Taylor, and Harry H. L. Kitano, eds. *Japanese Americans: From Relocation to Redress.* Rev. ed. Seattle: University of Washington Press, 1991.

Diggs, Nancy Brown. *Steel Butterflies: Japanese Women and the American Experience.* Albany: State University of New York Press, 1998.

Fugita, Stephen S., and David J. O'Brien. *Japanese American Ethnicity: The Persistence of Community.* Seattle: University of Washington Press, 1991.

Glenn, Evelyn Nakano. *Issei, Nisei, War Bride: Three Generations of Japanese American Women in Domestic Service.* Philadelphia: Temple University Press, 1986.

Grodzins, Morton. *Americans Betrayed: Politics and the Japanese Evacuation.* Chicago: University of Chicago Press, 1949.

Hatamiya, Leslie T. *Righting a Wrong: Japanese Americans and the Passage of the Civil Liberties Act of 1988.* Stanford, Calif.: Stanford University Press, 1993.

Herman, Masako. *The Japanese in America, 1843–1973: A*

Chronology & Fact Book. Dobbs Ferry, N.Y.: Oceana Publications, 1974.

HOSOKAWA, BILL. *JACL in Quest of Justice.* New York: William Morrow and Co., 1982.

———. *Nisei: The Quiet Americans.* New York: William Morrow and Company, 1969.

———. *Out of the Frying Pan: Reflections of a Japanese American.* Niwot: The University Press of Colorado, 1998.

HOSOKAWA, BILL, AND ROBERT A. WILSON. *East to America: A History of the Japanese in the United States.* New York: William Morrow & Company, 1980.

HOUSTON, JEANNE WAKATSUKI, AND JAMES D. HOUSTON. *Farewell to Manzanar.* Boston: Houghton Mifflin Company, 1973.

ICHIOKA, YUJI. *The Issei: The World of the First Generation Japanese Immigrants, 1885–1924.* New York: The Free Press, 1988.

JAMES, THOMAS. *Exile Within: The Schooling of Japanese Americans, 1942–1945.* Cambridge, Mass.: Harvard University Press, 1987.

KAWAKAMI, K. K. *The Real Japanese Question.* New York: Macmillan, 1921.

KESSLER, LAUREN. *Stubborn Twig: Three Generations in the Life of a Japanese-American Family.* New York: Plume, 1994.

KIKUMURA, AKEMI. *Promises Kept: The Life of an Issei Man.* Novato, Calif.: Chandler and Sharp Publishers, 1991.

———. *Through Harsh Winters: The Life of a Japanese Immigrant Woman.* Novato, Calif.: Chandler and Sharp Publishers, 1981.

KITANO, HARRY H. L. *Generations and Identity: The Japanese American.* Needham Heights, Mass.: Ginn Press, 1993.

———. *Japanese Americans: The Evolution of a Subculture.* 2nd ed. Englewood Cliffs, N.J.: Prentice-Hall, 1976.

LAVIOLETTE, FORREST E. *Americans of Japanese Ancestry: A Study of Assimilation in the American Community.* Toronto: The Canadian Institute of International Affairs, 1945.

MCWILLIAMS, CAREY. *Prejudice, Japanese-Americans: Symbol of Racial Intolerance.* Boston: Little, Brown and Company, 1944.

MINATOYA, LYDIA YURIKO. *Talking to High Monks in the Snow: An Asian American Odyssey*. New York: HarperCollins, 1992.

MONTERO, DARREL. *Japanese Americans: Changing Patterns of Ethnic Identification Over Three Generations*. Boulder, Colo.: Westview Press, 1980.

MURA, DAVID. *Turning Japanese: Memoirs of a Sansei*. New York: Atlantic Monthly Press, 1991.

NAKANO, MEI T. *Japanese American Women: Three Generations, 1890–1990*. Berkeley: Mina Press Publishing, 1990.

NIIYA, BRIAN, ed. *Japanese American History: An A-to-Z Reference from 1868 to the Present*. New York: Facts on File, 1993.

O'BRIEN, DAVID J., AND STEPHEN S. FUGITA. *The Japanese American Experience*. Bloomington: Indiana University Press, 1991.

PETERSEN, WILLIAM. *Japanese Americans: Oppression and Success*. New York: Random House, 1971.

SARASOHN, EILEEN SUNADA, ed. *The Issei: Portrait of a Pioneer*. Palo Alto, Calif.: Pacific Books, 1983.

SHIMONISHI-LAMB, MILI. *And Then a Rainbow*. Santa Barbara, Calif.: Fithian Press, 1990.

SMITH, BRADFORD. *Americans from Japan*. Philadelphia: J. B. Lippincott Company, 1948.

SPICKARD, PAUL R. *Japanese Americans: The Formation and Transformations of an Ethnic Group*. New York: Twayne, 1996.

STRONG, EDWARD K., JR. *The Second-Generation Japanese Problem*. Palo Alto, Calif.: Stanford University Press, 1934.

TAKAKI, RONALD. *Issei and Nisei: The Settling of Japanese America*. New York: Chelsea House Publishers, 1994.

TAKEZAWA, YASUKO I. *Breaking the Silence: Redress and Japanese American Ethnicity*. Ithaca, N.Y.: Cornell University Press, 1995.

TATEISHI, JOHN, ed. *And Justice for All: An Oral History of the Japanese American Detention Camps*. New York: Random House, 1984.

UCHIDA, YOSHIKO. *Desert Exile: The Uprooting of a Japanese American Family*. Seattle: University of Washington Press, 1982.

VAN SANT, JOHN E. *Pacific Pioneers: Japanese Journeys to Ameri-*

ca and Hawaii, 1850–80. Chicago: University of Illinois Press, 2000.

Wilson, Robert A., and Bill Hosokawa. *East to America: A History of the Japanese in the United States.* New York: William Morrow and Co., 1980.

KOREAN AMERICANS

Barringer, Herbert R., and Sung-Nam Cho. *Koreans in the United States: A Fact Book.* Honolulu: Center for Korean Studies, University of Hawaii, 1989.

Chin, Soo-Young. *Doing What Had to Be Done: The Life Narrative of Dora Yum Kim.* Philadelphia: Temple University Press, 1999.

Choy, Bong-youn. *Koreans in America.* Chicago: Nelson-Hall Publishers, 1979.

Hastings, Max. *The Korean War.* New York: Simon and Schuster, 1987.

Hurh, Won Moo, and Kwang Chung Kim. *Korean Immigrants in America: A Structural Analysis of Ethnic Confinement and Adhesive Adaptation.* Rutherford, N.J.: Fairleigh Dickinson University Press, 1984.

Jo, Moon H. *Korean Immigrants and the Challenge of Adjustment.* Westport, Conn.: Greenwood Press, 1999.

Kim, Elaine H., and Eui-Young Yu. *East to America: Korean American Life Stories.* New York: The New Press, 1996.

Kim, Elizabeth. *Ten Thousand Sorrows: The Extraordinary Journey of a Korean War Orphan.* New York: Doubleday, 2000.

Kim, Hyung-chan, ed. *The Korean Diaspora: Historical and Sociological Studies of Korean Immigration and Assimilation in North America.* Santa Barbara, Calif.: ABC-CLIO, 1977.

Kim, Hyung-chan, and Wayne Patterson. *The Koreans in America, 1882–1974.* Dobbs Ferry, N.Y.: Oceana Publications, 1974.

Kim, Illsoo. *New Urban Immigrants: The Korean Community in New York.* Princeton, N.J.: Princeton University Press, 1981.

KIM, KWANG CHUNG., ed. *Koreans in the Hood: Conflict with African Americans.* Baltimore: The Johns Hopkins University Press, 1999.

LEE, MARY PAIK. *Quiet Odyssey: A Pioneer Korean Woman in America.* Seattle: University of Washington Press, 1990.

LIGHT, IVAN, AND EDNA BONACICH. *Immigrant Entrepreneurs: Koreans in Los Angeles, 1965–1982.* Berkeley: University of California Press, 1988.

MARKS, COPELAND, WITH MANJO KIM. *The Korean Kitchen: Classic Recipes from the Land of the Morning Calm.* San Francisco: Chronicle Books, 1993.

TAKAKI, RONALD T. *From the Land of the Morning Calm: The Koreans in America.* New York: Chelsea House, 1994.

FILIPINO AMERICANS

ALAMAR, ESTRELLA RAVELO, AND WILFREDO BUHAY. *Filipinos in Chicago.* Charleston, S.C.: Arcadia, 2001.

BANDON, ALEXANDRA. *Filipino Americans.* New York: Macmillan, 1993.

BLOUNT, JAMES H. *The American Occupation of the Philippines, 1898–1912.* 1912. Reprint, New York: Oriole Editions, 1973.

BUAKEN, MANUEL. *I Have Lived with the American People.* Caldwell, Idaho: The Caxton Printers, Ltd., 1948.

BULOSAN, CARLOS. *America Is in the Heart, a Personal History.* 1946. Reprint, Seattle: University of Washington Press, 1973.

CORDOVA, FRED. *Filipinos, Forgotten Asian Americans: A Pictorial Essay, 1763–circa 1963.* Dubuque, Iowa: Kendall-Hunt, 1983.

CROUCHETT, LORRAINE JACOBS. *Filipinos in California: From the Days of the Galleons to the Present.* El Cerrito, Calif.: Downey Place Publishing House, 1982.

DEWITT, HOWARD A. *Anti-Filipino Movements in California: A History, Bibliography and Study Guide.* San Francisco: R and E Research Associates, 1976.

FILIPINO ORAL HISTORY PROJECT. *Voices: A Filipino American Oral History.* Stockton, Calif.: Filipino Oral History Project, 1984.

KARNOW, STANLEY. *In Our Image: America's Empire in the Philippines.* New York: Random House, 1989.

KIM, HYUNG-CHAN, AND CYNTHIA C. MEJIA. *The Filipinos in America, 1898–1974: A Chronology & Fact Book.* Dobbs Ferry, N.Y.: Oceana Publications, 1976.

LEROY, JAMES A. *The Americans in the Philippines: A History of the Conquest and First Years of Occupation with an Introductory Account of the Spanish Rule.* 2 vols. 1914. Reprint, New York: AMS Press, 1970.

NORIEGA, VIOLETA A. *Philippine Recipes Made Easy.* Kirkland, Wash.: Paperworks, 1993.

PIDO, ANTONIO J. A. *The Pilipinos in America: Macro/Micro Dimensions of Immigration and Integration.* New York: Center for Migration Studies, 1986.

POSADAS, BARBARA M. *The Filipino Americans.* Westport, Conn.: Greenwood Press, 1999.

QUINSAAT, JESSE, ed. *Letters in Exile: An Introductory Reader on the History of Pilipinos in America.* Los Angeles: UCLA Asian American Studies Center, 1976.

SAN JUAN, E. *From Exile to Diaspora: Versions of the Filipino Experience in the United States.* Boulder, Colo.: Westview Press, 1998.

TAKAKI, RONALD, REBECCA STEFOFF, AND CAROL TAKAKI. *In the Heart of Filipino America: Immigrants from the Pacific Isles.* New York: Chelsea House, 1994.

VALLANGCA, CARIDAD CONCEPCION. *The Second Wave: Pinay & Pinoy (1945–1960).* San Francisco: Strawberry Hill Press, 1987.

VALLANGCA, ROBERTO V. *Pinoy: The First Wave, 1898–1941.* San Francisco: Strawberry Hill Press, 1977.

SOUTH ASIAN AMERICANS

Asian-Indian Americans

ALEXANDER, MEENA. *Fault Lines: A Memoir.* New York: Feminist Press at the City University of New York, 1993.

CHANDRASEKHAR, S., ed. *From India to America: A Brief History of Immigration; Problems of Discrimination; Admission and Assimilation.* La Jolla, Calif.: Population Review Publications, 1982.

DASGUPTA, SATHI SENGUPTA. *On the Trail of an Uncertain Dream: Indian Immigrant Experience in America.* New York: AMS Press, 1989.

FENTON, JOHN Y. *Transplanting Religious Traditions: Asian Indians in America.* New York: Praeger, 1988.

FISHER, MAXINE P. *The Indians of New York City: A Study of Immigrants from India.* New Delhi: Heritage Publishers, 1980.

GIBSON, MARGARET A. *Accommodation Without Assimilation: Sikh Immigrants in an American High School.* Ithaca, N.Y.: Cornell University Press, 1988.

HELWEG, ARTHUR W., AND USHA M. HELWEG. *An Immigrant Success Story: East Indians in America.* Philadelphia: University of Pennsylvania Press, 1990.

JAFFREY, MADHUR. *A Taste of India.* London: Pavilion, 1985.

JENSEN, JOAN M. *Passage from India: Asian Indian Immigrants in North America.* New Haven, Conn.: Yale University Press, 1988.

LEONARD, KAREN ISAKSEN. *The South Asian Americans.* Westport, Conn.: Greenwood Press, 1997.

RUSTOMJI-KERNS, ROSHNI, ed. *Living in America: Poetry and Fiction by South Asian American Writers.* Boulder, Colo.: Westview Press, 1995.

SARAN, PARMATMA. *The Asian Indian Experience in the United States.* Cambridge, Mass.: Schenkman Publishing Company, 1985.

SARAN, PARMATMA, AND EDWIN EAMES, eds. *The New Ethnics: Asian Indians in the United States.* New York: Praeger, 1980.

SAUND, DALIP SINGH. *Congressman from India.* New York: E. P. Dutton and Company, 1960.

WILLIAMS, RAYMOND BRADY. *Religions of Immigrants from India and Pakistan: New Threads in the American Tapestry.* New York: Cambridge University Press, 1988.

WOMEN OF SOUTH ASIAN DESCENT COLLECTIVE, eds. *Our Feet*

Walk the Sky: Women of the South Asian Diaspora. San Francisco: Aunt Lute Books, 1993.

XENOS, PETER, HERBERT BARRINGER, AND MICHAEL J. LEVIN. *Asian Indians in the United States: A 1980 Census Profile.* Honolulu: East-West Center, 1989.

SOUTHEAST ASIAN AMERICANS

DOMMEN, ARTHUR J. *The Indochinese Experience of the French and the Americans: Nationalism and Communism in Cambodia, Laos, and Vietnam.* Bloomington: Indiana University Press, 2001.

HAINES, DAVID W., ed. *Refugees as Immigrants: Cambodians, Laotians, and Vietnamese in America.* Totowa, N.J.: Rowman & Littlefield Publishers, 1989.

HANSEN, BARBARA. *Taste of Southeast Asia: Brunei, Indonesia, Malaysia, the Philippines, Singapore, Thailand, and Vietnam.* Tucson, Ariz.: HPBooks, 1987.

HEIN, JEREMY. *From Vietnam, Laos, and Cambodia: A Refugee Experience in the United States.* New York: Twayne, 1995.

HIGGINS, JAMES, AND JOAN ROSS. *Southeast Asians: A New Beginning in Lowell.* Lowell, Mass.: Mill Town Graphics, 1986.

SARDESAI, D. R. *Southeast Asia.* 3rd ed. Boulder, Colo.: Westview Press, 1994.

SCOTT, JOANNA C. *Indochina's Refugees: Oral Histories from Laos, Cambodia and Vietnam.* Jefferson, N.C.: McFarland & Company, 1989.

STRAND, PAUL J., AND WOODROW JONES JR. *Indochinese Refugees in America: Problems of Adaptation and Assimilation.* Durham, N.C.: Duke University Press, 1985.

TENHULA, JOHN. *Voices from Southeast Asia: The Refugee Experience in the United States.* New York: Holmes & Meier, 1991.

VIETNAMESE AMERICANS

ADDINGTON, LARRY H. *America's War in Vietnam: A Short Narrative History.* Bloomington: Indiana University Press, 2000.

BACHE, ELLYN. *Culture Clash.* Yarmouth, Maine: Intercultural Press, 1989.

DUFFY, DAN, ed. *Not a War: American Vietnamese Fiction, Poetry and Essays.* Viet Nam Forum 16. New Haven, Conn.: Yale University Council on Southeast Asia Studies, 1997.

FREEMAN, JAMES M. *Hearts of Sorrow: Vietnamese-American Lives.* Stanford, Calif.: Stanford University Press, 1989.

HAYSLIP, LE LY, WITH JAMES HAYSLIP. *Child of War, Woman of Peace.* New York: Doubleday, 1993.

HAYSLIP, LE LY, WITH JAY WURTS. *When Heaven and Earth Changed Places: A Vietnamese Woman's Journey from War to Peace.* New York: Doubleday, 1989.

KARNOW, STANLEY. *Vietnam: A History.* New York: The Viking Press, 1983.

KIBRIA, NAZLI. *Family Tightrope: The Changing Lives of Vietnamese Americans.* Princeton, N.J.: Princeton University Press, 1993.

KUTLER, STANLEY, ed. *Encyclopedia of the Vietnam War.* New York: Charles Scribner's Sons, 1996.

MCNAMARA, ROBERT S., WITH BRIAN VANDEMARK. *In Retrospect: The Tragedy and Lessons of Vietnam.* New York: Random House, 1995.

MONTERO, DARREL. *Vietnamese Americans: Patterns of Resettlement and Socioeconomic Adaptation in the United States.* Boulder, Colo.: Westview Press, 1979.

MOORE, JOHN NORTON, ed. *The Vietnam Debate: A Fresh Look at the Arguments.* New York: University Press of America, 1990.

NEWELL, JEAN F. *Vietnamese Americans: A Needs Assessment.* Ann Arbor, Mich.: University Microfilms International, 1993.

ROUTHIER, NICOLE. *The Foods of Vietnam.* New York: Stewart, Tabori & Chang, 1989.

RUTLEDGE, PAUL JAMES. *The Vietnamese Experience in America.* Bloomington: Indiana University Press, 1992.

TRAN, DE, ANDREW LAM, AND HAI DAI NGUYEN, eds. *Once Upon a Dream: The Vietnamese American Experience.* Kansas City: Andrews and McMeel, 1995.

TUCKER, SPENCER, ed. *The Encyclopedia of the Vietnam War: A*

Political, Social, and Military History. Oxford: Oxford University Press, 1998.

LAOTIAN AMERICANS

CHAN, SUCHENG, ed. *Hmong Means Free: Life in Laos and America.* Philadelphia: Temple University Press, 1994.

DONNELLY, NANCY D. *Changing Lives of Refugee Hmong Women.* Seattle: University of Washington Press, 1994.

HAMILTON-MERRITT, JANE. *Tragic Mountains: The Hmong, the Americans, and the Secret Wars for Laos, 1942–1992.* Bloomington: Indiana University Press, 1993.

HENDRICKS, GLENN, BRUCE DOWNING, AND AMOS DEINARD, eds. *The Hmong in Transition.* Staten Island, N.Y.: Center for Migration Studies, 1986.

MOTTIN, JEAN. *History of the Hmong.* Bangkok: Odeon Store, 1980.

PROUDFOOT, ROBERT. *Even the Birds Don't Sound the Same Here: The Laotian Refugees' Search for Heart in American Culture.* New York: Peter Lang, 1990.

STUART-FOX, MARTIN. *Historical Dictionary of Laos.* 2nd ed. Asian/Oceanian Historical Dictionary Series No. 35. Lanham, Md.: The Scarecrow Press, 2001.

———. *Laos: Politics, Economics and Society.* Boulder, Colo.: Lynne Rienner Publishers, 1986.

CAMBODIAN AMERICANS

CHAN, SUCHENG, ed. *Not Just Victims: Conversations with Cambodian Community Leaders in the United States.* Urbana: University of Illinois Press, 2003.

CHANDLER, DAVID P. *A History of Cambodia.* Boulder, Colo.: Westview Press, 1983.

———. *The Tragedy of Cambodian History: Politics, War, and Revolution since 1945.* New Haven, Conn.: Yale University Press, 1991.

CRIDDLE, JOAN D., AND TEEDA BUTT MAM. *To Destroy You Is No*

Loss: The Odyssey of a Cambodian Family. New York: The Atlantic Monthly Press, 1987.

EBIHARA, MAY M., CAROL A. MORTLAND, AND JUDY LEDGERWOOD. *Cambodian Culture since 1975: Homeland and Exile.* Ithaca, N.Y.: Cornell University Press, 1994.

FIFFER, SHARON SLOAN. *Imagining America: Paul Thai's Journey From the Killing Fields of Cambodia to Freedom in the U.S.A.* New York: Paragon House, 1991.

GOTTESMAN, EVAN. *Cambodia After the Khmer Rouge: Inside the Politics of Nation Building.* New Haven, Conn.: Yale University Press, 2003.

HOPKINS, MARYCAROL. *Braving a New World: Cambodian (Khmer) Refugees in an American City.* Westport, Conn.: Bergin & Garvey, 1996.

MARTIN, MARIE ALEXANDRINE. *Cambodia: A Shattered Society.* Berkeley: University of California Press, 1994.

NGOR, HAING, WITH ROGER WARNER. *Haing Ngor: A Cambodian Odyssey.* New York: Macmillan, 1987.

RATLIFF, SHARON K. *Caring for Cambodian Americans: A Multidisciplinary Resource for the Helping Professions.* New York: Garland, 1997.

SCHANBERG, SYDNEY H. *The Death and Life of Dith Pran.* New York: Penguin, 1985.

SHAWCROSS, WILLIAM. *The Quality of Mercy: Cambodia, Holocaust and Modern Conscience.* New York: Simon and Schuster, 1984.

TOOZE, RUTH. *Cambodia: Land of Contrasts.* New York: The Viking Press, 1962.

WELARATNA, USHA. *Beyond the Killing Fields: Voices of Nine Cambodian Survivors in America.* Stanford, Calif.: Stanford University Press, 1993.

PACIFIC ISLANDER AMERICANS

GIBSON, ARRELL MORGAN, WITH JOHN S. WHITEHEAD. *Yankees in Paradise: The Pacific Basin Frontier.* Albuquerque: University of New Mexico Press, 1993.

HOWE, K. R., ROBERT C. KISTE, AND BRIJ V. LAL, eds. *Tides of History: The Pacific Islands in the Twentieth Century.* Honolulu: University of Hawaii Press, 1994.

ONG, PAUL, ed. *The State of Asian Pacific America: Economic Diversity, Issues & Policies.* Los Angeles: LEAP Asian Pacific American Public Policy Institute, 1994.

SPICKARD, PAUL, JOANNE L. RONDILLA, AND DEBBIE HIPPOLITE WRIGHT, eds. *Pacific Diaspora: Island Peoples in the United States and Across the Pacific.* Honolulu: University of Hawaii Press, 2002.

SAMOANS

GRAY, J. A. C. *Amerika Samoa: A History of American Samoa and Its United States Administration.* Annapolis, Md.: United States Naval Institute, 1960.

SETTER, FREDERIC KOEHLER. *America Samoa: An Anthropological Photo Essay.* Honolulu: University of Hawaii Press, 1984.

SWANEY, DEANNA. *Samoa: Western & American Samoa.* 2nd ed. Hawthorn, Australia: Lonely Planet Publications, 1994.

HAWAIIANS

ANDERSON, ROBERT N., WITH RICHARD COLLER AND REBECCA F. PESTANO. *Filipinos in Rural Hawaii.* Honolulu: University of Hawaii Press, 1984.

BURROWS, EDWIN G. *Hawaiian Americans: An Account of the Mingling of Japanese, Chinese, Polynesian, and American Cultures.* 1947. Reprint, Hamden, Conn.: Archon Books, 1970.

DAWS, GAVAN. *Shoal of Time: A History of the Hawaiian Islands.* New York: Macmillan, 1968.

GLICK, CLARENCE E. *Sojourners and Settlers: Chinese Migrants in Hawaii.* Honolulu: University Press of Hawaii, 1980.

GRAY, FRANCINE DU PLESSIX. *Hawaii: The Sugar-Coated Fortress.* New York: Random House, 1972.

HAZAMA, DOROTHY OCHIAI, AND JANE OKAMOTO KOMEIJI.

Okage Sama De: The Japanese in Hawai'i. Honolulu: Bess Press, 1986.

KIMURA, YUKIKO. *Issei: Japanese Immigrants in Hawaii.* Honolulu: University of Hawaii Press, 1988.

OKIHIRO, GARY Y. *Cane Fires: The Anti-Japanese Movement in Hawaii, 1865–1945.* Philadelphia: Temple University Press, 1991.

SAIKI, PATSY SUMIE. *Early Japanese Immigrants in Hawaii.* Honolulu: Japanese Cultural Center of Hawaii, 1993.

TAMURA, EILEEN H. *Americanization, Acculturation, and Ethnic Identity: The Nisei Generation in Hawaii.* Urbana: University of Illinois Press, 1994.

WAKUKAWA, ERNEST K. *A History of the Japanese People in Hawaii.* Honolulu: The Toyo Shoin, 1938.

TONGAN AMERICANS

RUTHERFORD, NOEL, ed. *Friendly Islands: A History of Tonga.* Melbourne: Oxford University Press, 1977.

SWANEY, DEANNA. *Tonga.* 2nd ed. Hawthorn, Australia: Lonely Planet Publications, 1994.

GUAMANIANS

THOMPSON, LAURA. *Guam and Its People.* Reprint, New York: Greenwood Press, 1970.

Index